PRENTICE HALL SERIES IN COMPUTER SHORTHAND

JEAN GONZALEZ, EDITOR

COMPUTER SHORTHAND THEORY AND TRANSCRIPTION, Second Edition
by Alan Roberts, John Walsh, Jean Gonzalez

READER TO ACCOMPANY Roberts/Walsh/Gonzalez,
COMPUTER SHORTHAND THEORY AND TRANSCRIPTION, Second Edition
by Jean Gonzalez

COMPUTER SHORTHAND: SKILL BUILDING
AND TRANSCRIPTION, Second Edition
by Carolee Freer

COMPUTER SHORTHAND: SPEED BUILDING
AND TRANSCRIPTION, Second Edition
by Carolee Freer

COMPUTER SHORTHAND: MEDICAL DICTATION
AND TRANSCRIPTION
by Catherine McCandless

THE COMPLETE COURT REPORTER'S HANDBOOK, Second Edition
by Mary H. Knapp

STUDY GUIDE TO ACCOMPANY THE COMPLETE
COURT REPORTER'S HANDBOOK, Second Edition
by Mary H. Knapp

THE COMPLETE COURT REPORTER'S HANDBOOK

Second Edition

MARY H. KNAPP

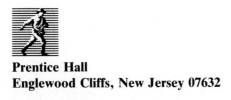

Prentice Hall
Englewood Cliffs, New Jersey 07632

Library of Congress Cataloging-in-Publication Data

Knapp, Mary H.
    The complete court reporter's handbook/by Mary H. Knapp.—2nd
ed.
        p.   cm.—(Prentice Hall series in computer shorthand)
    Includes bibliographical references and index.
    ISBN 0-13-159369-2
    1. Law reporting—United States.   2. Computer-aided transcription
systems. I. Title. II. Series.
KF255.K58   1991
347.73'16—dc20
[347.30716]   90–26504
                                                  CIP

Editorial/production supervision and interior design: Fred Dahl and Rose Kernan
Pre-press buyer: Ilene Levy
Manufacturing buyer: Edward O'Dougherty
Cover design: Bruce Kenselaar
Acquisition editor: Liz Kendall

© 1991 by Prentice-Hall, Inc.
a Simon & Schuster Company
Englewood Cliffs, New Jersey 07632

Printed in the United States of America
10 9 8 7 6 5 4 3 2

ISBN 0-13-159369-2

Prentice-Hall International (UK) Limited, *London*
Prentice-Hall of Australia Pty. Limited, *Sydney*
Prentice-Hall Canada Inc., *Toronto*
Prentice-Hall Hispanoamericana, S.A., *Mexico*
Prentice-Hall of India Private Limited, *New Delhi*
Prentice-Hall of Japan, Inc., *Tokyo*
Simon & Schuster Asia Pte. Ltd., *Singapore*
Editora Prentice-Hall do Brasil, Ltda., *Rio de Janeiro*

Contents

CHAPTER **25** **Exhibits,** 217

Preface

A popular expression of the day, "You've come a long way, baby," can certainly be applied to the court reporting profession. Following World War II, teachers blithely said "When in doubt, write it out." They then unleashed the unwary, petrified students upon the working world when they reached 200 words a minute, needing to learn on the job everything but speed in writing. A shortage of reporters existed then as now, and judges and law firm owners taught newcomers (then 90 percent men) all they needed to know to survive.

After I spent two years of reporting military statements, courts martial, and investigations, a fellow instructor taught me to use the shorthand machine while I directed the Office Practice Department of Rider College in Trenton, New Jersey. After three years of teaching and training at the Minnesota School of Business in Minneapolis, Minnesota, my husband and I entered court reporting as a career.

Knowing my background, judges and attorneys talked to me a great deal about the training of reporters. They discussed strengths and weaknesses of reporters they had known and worked with. One recurring comment was that the court reporters frequently had reasonable speed in writing shorthand when they left school, but they seemed to have little else. In many cases, judges and lawyers seemed to think beginning court reporters had to be taught everything (demeanor, procedures, transcript setups, manners, and even grammar and punctuation) on the job.

I determined that should I ever have an opportunity to train court reporters again, such comments would not apply to my graduates. Therefore, upon my return to the teaching field after my husband's death, I set up classes in courtroom procedure and office practice as separate subjects.

During the past 25 years of training court reporters I have had graduates return to visit and talk with my students countless times. Most of them have said during these sessions (or by letter) "The most important things we got in school were gleaned during courtroom procedures, office practice, and classtime when you would talk with us, bring in forms, check our transcripts and projects, and teach us how things are done out there."

Recent innovations have been many, and in the past ten years CAT (Computer-Aided Transcription), videotaping, closed captioning, realtime reporting, and study of voice activation have developed at a rapid rate. The reporter of today must be geared to change for we live in a technological world. We must always remember that the live reporter offers three things no alternative can: greater accuracy and savings of time and money. As long as we can provide these, our profession is secure.

This book is offered to help students bridge the gap from classroom to reporting work. It is not a learned treatise, nor does it cover everything a reporter needs to know. Forms and procedures vary according to locale, so there will still be much to learn out on the job. However, I hope this book will start you out with a clearer understanding of your part in the scheme of the reporting world.

Who knows? Perhaps this volume may even help some experienced reporters!

Acknowledgments

The author wishes to thank Carolee Freer of Cypress College, Sarah L. McKinney of Rose State College, Susan Segal of Segal Institute of Court Reporting, Elizabeth C. Waggoner of Sparks College, and Elaine C. Wojcik, Massachusetts Bay Community College for their diligent work in reviewing this text.

Introduction: A Career as a Reporter

The person seeking to become a reporter must be intelligent, highly literate, dedicated, and physically fit. This person must set reporting as a firm career objective and then work diligently to achieve a high degree of expertise and shorthand speed to qualify for this position.

In the span of the last 20 years, many new positions have opened up in addition to the traditional ones of courtroom official, freelance reporter, convention reporter, and legislative reporter. Today, thanks to the perfection of stand-alone CAT (Computer-Aided Transcription), machine writers present closed-captioned bylines for TV news and other programs, do realtime translations on CRT's for deaf students in classroom and other situations, provide immediate translations in courtrooms on monitors for judges and attorneys and judges of ongoing proceedings, accomplish entire daily copy assignments in courtrooms through CAT translation, using scopists to make corrections, and prepare exact transcripts of videotaped materials to accompany viewings of these.

Industry and government agencies are at last waking up to the fact that information can be put in at least four times as rapidly by using shorthand machine writers as an alternative to keyboarding by typewriter or word processor. Thus, new uses of the latest technology are creating diversified professional opportunities daily.

As you study reporting, keep in mind that you are learning a skill that will enable you to find a valued position in our technological society. During your training you will acquire a background diverse enough to enable you to enter many different professional areas.

Chapter 1   *So You Want To Be a Reporter*

Congratulations! You have decided to join the reporting profession. What a wise decision! Reporting is an interesting, rewarding, challenging occupation in which your earnings will be limited only by your ability and your desire to work.

Preparation for the Reporting Profession

Although you may devote full time and effort to development of high-speed machine shorthand skill, this accomplishment alone will not be enough to enable you to achieve success and happiness in the reporting profession. The following factors will also greatly influence your future in reporting.

Physical Attributes

Do you have keen hearing, good eyesight, and good reflexes? Be sure a thorough physical examination assures you that you are adequately endowed with these three because an instant's thought will convince you that they are, indeed, of paramount importance to your career.

How is your general health? Great physical stamina is needed in the long hours of work under stressful conditions which are frequently required. Travel is often a part of the reporter's life, and substitutes are not always available to cover assignments. Care and protection of your hands will always be a prime consideration because your livelihood will depend upon them.

English Skills

A reporter must have extraordinary English skills that include extensive vocabulary and fine spelling, grammar, and punctuation. Let's face it: English is the everything of court reporting. A reporter's whole business is words—getting them down, reading them back, and producing them in error-free printed form. It has been said that reporting is 5 percent writing it down and 95 percent writing it up. Since great proficiency in English is a requisite for this profession, a reporter must possess more than ordinary language skills. He or she must genuinely enjoy working with words. Examine yourself to see how you qualify in this respect by considering your reaction to the following questions:

- Do you like to read not only light fiction but also newspapers, *The Wall Street Journal*, *Newsweek*, and books of genuine substance?

1

- Do you have a feel for words and the way they flow together?
- Are you a fine speller?
- Do you look up unfamiliar words or just ignore them?
- Did you do exceptionally well in English classes in school?
- Do you like to work crossword puzzles and other word games?
- Are you a good typist who takes pride in producing perfectly typed pages?

If you can answer all these questions positively, you may be a good candidate for the reporting profession.

Attitude—A Necessity for Successful Reporting

Many people lose good jobs as reporters because they have negative attitudes. You can avoid that problem by developing a successful attitude while in school. You can begin by developing the skill of getting along amicably with your fellow students, your instructors, and all types of people.

In this profession you must display a positive, mature personality and exhibit a cheerful, pleasant demeanor under pressure. You must learn to accept and profit from criticism without becoming defensive. In court reporting there is no place for immature behavior.

A successful reporter does more than is asked. To be a good reporter, one must be a good person first. Be such a great person that "even the undertaker would hate to bury you."

Perseverance Wins!

In reporting, perseverance is vital. Put forth your utmost every minute each day, and believe that success will follow! It takes real determination to complete the training to become a court reporter and to overcome plateaus that may appear on the road to acquiring machine shorthand speed. Determine that you are going to master the shorthand machine and that it is not going to master you.

To prepare thoroughly for reporting, you must devote time to the study of medical, legal, and technical terminologies, since good knowledge of these subjects is required. A reporter must develop a minimum shorthand speed of 225–250 words per minute on testimony, 200 WPM on jury charge, and 180 WPM on difficult literary material. Hang in there, and keep your spirits high!

As a student, always keep your goal before you no matter how rigorous your training may seem, believing and knowing that you can do what you really want to do. Remember people just like you are doing this job well every day and loving every minute of it.

Appearance Is Highly Important

To be a successful reporter, you must look the part. John T. Molloy in his best-selling books *The Woman's Dress for Success Book* and *Dress for Success* (for men) explains how this look is achieved. Reporters should read these and current articles on proper dress because they must create a favorable image of themselves and of the entire court reporting profession. Reporters hold very responsible positions in our society today. As a reporter, you are an officer of the court and therefore contribute to the layman's respect for law and order. You will often be called upon to transcribe cases involving large sums of money and people's lives. Your appearance should instill confidence in those you meet that you can handle these responsibilities.

Begin with a well-scrubbed, neat look. If you are a woman, wear conservative, good quality, proper fitting business suits or dresses of reasonable length. Your dresses or suits should be short enough that everyone can tell you are a woman and long enough that they know you are a lady. The accepted norm is two inches below the kneecap. You may wear businesslike pantsuits if the court or freelance firm employing you allows these. Jumpsuits, halters, and shorts are not attire that will command the trust, confidence, and respect of others in the reporting workplace.

If you are a man, you should wear business suits or sports jackets and matching slacks. Flannel shirts, T-shirts, flashy colored shirts, or shirts with slightly frayed cuffs or missing buttons are totally inappropriate. A conservative tie should always be worn while working.

Blue jeans have no place in the working wardrobe of any reporter either male or female. There are reasons for excluding them. If a judge has banned improperly clad witnesses from his or her courtroom, how can he or she justify having an unprofessional looking reporter present?

Some judges request their reporters to dress in certain attire. For instance, a judge may insist the lady reporter dress in a black dress to add dignity to the courtroom setting. The reporter must either conform or look for work elsewhere, as this is the judge's prerogative.

Of course, situations alter cases somewhat. For example, in a situation where there is no air conditioning in a room and the attorneys remove their coats, a male reporter may do the same if so instructed by those hiring him. In certain areas that have freezing weather, reporters may choose to wear pantsuits or flannel shirts. Good judgment is what counts at all times.

Confidentiality Is a Must

Can you keep a secret? Reporters must never discuss anything that transpires at work with outsiders. Confidentiality is required—the slightest slip regarding something said or done in court or during a deposition or statement could be serious harm to someone's life or affect a case adversely. Even an innocent remark to a juror could cause a mistrial. Therefore, reporters must learn to avoid discussing their work.

Secrecy about your work extends to scopists, transcribers, binders, and go-fers, too. Reporters must never give others the opportunity to divulge information by leaving any matter lying about that might be discussed elsewhere or given to news reporters. They may never furnish news reporters or other outsiders with transcripts unless clearance has been arranged with the judge.

Statements recorded by reporters for attorneys or adjusters may never be discussed with others. Copies of such transcripts may not be sold or given to anyone without the authorization of the person who hired the reporter to take and transcribe them.

Deportment of Reporters

A reporter's deportment reflects not only on the individual reporter but upon the entire reporting profession. Reporters must respect and obey all laws, conduct themselves properly in social situations, and exhibit good manners and breeding at all times. In order to be properly informed as to appropriate conduct for all occasions, the aspiring reporter should secure standard etiquette books and study everything from how to introduce people to which fork to use when.

Reporters Must Exercise Courtesy

A reporter was once spoken of as "the silent man" when men dominated the industry. Today, women are in the majority, so the following statement applies to women reporters as well. Reporters do not interject themselves into the proceedings any more than is absolutely necessary to ensure a correct verbatim record.

Sometimes reporters must interrupt witnesses and ask them to repeat mumbled answers or replies that trail of for must stop counsel when everyone is talking at the same time. At other times they might have to interrupt the proceeding because people are speaking too rapidly. At such times reporters must learn to use courtesy and tact. Although reporters who must interrupt are just doing their job well, the way they handle interruptions makes all the difference.

Ability to Work with Attorneys. A reporter who respects attorneys will seldom lose them as clients. Reporters can show respect by not monopolizing conversations when attorneys are conversing, by stating opinions in an unobtrusive way, and by not engaging in arguments on religion or politics with others. Reporters who do not follow these guidelines will only make enemies and lose business. Although reporters should not act in a subservient manner, they must exercise good judgment and common sense at all times.

Use of Tact and Diplomacy. Develop tact and diplomacy in handling the diverse types of people you meet daily. For example, an attorney who has just lost a case asks you what you thought of the way he or she handled it. Never tell the attorney he did a poor job (even though you may feel that way). The attorney is probably already upset enought about losing the lawsuit and perhaps the contingency fee. Find something reassuring to say such as, "I thought you did as well as anyone could have with that situation," or "Your opening statement was certainly good, but the jury obviously felt sympathy for the plaintiff for all the injuries she sustained."

Tact will also help in collection of overdue bills. Reporters use collection measures more frequently today, but they should attempt to remain friendly with everyone under every situation possible. At depositions and hearings, reporters must be just as cordial to attorneys who are slow in paying bills as to the lawyers who pay promptly.

Reporters are the only individuals present at any proceeding at whom no one is angry; therefore, they must remain truly unbiased. They may not show facial expressions or other actions what they think of counsel's questioning, a witness's answers, or the judge's rulings, as such behavior could influence the jury in favor or one side or the other. Reporters are expected always to exhibit calm, unruffled expressions while writing, even under the most difficult circumstances.

Reporters may not allow jurors or witnesses to discuss cases with them because such conduct could lead to improper conversations concerning the lawsuit. Such talk might give the impression the reporter has an opinion regarding one side or the other.

It is also best for reporters not to spend a disproportionate amount of time talking to either counsel. Witnesses and jurors who observe the reporter talking lengthily to a particular counsel may feel that the reporter is partial to that attorney's position or regards that lawyer more highly than opposing counsel. This observation might affect the witnesses' or jurors' interpretation of the facts.

Reporters must always use discretion in dealing with everyone. Again, reporters who exhibit good judgment will never go wrong.

Loyalty—a Must

Reporters must be loyal to judges and members of the Bar. They should never speak adversely about any attoney or judge to others. They are expected to show respect for all other officers of the court with whom they work and never enter into negative discussions about judges or counsel, avoiding diligently the telling of any tales that create dissension between judges, counsel, and other associates.

Integrity

It is the reporter's duty to charge proper, uniform rates to all and to do work, generally, in the order in which notes are taken. Reporters should avoid the temptation of cutting rates.

Reporters are no longer permitted to publish a fee schedule, as this practice has been ruled restraint of trade. Reporters should check with other reputable firms on rates, do their best work, and charge according to going standards. They should avoid unethical practices such as overcharging or preparing pages with oversized margins or illegally large type. Reporters should all join and work with their local, state, and national associations to assure just compensation and working conditions for official reporters.

Those sent as overflow reporters to cover other reporters' jobs should not try to solicit the client's business for their firm or for themselves. When reporters leave one firm to set up private practice, they also should not solicit former clients.

Taking Reporting Seriously

One criticism occasionally made of beginners is that they are sometimes unbusinesslike, immature, and unprofessional. Reporting is a dignified profession, and reporters must act as adults and know when to "turn off the silly."

Many things occur during assignments which are truly amusing, but reporters must be careful to smile or laugh only when everyone else laughs. In court, the reporter should look at the judge. If he laughs, the reporter may laugh. At depositions, reporters must also be careful to treat all situations seriously. Lawsuits are nut funny to people involved in them no matter how petty or ridiculous they may seem to others.

Just by way of an example, I once took depositions in an alienation of affections suit where the attorneys began bantering back and forth. Their exchange went something like this:

Q: (By Mr. Weis) When did you first become aware that your wife and Mr. Holmes were having an affair?

A: When I went out in the hall on New Year's Eve and found him hugging and kissing her, and she was hugging and kissing him.

Q: Well, at a New Year's Eve party, isn't there always quite a bit of drinking going on?

MR. CATTELL: Now, Mr. Weis, don't judge the parties we have over here in Douglas County by the kind you have over in Madison County.

Q: (By Mr. Weis) All right. Well, anyway, isn't it customary for everyone just to grab anyone around them at midnight on New Year's Eve and kiss them and hug them?

A: Yes, but this was 7:00 o'clock at night, and we hadn't even had supper yet.

Now, ordinarily, this conversation would not have had any effect on me, but on this day I started to laugh. Then I looked over at the witness. Tears were streaming down his face, and I realized there was nothing funny to him about having his home broken up—a sobering realization.

Ability Is What Counts in Reporting

Reporters should secure work through ability and ability alone and should never depend on other factors such as friendship or sex to secure jobs. Reporters should keep their self-respect and the high regard of otrhers. Polonius's words still apply: "To thine own self be true, and it doth follow as the night the day, thou canst not then be false to any man."

Accuracy Is Vital

There is nothing so exasperating to an experienced reporter who is checking the transcript of a newcomer who keeps insisting, regarding something that does not make sense in a transcript, "But that is what I have in my notes."

What you first think you heard often turns out later to be something else. Provisions are made for correcting honest errors which may creep into the finished product. However, reporters may not change a judge's ruling or add or delete anything to favor someone involved in litigation. Above all else, accuracy is important in notetaking.

The Buck Stops with the Reporter!

Everything a reporter takes in shorthand must be transcribed if required. Reporters who have had a hard day or who feel tired cannot use such excuses as "I lost my notes," or "The dog chewed them up." Reporters must guard their notes diligently and never misplace them. Failure to deliver a transcript may result in the reporter being jailed until the transcript is completed or a malpractice action being instituted against the offender.

A tip for reporters who have a very difficult transcript to transcribe is do it right away. Reporters who follow this advice will discover that the transcript was not nearly so bad to produce as they feared.

Personality Traits Are Important

The reporter probably should be an ambivert. A reporter must be enough of an extrovert to meet people well and get repeat business as a freelancer and also get along with those he or she comes into contact with in various situations. However, reporters must be introvert enough to get transcripts out alone and one time. When a judge or head of the firm has to tell a reporter to get a transcript out, that person is in deep trouble. Reporters must organize their lives in order to produce a large volume of work efficiently.

Punctuality and Efficiency—Marks of an Excellent Reporter

Punctuality is essential. A court reporter may never be absent or late without serious cause once an assignment has been accepted. Most counsel never forget the one time a court reporter appeared late. Reporters should always arrive at least 15 minutes early to secure titles, venue, appearances, and to set up so they are ready on time.

As a student you can develop discipline right now! Go to class on time each day with your machine in good order, well stocked with paper, properly inked, ribbon checked, and pencil or pen ready to make notations and corrections.

Scotch tape an extra ribbon under the plate of your machine right now, and keep a 3″ x 5″ notepad taped to the top of it to insure efficiency in getting out a perfect record. As a student you can use that pad to jot down words you have difficulty writing; practice each time you sit down at your machine.

Have a regular daily practice time, and constantly strive to turn out greater amounts of perfect transcript during every class transcription period. Clients pay only for perfectly typed pages, so take pride in your work. Learn to spell and punctuate well long before you face the working world. Otherwise, attorneys are apt to say "Why should reporters who can't spell and punctuate make all the money they do? My secretary is far more capable than they are."

Reporting Requires Stamina

A reporter works under much pressure, so good health is essential. You cannot be like a student I once had who left almost every 50-minute class period because of a kidney condition. I could only advise her that she was in the wrong field.

Another man with a hearing impairment, discovered entering the study of reporting, insisted "I can do it, but it will just take me longer." Reporting demands acute hearing, and he was simply deluding himself.

Your presence is expected whenever scheduled. My husband had reported without absence for one judge for about two years to the complete satisfaction of both. However, one winter day, a week into a lengthy case, he became ill with the flu. Toward the end of the afternoon he said "Judge, I just don't think I may be able to make it tomorrow."

The judge replied "What good is a reporter to me if he can't be here when I need him?" Then he realized what he had said and laughed, adding "Well, I guess everyone gets sick once in awhile, but I hate to change reporters in the middle of this big case or have to continue it."

That situation is the extreme. In fact, some courts now hire swing reporters, and some change reporters after a certain number of days on a case to keep transcript current. Nonetheless, reporting demands a healthy constitution. If you do not work in a large city, there may be no substitute available; and if you do not show up after you have agreed to report a matter, you may be held guilty of contempt of court.

Remember, you are going to be doing very responsible work. Be guided accordingly.

Stop Now and Consider Your Future

After you have thought awhile about the foregoing discussion of reporting, only you can make the decision as to whether reporting is your ideal career. I hope you will decide that it is, for there will always be a shortage of truly fine court reporters. As long as court reporters can furnish the service and save consumers time and money, the future of the reporting profession is secure.

I Dare You To Be Great!

When you finish school, begin work with the idea that you are going to be a truly great reporter and a real contributor to your profession. It may seem easy for you to bask in the protection of your local, state, and national associations, taking benefits out and putting nothing back in. Still, I say to you GET INVOLVED!

Join your associations, and give of your time and your money. Be proud of your profession, and work to maintain the high esteem of your fellow reporters and the public. Pay your dues; go to state and national conventions and local meetings. Always try to improve yourself throughout your career through study, seminars, and reading experience. Obtain the National Court Reporters Association (NCRA) Certificate of Proficiency (while in school, if possible) and take the NCRA Merit Examination, and possibly sit for the NCRA Championship after that. Certified Shorthand Reporter (CSR) examinations are given in some states. Take these examinations and prove to yourself and others that you are proficient. Aim high! You will be so glad you did, and your life will be richer and fuller for it.

Again, I DARE YOU TO BE GREAT!

Chapter 2   *What's In Reporting For Me?*

Benefits of the Profession

The student who begins to study reporting, like the general public, knows little about what the profession really entails, what jobs exist, or how one goes about getting into the field. Somewhere he or she has heard that court reporting is a profession that takes just two years of training (or maybe less), that offers a huge salary, and that provides a chance to hear fascinating tales of murder and intrigue. Those impressions have been around for a long time, and many of them are correct, but there are additional benefits I wish to stress in the following paragraphs.

Low Cost of Entry

You will need far less of an investment in time (perhaps) or money to enter the field of court reporting than to enter other professional fields. Doctors, lawyers, and engineers spend many years in preparation. Then, when they enter private practice at the end of their studies, they must rent offices; pay electric bills, telephone bills, and water bills; buy equipment; pay secretaries or assistants; and wait for the elusive butterfly of success.

With the skills you have developed and your computer input machine, you will enter a high-paying field as a professional. You can instantly become a judge's official reporter or join a freelance agency which will furnish you with all the work you can handle and everything you need to start at no further cost to you. Or you may choose to enter the closed-captioning or legislative reporting area of the profession. Opportunity is yours for the taking!

Fascinating Work

As a reporter, you will meet and learn from famous people, professionals, blue-collar workers, merchants, farmers, oil drillers, entrepreneurs, the highly literate, the most illiterate—those from every type of background imaginable.

In what other field of work could you ever absorb so much, perform such great service in our country's legal processes, be present during the making of history and record it being made, and have such a fascinating time doing it?

Absence of Discrimination

Reporting is the one profession where women earn the same pay as men, and no discrimination exists as to religion or sex, although some individuals or firms may prefer to hire a male or female reporter for a particular reason. There is a place in reporting for everybody. You simply have to find the niche that fits your personality best.

A reporter does not have to retire at a certain age because competence is the real criterion in the reporting business. A person can also enter this profession at an early age provided he or she develops the necessary skills of speed and proven transcription ability. Some states, however, have minimum age requirements for certification.

A Nonroutine Job

As a court reporter you will not be bound by an 8:00 to 5:00 schedule as are most people. Oh, no! In the beginning you will spend more than eight hours a day; but if this profession is for you, you will love every interesting minute of it. How much more time your work will take will depend upon your own situation, how organized you are, and what talent you bring to the profession.

In any event, if you are a good reporter, you are going to be very busy. If you are mediocre, you will not be busy and will not be respected by members of your profession and those associated with the law. So, do insist on perfection from yourself while you are in school, and then be willing to work hard to be successful. What you learn from your cases and the people involved in them will add an extra dimension to your life and provide you with a liberal education.

Perhaps your ideas of what a reporter does are founded mainly on what you have seen on courtroom-related shows. Much of what you will report will be exciting and dramatic, but re-member some material will be dull, such as condemnation suits where you will be writing figures and land descriptions over lengthy periods. Accept that reporting is not going to be all fun and games. However, if you are a dedicated professional, you will accept every assignment as part of the work to be done, and you will do it well.

Training Required

It is hoped by NSRA that within reasonable time all reporters will be four-year college graduates, and I personally feel it would raise the respect held for reporters greatly if all aspirants to enter the profession would have a four-year degree in liberal arts before beginning training for the specific field of reporting.

Reporting, at this time, is still a profession that can be entered upon completion of a rea-sonable period of training. Recent studies have shown the average length of training to be 31 months. If I were a beginning student, I would discount all stories about people who taught themselves (half taught is more like it) and those that required only eight or nine months to prepare for this field. At best, such people could not have been very competent beginning re-porters. There are very few geniuses around who are competent enough to enter the profession with skills developed within such a short time.

My advice is to enter the best approved, reputable court reporting school you can find and devote yourself to practicing night and day for whatever time you need to develop your skills. Ask a number of reporters which are the better schools, for that is the best way to judge a school. Enter the field fully qualified. Only the best will survive in this age of technology and change.

Required Testing for Reporting

In states having Certified Shorthand Reporter (CSR) laws that make reporting work contin-gent upon passing a test given under auspices of the state CSR board, it may be a felony to practice without proof of passing such a test on file.

If the CSR is linked to civil service, the reporter cannot lose a position when a judge changes due to retirement, death, or politics.

Tests vary within the various states. Most CSR states require a written knowledge examination (WKT) and five minute tests at speeds of 225 WPM on testimony with no more than 57 errors, 200 WPM on jury charge with no more than 50 errors, and 180 WPM on literary material with a maximum of 45 errors. The entry level test given by NCRA twice a year is also based upon that standard. Still other states require four-voice tests with a portion to be typed and/or read, medical or technical takes with transcription or readback required, and jury charge readback on an entire take. Promotion tests are given in New York City.

To secure information about required testing and vacancies in any given location, write to the secretary of that state's reporting association. A list of these officers is provided at the end of the NCRA manual listing members of the association.

Freelance Reporting

Most reporters work as either freelance reporters or official reporters for courts. The bulk of work in most freelance firms is reporting statements, interrogatories, and depositions, with occasional other assignments. Freelance reporters substitute in court; do convention reporting; take minutes of public stockholder and board of directors' meetings; report zoning variances and condemnations; participate in arbitrations, in unemployment compensation hearings and disability claims, and so on.

Some freelance firms also service courts and do contract work for the government. The firms that service courts usually allot each reporter a certain number of days in court monthly to ensure that each reporter receives a steady monthly salary.

Method of Payment

It is customary for freelance businesses to pay reporters using a split percentage system (such as 40 percent to the firm and 60 percent to the reporter, or 50 percent to the firm and 50 percent to the reporter) based upon how much the firm contributes to the reporter's work.

In this system, the firm furnishes supplies; office functions such as booking, billing, and collecting; computers, and sometimes scopists or transcribers for dictated material. The reporter furnishes a proper shorthand machine and sometimes dictation equipment or computer equipment. Some firms also provide notereaders.

Another prevalent system is for the firm to pay the reporter 80 percent and keep 20 percent. The reporter then must furnish and pay his transcriber, notereader, or typist and provide his or her own office space at home, which allows certain tax breaks.

Reporters may be deemed employees or independent contractors, and for tax purposes it is highly important that this be agreed upon from the start between the firm and the reporter.

After a reporter is employed for a time by a firm, he or she may be made a partner in the firm and share in the profits.

Advantages of Freelance Reporting

1. The reporter's return in freelance reporting is limited strictly by how much he or she desires to work—the more pages produced, the more pay.

2. A reporter has more freedom from set routine in a freelance office.

3. Another reporter is usually available to appear for any assignment should the scheduled reporter become ill or desire to take a vacation at any particular time.

4. Freelance reporters often have opportunities to specialize in the particular field of work that they enjoy, such as medical or maritime reporting.

5. Opportunities for overseas travel, reporting in other areas, and highly profitable daily copy work frequently are offered to freelance reporters.

6. On many freelance assignments there are fewer people to identify than in court work, where the judge must also be designated.

7. Freelance firms usually book jobs for reporters and provide hearing rooms and office space, telephone service, electricity, water, billing and bookkeeping services, paper, carbons, ink, supplies, copying machines (and sometimes typewriters), computers, dictating equipment, typists, notereaders, and sometimes scopists. Proofreaders are also on the payrolls of many firms today. Many freelance businesses offer all computer transcription and video facilities for their reporters and assist new reporters in securing financing for equipment. Today students leave schools with their dictionaries in hand, ready to begin work, but some firms are willing to help newcomers prepare theirs.

8. Freelance firms may provide fringe benefits such as insurance and hospitalization, but this is not customary.

9. In a freelance office there are always seasoned reporters available to instruct and help the beginner.

10. Better freelance firms start beginners on easier jobs as a rule and train them for increasing responsibility. During the training period jobs are assigned in accordance with background and ability, and an experienced reporter proofreads transcripts and makes suggestions. An effort is made to instruct the novice on all matters of setups, English, certificates, procedures, and methods of dealing with problems.

    Normally, each firm has a form book to guide reporters that will answer many questions. The beginning reporter usually goes out at first with an experienced reporter who will have him or her read notes back, comparing them with the notes of the expert trainer. Transcripts are reviewed carefully and discussed with the training reporter. Preferred ways to identify speakers, to handle false starts, to edit, to bill, to fill out forms, and to handle emergencies are taught. This training is invaluable to the success of a beginning reporter.

11. Many firms assign very experienced typists, notereaders, or scopists to beginners. These people are the reporter's best friend, offering constructive criticism of word usage, transcription techniques, and handling of office routine. Many errors are caught by these alert people, so the smart reporter will treat these fine members of the firm with the respect they have earned.

12. Payment in a freelance firm is usually biweekly or monthly. Some firms pay for all work done whether they receive payment or not, reserving a percentage for bad debts. Some companies pay when the clients pay.

13. Good freelance firms screen work to be sure poor-paying accounts are kept to a minimum.

14. Better reporting organizations distribute the work equitably, according to the reporters' abilities, to ensure that each reporter shares equally in the top-paying jobs.

15. A freelance firm finds the jobs for its reporters and tries to ensure each reporter as much work as he or she can handle.

16. Often fine officialships in courts come to freelance reporters who have worked for better attorneys who are eventually appointed to the bench. A lawyer who has become a judge will often choose as a reporter a freelancer with whom he or she particularly enjoyed working or one who has proven to have exceptional ability in reporting and good rapport with people.

17. A freelance reporter may work with a wider range of lawyers than the official reporter, since many of the finest attorneys spend little time in court, preferring to settle the majority of their cases rather than try lawsuits. Days in court often earn attorneys far less than office work, unless they are famous trial lawyers.

Disadvantages of Freelance Reporting

1. Many freelance companies provide no fringe benefits, such as insurance, hospitalization, tax withholding, or retirement benefits.

2. Since freelance reporters are paid for pages produced, most reporters take vacations without pay. A rare firm may have a provision for vacations.

3. A reporter may enter upon what appears to be an ideal freelance situation only to have the owner die, retire, or withdraw from business, leaving the reporter to work with people he or she may not like or respect. The reporter then must seek work elsewhere or remain in an unsatisfactory circumstance.

4. Some firms do not screen work sufficiently to ensure prompt payment of bills, and the financial arrangement they make with reporters may reflect this inadequacy.

5. The reserve for unpaid accounts may be too high in a firm.

6. Petty jealousies may develop among reporters in a freelance firm because some may feel work is being unevenly distributed. These feelings may result from real or imagined partiality being shown to certain reporters. Nevertheless, an uncomfortable atmosphere can be created.

7. If the work of a freelance firm consists solely of government contracted work, and the contract bid goes to someone else, the firm may not be able to continue to employ all of its employees. Layoffs will result.

8. In depositions, attorneys may represent various parties and interests. Consequently, the reporter is the person solely responsible for getting the record and keeping the procedures under control. In court, however, the judge usually has control of the proceedings. Since many meetings are very unstructured, the reporter must stay in charge at all times in the interest of securing a complete record.

9. Some freelance firms require that a reporter sign a contract. Think hard before signing a contract. If you are doing a good job, the firm will want desperately to retain you. If you are treated well and have an opportunity to progress in the firm, you will never want to leave.

    Usually less ethical firms require contracts totally slanted to benefit the employers and exploit the beginner. If you are so enamored of a firm or a location that you feel you want to work there regardless of the required contract, take the contract to your instructors, to your attorney, and to a trusted reporter and have them read it and advise you. If all three say to sign it, perhaps—and it is a *big* perhaps—you should sign it.

    Remember most of the contracts required by freelance firms have clauses restricting you from practicing in a large area around the city where the firm is located, as well as within it, for years after you leave the firm. Although in most instances these contracts are thrown out of court as restraint of trade, who wants the trouble of litigation and the grudges that follow a parting of the ways?

10. Office space may be limited, and the reporters may be forced to work at home after taking assignments. An advantage is that having an office in the home qualifies reporters for a tax deduction (and more frequent audits than those not claiming a home office). The reporter goes to the office only to report in for job assignments and to deliver transcripts, have them signed, and take care of miscellaneous related business such as picking up his or her paychecks. However, working at home means interruptions and the inconvenience of having one's home taken over as a place of business.

Official Reporting

Some graduate reporters want only one thing by way of employment: an officialship with a judge.

All officials must meet the CSR or other certification requirements, while the U.S. District Courts (federal courts) normally require three to four years' experience and testing.

Some judges prefer to hire beginners so they can train them to do things their way. Other jurists hire only reporters who have had freelance experience or training by some other judge. Some judges prefer men reporters; others feel that women add "class" to the courtroom setting.

One thing is certain: The judge and the judge's reporter must have a good rapport since they must spend much time together. Ordinarily, an official reporter accompanies the judge at all hearings at which the judge presides, either in the city or county wherein they reside or elsewhere (although the tendency is more and more toward pooling reporters and using "swing reporters" to keep transcripts current).

Advantages of Official Reporting

1. A reporter possessing good rapport with a judge can have a very enjoyable work life since the reporter is the judge's confidant and right-hand helper. As an official reporter, you will find background knowledge gained through association with the judge helpful in preparing transcripts. A judge will assist his very competent reporter with problems and collections and grant many privileges to try to keep such a jewel.

2. The official reporter receives a steady yearly salary and paid vacations, pension plans, life insurance, and hospitalization.

3. An official reporter is given all legal holidays.

4. When cases are settled or dismissed, the official reporter often gains unexpected time off.

5. The official reporter not only gets the base salary, but also receives fees for records ordered by the attorneys, expense reimbursement, and sometimes per diems when working away from home.

6. Many judges allow official reporters to do freelance work as long as it does not interfere with duties connected with court work, thus greatly supplementing the official's salary. In some places the reporter may be the only reporter for many miles, and it may be considered as a required part of the work to do the freelance reporting. These reporters have the best of all worlds.

7. Official court reporters are held in great esteem because the general public realizes that it takes a high degree of intelligence and training to do the exacting job of court reporting.

8. Official court reporters constantly meet interesting, highly important people through their work and through their association with the judge. A fringe benefit of the position is that the reporter often has a chance to socialize with the attorneys and other judges at bar meetings, luncheons, and social gatherings.

9. Attorneys tend to pay official court reporters promptly because they do not want judges to think that they do not pay their bills.

10. An official records many interesting, even history-making, cases as justice is dispensed.

11. The official reporter is furnished with an office, telephone service, electricity, supplies for required court work, and usually some equipment—even a computer and scopist service in some instances. In some locations, the home county may furnish supplies for deposition and statement work to make the official position more enticing, but this situation is rare.

12. Associations with other courthouse personnel may be very enjoyable for a judge's official reporter.

13. Through association with attorneys and the court and information learned through cases being tried, an official reporter may often acquire information that can lead to good investments.

Disadvantages of Official Reporting

1. In a large city, when a judge dies, resigns, or retires, the new judge may bring in another reporter, forcing the previous official to seek other employment.

2. A judge who replaces a previous employer may be tyrannical or unpleasant or work so many hours the reporter cannot get out transcripts. Then, the reporter might choose to change employment.

3. Some judges do not allow their official reporter to do any freelance work, feeling that extra work may detract from the reporter's effectiveness.

4. In some jurisdictions an official court reporter is also the judge's secretary. If the judge is male, this may include filling His Honor's pens, tearing off used calendar pages, running out and getting the judge's briefcase from his car, buying presents for his wife or ordering flowers, doing his correspondence, preparing and/or typing the judge's tax returns, picking up his children from school or piano lessons, or typing reams of legal material the judge wants for any kind of reference. A female judge might also require that the reporter perform many similarly unchallenging, but demeaning, tasks.

5. When traveling, court reporters may be required to go to meals with the judge and attorneys.

6. Official court reporters may be required to take their vacations at the same time as the judge, whether the time is convenient or not.

7. An official may be required to do a great deal of driving, particularly if the judge is old or infirm.

8. An official reporter must be competent enough to make an excellent record of a judge, at least two and often more attorneys, and a witness at all times. Since there are four people participating in any ordinary trial, objections and rulings occur frequently. In many cases there are large numbers of attorneys to identify.

9. Much more exhibit marking is required in court than there is in most freelance work. The reporter must be able to keep all exhibits marked and maintained properly throughout the trial.

10. Travel in a large district may become very wearing, particularly since transcripts may be reaching deadlines and sufficient computer time may not be available. Time spent driving cannot be used for transcribing or proofreading. Hotel or motel rooms become cheerless places after a time.

Other Reporting Position Possibilities

Reporting is not limited to court and related freelance reporting. Reporters are sought after to fill positions in areas described in the following paragraphs.

Closed Captioning Reporter

The closed captioning reporter writes news programs and other materials that are translated instantly through a scopist on T.V. screens for the hearing impaired.

College Captioning Reporter

Reporters are now hired in some universities and other colleges to take lectures, which are shown on a screen, and to prepare transcripts for the benefit of deaf students.

Data Storage Reporter

Industrial concerns and government agencies are at last realizing that machine shorthand writers can input figures and other materials over four times as rapidly as those using conventional methods. This development has great possibilities for future employment of specially trained personnel.

Specialized Freelance Reporting

Many freelance firms specialize in convention and seminar reporting; others, in public meeting reporting, medical interrogatories, or taking statements exclusively.

Medical, chemical, or other technical conventions, especially those devoted to space-age technology, computer language and development, mathematics, and the like are difficult because of the specialized terminology. Only beginners possessing excellent English skills and wide background knowledge should tackle such work directly from school as the material may be very difficult.

Commission Reporting

The various commissions, such as railroad and warehouse commissions, the water commissions, and railroads hire their own reporters. In these positions extra pay is usually not provided for transcripts, but the work is not as high-pressured as some other reporting. Since there is a reasonable amount of travel involved, the jobs are quite enjoyable.

In these positions transcripts are usually completed within set working hours. The same applies regarding transcripts of hearing reporters who take preliminary examinations in some areas.

Military Reporting

The military branches are seeking machine reporters much more since the advent of CAT (Computer-Aided Transcription) because the work can now be produced much more efficiently that way. However, Stenomask systems using military personnel trained by the branch are used primarily because the federal government has always offered a very low pay scale for reporting services.

It matters little to the military that this method is cumbersome, unreliable, and inferior or that it requires an inordinate amount of time for production of transcript. All parties are readily available again should the system fail to function, as is often the case. Most proceedings are quite cut and dried anyway. As with all electronic systems, if the electricity goes off, no record is possible.

Scopist and/or Proofreader

The tremendous popularity of Computer-Aided Transcription has led to the emergence of new positions related to the reporting field. As a reporter proofreads, he or she may mark all changes and then hand the pages to a scopist to make corrections, deletions, or additions. This is a highly responsible position, and many expert scopists command middle five-figure salaries. A number of firms also hire proofreaders to ensure correctness of all records. These people are highly literate individuals, and they are paid in accordance with their high abilities. Normally, both scopists and proofreaders are paid by the page.

Legislative Reporting

High on the scale of reporting pay is legislative reporting in the U.S. Senate and the House of Representatives. The salary earned reaches $60,000 per year.

These positions are considered very desirable, and the reporter is at the center of where it all happens—Washington, D.C. The reporter writes ten minutes of each hour and provides immediate copy on the desks of the lawmakers for revision and same-day printing by the Government Printing Office.

Beginners usually do not aspire to these positions immediately because they may be reserved for experienced individuals with contacts, but they are available and something to aim at should you be interested. Now that freelance reporters who are great can easily exceed this salary range, these jobs are much more available than they once were.

The Carrot at the End of the Stick

This chapter has described different fields available within the reporting profession, and new opportunities are opening up everyday. Having read this far, you may already have decided which of these careers is for you.

You are probably saying "What about the money?" Money is what one hears most about when the topic of reporting comes up. After all, reporting is a comparatively high-paying job. Reporters earn from $25,000 upward their first year if they become freelance reporters. They earn much more if they use a computer for transcription, once they have secured their basic equipment and a few months' experience. From the first year on, earnings should rise yearly with fewer hours or work essential to produce the pages of transcript.

The pay schedules for courtroom officials are carefully set out in each state, and transcript fees are added to the basic salary. In some places the county commissioners set the remuneration, and in many instances the salaries and transcript fees are set by the legislature.

A court reporter will make a good comfortable living, although most will not become millionaires—that is, from their reporting. However, hard work plus good investments may do it.

Reporting is a challenging, rewarding career that will provide you with satisfying experiences, friendships, self-esteem, and enough money to allow you to appreciate many of the fine things you have the discrimination to appreciate.

REPORTING HAS A LOT TO GIVE YOU! GO GET IT!

Chapter 3

A Court Reporter Is Literate

The Need for Reading

Anyone entering the career of court reporting should read a wide variety of materials, including a good daily newspaper (news and editorials, not just the comics). Other recommended choices are *Time, Newsweek, The National Shorthand Reporter, The Wall Street Journal, Barron's, Vital Speeches of the Day, Scientific American,* and *The Journal of the American Medical Association.* Trade publications and annual reports of corporations also are worthwhile reading.

Occasionally a student with limited English skills and little time to practice on the shorthand machine, upon being told to read more, will remark "But I don't have any time to read!" The only possible retort to this is "You do not have time *not* to read if you are going to be successful in this profession. A court reporter must have an excellent background in English and be knowledgeable about many subjects."

It has been said that the ideal court reporter is a 50-year-old person who has been everywhere and done everything. Not necessarily so! But the broader your background, the easier your job. The topics that come up in reporting are infinite, and the work is becoming more complex as the world becomes more scientifically oriented.

Make it a habit to fit some reading of worthwhile matter into every day until you feel at ease with the professionals you come into contact with each day. Remember, you are joining one of the top professions.

Research Books

No one can possibly know everything, and your ability as a reporter will be judged by how well you can research specialized material in the interest of a truly verbatim transcript that accurately portrays what a technical or medical expert intended to convey.

Many times you will realize in the afternoon court or deposition session that a word you thought you heard 50 times during the morning session now does not make sense in the context of the further proceedings. You will have to find what that expression really is, as well as its exact meaning. The "coaming" of a ship is different from "combing" the hair.

It is difficult for the student to comprehend how much research may go into a transcript in the reporter's search for total accuracy, but a good reporter will go to extreme lengths to be absolutely sure of everything in the transcript he or she delivers.

Reporters cultivate doctors, druggists, librarians, and specialists as friends with whom they can verify facts as a last resort. For everyday purposes, reporters need to build a good reference library particularly suited to their type of reporting and the locality in which they work.

The following list will give you an idea of the types of books to start collecting while you are a student. There will be many other useful books you will discover while wandering about bookstores, secondhand shops, or even garage sales.

You will probably not want to get all the books listed here because some are duplicates, but the ones named are representative of the books reporters use to prepare their transcripts.

Dictionaries

Court reporters employ a variety of different types of dictionaries. The first spelling given under each definition is always preferred, and the reporter must be alert to changes in our ever evolving language.

Unabridged Dictionaries. *Webster's Third New International Dictionary* (Merriam Webster, Inc., Springfield, MA) is the unabridged dictionary of choice of many fine reporters. *The Oxford Dictionary* is a very complete unabridged version except that is has British spellings with double "l's" that are no longer used in Americanized past tenses and participles. Therefore, it is not recommended.

Desk Dictionaries. *Webster's Ninth New Collegiate Dictionary* (Merriam Webster, Inc., Springfield, MA) is an adequate smaller dictionary for general use, although it disagrees with the unabridged dictionary listed above in a number of small ways.

Funk & Wagnall's New College Dictionary (Wilfred Funk; New York, NY) and *Webster's New World Dictionary of the American Language* (Southwestern Co., Nashville, TN) are two smaller desk-size dictionaries of quality. The latter has a good print size.

The American Heritage Dictionary, 2d College Edition (Houghton Mifflin, Boston, MA) contains derivations.

The Dictionary of Cultural Literacy (Houghton Mifflin, Boston, MA) discusses in encyclopedic style thousands of cultural references the reporter may need to research, although there are some misquotations.

Biology Dictionary. *Biology Dictionary* by Sister Rita Blanche St. Pierre, RSM (5,000 terms) (National Book Co. Portland, OR) has good variety of terms and carefully marked pronunciations.

Synonyms. *Webster's Dictionary of Synonyms* (B. C. Merriam Co., Springfield, MA) will help with words that have similar meanings.

Slang. Reporters doing criminal work may find the *Dictionary of American Slang* (Pocket Books, New York, N.Y.) helpful, although it is somewhat limited.

Computers. *Webster's New World Dictionary of Computer Terms* (Simon & Schuster, Inc., One Gulf & Western Plaza, New York, NY) helps research terms and definitions.

Computer-Compatible Stenograph Theory, Dictionary I Reference Guide (Stenograph Corp., 1500 Bishop Court, Mt. Pleasant, IL) is reliable for dictionary building, although this is not a "reading" book. *The Campbell Machine Shorthand Dictionary*, 2d Edition (Obsidian Press, Las Vegas, NV) falls into the same category.

Chemicals. *Hack's Chemical Dictionary* (McGraw-Hill Book Co., New York, NY) is of use in scientific case research.

Scientific Terms. *The Dictionary of Scientific Terms* (D. Van Nostrand Co., Inc., Princeton, NJ) covers many technical topics.

Legal Dictionaries. *Black's Law Dictionary* (West Publishing Co., St. Paul, MN) is the most popular large volume of this type.

Law Dictionary by Steven H. Gifis (Barron's Educational Series, Inc.) is a smaller volume recommended for those who deal extensively with legal terminology.

Cochran's Law Lexicon (W. H. Anderson Co., Cincinnati, OH) is a handy pocket-sized volume.

In addition, all potential court reporters should work through *Legal Terminology, A Programmed Approach* by Mary H. Knapp (Stenograph Corp., 1500 Bishop Court, Mt. Pleasant, IL) to secure the necessary basic background in legal terminology.

Atlases. A good atlas is a must, and the most commonly used ones in the recommended order are:

Hammond's Ambassador World Atlas (C. S. Hammond & Co., Maplewood, NJ).
World Atlas (Rand-McNally, New York, NY)
Encyclopedia Britannica World Atlas (Encyclopedia Britannica, Chicago, IL).

Legal Directories

The Legal Directories Publishing Co., Inc., 2122 Kidwell Street, P.O. Box 140200, Dallas, TX 75214-0200, publishes 26 directories covering 42 states. These are often called the "Blue Books," and they contain listings by names of all judges; attorneys, with addresses; justices of the peace; sheriffs; county officers (auditors, treasurers, county clerks, constables, probation officers, etc); commissioners; and court reporters by counties, together with much other information.

General Local References

Wherever you go, collect city directories, telephone books (white and yellow pages), and comprehensive maps of the city you are in and all the surrounding areas. Then, at midnight when you are preparing a "rush" and you find you did not verify a name in your notes that looks like "Ronnie Moose," you can find that it is "Ronemus" and solve your problem.

Encyclopedias

A good set of encyclopedias can be most useful in verifying strata of rocks in oil drilling cases, finding families of insects in contaminated grain cases, looking up past historical events, and locating a myriad of miscellaneous items. Several of these follow:

Encyclopedia Britannica (Encyclopedia Britannica, Inc., Chicago, IL).
Columbia-Viking Desk Encyclopedia (two volumes) (Viking Press, New York, NY).
Lincoln Library of Essential Information (The Frontier Press, Buffalo, NY).
Grolier Encyclopedia (The Grolier Society, New York, NY).

Medical Reference Books

A reporter can never have too many medical reference books because of the unlimited subject matter brought forth in the many medical cases reported. Some medical material comes up in probably 75 to 80 percent of the cases in the courts today. The following are some suggestions:

Gray's Anatomy, by Henry Gray, FRS (Running Press, Philadelphia, PA).

Taber's Cyclopedic Medical Dictionary (F. A. Davis Co., Philadelphia, PA). Long vowels are clearly marked.

Dorland's Medical Dictionary (W. B. Sanders, Philadelphia, PA)

Blakiston's New Gould Medical Dictionary (The Blakiston Co., Philadelphia, PA).

Stedman's Medical Dictionary (The Williams & Wilkins Co., Baltimore, MD).

Mosby's Medical and Nursing Dictionary (C. V. Mosby Co., St. Louis, MO). This is written in full encyclopedic style.

Webster's Medical Desk Dictionary (Merriam Webster, Inc., Springfield, MA).

The New American Medical Dictionary and Health Manual by Robert Rothenberg (The New American Library, New York, NY). This contains 7,500 definitions, medical slang, and numerous charts.

The American Medical Association Guide to Prescription and Over-the-Counter Drugs, edited by Charles B. Clayman, M.D. (Random House, New York, NY).

Learning Medical Terminology by Young & Astrin (C.V. Mosby Co., St. Louis, MO).

Mastering Medical Language by Anthony L. Spatold (Prentice-Hall, Englewood Cliffs, NJ)

Physician's Desk Reference (PDR). This annual is a must when researching medications, uses of drugs, contraindications, etc. (PDR, Box 58, Oradell, NJ).

The Merck Index (Merck Co., Rahway, NJ).

The Pharmacist's Guide to Products and Prices (American Pharmaceutical Association).

The Reverse Medical Secretary by Richard Franks (Medical Economics Co., NJ). This book categorizes medical terms according to their roots.

Medical Terminology for Court Reporters by Nathaniel Weiss (NCRA, 118 Park Street, S.E., Vienna, VA).

Medical Aspects of Negligence Cases (2d ed.) and *The Defense of Personal Injury Actions* (The Practicing Law Institute, New York, NY) provide good background reading.

The Practicing Law Institute, New York, NY, publishes such books as *The Medical Aspects of Negligence Cases* and *The Defense of Personal Injury Actions*. Callaghan & Co., 6141 North Cicero Avenue, Chicago, IL publishes *Medical Trial Technique Quarterly, Trial Lawyer's Guide*, and *Goldstein's Trial Technique*. These sets have actual case testimony and fine articles on new developments in lawsuit subject matter. Your county law library will welcome you to read these and other background books.

The *NCRA Professional Education Series* consisting of English, law, and medical volumes is now in process of revision, but the medical book has good references regarding treatment of fractures and a lot of general knowledge that is still pertinent.

Medical Directories

The medical societies of your state issue directories of doctors, dentists, anesthetists, nurses, physical therapists, psychologists, and psychiatrists. These publications often list background information as well as names and addresses of professionals.

English

Morson's English Guide for Court Reporters by Lillian I. Morson, New Egypt, NJ, is universally accepted as authority for court reporters.

Court Reporting: Grammar and Punctuation by Diane Castilow-Palliser (Southwestern Publishing Co., Cincinnati, OH) and *The Complete Guide to Punctuation* by Margaret Enright Wye (Prentice-Hall Press, Englewood Cliffs, NJ) are handy volumes of advice as to perfect punctuation. Another is *Discovering English Grammar* by Richard Veit (Houghton Mifflin, Boston, MA).

Everyone needs a good style handbook. *The Little, Brown Handbook* by H. Ramsey Fowler (Little, Brown, Boston, MA) is an excellent one.

Of course, the reporter's accepted final authority as to grammar and punctuation has always been the *Style Manual of the Government Printing Office,* which can be secured from the Superintendent of Documents, Government Printing Office, Washington, D.C. Others of merit include: *A Manual of Style* (University of Chicago Press, Chicago, IL), *The Writer's Manual* (ETC Publications, Palm Springs, CA), *A Rhetoric and Composition Handbook* by Richard M. Weaver (Quill, New York, NY), *A New Guide to Better Writing* by Flesch & Lass (Popular Library, New York, NY) and *The Practical Stylist*, 2d ed. by Sheridan Baker (Thomas Y. Crowell, New York, NY).

Proofreading

An area of high importance today because of the intricacies of computer translation is proofreading. Some recommended helpers are *Developing Proofreading Skill* by Sue C. Camp (Gregg Division, McGraw Hill, New York, NY), *Proofreading* By Kruse, Herlinger & Lawry (Glencoe Publishing Company, Mission Hills, CA), and *Proofreading/Editing Proficiency* by Judith C. Simon (Glencoe Publishing Company).

Shorthand Writing

Glossary of Words, Abbreviations, and Phrases by Mary H. Knapp (College Store, Alvin Community College, 3110 Mustang Road, Alvin, TX 77511).

Miscellaneous English Sources

The Creative Writer's Phrase Finder by Edward Prestwood (ETC Publications, Palm Springs, CA).

Encyclopedic Dictionary of English Usage by Mager & Mager (Prentice-Hall, Englewood Cliffs, NJ).

The Joy of Lex by Gyles Brandreth (William Morrow & Co., Inc., New York, NY). After all, English should be fun!

I Always Look Up the Word "Egregious" by Maxwell Nurnberg (Prentice-Hall, Englewood Cliffs, NJ).

A Pleasure in Words by Eugene T. Maleska (Simon & Schuster, New York, NY).

Mythology

Greek Mythology for Everyone by Donald Richardson (Avnel Books, New York; Crown, New York, NY)

Quotations

Bartlett's Familiar Quotations (Little, Brown, Boston, MA) is the most commonly used reference for quoted matter. Another one is *The Home Book of Quotations* by Burton Stevenson (Dodd, Mead & Co., New York, NY).

Thesaurus

No reporter should be without *Roget's International Thesaurus* (Thomas Y. Crowell, New York, NY) because it is a ready reference when you know the meaning of a word but you cannot think of the exact word.

The Bible

Many references are made to passages from The Bible, so secure both the King James version and the American Standard version.

Shakespeare

The words of Shakespeare seem to be cited more than Biblical passages. The Rockwell Kent edition of the *Complete Works of Shakespeare* (Garden City Books, Garden City, NY) is recommended because of its large print and compact, one-volume size.

Foreign Languages

Lyall's Guide to the Languages of Europe (David McKay Company, Inc., New York, NY) will provide help with occasional foreign words and phrases.

Pronunciation

There Is No Zoo In Zoology by Charles Harrington Elster (Collier, McMillan, New York, NY).

Word Derivations

Word Mysteries and Histories by Barry Moser (Houghton Mifflin, Boston, MA).

Biographies

Who's Who In America (and Regional and World volumes) is published by A. N. Marquis Co., Chicago, IL. Many outstanding people have memorized their biographies or curriculum vitae almost verbatim as it appears in *Who's Who*.

The Congressional Directory (Superintendent of Documents, GPO, Washington, D.C.) includes biographies of state and federal government notables and listing of members of Congressional committees.

NCRA publishes a somewhat useful *Reporter's Desk Reference*; and everyone in reporting circles has heard of the *Philadelphia Clinic*, which can be secured from Harry Foster, 102 Center Building, York Road & Greenwood Avenue, Jenkintown, PA. This book is a treasure of writing and reporting essentials.

Etiquette

Attorneys and judges place a high value on observing excellent business etiquette, so every reporter should secure one of the following books or a similar high-quality one and study it:

Manners in Business (MacMillan, New York, NY)
The Encyclopedia of Etiquette (Crown, New York, NY)
Business Etiquette Handbook (Prentice-Hall, Englewood Cliffs, NJ)
Charm: The Career Girl's Guide to Business and Personal Success (McGraw-Hill, New York, NY)

Financial

Barron's, a weekly market publication, contains articles on stocks, bonds, futures, money markets, business matters, dividends, etc. *The Wall Street Journal* should be read by every reporter to keep up on these topics. Standard & Poor's Corporation publishes many publications pertaining to investments. *Dun & Bradstreet Ratings and Reports* and *Moody's Manuals* help with references needed in civil and probate reporting.

Hotels

The Hotel Red Book (American Hotel Association Directory Corp., New York, NY) lists hotels alphabetically by city and state, giving managers' names, rates, services, and types of accommodations offered. Since reporters and judges travel extensively, it pays to compare offerings. Some hotel chains and airlines offer free accommodations, air travel, and lower rental auto deals to frequent travelers. Check into these by all means and save yourself money.

Legal Helpers

A Uniform System of Citation (The Harvard Law Review Association, Cambridge, MA) is everyone's authority for listing cites. Also secure *Shepard's Citations* (Shepard's Citations, Inc., Colorado Springs, CO).
Using Law Books by Alfred J. Lewis (Kendall/Hunt Publishing Company, Dubuque, IA)
West's Law Finder (West Publishing Company, St. Paul, MN) will also prove invaluable.
Introduction to the Criminal Justice System by Gerald D. Robin (Harper & Row, New York, NY) will instruct you regarding criminal principles, procedures, and practice. This valuable book will teach court systems, provide references and citations for many famous criminal cases, and give you a good glossary of terms.
Paralegal's Litigation Handbook by Carole A. Bruno (Institute for Business Planning, Englewood Cliffs, NJ).
The Deposition Handbook by Lynn Brooks (NCRA, 118 Park Street, S.E., Vienna, VA) is a thorough volume for all freelancers. Although the taking of depositions is covered at length in this book, another writer's slant can be very helpful.
Legal Office Procedures, College Series by Bate & Casey (Gregg Division, McGraw-Hill, New York, NY) is a good addition to a reporter's library.
Federal Rules of Civil Procedure and Title 28, U.S. Code, Judiciary and Judicial Procedure (West Publishing Co., St. Paul, MN) is just what its name implies.

Automobile Values, etc.

The Kelley Blue Book—Automobile Market Report (Kelley Blue Book Co., Costa Mesa, CA) is a good investment for reference use in personal injury automobile negligence cases.

Organization

How To Be Organized in Spite of Yourself by Schlenger & Roesch (NAL books, a division of Penguin Books, USA, Inc., New York, NY). Maybe you don't need it, but most of us do!

Word Processing

The ABC's of Word Perfect 5 by Alan R. Neibauer (SYBEX, San Francisco, CA) was so clear it taught me to use Word Perfect in half a day!
Word Processing and Information Systems by Marilyn K. Popyk (Gregg Division, McGraw-Hill, New York, NY).

Secretarial References

Do not refuse to add books to your library simply because they say "legal secretary." Some of these can be your most valuable books at times, particularly if you are also secretary to a judge. A well-trained reporter is as high above a secretary in training and qualifications as a nuclear scientist is above a nature counselor in a scout camp, but that does not mean we can't use every resource we can find. Some useful books are listed below.

Sletwold's Manual of Documents and Forms for the Legal Secretary (Prentice-Hall, Englewood Cliffs, NJ).

Legal Secretary's Complete Handbook by Besse Mae Miller (Prentice-Hall, Englewood Cliffs, NJ).

Legal Secretarial Procedures by Joyce Morton (Prentice-Hall, Englewood Cliffs, NJ).

Handbook for the Legal Secretary by Leslie & Coffin (McGraw-Hill, New York, NY).

The Career Legal Secretary, National Association of Legal Secretaries International (West Publishing Co., St. Paul, MN).

Secretary's Modern Guide to English Usage by Jean C. Vermes, (Parker Publishing Co., Inc., West Nyack, NY).

New World Secretarial Handbook (World Publishing, Cleveland, OH).

Secretary's Desk Book (Parker Publishing Co., West Nyack, NY).

Parliamentary Procedures

Robert's Rules of Order, Revised ed., by H. M. Robert (William Morrow & Co., New York, NY) provides rules for conducting meetings, conventions, and conferences.

Newspapers and Periodicals

N. W. Ayers & Sons' Directory of Newspapers & Periodicals (N. W. Ayers & Sons, Philadelphia, PA) is an extensive alphabetical listing source, grouped by city and state, of every periodical and newspaper published in the United States, Canada, and some foreign countries. Names and addresses of publishers and editors are included.

Post Offices

The United States Directory of Post Offices, Publication No. 26 (Superintendent of Documents, GPO, Washington, D.C.) contains all cities and towns having post offices, street names, and zip code listings, and essential postal information.

Maritime

Should you be located where maritime work is frequent, you may need *Kelly's Directory of Merchants, Manufacturers, and Shippers* (Kelly Directories, Ltd., London, England). *The Bluejacket's Manual* of the United States is helpful in searching out many maritime terms which are not encountered in everyday work. De Kerchoven's *Maritime Dictionary* or one of the many other such books, although expensive, should be secured if your work involves extensive admiralty terminology.

Jury Charges and Jury Selection

If you secure the *Pattern Civil and Criminal Jury Charges* for your state, the function of taking jury charges will become easier, especially if your judge seems to exemplify "The Charge of the Light Brigade." *Jury Selection* by V. Hale Starr and Mark McCormick (Little, Brown & Co., Boston, MA) will assist you to learn how attorneys arrive at decisions in selecting jury panels.

Science and Engineering

The Science-Engineering Secretary by Stafford & Culpepper (Prentice-Hall, Englewood Cliffs, NJ) is great for showing how to type mathematical symbols, technical abbreviations, formulae, numbers (including superscripts and subscripts) and teaching technical terms and fundamentals (good sections on hyphen usage, confused words, etc.).

Manufacturers

Thomas' Register of American Manufacturers (Thomas Publishing Co., New York, NY) lists products and their manufacturers.

Foundations

The Foundation Directory (Russell Sage Foundation, New York, NY) lists large and small, the type, and names and addresses of officers.

Reference Guides

Much research time can be saved by using a reference guide such as *Guide to Reference Materials* by Mona McCormick, published by *The New York Times*, or *Find it Fast* by Robert I. Berkman (Harper & Row, New York, NY)

Then, because all reporters need a little stimulation once in awhile, *A Whack on the Side of the Head* by Roger von Oech, Ph.D., from Warner Books, P.O. Box 690, New York, NY 10019, will provide motivation.

The volume of court reporting work has increased so greatly since the advent of Computer-Aided Transcription (CAT) that improved management of freelance offices and official reporters' practices has become of paramount importance. *The Court and Freelance Reporter Profession—Improved Management Strategies* by David J. Saari, Published by Quorum Books, Greenwood Press, Inc., 88 Post Road West, Westport, CT 06881, will provide worthwhile reading for any court reporter and student.

Many freelance reporting firms have extensive resource libraries, and the courthouse law library is available to the public as well as to those connected with the legal profession as long as conditions for its use are observed, since tax money and assessments from attorneys support the library. However, you should begin to build as early possible as extensive a library as you can afford, to save time in research and producing your own work.

The above list is only representative and should give you an idea of the type of books you should acquire to assist you with transcript research. As you secure such books, read and study them, and you will save yourself hours of researching later.

BY THE QUALITY OF YOUR TRANSCRIPTS SHALL THE LEGAL PROFESSION KNOW YOU.

Chapter 4

The Notary Public

Since reporting is such responsible work, some type of performance bond is usually required of the reporter to insure faithful carrying out of the duties of the office.

Bonding for the Reporter

As an official court reporter for a judge, you may be required to take an oath and secure a performance bond, which will be recorded by the appropriate clerk of court. Your signature as certification of your transcripts will then meet all requirements of the law. Upon appointment, you should check with the judge for whom you work as to bonding requirements for your position as they vary widely from state to state and court to court.

In some states, your Certified Shorthand Reporter (CSR) certificate and seal imprint make your official signature valid on the certificate of any of your work; but in some states, as an official or freelance reporter, your authority will stem from the fact that you are a notary public. The notary public is the officer whose duty it is to attest to the genuineness of legal instruments in order to render them available as evidence of the facts contained therein.

A notary acts in a ministerial rather than in a judicial capacity, and a notary public may not practice any form of law. You should check with the clerk of court as to the procedure for securing a notary public commission in the locale where you plan to practice. Most official reporters secure a notarial commission for the convenience it affords the judge and the attorneys, even though it may not be required for certification of transcripts in their particular states.

History of Office of Notary Public

The office of notary public goes back to the ancient Roman days. In the beginning, the notary was merely a scribe who took notes and minutes and made short drafts of public and private instruments. The notary was a particularly important officer in the early days of the law merchant because it was necessary to have someone with respected authority to vouch for acts performed between people of nations far apart from one another.

This office exists today in most Christian nations. Although the powers and duties of the office vary from country to country, the notary public today is authorized by law to perform functions of wider scope.

Restrictions of Notary Public Commission

In some states, notaries are appointed to act only in the county in which they reside. In case you are a court reporter holding such a restricted notarial commission, at the beginning of every statement or deposition you take in a county outside your jurisdiction, you must remember to have the attorneys stipulate on the record that this restriction is waived. Such a stipulation in the front of your transcript may read "IT WAS STIPULATED AND AGREED by and between counsel for the respective parties hereto that the officer taking the deposition could swear the witness with the same force and effect as though (he) (she) were a notary public in and for the County of _____, State of _____." There are very few states today which have the county type of appointment.

A notary public may otherwise not perform the duties of the office in any state other than that for which he or she is appointed. Should you take a deposition in a state outside your residence, again, a stipulation similar to the above will be required.

Any person who is a party to an instrument, no matter how small or nominal the interest, cannot act as a notary public on it. Neither may a notary public sign an acknowledgment to his or her own signature on any document.

Requirements of Office

To be eligible for appointment as a notary public, a person must be of legal age and a resident citizen of the state in which the commission is to be granted. An alien may not be appointed a notary public. Of course, it goes without saying that an applicant for a notary public commission may have no criminal record and must possess a good reputation in the community, for this is a very responsible position.

Appointing Procedures

The method of securing appointment as a notary public is set forth in the statutes of each state. Beginning court reporters should familiarize themselves fully with these rules in order to understand fully the specific requirements of the jurisdiction in which such power is sought.

Ordinarily, authority for appointment of notaries is vested in the State's Secretary of State, who is empowered to appoint a convenient number of notaries public for each county of the state. These appointments may be made at any time.

To secure your commission, go to the county clerk of your residence county and satisfy the county clerk as to your eligibility to become a notary public. Fill out the essential forms before the clerk, who will then forward your name and forms to the Secretary of State with a certificate as to your eligibility for appointment.

The Secretary of State will act on this application at the earliest practicable time and notify the clerk that the appointment has or has not been made. The clerk will then inform you to appear to give oath and bond and qualify for the appointment by paying all fees required within the number of days set by the statute.

When the applicant for appointment has qualified for office, the county clerk must notify the Secretary of State of the fact and remit the fees to him. Upon receipt of notice, the Secretary of State will issue the commission, either by sending it to the clerk of court to transmit to the new notary public or by mailing it directly to the notary public, according to custom. The commission will be dated as effective on the date of qualification.

A qualified notary public may perform the duties of the office from the time of qualification, even before receiving the commission.

Execution of Bond

Any person appointed as a notary public must, before entering upon official duties, execute a bond with a solvent surety company. The company must be acceptable to the Secretary of State and authorized to do business in the state. The bond is to insure faithful performance of the duties of the office.

The State Board of Insurance normally approves the rate for notary public bonds. This bond must be approved, entered, and deposited in the clerk's office. The appointee must also take an official oath of office to which he or she must subscribe. This oath is endorsed on the bond with the certificate of the official who administers it.

An application for renewal of notary public bond must be made at the expiration of each statutory period of appointment. The bond is automatically renewed with the commission (upon payment of proper fees) by the Secretary of State, as long as no reason is presented against its renewal.

A notary public must notify the Secretary of State of any change of address within the statutory period of time after such change. If a notary removes his or her residence or principal place of business from the state, the office is automatically vacated, at which time any necessary record books and instruments in the notary's possession should be turned over to the clerk of court.

Maintenance of Book of Records

Each notary public should keep a well-bound book of records of all acknowledgments of record taken before him or her. However, failure of the notary to maintain such a record of any acknowledgment will not invalidate the instrument.

Check your state statutes carefully regarding this procedure as it is possible you may fulfill other notarial duties than merely certifying depositions, statements, and records, and placing jurats to witnesses' signatures on such instruments.

Making Documents Official

The signature of the notary is what gives an instrument executed before him or her its character, and the paper cannot be considered authentic without such signature. Beneath the signature on acknowledgments, proofs of written instruments, protest documents, oaths, affidavits, and depositions, the notary public is required to type, print, or stamp his or her name. However, failure to do so will not invalidate the acknowledgment.

In most states it is essential to show the date of expiration of the notary's commission on all instruments signed by the notary.

A Rubber Stamp Saves Time

Most reporters use a rubber stamp beneath their signatures on the original and all copies of every document signed as a notary public. Of course, this information may be typed on each document instead of stamped. The rubber stamp and its location should be as follows:

NEAT N. FINE, CSR, Notary Public
County of Cooper, State of New York
My commission expires _____

Of course, the size of the type on your rubber stamp will correspond to the space of the signature.

State statutes also indicate that each notary public must provide a seal of office which conforms to the laws as to the engraved matter thereon to use for authentication of all official acts.

In some states it is the custom to inscribe the name of the notary public on the metal notarial seal. In a few states provision is now made for the notary to be allowed to use a properly designed rubber-stamp seal instead of the metal one which impresses the design into the paper. This method is cheaper, but it certainly does not add to the dignity and appearance of any instrument.

The proper place to affix the notarial seal on any instrument is over the notary public's signature. The seal may be impressed either on the paper or on some substance as sealing wax attached to the paper (susceptible of a definite, uniform impression) or a gilt paper seal pasted to the document.

It is doubtful that the sealing-wax method is used frequently in this country, but many European legal documents have a wax seal with ribbons imbedded therein.

Procedures for Certifying and Filing Depositions

The reporter before whom depositions are taken should inscribe on the manila envelope containing the originals of the depositions the following: (1) case number, (2) venue, (3) title of case, (4) names of persons deposed, (5) date taken, and in some cases (6) costs and by whom paid. The reporter must also certify that he or she is the person who deposited the same in the mail for transmission or delivered same, sign the certificate on the envelope, and place his or her notarial seal over signature.

The deposition originals should then be sealed in a larger manila envelope addressed to the clerk of the proper court. All mailed depositions should be sent first class with a return receipt requested.

If deposition originals are hand carried for filing, a receipt should be prepared by the reporter. The clerk receiving the depositions should be requested to sign the receipt to protect the reporter against blame in case misfiling should occur or the depositions be lost or borrowed and not returned by another party.

A good technique to use is to place several staples across the top of the inner envelope and tape the top shut, since in some states depositions may not be opened prior to trial. It is difficult to open an envelope secured this way without it being evident that the envelope has been tampered with. This technique does deter some unscrupulous attorneys from removing the originals and copying them to avoid paying for copies.

Procedures vary from place to place regarding what the notary places on the outside of the envelopes, but the previous procedure will certainly be acceptable in any jurisdiction.

Responsibilities of Notary Public

A notary public must never sign an acknowledgment unless the person whose signature appears on the instrument signs the paper in his or her presence. If the person is not present to sign the document, he or she might be a fraud or murder victim. Someone seeking to get possession of property owned by the person purportedly signing the document might go to extremes to get the property is question.

One notary signed an acknowledgment upon representation by an attorney who said the signature of the person who was not present was genuine. The notary public lost his commission when it was determined that the signature was forged. So, protect yourself. Follow the letter of the law!

Penalties for Misuses of Notarial Power

Any person directly or proximately injured by a notary public's official misconduct or negligence may recover against the notary individually and against his or her official bond. Official misconduct on the part of the notary public may result also in imposition of criminal liability.

These penalties should persuade you that you are entering a very responsible type of work and that you should be well qualified upon entry into the profession of court reporting. As a court reporter, should you fail to deliver transcript or should you bill for services you do not perform, you may be deprived of your notary commission or Certified Shorthand Reporter (CSR) license as well as required to face criminal charges, including incarceration to complete unfinished transcripts.

Any notary public who shall be guilty of any willful neglect of duty or malfeasance in office may be removed from office in the manner provided by law. To impeach a notary public's certificate, evidence must be clearly cogent and convincing beyond any reasonable controversy. However, when a notary public has been indicted for, and convicted of, any wilful neglect of duty or official misconduct, he or she must be removed from office, in which case the order for removal in embodied in the judgment of the court.

All court reporters should carry malpractice insurance today (just as other professionals do) to protect themselves against the consequences of such things as having their cars stolen with their notes inside, persons bringing false charges, and so on.

Guard your notarial commission jealously as a court reporter. If you are a freelance reporter, it may be the instrument that grants you the right to work. Along with your required certification, it lends credence to the records you produce.

BE WISE! GUARD YOUR NOTARIAL COMMISSION!

Administering the Oath and Reading Back

In this book, the chapters will progress from the simplest forms of reporting to the more complex types. One of the duties of the court reporter is to administer oaths to witnesses on interrogatories, statements, and depositions.

In a court of record (a court having a court reporter), the clerk of court will administer oaths. On rare occasions the judge may administer the oath. If ever the judge might be busy signing papers and the clerk be absent, the judge might request the reporter to swear the witness. In such a case, you will be thankful not to have to ask the witness to swear to the following oath which was administered in the courts of Siam as late as 1910:

Example

"May the blood flow from every vein in my body;
May the lightning cut me in two parts;
May the crocodiles eat me;
May I be condemned to carry water towards the flames of hell in panniers without
   bottoms;
May I pass after my death into the body of a slave;
May I suffer the most dire treatment during years as numerous as the grains of
   sand in the Four Seas;
May I be born again deaf, dumb, and blind, my body covered with wounds most
   repulsive;
May I also be cast to Narok (hell) and tortured excruciatingly by Pres Yom (The
   Devil) if I shall ever break my oath."

Suitable Reporter's Oath

When you report statements, the adjuster or attorney you accompany will tell you whether or not to swear the witness. Written interrogatories are a form of deposition, so you will always swear the witness just as though a regular deposition were taking place since you are the officer of the Court while reporting them. There is one place where you must be very sure to swear each witness, and that is at the beginning of every deposition you report.

Some reporters simply ask the witness to rise and say "Do you swear to tell the truth, the whole truth, and nothing but the truth, so help you God?" Then, upon securing an affirmative answer, they say "You may sit down," and the questioning begins. However, in every state, a little pamphlet concerning the notary public's duties, which every clerk of court can furnish you, ordinarily gives the correct form of oath for that state. Be sure to follow the correct wording to avoid being embarrassed by some smart-aleck attorney who is a purist for form.

The usual form of oath administered by the court reporter before a sworn statement, interrogatory, or deposition is:

Example
"You do solemnly swear that the testimony you are about to offer regarding the cause hereinunder consideration shall be the truth, the whole truth, and nothing but the truth, so help you God?"

Affirmation. On occasion you will be confronted by witnesses who will refuse to swear, stating that their religion prevents their taking an oath. In such cases simply ask them if they will affirm that they will tell the truth. Then, proceed with the affirmation, which should be similar in wording to the following:

Example
"You do solemnly affirm that the testimony you are about to offer regarding the cause hereinunder consideration shall be the truth, the whole truth, and nothing but the truth? This you do under the pains and penalties of perjury."

Be sure to leave the "so help you God" off every affirmation.

Tips for Administering the Oath

Always make enough of a production of swearing the witness that he or she will definitely remember having been sworn.

Be sure to look at the witness and assess any physical limitations before you administer the oath.

Unless the person is incapacitated (a person in traction or with crutches should not be asked to stand) say "Will you please rise and raise your right hand and be sworn?" To a one-armed person, say "Please raise your hand and be sworn." Try to avoid embarrassing situations by using tact and common sense and keep your mind on what you are doing. Should you make a mistake at any time when administering the oath, do not intensify the situation by apologizing too much.

Upon receiving an affirmative answer to either oath or affirmation, you should say "You may be seated," and the proceedings will begin immediately, so be ready to write at once. The attorneys often forget that you are there once they start their questioning, so be totally prepared.

The Courtroom Oath

Some states still have rather long, complicated oaths to be administered to witnesses. In some jurisdictions, witnesses must place their right hand on the Bible while swearing. In case you are ever requested to swear a witness or witnesses in a courtroom, a suitable oath would be:

Example
"You do solemnly swear that the testimony you shall give in the cause now pending before this Court shall be the truth, the whole truth, and nothing but the truth, so help you God."

If you are swearing more than one witness at the same time, you will start off by saying: "You, and each of you, do solemnly swear . . .," and so on. Affirmations may also be given.

Do Not Assume the Duty. When you are hired by attorneys or adjusters to report cases in courts of lower jurisdictions (those not courts of record, such as small justice courts), there may be no clerk present to swear the witnesses.

Do not make the mistake I did on my first one. I was reporting a contested case in which civil matters also had been filed. The municipal judge, probably fearful of being reversed if the defendants were convicted by the six-man jury, looked up in annoyance upon seeing a court reporter present to make a verbatim record.

Seeing no clerk, I stood up to swear the first witness when he was called and got as far as "Would you please raise your right hand and be sworn?" when the judge asked "What do you think you are doing?" I said "Swearing the witness." "Not in my court," he bellowed.

I sat down meekly, quiet for the rest of the morning, thinking everyone present must be wondering where I came from.

During the course of the day, the judge asked me repeatedly for readbacks (probably hoping the worst would happen) and, luckily, each time I responded promptly and correctly.

Fortunately, the defendants were acquitted, and by afternoon the judge was in a jovial mood. He apologized and told me what a great job I had done. Then, he asked if he could recommend me to attorneys and request my presence in the future. I worked for him and with him for ten very enjoyable years, so all was well that ended well. But it is better to know the proper procedure and not make errors.

In a lower court wait to be asked to swear the witnesses or to mark the exhibits. If a clerk is present, ask him or her what the judge prefers. Usually the judge will prefer that you handle these items in the absence of a clerk. You will be expected to do these chores willingly and carefully when asked.

Sometimes the judge will administer an oath to you before the proceedings begin; so, be prepared.

When the Witness Has Not Been Sworn. Should you ever discover you have started reporting a deposition and the witness has not been sworn, do not become flustered. At the first opportunity say calmly "I don't believe 'we' have had this witness sworn," which spreads the blame around. After all, it is counsels' duty to see that proper procedures are followed. If no one objects, administer the following oath retroactively: "Do you solemnly swear that the answers you have given and will give to the questions regarding the cause hereinunder consideration are and will be the truth, the whole truth, and nothing but the truth, so help you God?" Should any attorney object to the oath being retroactive, that is a matter for the attorneys to decide between themselves. Be sure to include in your shorthand notes *witness sworn* at the time you administer the oath to serve as proof if any question should come up later concerning this.

Attorneys are frequently forgetful and will not discuss swearing witnesses or stipulations governing the taking (discussed in a later chapter), but will start right off with questions. So, do not hesitate to mention either of these topics before they launch into questioning. You can, of course, get the stipulations later; but you might forget, too. Try always to keep the same orderly procedure, and it will become a habit with you.

Administering the Oath to Children

Prior to administering the oath to small children, if no mention is made by counsel about qualifying the child before starting to take a statement or deposition, ask the attorneys or adjusters if they would like to do so or whether they would prefer that you do it.

They or you will then ask questions to determine whether the child understands the difference between right and wrong and whether the youngster is competent to give truthful answers regarding the pending matter. Then, you will be told to administer the oath. Most reporters ask a very simple oath of a child, saying:

Example   "Do you promise (or swear) that everything you say here and now will be the truth, so help you God?"

In court, judges usually do some voir dire questioning of a child and then administer the oath themselves, although sometimes the clerk of court is asked to do it. The reason judges administer the oath to a child is because they try to put the child at ease and at the same time impress the child with the seriousness of the matter at hand.

Special Admonitions

In some jurisdictions, it is customary for court reporters to explain to affiants being deposed that they are subject to the pains and penalties of perjury should they testify falsely, since they are now under oath.

In other places, lawyers will object if reporters do this, feeling that the reporter is usurping the lawyers' function. The best advice with regard to this is "When in Rome, do as the Romans do," and find out what is done from the statutes and other practicing reporters.

Upon beginning work anywhere, check with your employer (court reporter in charge of freelance office; judge or court clerk in the courtroom) to secure the absolutely correct form of oath and accepted procedure, for while it will not affect a case adversely if you do not use a certain form, you should do everything in the most professional way.

Be dignified when swearing the witness, for this is a very serious matter. Should the person being sworn raise the wrong hand, simply say quietly "The other hand, please." The professional way you administer the oath to witnesses will help stamp you as a person who belongs in the position of court reporter.

Reading Back

Attorneys and judges often ask for readbacks, and your ability will be judged to a large extent upon how well you perform this part of your duties.

You cannot be like an old-time reporter who, when requested to read from his notes in court and finding it an impossible task, remarked something to the effect that his notes were not meant for immediate translation. Today all notes must be meant for immediate transcription, so get ready for instant readbacks.

Sometimes whole sessions will go by without anyone asking for a single readback. Then, again, during other depositions and hearings, it will seem that requests to review testimony are endless as attorneys cut in to object (cutting off the answer) or witnesses fail to speak out. You may be asked to read an entire day's testimony or a long statement by counsel to the jury or to the court and counsel in chambers.

I once worked for a judge who had recently suffered a stroke which left him with a poor memory. He would ask me to come in and read hours of proceedings to refresh his memory.

Practice Develops Readback Ability

To a nervous beginner, readbacks may seem like nightmares. However, if you have done lots of reading in school and while practicing at home have practiced taking good, clean notes all the way (as you should have done) this phase of your work should not be fearsome.

To be a good shorthand reader, you must be able to read from print accurately, loudly, and clearly at an acceptable rate. These prerequisites are musts. No noticeable speech impediments should exist. You cannot, like Mel Tillis, sing your readbacks to overcome stuttering.

About the only places where readbacks do not occur are in conventions and legislative work. Even there, public relations are important. You will have frequent conversations with those running the convention.

The following paragraphs provide some tips for reading back.

Develop a Booming Voice! Many students read so softly they cannot be heard two rows away. You must read very loudly because courtrooms are big, and judges or attorneys may be old and slightly (or exceedingly) deaf. If you mutter or mumble and half-whisper, everyone will feel that you are not sure of yourself. Besides, it will give you much needed confidence to let your voice ring out loudly.

Take Your Time. Always carefully find the place you were requested to read. Then, read slowly, deliberately, and loudly. When you think you are reading loud enough, increase the intensity of your voice a little more and read louder. This technique helps keep your reading speed slow enough to enable you to look ahead constantly in your notes so that you can spot bad outlines and decipher them in advance. When you use this technique, you will have no pauses as you read along. If you read rapidly and then stop suddenly, it may appear that you are having trouble with your notes.

Usually, the reason you are requested to read back is that questions have become garbled, that two or more people have been talking at once, or that because the questioning has become involved, the witness cannot or does not want to understand the question. Sometimes the witness speaks very softly or his or her voice trails off, and the reporter is the only one in a position to hear what was said. So, take readbacks in your stride and read carefully.

Remember, you are just a cog (a very important one, nevertheless) in the wheels of justice. Should you make an occasional error, the world will not come to an end. If you simply cannot read an outline you think is essential, look hopefully at the attorney who said it, and he or she will often supply the word or phrase. Sometimes the judge will just say "That's all we need. Rephrase the question," or something to that effect. However, you must not minimize the importance of having everything in your notes and reading excellently. If you do not read back well, everyone at the proceeding will be ill at ease, and the discomfort will rub off on everyone. The judge and the attorneys will ask you to read back all the time just to be sure you are getting the record down properly, and the attorneys will ask the same questions over and over to ensure a complete record.

So, become highly proficient at the skill of speed writing and notereading. It is also imperative that you read your notes well in order that you can dictate well for a transcriber if your computer ever is out of commission.

Read Only the Facts. Do not insert extraneous remarks in your readbacks while in school when your instructor corrects you or when you notice you have erred in reading because it might become a habit.

One day while I was reading back, I came to a word outline which represented two different words, both of which made sense. The attorney corrected me when I selected one; and I, much chagrined, said "Oh, that is what I have in my notes," a remark I never should have added.

He said "Well, if that is what you have, why didn't you read it that way?" It did not seem to matter that he and I had worked together for over six years and that all my previous readbacks were flawless. At recess he apologized repeatedly for embarrassing me in front of a courtroom full of people; but, you know, I realized that I brought the problem on myself.

When you are asked for a readback, just read the material you were asked to read. If any corrections are made, say "Thank you," and just continue.

Use Proper Expression When Reading. Cultivate a pleasant, well-modulated voice with just enough expression to ensure everyone's understanding the words you speak. If a witness has been highly dramatic, don't read back dramatically. Simply read the material in the same matter-of-fact way as you read anything else.

Witnesses often say, when asked to testify to lurid material, "I don't want to say that in front of this lady," or "I don't know if I should use language like that in front of all these people." The judge or the attorneys will instruct witnesses to answer in such instances, assuring them that the woman reporter hears this type of language everyday.

Do not act ill at ease, blush, or make any remarks or gestures which might distract witnesses during any testimony. Act as though you hear the language used in the testimony every day. When you read such material back, do so just as you would any other testimony. Some attorneys like to see if they can embarrass reporters, but just treat sensational material they request read back as ordinary material. You will not be reporting long before any embarrassment in reading anything vanishes, but do not let anyone know by your demeanor or readback that you are a beginner.

Keep Only Current Notes in the Courtroom. Before you begin to work as a judge's official, request permission to keep only the notes of your current session in the courtroom. This practice will ensure the safety of notes taken during recesses and assist you when readbacks are requested from notes taken in past days.

Counsel frequently disagree about what was testified previously. They will blithely say "Well, we will just have the court reporter read to you what the witness said two days ago." It is very harrowing to have to hunt the spot amid the deadly silence that follows. Every minute seems like an hour.

If the notes are in your office (for security purposes, of course!), you may say "Your Honor, may we have a brief recess so that I may go to my office and secure the notes to locate the requested testimony?" The judge will then send the jurors to the jury room where they can talk and relax, and you can locate the portion to be read without extreme pressure.

Do Not Make Reporting Look Too Easy. Nathaniel Weiss tells the story about a time he was requested to read something which had occurred several days before. He just happened to have his notes from that previous day lying on the table beside him. As he looked down at the notes, he noticed he was as the place that was requested. He began to read immediately. He finished, thinking what a good impression he must have made on all present. Unfortunately, everyone was so amazed at his uncanny ability to find the requested place that they wanted to see if he could do it that fast again. He was kept busy reading back all through the case.

Moral: Never make your job look too easy! Keep everyone aware that it takes a great deal of ability to be a court reporter.

Who Requests Readbacks?

During statements and depositions, the questioner and even sometimes the witness may ask for something to be read back.

There are many judges who conduct a formal court and insist attorneys address all requests for readbacks to the judge, who, in turn, directs the court reporter to read. In other courts such informality prevails that any counsel, welfare director, probation officer, or even the witness may ask the court reporter to read matter without censure from the judge.

Procedures at Recess

Let's suppose it has been a very busy morning of depositions or court work, and you have been writing steadily from 9:00 to 10:30 A.M. To your joy, the attorneys or the judge announce a 15-minute recess. Do you rush right out for a cup of coffee and a chat with your old friends, the attorneys or the courtroom clerk? Later, perhaps, but not right away.

Before you leave your machine, put a fresh pack of paper in it and carefully put your used notes where they are safe. Count the exhibits if they have been placed in your care. Now, read the last few questions and answers so when counsel return and say "Where did we leave off?" you can instantly give them the last portion of the testimony or colloquy. Do remember you were probably tired before recess, and your notes may have become a little "shaggy." Pen in missing letters before leaving your machine. Also, check your "hot spots" and verify spellings or words you misunderstood or misheard, such as the name of that ten-word school in Switzerland the expert witness attended. After you have secured your notes and exhibits safely in a locked drawer or in your office, you have earned that long-awaited break.

Finding the Readback Spot

It will be necessary for you to devise a good method of finding a certain place in your notes for instant readback.

You can be quite sure a readback may be called for after an objection, so hit the StenoMark or toss a little red card, a rubber band, or some other item into your tray immediately when an objections begins. Some reporters draw a line across their notes at such a point, but since objections are spontaneous and rapid, this is not always possible. At any rate, do something to help you find the question and/or answer preceding the objection at the end of the colloquy.

Keep your mind on what is happening, and you will usually remember the general vicinity of any passage that may be requested. Many reporters prefer the number bar to a word system for numerals because dates and figures are often requested to be verified, and the figures stand out in the notes.

You will soon develop a sixth sense that warns you that a readback is imminent regarding testimony or a controversial argument. During your four-voice classes in school and your apprenticeship with practicing reporters, do a great deal of readback. You will become quite adept at finding requested material.

When readbacks are requested that have long preliminary statements, dispense with these statements and just read the question. If counsel asks for a question to be read back and the last question is only one word or does not make sense by itself, read the preceding question and answer also.

Marking the Readback Spot

When readback is requested, write down who (counsel or the Court) requested it in your notes. Mark on your notes with a straight horizontal line (red stands out) across your notes at the beginning of the portion read and at the end so you can insert the proper parenthetical and readback material, if necessary.

As you finish reading, write in your notes "KWERD" for "Question read" or "KWARD" for Question and answer read", or use another suitable designation. Be sure your parentheticals are placed in your computer dictionary if you are on a CAT system.

Reading to the Jury and to Witnesses

Juries often forget what was said during a witness's testimony or they cannot remember which witness said a certain thing. Sometimes, too, they think they heard a certain thing said, but their memories are faulty. Then, the reporter will be called upon to read the appropriate question, answer, or entire testimony back for clarification.

The jury will send a note to the judge through the bailiff or matron that it desires the reporter to read something back from the trial. The judge and the attorneys must agree that what is asked for was actually testified to and is part of the record. In that case, the reporter will first have to search through the notes and read to them after finding the requested material or verifying that such requested material did not take place.

Normally, you will be called back in open court with all parties present and be seated on the witness stand to read requested portions of material, but on occasion you may be summoned to the jury room for this purpose. Face the jury and use the microphone if one is provided. Go slowly because jurors may want to take notes as you read.

If possible, go through your notes before going in to read, and mark areas that should not be read. When you are reading testimony to the jury, do not read questions which were objected to, objections that were sustained, ensuing colloquy, and places where the witness was not allowed to answer. Bench conferences also are not read back. Marking portions to be omitted with paper clips or red Marks-A-Lot will help when you begin reading. As you review your notes, clean up any poor outlines and punctuate where necessary to make sense of long, confusing questions or answers.

If you are reading back to the jury in the jury deliberation room without having counsel and the judge present, read back only what has been requested. If the jury wishes additional testimony read, have the foreman make a request in writing to the judge.

Many times an opportunity will not present itself to review the notes prior to going in to read. Always be looking ahead as you read to see if objections are coming up, and if they are sustained, skip the question, ruling, and colloquy.

When you are called upon to do long readbacks, state to the jury "I will now read to you the testimony of Henry Hanks, which was heard on Wednesday, March 15, 1990. I will start with the direct examination by the District Attorney, Mr. Harelson." Read the words "question" and "answer" as you read back.

It is vital that your reading be totally verbatim, as the outcome of the case may hinge upon the matter requested to be read. Read fluently, clearly, and loud enough to be heard well. Do not show emotion because you might have an influence over the jury by doing so, and you must be impartial at all times.

Because a reporter may be called upon at any time to read back material, it is vital that you make it known at once if you are having difficulty understanding a foreign witness with a thick accent or highly technical matter or you cannot grasp the context of any testimony. Mark your notes and check doubtful passages during recess if necessary. Do not just hope that the problem will just go away. You are there for one purpose only—to get the record.

If you come to very poor spots in your notes (God forbid!) and have been reading a lengthy portion of the record, it has been suggested that you might say "Have I read the part you wished now?" or something similar. If the requesting party says "Yes," you need read no more. Of course, the more speed in writing and facility you have in reading back, the less likely such an occasion will arise. I would certainly not count on handling it that way.

Another suggestion has been made that when an answer is read back to a witness, the reporter should look directly at the witness and say "Right?" Of course, the witness will agree, which will make everyone feel admiration for the court reporter who possesses all that skill.

Good reporters read with such authority, vigor, and clarity that no one would dare dispute their accuracy. I suggest you be one of these reporters.

When you have concluded reading back to the jury, excuse yourself and leave the courtroom or jury room promptly. Do not converse with the jury about anything related to the trial. You may not be present during any of the jury deliberations. If they begin to discuss anything about the case before you have completed your readback in the jury room, remind them of your duty and ask the foreman if you should leave or continue reading. If you leave without concluding the readback, mark in your notes where you stopped and advise the judge and counsel of what transpired.

When you begin reporting, keep your cool, never panic, read loudly and clearly, and take your time. They cannot proceed until you finish, and it is your moment to shine and impress everybody. Soon, you will be at ease. Then, readbacks may even become an enjoyable part of your day.

AT THAT POINT, YOU CAN CALL YOURSELF AN OLD PRO!

Chapter 6 *Interrogatories*

After I had been freelancing about six months, a Brother of a Catholic order came into the office one morning to inquire if I were a notary public and a court reporter. Upon my affirmative response, he produced about ten pages of questions with long spaces provided beneath each, neatly typed on legal-sized paper, titled and venued in proper form.

He stated that he had been served with this set of interrogatories which had to be completed before a notary public and returned to the requesting attorney. The interrogatories were about a large tract of land which had been willed to the monastery.

I took down his answers in shorthand, after which he left for a few hours. Then I typed them up and appended my certificate. When he returned, he inspected the document and said, "Very nice. How much do I owe you?" I said, "$25," and he said, "The lawyer sent $50, so I assume that is what most people charge. Will that be all right?" Now, in those days $50 was a great fee for about an hour's work, so I thanked him profusely.

Not long afterward I asked an attorney how to build up a volume of interrogatory business since it was so easy and seemed to pay so well. He just laughed and said, "You'd starve to death if you depended upon the written interrogatories you would take here."

He went on to explain about interrogatories to me.

What Interrogatories Are

Written interrogatories are a discovery device used by attorneys which have the same force and effect as a deposition, although ordinarily no attorneys are present when they are taken.

Types of Interrogatories

There are basically three different types of written interrogatories:

1. Interrogatories taken simply for the purpose of securing records from a medical custodian or other person entrusted with care, custody, and control of the records.

2. A set of standard questions used over and over to secure information regarding various frequently occurring situations, such as automobile accidents, pedestrian mishaps, falls, food poisoning lawsuits, and passenger claims.

3. Involved questions asked of medical or other expert witnesses regarding specialized situations.

Answers to Interrogatories

The opposing party can respond to written interrogatories being served in several ways. The opposing party can:

1. File for a motion to quash after having seen the direct questions to be propounded.
2. Send the reporter cross-questions to be asked by the reporter at the same time as the reporter gets the answers to the direct questions. These questions and answers are typed at the end of the direct questions as cross-interrogatories.
3. Initiate cross-interrogatories in response to the answers given on the direct interrogatories when he or she receives his or her copy of the answers to the direct interrogatories.

Who Pays the Cost?

All this is paid for by the attorney who initiated the direct interrogatories. The attorney who started the process must pay the cost for all cross-interrogatories as well as the direct questions. This procedure may seem highly unfair, but the Rules of Civil Procedure make this provision.

Taking Interrogatories Could Get a Little More Complicated

At the outside possibility, there may be occasions when the reporter will appear to depose the witness on direct questions, and the attorney for the opposing side will be present or appear prior to the set time. He or she will listen to the answers to the direct interrogatories and thereupon proceed to depose the witness on cross-questions. This rarely happens, but it does occur occasionally.

Frequently depositions are taken following the securing of interrogatories to develop matters related to a case which appeared germane from the answers to the interrogatories.

Handling of Interrogatories in Various-Sized Cities

The attorney I questioned further explained that, as a general rule, in medium-sized cities attorneys, doctors, scientists, and businesspeople are friendly and know one another well. In such places the attorney simply has his or her secretary prepare the interrogatories, and they are mailed to counsel for the opposing party.

The lawyer receiving these interrogatories has his or her client answer the questions by phone, letter, or office visit; then the attorney's secretary types them in proper form within the statutory period, which ranges from 15 to 30 days in the various states. The answers are mailed back to the initiating attorney, and no reporter's fee is involved.

The only times written interrogatories would be prepared by a court reporter in such places would be in those cases where it became apparent that cooperation would be secured in no other way or when attorneys for cases in distant places were involved. If counsel feel any questions are improper in interrogatories, they secure the judge's ruling as to whether or not objectionable questions should be answered.

By the way, in over nine years' reporting in that area, I can remember only six sets of written interrogatories crossing my desk; so, it turned out that the attorney was correct.

In large cities where people are not trusting and do not cooperate on a friendly basis, written interrogatories may supply much of a firm's business. Therefore, in cities, it is customary for law firms or the reporter to secure a commission and a subpoena. The subpoena provides for the court reporter to appear at the set time and place to secure answers to questions or pick up records of hospitals, doctors, accounting papers, or such other documents as may be involved in a case to gain information required to settle or go forward with the case.

The court reporter is frequently requested to handle this entire procedure down to securing the subpoena since many doctors and other experts do not like to take time away from their business to testify.

Always keep in mind that doctors are overworked, beset by paperwork required by the government, and working under great pressure in many instances. Maintain a good relationship with doctors and other expert witnesses who may be called to testify so they will be considerate of you and speak slowly when they use unfamiliar terms. Also, you may need to obtain copies of originals of medical records at the end of the session and obtain signatures and copies of needed papers. Being on good terms with them will prevent you from spending time searching for information that they could provide you. It is customary for the reporter to ask for and receive medical record copies at the end of the proceedings to save verification time, but I have known reporters who angered doctors and, as a result, did not receive such cooperation.

Purpose of Interrogatories

Written interrogatories are often directed to securing records to assess the value of a case and possibly settle without costly litigation. It is less expensive to schedule interrogatories than it is to set depositions, and for many cases they provide a valuable discovery tool that shows the strengths and weaknesses of a case.

Written interrogatories are also useful for impeachment purposes should a witness change his or her answers at the time of trial. Answers to interrogatories are almost universally considered as prior admissions by a party against his or her interest, so they constitute an exception to the hearsay rule. Therefore, they may be admitted into evidence and referred to during the closing arguments, serving as a very real piece of evidence for consideration of the jury during their deliberations.

Procedures to Be Followed Regarding Interrogatories

The lawyer requesting interrogatories may handle all preliminaries, such as securing the commission if required in his or her state, subpoenaing the witness, and notifying the opposing attorney. Increasingly, however, attorneys are requesting the court reporter to take care of all such details.

In Texas the reporter fills out a Request for Commission to Take Written Interrogatories (Figure 1). When this is granted, the Notice of Taking Depositions on Written Questions (Figure 2) is prepared and served on opposing counsel.

Methods and forms vary widely from state to state, so check the procedures and forms for your particular state should you be called upon to perform these duties. You will observe that you are noticing the opposite side from the party initiating the written interrogatory; this form is used in county and district courts only.

After Notice of Taking Deposition on Written Questions has been mailed by certified mail with a return receipt requested, postage prepaid, whether the person to be questioned is a mere witness or a party to the suit, that individual is subpoenaed to ensure he or she will appear when the reporter arrives to report the answers.

The reporter must prepare the subpoenas if requested to do so. Firms that do many written interrogatories keep printed forms for ordinary subpoenas and subpoenas duces tecum. These may be totally typed, double-spaced, worded generally as shown on the forms herein, but in compliance with each state's particular regulations. Figure 3 is an example of a subpoena used in Texas.

Service of Subpoenas

In Texas, if the reporter serves the subpoena, $1 is attached to the first copy, which is presented to the witness at service. If the witness will not cooperate, the reporter must prepare

FIGURE 1
Request for Commission To Take Written Interrogatories

```
                              No. 461.397

PATSY R. COSTAIN, ET AL.        ∮       IN THE DISTRICT COURT OF
                                ∮
         -vs-                   ∮       HARRIS COUNTY, T E X A S
                                ∮
JANET REIM                      ∮       145TH JUDICIAL DISTRICT

                       REQUEST FOR COMMISSION
                  TO TAKE WRITTEN INTERROGATORIES

TO THE DISTRICT CLERK FOR THE 145TH JUDICIAL DISTRICT COURT:

         I, Lightning Digits, on behalf of the attorney for the

defendant in the above-numbered and captioned cause, desire to

take Written Interrogatories of JANE HOUGH, a resident of Harris

County, Texas, on the 25th day of July, A.D. 19__, commencing at

2:00 o'clock p.m., in the offices of Dr. Robert E. Dahl, 1384

Essex, Houston, Texas  77001, and hereby request that you issue

a commission to take such interrogatories.

                           Respectfully submitted,



                       By:_____
                          LIGHTNING DIGITS, CSR
                          Notary Public in and for
                          Harris County, Texas
                          My Commission Expires 6/30/__
```

an original and two copies of the subpoena and handle it as for a regular oral deposition by service through the sheriff or constable.

When a reporter has the subpoena or subpoena duces tecum served by a sheriff or constable, it is his or her duty to pay in advance the proper fee to have service performed, usually ten days prior to date of the taking of the written interrogatories.

When return is made of service of the subpoena or subpoena duces tecum (Figure 4), the reporter simply appears at the stated address at the set time with a copy of the interrogatories and a well-stocked, properly inked machine, ready to write the answers of the witness.

Federal Court Procedure

In the U.S. District Courts (federal courts), if the person to be deposed upon written interrogatories is a party to the suit, only his or her attorney of record is formally noticed (Figure 5). Either the witness or a party to the suit who is being questioned is subpoenaed by the form used throughout the federal process in accordance with the Federal Rules of Procedure.

Interrogatories May Be the Beginning Step into Reporting. Some advanced students of better court reporting schools earn good money and gain an introduction to the reporting profession, as well as excellent transcribing experience on medical and technical material, by taking written interrogatories for a freelance firm. This work is just a step above secretarial work, for interrogatories are simpler than statement taking in that the reporter propounds the questions and, thus, can govern the speed to some degree.

However, a person entering upon this work should write at least 180 words per minute in shorthand with good accuracy and possess excellent English ability, medical background, and tact,

FIGURE 2
Notice of Taking Depositions on Written Questions

```
            IN THE DISTRICT COURT OF HARRIS COUNTY, TEXAS

                      122ND JUDICIAL DISTRICT

C. KING REMEDY                      0
                                    0
          Plaintiff,                0
                                    0
     -vs-                           0          No. 345,678
                                    0
GILT T. PARTEE,                     0
                                    0
          Defendant.                0

          NOTICE OF TAKING DEPOSITION ON WRITTEN QUESTIONS

TO:  TAIKES A CUTT, ESQUIRE
     Attorney at Law
     1405 Knowlton Street
     Houston, Texas  77001

     You will take notice that ten (10) days after the service
hereof and the attached questions, pursuant to Rule 189, Texas
Rules of Civil Procedure, the answers of the witness.

                      TELLE T. TRUTHE

will be taken before Ima Golden, Court Reporter, Houston Law Center,
122 Main Street, Houston, Texas  77002, a duly authorized officer,
to be used in the above-styled and numbered cause.

     The above officer is requested to secure a proper subpoena
duces tecum and direct the witness to produce at a time and place
to be specified by the aforementioned officer the following:

          All medical records in his office for medical
          treatment rendered by him to plaintiff, C. King
          Remedy, during the period of June 1, 19__-December
          21, 19___, inclusive.

                   CERTIFICATE OF SERVICE

     I, Ima Golden, a notary public in and for the County of Harris,
State of Texas, do hereby certify that I nailed a copy of this
notice by certified mail, return receipt requested, postage pre-
paid, properly addressed to:

               TAIKES A CUTT, ESQUIRE
               Attorney at Law
               1405 Knowlton Street
               Houston, Texas  77001


               _____
               IMA GOLDEN, Notary Public
               Harris County, Texas
               My Commission Expires 6/30/__
```

since doctors and experts tend to talk rapidly, using terminologies peculiar to their professions, and they are sometimes impatient.

Due to the irregularities of expert witnesses' hours, several trips may be required to secure the required signatures on completed work, so it is a good idea to telephone first.

Points to Observe Concerning Interrogatories

Be sure to mark the number of each answer to an interrogatory carefully in your notes. Secure all records to be copied or all copies the witness provides. Carefully check them as you put them in your briefcase. Make sure you have everything, but that you have not picked up any extra documents or materials from anyone's desk. Always ask the witness if signature will be required. Signature may be waived, but it is usually required by doctors and other experts.

FIGURE 3
Subpoena

```
          IN THE DISTRICT COURT OF HARRIS COUNTY, TEXAS
                    159TH JUDICIAL DISTRICT

CLOUDEE OUTLOOK,                     0
                                     0
          Plaintiff,                 0
     -vs-                            0        No. 800,475
                                     0
SUE DOFFEN,                          0        SUBPOENA
                                     0
          Defendant.                 0

TO ANY SHERIFF OR CONSTABLE OF THE STATE OF TEXAS, GREETING:

     You are hereby commanded to summon CUSTODIAN OF MEDICAL RECORDS
for Dr. Jacob Gray, 555 Montrose Boulevard, Houston, Texas, a resident
of Harris County, Texas, to be and appear before me, a notary public
in and for the County of Harris, State of Texas, or any other person
authorized to administer oaths in Harris County, Texas, at 11:00 a.m.
on the 14th day of January 19_, in the offices of said Custodian,
then and there to make answers under oath to written questions now
in my possession; said Custodian being summoned at the instance of
the Defendant's Attorney, and that she bring with her and produce at
said time and place the following:

        Any and all office records, reports, or other writing
        in the custody or subject to the control of said
        custodian pertaining to treatment or examination of
        Cloudee Outlook by Dr. Jacob Gray,

and that said witness continue in attendance from day to day until
discharged by me.

     Herein fail not, but make due return to me on or before the
14th day of January 19_, showing how you have executed the same.

     Given and issued under my official hand and seal of office on
this 1st day of January, 19__, acting under and pursuant to Notice
served on the 30th day of December, 19__.


                              _____
                              EZEE WRITER, Notary Public
                              Harris County, Texas
                              My Commission Expires 3/2/___.

            OFFICER'S RETURN

     Came to hand the _____ day of _____, 19__, and executed
the ____ day of _____, 19__, by handing the above-named a true
copy of this subpoena and by tendering the above-named witness fee of
$1.00, which he accepted.

     Returned this _____ day of _____, 19__.
Mileage _____              C. V. "BUSTER" KERN,
Sheriff                            Harris County, Texas
Service _____
Total              $_____  BY: _____
                                        Deputy Sheriff

Make Return to:  Ezee Writer
                 Ace Reporting, Inc.
                 1411 Westheimer Street
                 Houston, Texas  77036
```

When you return to your office, transcribe the material promptly, inserting proper parentheticals. Do all photocopying promptly, and be sure all materials to be returned are transmitted in a timely manner to the proper office.

If required, prepare the written interrogatories for signature of the witness and complete and sign your certificate. Should signature have been requested by the witness, be sure signature is secured before filing the interrogatories. Most reporters who have a large volume of this type of work arrange to secure signatures on several sets of interrogatories on the same trip whenever possible.

You may notice the venue is placed at the top of some instruments and at the right of the title box on others. This is simply a matter of preference as firms and judges use the form of setup that appeals to them. You will, of course, follow your employer's instructions as to setups at all times because there is no one set way to draw up most legal papers as to spacing, headings,

FIGURE 4
Subpoena Duces Tecum

```
                    SUBPOENA DUCES TECUM

                     THE STATE OF TEXAS

TO THE SHERIFF OR ANY CONSTABLE OF HARRIS COUNTY, TEXAS, GREETING:

       You are hereby commanded that you summon JANE HOUGH to be and
appear before me, Lightning Digits, Notary Public in and for Harris
County, Texas, or any Notary Public of my designation, in the offices
of Dr. Robert E. Dahl, 1348 Essex, Houston, Texas  77001, on the 25th
day of July, A.D. 19__, at 2:00 p.m., and there to make answers under
oath to certain written Interrogatories to be propounded to her at
the instance of the defendant, Janet Reim, in a certain suit now
pending in the 145th Judicial district Court, wherein Patsy R.
Costain, et al., Plaintiffs and Kamet Reim, Defendant, appear, being
No. 461,397 on the docket of said Court, and that she bring with her
and produce at said time and place the following, to-wit:

       All records in the office of Dr. Robert E. Dahl pertaining
       to care and treatment of Patsy R. Costain from the very
       earliest to the most recent one;

and that she continue in attendance before me from day to day until
discharged by me.

       This Subpoena is issued under and by virtue of authority of a
Commission issued out of the Honorable 145th Judicial District Court
of Harris County, Texas, and now in my possession.

       Herein fail not, but have you then and there before me at said
time and place this Writ, with your return thereon, showing how you
have executed the same.

       WITNESS MY HAND AND SEAL OF OFFICE at Houston, Texas, County of
Harris, on this the 14th day of July, A.D. 19__.



                            _____
                            LIGHTNING DIGITS, Notary Public
                            in and for Harris County, Texas
                            My Commission Expires 6/30/__

              OFFICER'S RETURN

Came to hand on this the 14th day of July, A. D. 19__, at 10:00
o'clock a.m., and executed the 14th day of July, A.D. 19__, at 11:00
o'clock a.m., by reading the within Subpoena to the said Jane Hough
at 1384 Essex, Houston, Texas  77002, the said _____
accepting the tender of $1.00.


Fees:  Service Writ _____
```

and placement. Just be sure all your work is well centered and pleasing to the eye, with no erasures, strikeovers, or misspelled words.

Remember, 50 years from today someone may pull some of your work out of a file. By your product shall you be known!

Examples to Follow

Figure 6 is a form for a title page of a written interrogatory. Figure 7 is a sample page of a setup, and a sample reporter's certificate is shown in Figure 8 to assist you in setting up written interrogatories, although these are but one type of format used. There probably are as many formats as there are court reporting firms in the country.

You will notice that Figure 6 provides for cross-written interrogatories.

Written interrogatories should be bound in a proper cover just as any deposition should be.

The originals of written interrogatories are filed with the proper court clerk. Be sure to send a letter of transmittal with mailed copies or request a receipt if you hand carry them to the attorneys' offices. Prepare these before you leave your office.

FIGURE 5
Federal Court Notice

IN THE DISTRICT COURT OF THE UNITED STATES

FOR THE SOUTHERN DISTRICT OF TEXAS

HOUSTON DIVISION

IMA SADDE VICTUMM,   §

      Plaintiff,   §

    -vs-   §   CIVIL ACTION NO. H-80-123

JAYBIRD CHEMICAL, INC.,   §

      Defendant.   §

TO: Louis R. Koerner, Esquire
     Attorney at Law
     730 Camp Street
     Houston, Texas 77002

You are hereby notified that after the expiration of a reasonable time from the date of service hereof, Defendant, Jaybird Chemical, Inc., intends to take the oral deposition of Cyril Sawitt, commencing at 1:00 p.m. on the 30th day of November, 19__, in the office of:

        James E. Stanton, Esquire
        Attorney at Law
        1450 Van Buren Street
        Houston, Texas 77006

CERTIFICATE OF SERVICE

I, Wry Ting Righte, a notary public in and for the County of Harris, State of Texas, do hereby certify that I mailed a copy of this notice by certified mail, return receipt requested, postage prepaid, properly addressed to:

        Louis R. Koerner, Esquire
        Attorney at Law
        730 Camp Street
        Houston, Texas 77002

on November 10, 19__

                     _____
                     WRY TING RIGHTE, Notary Public
                     Harris County, Texas
                     My Commission Expires 9/21/__

Wry Ting Righte
Court Reporter
116 Main Street, Suite 1416
Houston, Texas 77001
Telephone: 495-1893

FIGURE 6
Title Page

1	NO. 345,932
2	
3	IMA SICKE, X IN THE DISTRICT COURT OF
	X
4	PLAINTIFF, X HARRIS COUNTY, T E X A S
	X
5	-vs- X 136TH JUDICIAL DISTRICT
	X
6	R.E. SISTING, X
	X
7	DEFENDANT. X
8	
9	ANSWERS TO DIRECT WRITTEN INTERROGATORIES
10	OF
11	DR. FIXUMM UPP
12	
13	DEPOSITION AND ANSWERS of Dr. Fixumm Upp, taken on
14	behalf of the defendant to the accompanying direct (or
15	direct and cross-) interrogatories propounded to him in the
16	above-styled and numbered cause, taken before Uva Goodcase,
17	a notary public in and for Harris County, Texas, on the
18	6th day of October, 19_ _, at the offices of Dr. Fixumm Upp,
19	4857 East Woodglade, Suite 384, Houston, Texas 77042,
20	pursuant to the Notice and Interrogatories herein contained.
21	
22	
23	
24	
25	

FIGURE 7
Sample Page Set-Up

```
 1                          DR. FIXUMM UPP,

 2   called as a witness in behalf of the defendant, having been

 3   first duly sworn, testified as follows:

 4   DIRECT INTERROGATORY NO. 1:

 5           Please state your name, address, and occupation

 6           or profession.

 7   ANSWER:  Fixumm Upp, 4857 East Woodglade, Suite 384,

 8           Houston, Texas  77042

 9   DIRECT INTERROGATORY NO. 2:

10           In the course of your medical practice, have you

11           had as a patient a man named Ima Sicke?

12   ANSWER:  Yes, I have.

13           Etc., etc.

14

15               CROSS-WRITTEN INTERROGATORIES

16   Cross Interrogatory No. 1:

17           Are you aware that Mr. Sicke sought medical aid

18           from Dr. Aaron Goodly on December 23, 19__,

19           for this same condition for which you were treating

20           him?

21   ANSWER:  I am.

22           Etc., etc.

23

24

25
```

FIGURE 8
Reporter's Certificate

1	THE STATE OF TEXAS)
	)
2	COUNTY OF HARRIS)
3	I, Uva Goodcase, a certified shorthand reporter and
4	notary public in and for the County of Harris, State of Texas,
5	do hereby certify that I took in shorthand the foregoing
6	testimony of the witness, DR. FIXUMM UPP, who was first duly
7	sworn, and that it was reduced to typewriting under my
8	direction.
9	I further certify that I am not, in any capacity, a
10	regular employee of the party in whose behalf this deposition
11	is taken, nor in the regular employ of his attorney; and I
12	certify that I am not interested in the cause, nor of kin or
13	counsel to either of the parties.
14	I sealed up said deposition and delivered it to the
15	Clerk of the Court in which said cause is pending without it
16	having been out of my possession or altered after it was read
17	and approved by the witness on the 8th day of October, 19__.
18	GIVEN UNDER MY HEAD AND SEAL OF OFFICE on this, the
19	8th day of October, 19__.
20	
21	
22	
23	_____ UVA GOODCASE, Notary Public Harris County, Texas My Commission Expires 5/31/__
24	
25	

Figure 9 shows you how a complete written interrogatory of a witness, Jan Hough, would appear before having the copies of medical records placed at the back and being bound up in the firm's covers. This is the most common type of interrogatory.

It could happen that the reporter might secure a commission from the clerk of court to take written interrogatories, but due to some unforeseen factor, the witness might be unavailable when you appear to take the interrogatories. In order that the file may be complete in such a case, the reporter must file an affidavit setting out the facts concerning the matter. Figure 10 shows a form for this affidavit.

FIGURE 9-A
Written Interrogatory

```
No. 461,397                    IN THE DISTRICT COURT OF

PATSY R. COSTAIN, ET AL.,      HARRIS COUNTY, T E X A S
         Plaintiffs,           145TH JUDICIAL DISTRICT
         -vs-
JANET REIM,
         Defendant.
```

ANSWERS TO DIRECT WRITTEN INTERROGATORIES
of
JANE HOUGH

The following deposition was taken before the undersigned at the offices of Dr. Robert E. Dahl, 1384 Essex, Houston, Texas 77001, on the 25th day of July, A.D. 19--, the same being taken upon interrogatories duly certified by the Clerk of the Court in which said cause is pending.

Said witness, having been duly sworn by me before the examination, deposed as follows:

FIGURE 9-B

JANET HOUGH,

being first duly cautioned and sworn to testify the truth, the whole truth and nothing but the truth in answer to the direct questions as hereinafter indicated, deposes and says as follows:

Direct Interrogatory No. 1:

Please state your name.

A   Jane Hough.

Direct Interrogatory No. 2:

Please state whether you have under your care and custody any and all records in your office pertaining to the care and treatment of Patsy R. Costain.

A   Yes.

Direct Interrogatory No. 3:

Please state whether or not these records have been under the care, custody, and control of any other individual since Ocbtober 1, 19--.

A   No. I have been the sole custodian of these records at all times since that date.

Direct Interrogatory No. 4:

If you have stated that you have such records, please pass all records, from the very earliest to the most recent one to the court reporter taking this deposition.

A   (Complied.)

FIGURE 9-C

```
 1
 2                (Copies of records are attached
 3            hereto and made a part of this
 4            deposition.)
 5
 6                                    JANE HOUGH
 7   STATE OF TEXAS
 8   COUNTY OF HARRIS
 9
10       Subscribed and sworn to before me, the undersigned
11   authority, on this the 27th day of July, 19__.
12
13            LIGHTNING DIGITS, Notary Public
14            in and for Harris County, Texas
             My Commission Expires 6/30/__
15
16
17
18
19
20
21
22
23
24
25
```

FIGURE 9-D

```
 1
 2   THE STATE OF TEXAS
 3   COUNTY OF HARRIS
 4       I, Lightning Digits, a notary public in and for
 5   the County of Harris, State of Texas, do hereby certify
 6   that I took in shorthand the foregoing testimony of the
 7   witness, JANE HOUGH, and that it was reduced to typewriting
 8   under my direction.
 9       I further certify that I am not, in any capacity,
10   a regular employee of the party in whose behalf this
11   deposition is taken, nor in the regular employ of his at-
12   torney; and I certify that I am not interested in the
13   cause, nor of kin or counsel to either of the parties.
14       I further certify that I sealed up said deposition
15   and delivered it to the Clerk of the Court in which said
16   cause is pending without it having been out of my possession
17   or altered after the transcript was prepared and it was
18   read and approved by the witness in my presence on this
19   27th day of July, 19__.
20
21
22            LIGHTNING DIGITS, Notary Public
23            in and for Harris County, Texas
24            My Commission Expires 6/30/__
25
```

FIGURE 10-A
Affidavit

```
 1   IN THE DISTRICT COURT OF HARRIS COUNTY, TEXAS
 2           162ND JUDICIAL DISTRICT
 3
 4   HARRISON C. CADY,
 5        Plaintiff,
 6                          CIVIL NO. 736,057
 7   READERS PERIODICALS, INC.
 8        Defendant.
 9
10            A F F I D A V I T
11
12       I, Ima Copperplate, a notary public in and for
13   the County of Harris, State of Texas, do hereby certify
14   that a commission was issued out of the 162nd Judicial
15   District Court of Harris County, Texas, to take the written
16   deposition of Dr. Cuttem Upp, Alief, Harris County, Texas.
17       Pursuant to the aforementioned commission to
18   take written deposition, on the 31st day of August, 19--,
19   I called the residence of said Dr. Cuttem Upp, retired,
20   in order to set up an appointment for the purpose of taking
21   said deposition and issuance of subpoena, and was informed
22   by Mrs. C. Upp that the Doctor had suffered a stroke and
23   was unable to talk over the telephone or make answers to
24   written interrogatories.
25       I further certify that the attached instrument is
```

FIGURE 10-B

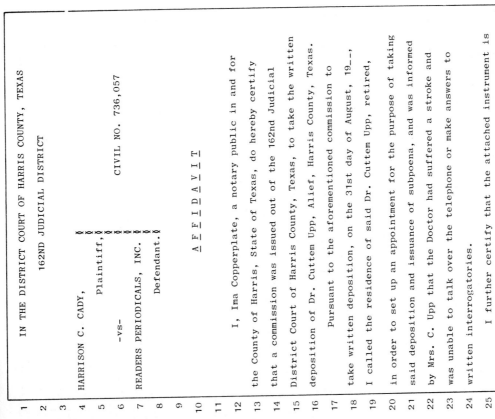

```
 1   the commission referred to in the above and foregoing
 2   affidavit.
 3
 4
 5   IMA COPPERPLATE, Notary Public
 6   in and for Harris County, Texas
 7   My Commission Expires 6/30/--
 8
 9
10
11
12
13
14
15
16
17
18
19
20
21
22
23
24
25
```

Chapter 7

Statement Reporting

An interesting, lucrative form of court reporting that is a cut above reporting interrogatories is statement work. Statement reporting is simpler than deposition or courtroom reporting since it involves only taking the questions of the examiner, who will be an attorney, insurance adjuster, or other investigator, and the answers of the witness or witnesses.

Getting Started In Statement Reporting

You must be a notary public in most states to give validity to the statements you will report. If you start on your own, visit insurance companies and adjusting firms listed in the yellow pages and leave your card. Briefly inform them that you would like to do their statement reporting. It is a good idea to make up an attractive announcement card or brochure and send it out to solicit business. After a visit to any company, write a nice letter thanking them for their time and state that you will be happy to serve them.

You must have a telephone number or answering service that can reach you at all times because accidents, ship collisions, and crimes happen at any time of day or night. Be dressed in a suit and comfortable shoes with your equipment ready to go quickly because you will be called at your office or home by adjusters who will announce, "There's been a bad two-car collision over at Milby. Three people have been killed. I want to beat the other adjuster out there to get statements from the remaining parties and any witnesses. Can you go with me right away?" Soon, they will simply appear to pick you up, and you will be on your way.

Generally speaking, the main field you will be reporting statements in will be accidents—automobile, industrial, marine, pedestrian, and so on. Certain reporters, however, are hired by police departments specifically to report criminal confessions and statements. You may be hired on occasion to report criminal statements.

Order of Inquiries

Most statements follow the same order:

1. The questioner identifies the witness and gets the location the statement is taken at in the record.
2. The reason for taking the statement is discussed.

3. Qualification of the witness is established: Was that person present at the scene at the time of occurrence? What did he or she see or hear?

4. Questioning will show on the record that the witness gave the statement freely and voluntarily, that the witness was not under the influence of liquor or drugs at the time the statement was taken, and that he or she understood all the questions and answered them truthfully to the best of his or her ability. The witness will also be asked if there are any additions he or she cares to state.

Preparing in Advance

Many times you will ride with the interviewer to the spot where the statements are to be taken, although sometimes you will be instructed to meet him or her at a designated place.

Find out all you can about the matter while you are en route. Sometimes the adjuster will open his or her briefcase and let you jot down names, places, and general information from his or her file as you ride. Getting information beforehand saves time later when you do not have to verify spellings or numbers. It also helps you to understand the location and conditions of a happening in advance. Occasionally an investigator will even drive out to the place in question to survey it or take pictures before seeing anyone to focus the situation in his or her own mind.

Always arrange with the examiner in advance just when you are to start writing anything down. Usually he or she will have a little preliminary discussion and have the reporter start to write when he or she says, "What is your name?"

Sometimes an adjuster or attorney will introduce you as his or her secretary or stenographer that he or she just brought along to save time and to keep him or her from having to handwrite everything. Avoid saying, "I'm a court reporter." The investigator might say you are a secretary or stenographer to keep the person interviewed from becoming uncomfortable. The adjuster does not want the person being questioned to have to worry about having to appear in court in the future. The questioner is not being deceitful. He or she simply wants honest, straightforward answers regarding what a witness saw or knows about the matter or the truthful statement that the person knows nothing about the matter at all.

Usefulness of the Statement

Statements do not carry the force of a deposition, but they are helpful for impeachment purposes. Sometimes a person will give a statement, but at the time of trial he or she will forget or purposely tell a different story. When that person is confronted with the statement given close to the time of the occurrence of the incident, should there be a conflict, he or she is impeached as a witness.

Usually quite a bit of money is involved when statements are taken regarding a case, and much of your time will be used in canvassing the vicinity of an accident or crime, as much to get negative statements as to secure complete eyewitness accounts of what happened.

Negative statements are those in which a witness avers that he or she did not see or hear the incident involved and that his or her knowledge is only of a hearsay nature.

All statements of both positive and negative nature will be evaluated to try to settle the cases without going to court, or they are carefully studied for information purposes in preparing for court trial.

Procedures In Statement Reporting

Arrange in advance with the interviewer whether or not you are to swear the witnesses. Many statements are unsworn, and their value rests upon your certification as the reporter or as a notary public. If the witness is sworn, use the proper form, and make the swearing formal enough that the individual will remember being sworn.

In those cases where the investigator asks you to swear the witness and the witness refuses to be sworn because of religious beliefs, affirm the person as described previously. When you transcribe the statement, word your introductory clause accordingly so that the statement will be accurate in every respect.

Inject yourself into the proceeding as little as possible because your attitude could influence a witness not to give a statement if the witness thinks you are rude or forward. Do not eat, chew gum, make noises of any kind, show any feeling, or make any comments about any of the stories you may hear.

There will be times when you may have difficulty hearing above the noise of farm machinery, traffic, TV, children, and husband and wife or others trying to answer at the same time. Sit close to the witness. Be tactful if children try to touch your shorthand machine, but be firm about not letting them play with your machine.

The interviewer's duty is to have the individuals questioned one at a time so that you are reporting only one individual at once. However, should remarks be offered by a third party, take them down carefully and transcribe them as part of the record, identifying the speakers. If the interruptions get out of hand, with several people talking at once, tactfully control the situation.

When a hospital patient is interviewed, he or she may have a tube protruding from the throat. I always state to these people, who may have great difficulty speaking, "I will read each of your answers back to you after I have taken them down. If you raise your hand, I will take any answer or correction you then make or any addition you care to offer. I know it must be difficult for you to speak." I then position myself as close to the bedside as possible for maximum opportunity to hear what is answered.

Special Equipment for Statement Taking

You may want to purchase a harness-type apparatus made by Stenograph, 1500 Bishop Court, Mount Prospect, IL, 60056-6039, to suspend your machine in front of you if you take many statements. This company also manufactures a Hi-Boy Tripod which extends so that one may write easily while standing. However, I have found an ingenious person can write with the machine on his or her lap, on tables, counters, bars, inside cars, at roadsides, and under all sorts of conditions.

Statement reporting can be fun, and the examiners are usually great people who often become top deposition-taking attorneys or even judges later in their career. Statement taking will take you to all kinds of places, so be versatile. You entered court reporting for the variety it offers, didn't you?

Figure 11 shows a sample first page for a sworn statement. Figure 12 is a first page of an unsworn statement having several statements from the same case bound in a single cover, and Figure 13 is a certificate suitable for statements by the reporter.

FIGURE 11
First Page of Sworn Statement

```
1                    SWORN STATEMENT
                           OF
2                    TELLING WILLINGLY

3

4       TAKEN AT:              609 Seeall Avenue
                               Erie, Pennsylvania  18201
5
        TAKEN ON:              January 18, 19--
6                              2:00 p.m.

7       QUESTIONS BY:          Mr. Just T. Fax, Jr.
                               Knight, Day, & Fax
8                              2300 Indictment Road
                               Erie, Pennsylvania  18201
9
        ALSO PRESENT:          Mr. C. King Truth, Attorney
10
                               Mrs. Annie Rooney
11
        REPORTED BY:           Ima Verbatim
12

13                    TELLING WILLINGLY,

14      having been first duly sworn by the reporter, testified

15      on her oath as follows:

16

17                        EXAMINATION

18      BY MR. FAX:

19      Q   Let's get your full name down for the record.

20      A   Telling Willingly.

21      Q   Mrs. Willingly, let me first introduce myself and

22      tell you why we're here and what we are doing.

23          My name is Just T. Fax, Jr., and I'm a lawyer.  I

24      will be asking you questions.  You have been put under

25      oath, and the court reporter here will be writing
```

FIGURE 12
First page of Unsworn Statement
Several Statements in same case bound in single cover

1

2   S T A T E M E N T S   O F:

3   CUT M. UPP, M.D.
                           NURSEM TEW HEALTH
4   JENTILLE THERAPY
                           DELIGHTFUL RECOVERY
5

6

7   Taken on Wednesday, May 22, 19--, in the

8   offices of C. A. Malpractice, M.D., West Slicem General

9   Hospital, 7843 Traction Street, New Orleans, Louisiana,

10   at 10:00 a.m., before Lively Digits, Court Reporter.

11

12

13   * * * * * * *

14

15   APPEARANCES:

16   TRYING A CASE, ESQ.
                       123456 Contingency Circle
17   New Orleans, Louisiana   70112

18   ALSO PRESENT: MAY PAY MUNEE,
                       Representative, Liberal Insurance Company
19

20

21

22

23

24

25

FIGURE 13
Statement Certificate

1

2

3

4 C E R T I F I C A T E

5

6 I, LIVELY DIGITS, Certified Shorthand Reporter

7 in and for the Parish of Jefferson, State of Louisiana,

8 do hereby certify that the foregoing statements

9 consisting of _____ pages were reported by me in machine

10 shorthand and transcribed (by me) (under my personal

11 direction and supervision) and are a true and correct

12 transcript, to the best of my ability and understanding.

13 I hereby certify that I am not of counsel,

14 not related to counsel or the parties hereto, and am in

15 no way interested in the outcome of this matter.

16

17

18 _____
LIVELY DIGITS
19 Certified Shorthand Reporter
Parish of Jefferson
20 State of Louisiana

21

22

23

24

25

Chapter 8

Depositions: Examinations Before Trial

A deposition or examination before trial (EBT or XBT) is the testimony of parties or witnesses in the form of questions and answers, taken in writing, under oath or affirmation, before a legally designated judicial officer. Depositions are typewritten or transcribed by computer for the most part these days, although handwriting is legally acceptable. The parties appear for the deposition as a result of a Notice, a Dedimus (Commission), or an Order of the Court.

Depositions make up the bulk of many freelance reporting firms' businesses, for they are, indeed, big business, being of such value in the discovery process. Without them, litigation in the United States would be hopelessly slowed. With the advent of CAT (Computer-Aided Transcription) the taking of depositions has multiplied many times, and as reporters advance more fully to real time, it is inevitable that reporting of depositions will continue to grow rapidly.

Types of Depositions

The four main types of depositions are:

1. interrogatories,
2. de bene esse, or perpetuation of testimony,
3. discovery, and
4. depositions in aid of execution.

De bene esse depositions, discovery depositions, and interrogatories are taken prior to trial to assist in preparation for trial and to dispose of cases by settlement wherever possible in accordance with facts developed by their taking. Depositions in aid of execution are taken after a lawsuit is completed.

De Bene Esse Depositions

A de bene esse deposition is one which may be used at the time of trial should the person testifying not be available at the time of trial, as may be the case if a witness should die, a maritime or military person be sent overseas, an individual become too ill or infirm to be present, or a person reside a great distance from the place of trial, as in a far-away state or a foreign country.

Counsel must be able to prove these facts to the Court's satisfaction before these depositions are taken for perpetuation of testimony to be admitted into evidence.

Discovery Depositions

Discovery depositions are reported to elicit, before trial, evidence which will give information concerning the facts. These depositions act as a settlement device wherever possible, thus saving the court time and money. They also serve as a preparation aid for counsel in conducting the trial of the case should it go to trial. They prevent witnesses and parties from changing their testimony at time of trial and serve as the basis for impeachment should such occur. Discovery depositions delineate and narrow the issues of a case and allow opposing counsel to ascertain their adversary's theory of the case.

Depositions may be taken of all parties to a case; witnesses, such as doctors and experts to prove related matters; those who saw or heard the matter forming the basis of suit; and all other parties without whom the case could not be proved. Any party to a lawsuit in a court of record or who expects to be a party in such a proceeding may ask to have pretrial deposition testimony taken through his or her attorney.

Discovery depositions are increasingly being taken in criminal cases, although the work product of law enforcement officers may not be secured through deposition questioning. Also, privileged matter or self-incriminatory material cannot be obtained through depositions. Depositions do lessen the possibility of surprise during the suit in court.

Discovery depositions may not be used as "fishing expeditions." That is, irrelevant and immaterial questions may not be asked in the hope that something of importance to the case will come out in the answers thereto.

Depositions in Aid of Execution

Depositions in aid of execution may be taken after a case is completed, and the Court has ordered a money judgment against a party to determine what assets the losing party may have that could be levied upon to pay the judgment. These are also called disclosure depositions.

Court-Ordered Depositions

Depositions taken by order of a court require a court order which states the time, place, and manner of taking the deposition. When a case approaches the trial date and the attorneys have not taken the initiative to secure essential depositions, the judge will order these depositions taken to avoid continuing cases unduly.

Procedures Used in Taking Depositions. Where statutes do not require written notice of taking depositions, many are set up by friendly telephone calls between counsel, who agree upon time, place, witnesses to be deposed, and the court reporter to be used. Then the court reporter is called and asked to be present. Sometimes the attorneys will verify this with a letter, mailing a carbon copy to the reporter. Upon receipt of such a phone call or letter, the court reporter marks it on his or her calendar or in the appointment book. The court reporter must then be there or have an alternate reporter appear to cover the assignment.

All reporting firms maintain an appointment book in which every setting is listed under proper date, giving the time, place of taking, name of reporter assigned, and any other pertinent information. To avoid any deposition appointment not being met, provision must always be made in listing the settings to insure that a replacement is sent in a timely manner for reporters who may be ill, absent, or whose assignment for morning depositions lasts into the afternoon or another day.

A written Notice of Taking Deposition must be prepared stating the title and venue of the action, name and address of the person giving the notice, the person before whom the testimony will be taken, time and place of deposition, name or names of person or persons to be deposed, and the matters upon which such person or persons will testify. Figure 14 contains an example

FIGURE 14
Written Notice

```
 1    24TH JUDICIAL DISTRICT COURT FOR THE PARISH OF JEFFERSON

 2                    STATE OF LOUISIANA

 3                       DIVISION E

 4  NO. 138-495

 5  HAGGLING FUTELY,        )(
                            )(
 6           Plaintiff,)(
                            )(
 7      -vs-                )(
                            )(
 8  REE SISTING,            )(
                            )(
 9           Defendant.)(

10  FILED:_____DEPUTY CLERK:_____

11                  NOTICE TO TAKE DEPOSITION

12  TO:  LITIGATIOUS DAILY, ESQ.
            Contentious Building
13          411 Lawsuit Avenue
            New Orleans, Louisiana  70130
14
         PLEASE TAKE NOTICE that undersigned counsel for defendant
15
    REE SISTING will take the oral deposition of the following-
16
    named person before an authorized officer on July 22, 19--,
17
    at 3:00 o'clock p.m., at 1024 Legal Lane, New Orleans,
18
    Louisiana:
19                  Miss Mary M. Contrary
                    4243 Seesitall Road
20                  Metairie, Louisiana   70132

21  Dated this 17th day of June, 19__.

22

23
                         _____
24                       LYKE LEE WINNER
                         Attorney for Defendant
25                       1024 Legal Lane
                         New Orleans, Louisiana   70130
```

of such a written notice. Almost universally now all legal forms and papers are placed on 8½″ x 11″ paper, and these are double-spaced.

As is the case in interrogatories, attendance of witnesses for deposition purposes can be demanded by subpoenas. In the case of a subpoena duces tecum, the required books and records or other objects demanded must be brought by the witness to the deposition room.

The reporter may be requested to prepare these forms and arrange for proper service. Care must be taken to prepare the forms properly and to follow all required procedures carefully in accordance with each state's requirements to prevent a witness from not appearing at the proper time and place.

Before you leave your office to go on a deposition, be sure you are dressed as a professional. A good suit is always in order. Be sure all items of clothing are scrupulously clean and neat. Flashy or dangling jewelry is out of place, and makeup should be subdued.

Then make sure you are fully equipped to do the job. You should have with you a full pack of paper in your shorthand machine and several extra packs; or, if you are a pen writer, take an extra notebook. Take at least four cassette tapes if your CAT system uses them. Check your machine to be certain it is well inked, but not overinked. A spare ribbon should be taped to the underside of the plate on your machine, and you should carry a bottle of ink along. Your case should contain your exhibit stamp and a stamp pad plus exhibit stickers. You should take a supply of your business cards, a grease pencil for marking X-rays, ball point pens that really work, and red or other colored pencils to mark any readbacks. Of course, your machine will be equipped with a StenoMark so you can mark places to be verified. Have your information sheet with you, already filled out with any information you already have about the matter, and take some extra paper, such as a tablet, in case you are required to note other information. If it is a noticed deposition, take your copy of the notice along with you. Reporters also carry the following items which may be useful: Post-it Notes (which do not require glue and do not deface papers), paper clips, a stapler and staples, and an extension cord to use if the electrical outlet is too far away. A small screwdriver is handy if you need to change a ribbon that suddenly splits. You might also want to take along a crossword puzzle magazine, a book to read, or proofreading to do if you have a lengthy wait before the start of the deposition. If another reporter has worked on the case previously or if you have taken previous depositions in the matter, check for spellings, locations, appearances, and any other information you may need.

Be there at least 15 minutes early! To be on time is to be late is an expression often used in relation to this. When you enter the appointed place to take the depositions, identify yourself courteously to the secretary or legal assistant who greets you. She or he is a very important person to you, so give her or him your card and explain that you are there to take the depositions scheduled identifying the case.

The secretary or receptionist is very important because many attorneys simply come out of their offices and tell their secretaries, "I have set down the depositions in the Hall case for Wednesday at 2:30. Get me a reporter." Naturally, if your card is before the secretary, receptionist, or paralegal, and if you have made a good impression, she or he is going to call you next time.

Eventually you will be ushered into the deposition room, where you will ordinarily meet the attorney who hired you or his designate and his client or clients, who have been having a coaching session. Perhaps opposing counsel, all witnesses, and the attorney who hired you are all there. If so, you are lucky, for opposing counsel and/or his or her clients are often late. Do not show any annoyance should this be the case.

Identify yourself to these people and hand your business card to each attorney. Ask each counsel present for his or her business card, and mark on each card whom the lawyer is representing—plaintiff or defendant. If any attorney does not have a business card, mark down his name, address, phone number, and whom he or she represents carefully on your information sheet.

If you do not have venue, style or title, case number, and the name of the individual to be deposed from the notice, ask for a copy of the pleadings or a paper with this information.

From whatever you are handed, note all information carefully in longhand on your information sheet. I always specifically ask for a copy of the pleadings because everything will normally be spelled correctly and I can note unusual names and spellings, locations, etc., while they are talking preliminarily. Whatever they hand me with the necessary information on it, I accept.

Be sure to note any extra people, such as insurance adjusters, family members, co-counsel, and representatives of parties to the suit on your information sheet and list them on your appearance page when the deposition is printed.

Counsel will often ask you if it makes any difference to you where you sit and what kind of chair you prefer. Request that you be seated next to the witness and also next to or across from the questioning attorney. It is vital that you be in a good position to see both of them and particularly to hear them well. If the witness is a "murmurer" or "whisperer," move closer to the point where you can hear everything well. It is imperative that the record be complete, and you must do whatever is necessary to secure such a record. You cannot be too timid and be a good reporter.

If possible, look for a straight chair with no arms unless such an item is not readily available in the office. Then, you will have to do the best you can with whatever is available. Do not make an issue of petty things, or the next time depositions are to be scheduled a different reporter or firm will be requested.

Be sure to note the time the deposition actually begins. Ask when the trial date is so that it can be resolved if they are going to require daily or rush delivery of the transcript. Ask if the deposition is being taken pursuant to written notice or agreement in order that your transcript may correctly reflect this.

You should then inquire about stipulations. Do this at the very beginning if they do not introduce the subject. If counsel say, "Usual stipulations," pin them down because what may be usual stipulations in one place or one circumstance may not be what they mean at another time and place.

Stipulations

At the very beginning of the first deposition I ever reported, as soon as I had sworn the witness, plaintiff's attorney said, "Usual stips?" to which defense counsel replied "Okay."

I wrote this down, figuring "stips" meant "stipulations," and I knew that stipulations were agreements. I had no idea what they were talking about; but I kept quiet, not wanting to show my ignorance. Right after the depositions were over, I went out and asked an experienced reporter, "What are the usual stips?"

He explained to me that the stipulations were to be placed at the front of each deposition after the appearance page and that these stipulations give the "ground rules," so to speak, governing the taking and uses of the deposition.

Some Usual Stipulations

It is usual for counsel for the respective parties to stipulate that written notice of taking the deposition be waived if they have simply agreed orally to the time and place of the taking of the matter. They also usually stipulate that notice of filing is waived, which means that the reporter need not notify the attorneys when the original is filed with the appropriate court clerk.

Counsel will tell you if you ask:

1. If the deposition is being taken by agreement, normally usual stipulations will apply as follows:
    (a) Objections are waived until the time of trial except as to the form of the question;
    (b) Signature of the witness is waived; and
    (c) Formalities as to Notice of Taking and Notice of Filing are waived.

2. If the deposition is being taken by notice, you will still ask if usual stipulations listed above will apply. If the usual stipulations do not apply, this will mean any or all of the following:
    (a) Objections are not waived;
    (b) The witness must read and sign the deposition before a notary public before the original is filed;

(c) It will be necessary for you to notify the attorneys when you have filed the original of the deposition; and

(d) Other stipulations may be dictated to you in addition to the above.

If the attorneys do not discuss stipulations at the beginning of the deposition, and you have no opportunity to secure stipulations at the outset, do not assume stipulations apply. Just inquire tactfully at the end of taking the matter if any stipulations are to be included in the transcript. This may be important, so include any directions on the record, such as it is to apply to only one case or be used for some special purpose only, and so on.

Usual stipulations also mean that the deposition may be used for all purposes contemplated under the statutes of the state (or federal rules governing U.S. District Courts) and that objections need be made at the time of the taking of the deposition only as to the form of the question (leading and suggestive, for instance) and that signature of the witness is or is not requested.

Discussion about signing of the deposition by the witness usually takes place at the conclusion. In some states the witness must be asked directly by the reporter if he or she waives signature; in other states, the attorney for any party may state on the record that signature is waived. Be sure to include this in your notes.

Where Stipulations Are Placed

In most freelance firms the title page is page 1, which is never numbered. The appearance page, which contains names and addresses of the attorneys and whom they represent, is page 2; and the stipulations page is page 3. Pages of depositions are numbered in the upper right-hand corner above the ruled line, at the bottom of the page at the right below the ruled line, or at the center bottom of the page below the ruled line, whichever is the custom or stated statutory requirement in a jurisdiction.

Figure 15 shows a sample stipulation page. The reporters in some firms take sheets with them that list a number of common stipulations, and the attorneys check or circle the applicable ones and return the sheet to the reporter. (See Figures 16 and 17)

Some counsel prefer to dictate the stipulations into the record. Figure 18 is a sample of such a dictated stipulations page.

Deposition Worksheet

Every reporter should tape a 3″ x 5″ note pad to the plate on top of his or her shorthand machine for notations. However, this will not take the place of a reporter's worksheet, which the reporter fills in completely as an aid in preparing an orderly transcript.

Worksheets may take many forms, but those included will provide useful examples for your student use and reporting assignments, should a different form not be provided you, as they will cover the essentials for deposition use. As a student you should prepare a number of worksheets so the routine becomes habitual to you.

Contents of the Worksheet

Reporters' worksheets are usually placed on legal-sized paper. They should provide a place for the reporter's name, date and time the deposition was taken, court file number given the case by the clerk or courts, office job number and computer information required, title and venue of the case, appearances of counsel and their addresses and whom they represent, witnesses' names, exhibit listing, stipulation information, and billing requirements.

At the bottom of the page, space is provided for verified spellings, remarks, and arbitrary forms made up by the reporter (such as PLA for Piscataway Savings & Loan Association). The

FIGURE 15
Sample Stipulation Page

```
 1                    S T I P U L A T I O N S

 2

 3            IT WAS STIPULATED AND AGREED by and between

 4   counsel for the respective parties that notice, time,

 5   and all other statutory prerequisites incident to the

 6   taking and return of said deposition, including notice

 7   of filing, *(as well as the signing of same by the witness,)

 8   are hereby waived; that same may be taken at the time and

 9   place set forth, and when reduced to writing and returned

10   into court, may be used by either party upon the trial

11   of said cause, said deposition, however, to be subject to

12   all other legal objections, which need not be reserved

13   at the time of taking the deposition, but may be urged

14   at the time of trial the same as if the witness were

15   present, testifying in person.

16

17   _____

18   *Add the following if the signature of the witness is

19   required, deleting the material between parentheses above:

20

21            IT WAS FURTHER STIPULATED AND AGREED by and

22   between Counsel that the said witness shall read and

23   sign the deposition before filing.

24

25
```

opposite side of the information sheet or continuation pages are used to designate extra counsel, others present, and for further spellings and remarks. For lengthy work, more than one sheet may be needed.

Preservation of Worksheet and Notes

At the end of the depositions, the worksheet and any extensions are wrapped around the notes of the proceeding, secured by elastic bands. The date, case title, venue, case number, and such information as "Pack 3 of 5 packs" should be written on top of the wrapped worksheet. It is customary to place the date of taking the notes in large black Marks-A-Lot letters on the ends of each pack of notes so required notes can be found easily in chronologically filed stacks of notes.

FIGURE 16
Common Stipulations Form

COMMON STIPULATIONS

STIPULATIONS (Insert proper numbers.)

IT IS STIPULATED AND AGREED by and between counsel for the respective parties hereto that this deposition is taken pursuant to the paragraphs below, number _____.

(1) That the deposition of the witness named in the caption hereto may be taken at this time and place before the herein named notary public of _____ County, State of _____; time notice, and the issuance of a commission being waived; and that the said deposition or any part thereof, when so taken, may be used on the trial of this case with the same force and effect as if the witness were present in court and testifying in person;

(2) That the necessity for the witness to read and sign this deposition is waived;

(3) That the necessity for preserving objections at the time of taking is waived, and that any and all legal objections to this deposition or any part thereof may be urged at the time same is sought to be offered in evidence on the trial of this cause;

(4) That this deposition may be filed with the clerk of the court prior to reading and signing of same by the witness; provided further, however, that the witness shall read and subscribe to same at or before the time of the commencement of the trial;

(5) That the witness shall read and sign this deposition before a notary public prior to the time of filing same with the clerk of the court; and/or

(6) That the necessity for preserving objections at the time of taking is waived and that any and all legal objections to this deposition or any part thereof may be urged at the time same is sought to be offered in evidence on the trial of this cause; except, however, that objections to the form of the questions and/or responsiveness of the answers must be made at the time of taking or else such objections are specifically waived.

FIGURE 17
Common Stipulations Form

COMMON STIPULATIONS

(Check applicable stipulations for inclusion in the record.)

_____ 1. It is hereby stipulated and agreed by and between counsel for the respective parties that the deposition of the above-named witness may be taken on behalf of the (plaintiff - defendant) at the time and place set forth herein before the notary public herein mentioned and be reported by _____, a competent shorthand reporter and disinterested person, and thereafter reduced to typewritten form under (his-her) direction;

_____ 2. That all objections as to notice of time and place of the taking of this deposition are expressly waived;

_____ 3. That all objections except as to the form of the questions are reserved to the time of trial;

_____ 4. That this deposition, when transcribed, may be used for all purposes contemplated under the Rules;

_____ 5. That the reading of this deposition to, or by, the witness and the signing thereof by the witness are hereby expressly waived;

_____ 6. That it is hereby expressly stipulated that the signature of the witness shall be subscribed to the transcript of this deposition in the presence of a notary public; and/or

_____ 7. That in the event this deposition is not corrected and signed by the witness at the time of trial, reasonable opportunity having been given to do so, it may be introduced by either party with the same force and effect as though signed.

FIGURE 18
Dictated Stipulations

```
 1              MR. VELTA:  May it be stipulated, counsel,

 2       that the deposition of John Doyle is being

 3       taken here on the 12th day of February, 1982,

 4       pursuant to agreement, and may be used in the

 5       cases of S. E. Jensen v. John Doyle, Eva Jensen

 6       v. John Doyle, and also in the case brought by

 7       John Doyle against both of the Jensens, for

 8       all of the purposes which are contemplated by

 9       the Rules of Civil Procedure for the District

10       Courts of the State of Minnesota, for discovery

11       purposes, and that all formalities as to

12       signing and filing of the deposition may be

13       waived?

14              MR. GALLAGHER:  Just one thing:  That

15       does not contemplate use of it in case of the

16       inability of the person to be in Court, does

17       it?

18              MR. LUNDQUIST:  As I understood it, you

19       said in regard to discovery only.

20              MR. VELTA:  I guess I did.  I stand cor-

21       rected.

22              MR. LUNDQUIST:  That stipulation is

23       satisfactory with me.

24              MR. BLATTI:  It may be so stipulated so far

25       as we are concerned.
```

As the reporter dictates, transcribes, or has computer work done on a transcript, he or she may place other information on the worksheet so the necessary data will be on hand to produce a perfect transcript or make future references which may be required. Information sheets are also called "Dog sheets," "Poop sheets," and a number of other more uncomplimentary names, but they are an invaluable aid in producing transcripts.

Figures 19, 20, 21, and 22 are examples of worksheets used by some prominent firms. A number of other examples of information sheets are found at the back of *The Deposition* by Lynn Brooks, which book is sold by NCRA. Figure 19 is a good form for students to use during training and internship to acquire practice in securing basic essential information for preparation of the transcript since it is simple and quite comprehensive.

Swearing the Witness

Ask the attorneys if they would like you to swear the witness when these preliminaries are completed. Upon affirmative reply, proceed to swear or affirm the witness, following all of the instructions given in Chapter 5.

When taking a deposition, never forget to swear the witness unless you are willing to be the

FIGURE 19
Worksheet

DEPOSITION WORKSHEET

REPORTER _____

DATE _____ JOB NUMBER _____

CASE NUMBER _____

VENUE _____

Style

_____

_____

-vs-

_____

_____

PLAINTIFF'S   *Witnesses*   DEFENDANT'S

_____   _____

_____   _____

_____   _____

_____   _____

Appearances

_____   _____

_____   _____

_____   _____

_____ EXHIBITS _____ COPIES OF EACH

WAIVE SIGNATURE   (   )   PURSUANT TO AGREEMENT   (   )
SIGNATURE ANYTIME BEFORE   PURSUANT TO NOTICE   (   )
  TRIAL   (   )   USUAL STIPULATION   (   )
SIGNATURE BEFORE FILING   (   )
COMMISSION   (   )

BILLING TO PLAINTIFF:
    ORIG & _____ OF _____
    ORIG & _____ OF _____
    ORIG & _____ OF _____
BILLING TO DEFENDANT
    ORIG & _____ OF _____
    ORIG & _____ OF _____
    ORIG & _____ OF _____

SPELLING, REMARKS, AND ARBITRARY FORMS:

FIGURE 20-A
Side 1

CAT WORKSHEET

Reporter: _____

Note No.: _____   Date Needed

Tape Name(s) _____   _____

Style of Case: _____

_____

_____

Date Taken: _____   Date Ordered: _____

Stipulations: (1)   (2)   (3)   (4)   (None)

Estimated Pages: _____   Translated Pages: _____

Reading Instructions   Start/Stop Times   Job Name(s)

_____   _____

_____   _____

_____   _____

_____   _____

Steno Outlines   *English*

_____   _____

_____   _____

_____   _____

_____   _____

_____   _____

_____   _____

Functions   *Scoper/Date*

_____   _____

_____   _____

_____   _____

_____   _____

_____   _____

RUN FINAL: Orig. &   Copies   _____
RUN FINAL: Index (   )   Cert. Ques. (   )   _____

FIGURE 20-B
Side 2

Steno Outlines   *English*

_____   _____

_____   _____

_____   _____

_____   _____

_____   _____

_____   _____

_____   _____

_____   _____

_____   _____

_____   _____

_____   _____

_____   _____

_____   _____

_____   _____

Index Information:
Direct _____   *Exhibits*   *Certified*
Cross _____   *Questions*:
Redirect _____
Recross _____

DATE BILLED: _____ DATE DELETED _____

possible object of a malpractice suit. If the attorneys are antagonistic, the adversary may refuse to allow the testimony to be used in court.

Taking the Record

As soon as the oath is administered, get in there and write steadily, interrupting only for something you cannot hear or cannot possibly verify any other way. As you are saying, "You may be seated" to the witness, be getting in position to sit quickly and start writing because questioning usually begins at once. Needless to say, you must have your machine in such a location that you do not knock it over when you sit down, or you may delay the proceedings or put them off until another day if your machine should be broken.

Mark your "hot spots" with your StenoMark as you go along, read back like a veteran if called upon to do so, and cease to write only when all attorneys present agree to go off the record; never when they say, "Strike that."

FIGURE 21

GENERAL DOG SHEET

_____   REPORTER: _____

_____   DATE TAKEN: _____
vs.

_____   ESTIMATED PAGES: _____

_____

CASE NO: _____ filed in _____ COUNTY

BILL TO: _____   Deposition of

_____   _____ _____ pgs.

_____   _____ _____ pgs.

Attn: _____   _____ _____ pgs.

Orig. _____ pgs. @ $_____ . ___ pp. $ _____ . ___

(   ) Copy(s) _____ pgs. @ . ___ pp.   _____ . ___

Per Diem (Time) _____   _____ . ___ $ _____ . ___

_____ Xerox Copies @ . _____ pp.   _____ . ___ $ _____ . ___

Postage . . . .

BILL TO: _____

_____

_____

Attn: _____

Orig. _____ pgs. @ $_____ . ___ pp. $ _____ . ___

(   ) Copy(s) _____ pgs. @ . ___ pp.   _____ . ___

Per Diem (Time) _____   _____ . ___ $ _____ . ___

_____ Xerox Copies @ . _____ pp.   _____ . ___ $ _____ . ___

Postage . . . .

SPECIAL INSTRUCTIONS: To Be Signed: _____

                                 Extra Copy Made: _____

                                 File Orig: _____

                                 Orig. to Atty.: _____

                                 Job Saved: _____

                                 Exhibits: _____

Date Billed _____   Note Number _____

FIGURE 22

INFORMATION SHEET

ORIG & _____

PAPER _____

PHOTOCOPIED _____

S¼EC   Y _____ N _____

DAILY _____ EXP _____

TURN-IN DATE _____

PROOFREAD _____ DEPOSITION OF _____ pp. _____

DEPOSITION OF _____ pp. _____

_____ Hearing   (Place) _____ (Date) _____

_____ Deposition

_____ Videotape Deposition   of _____

_____ Pretrial Examination

_____ Sworn Statement

_____ Oral Examination Under Oath

held in the offices of _____ Building, at _____

on the above date before

a Registered Professional Reporter _____

a Certified Shorthand Reporter _____

a Commissioner—a Notary Public _____

a Court Reporter _____

*of the _____

of _____   or an Approved Reporter of the

APPEARANCES: U.S. District Court _____

_____

ATTY'S FULL NAME	DATE SENT	HOW/ LBS	CLIENT	ATTY #	RATE	INVOICE	AMOUNT
O&1cc							
COPY							
COPY							
COPY							
COPY							
COPY							

EXHIBITS RETAINED BY _____   # OF EXHIBITS _____   PAGES EXHIBITS COPIED _____

SPECIAL INSTRUCTIONS: STIPS: YES _____ NO _____

_____ CHARGE ATTENDANCE FEE

_____ SIGNATURE PAGE FOR WITNESS

_____ SIGNATURE PAGE FOR YOURSELF MADE UP IF WITNESS DOES NOT SIGN

_____ ATTACH ORIGINAL EXHIBITS TO ORIGINAL TRANSCRIPT

_____ ATTACH PHOTOCOPIES OF EXHIBITS TO COPIES OF TRANSCRIPTS

_____ ATTORNEY MADE PHOTOCOPIES OF EXHIBITS

_____ NAME OF ATTORNEY WHO RECEIVES EXTRA COPY FOR SIGNING _____

_____ NAME OF WITNESS WHO RECEIVES EXTRA COPY FOR SIGNING

NAME _____

ADDRESS _____

ADDRESS _____

CITY, STATE, ZIP _____

_____ NAME OF ATTORNEY WHO RECEIVES ORIGINAL FOR SIGNING _____

(ALL COUNSEL MUST AGREE TO THIS)

_____ SEND SIGNED TRANSCRIPT TO ATTORNEY _____

_____ FILE ORIGINAL TRANSCRIPT (WHETHER OR NOT IT HAS TO BE SIGNED)

CLERK OF COURT _____

COURT _____

ADDRESS _____

Off-the-Record Discussions

Some reporters stand when an off-the-record discussion is announced and remain standing until the attorneys state "back on the record." I do not do this, as I feel it might make the lawyers feel uncomfortable to see the lady reporter standing, and it might cut short their discussions.

Some reporters sit with their hands obviously raised enough that counsel can always see that they are not writing on such occasions. Still others merely sit quietly during these periods. You will soon determine your own most effective way of handling off-the-record situations.

If at any time you are uncertain as to whether an off-the-record discussion is still going on, ask. You will learn to sense that they have forgotten to inform you, for instance, by the fact that they turn and resume questioning the witness and forget to inform you they want to be back on the record.

At such times, simply say quietly to the attorney nearest you "Is this on the record?" Never continue to let the deposition go on while you are in doubt, or you may risk their ire ten minutes later when they realize they have no record of important matters. They well know a witness will probably never say anything the same way a second time or resist adding some qualifying remark that may negate the very point they have just made.

Marking Exhibits

The matter of marking exhibits will be taken up thoroughly in another chapter. Mark all deposition exhibits carefully, being very careful not to become confused with markings placed on them during previous depositions or cases. Keep possession of exhibits if you are requested to file them with the deposition, as all documentary evidence should be attached at the back of the deposition unless there is an agreement to the contrary between counsel or judges requesting that exhibits not be filed with depositions because of file space.

The attorneys may also stipulate that copies may be substituted for original exhibits, in which case the reporter prepares the copies, making a proper charge therefor, and returns the original exhibits promptly to counsel furnishing them.

Chapter 9

Taking the Deposition

Designation of Counsel

It is essential that the court reporter identify counsel properly at all times in the record, so it behooves you to get all identifications down in your notes correctly as you take any deposition or hearing.

When you enter the deposition room, mark on the cards you secure from the attorneys whom they represent. Then write the appearances on your information sheet, together with their addresses and phone numbers. On the little 3″ x 5″ pad you keep taped to the top plate of your machine mark how you will designate each counsel. Somehow, writing a name in longhand helps to impress it upon your memory.

When I have completed securing and recording the information, I fix my attention upon attaching the names to counsel if they are unknown to me from previous work. I look at my information sheet or cards and say to myself, "Mr. Barrow is an older, gray-haired man; and Mr. Arthur is the young man with black-rimmed glasses. Mr. Barrow will be asking the questions, and Mr. Arthur will be making the objections. Mr. Barrow has on a charcoal gray suit and tie, and Mr. Arthur has on a blue suit and a red tie." Of course, you must never stare as you do this, but you will find after a few depositions you will readily attach names to attorneys in short order.

When you walk into a deposition room and find a large number of attorneys there, look around; and you will see one or two counsel to whom the rest seem to be deferring. You will know they are the important attorneys, and you can normally figure they will be doing most of the questioning, objecting, and talking.

Identify them in your mind, concentrating on the important ones. You can tell a lot about the tenor of the depositions just by observing a while before they start. Don't panic because only one attorney will be questioning at a time. Stay calm. Draw a picture of where each attorney is seated, and be sure to identify each one carefully.

First Syllable Designation of Counsel

When you have several attorneys, you may use the first syllable of each attorney's name, struck twice, as identification of counsel. In the above example, you would strike BAR/BAR for Mr. Barrow and ART/ART for Mr. Arthur. If you use the first-syllable-twice method of identification, you must be very careful that two attorneys do not have a last name that starts with the same syllable. Fathers and sons are often present at depositions. Should this happen, substitute the first name of one lawyer.

Reporters have been known to designate attorneys by physical characteristics when their memory has failed them, writing BALD/BALD for a bald-headed lawyer, etc. Whatever you use, be sure you can properly state the attorney's name if you are called upon to read back during proceedings.

Another method of identifying counsel is to use STPHAO for plaintiff's attorney and SKWRAO for defendant's attorney. Then, you can use STPHAO-F, STPHAO-P, STPHAO-L, STPHAO-T and STPHAO-D for additional plaintiff's attorneys and SKWRAO-R, SKWRAO-B, SKWRAO-G, SKWRAO-S, and SKWRAO-Z for additional defense attorneys.

Designating Counsel by Numbers

A widely used system of designating counsel is by use of numerals. When using this method, 1234 would represent the first plaintiff's counsel; and 1234-5, 1234-6, 1234-7, 1234-8, 1234-9, etc., would represent other plaintiff's counsel.

Defendant's attorneys would be designated by 6789, 1-6789, 2-6789, 3-6789, 4-6789, 5-6789, and so on. This system is effective and easy to master.

Some reporters write 1234-6 to imply Franklin, who is represented by "F" under "6," and 1234-7 to designate Peters, who is represented by "P" under "7," etc. This method is rather complicated, so many reporters simply use the numbers consecutively down the sides of the table. Whatever you do, always keep your chart before you showing designations when you have more than two attorneys.

Depositions Having Multiple Attorneys

It is rather frightening to walk into a deposition room the first time and see a large number of attorneys, but do not worry! If there are numerous lawyers, the matter will involve greater investment, and they will all be more conscious of the record than attorneys in smaller lawsuits. Keep thinking of all the copies you will sell!

The worst attorney to report is a brand new one who has been sent out by an important senior partner to take his or her first deposition. Being afraid of making errors, he or she will ask questions out of sequence and cut in to try to head off unfavorable answers, make false starts, and phrase questions poorly. Such a person's nervousness rubs off on everyone, particularly the witness.

The best attorneys to report are the seasoned professionals, for they may go fast, but they never forget about the record. They will ask questions in sequence, keep the proceeding orderly, and phrase their questions expertly.

If you have a number of attorneys, never let the proceedings get out of hand and permit several people to speak at once to prevent your hearing the answers. Be firm, but always be polite about it. They will realize you are protecting their record and respect you for it. It is the printed record that matters and not your instant of wounded pride.

Using a Chart as a Visual Aid

Any time you have several attorneys to keep straight, draw a picture of where they are seated and mark on it the names and designations you will use for each.

Should a deposition or hearing last more than one day, check your drawing each session to be sure nobody has changed seats without your knowing. Also, be careful in large gatherings that no one slips in late causing everyone else to move down one seat, unnoticed by you. Occasionally someone will leave to phone or for another reason. Make notes of these things and be sure to keep your chart straight. Keep the chart constantly before you for reference.

Figure 23 shows a typical diagram of a case or deposition having a number of attorneys. You will soon devise a good method to fit your own specific needs in this regard.

Your daily practice in your four-voice classes will provide good experience in designation of counsel, so welcome every opportunity to keep your information sheets properly, mark designations in your notes, and practice drawing up charts for multi-counsel depositions and cases.

FIGURE 23

SAMPLE CHART FOR DESIGNATION OF COUNSEL

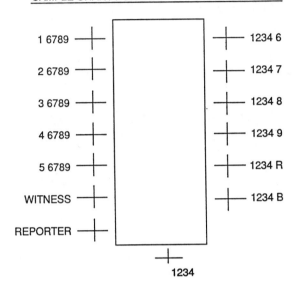

1 6789	1234 6
2 6789	1234 7
3 6789	1234 8
4 6789	1234 9
5 6789	1234 R
WITNESS	1234 B
REPORTER	

1234

Interrupting the Proceedings

Whether or not to stop proceedings because of speed or mishearing is always a problem to the beginning reporter. Sometimes it will seem that the attorneys have strained you to the breaking point, and you feel you simply must stop them for speed or because they are talking several at a time. Hold on as long as you can, and then force yourself just a shade longer, and you will make it. You will have avoided breaking in because they do have to come up for air or to consult their papers or to consider their next question.

Fix your eyes firmly on the point of your table, concentrate hard, and push and force yourself beyond your capacity, and you will have weathered the storm in most cases.

There are times, however (particularly when you are a beginner) when you need to interrupt. Sometimes you must say, "Excuse me. I got what Mr. Mason said, but I couldn't hear you, Mr. Marshall," or, "You said you entered the room and what?" or "Speak up, please," to a whispering or muttering witness. When appropriate, ask, "Which of you four gentlemen shall I record?" because you must have a complete record.

As a beginner you will not have the discrimination to tell what is vital, so use your judgment. Be sure to get the attention of the participants if you feel the record is slipping away from you. You cannot be like a timid beginner who, when the judge asked, "Are we going too fast for you?" said "No" over and over again. The judge came in the office at recess and said, "Boy, I kept going faster and faster this morning, and that new little reporter kept saying it wasn't too fast. She is unbelievable." Well, a few weeks later he came in with the record, screaming that he had to have a rehearing because the reporter had left out over half the record and what was in the transcript was not even right.

So, use your head, stay calm, and have the courage and intelligence to know your limits. The printed transcript of the record is what is important.

Avoid Interrupting Cross-Examination

It is difficult for attorneys to regain their train of thought if they are broken in on when cross-examining, so reporters try very hard not to interrupt them. By the time cross-examination is reached, tempers are often flaring, and it is best not to add to the feeling of ill will. However, you must use good judgment. The record must be complete.

Editing While Writing

Most competent reporters do a certain amount of editing as they go along, improving an attorney's or judge's grammar when it will not change the record, but be careful. Some freelance firms have their reporters change all "uh-huhs" to "yes" and all the "un-unhs" to "no" because depositions are simply "to get the facts."

One day I was taking a deposition, and suddenly counsel yelled, "I want this record to show every one of these 'uh-huhs' and 'un-unhs' because I can't tell which is 'yes' and which is 'no,' and I don't think the reporter can either." After that, I wrote everything down as said and decided what to do about it later, because that time I had to go back and insert a lot of "uh-huhs" and "un-unhs" in the transcript.

I reported several proceedings where one attorney would make little comments "sotto voce" during court cases and depositions. Everyone disregarded them, including me. One day opposing counsel bellowed, "I want every one of these remarks counsel is making in the record." Offending counsel made no comments after that, but I spent a miserable recess inserting every remark I could remember that he had made in my notes.

So, write down all that is said and then decide how to handle it when you prepare the transcript.

Of course, if counsel starts every question with "Well," "And. . .," or "Okay," it is a good idea to omit some of those because they make for a cluttered, not-too literate record. Attorneys do this to establish a "folksy," comfortable rapport with the witness. Even on videotaped depositions some reporters drop some of these, although many are purists on these.

Shakes and Nods of the Head Are Another Problem

The question sometimes comes up as to how to handle the fact that a witness shakes or nods his or her head. At a recent seminar, a speaker from the Texas Court of Appeals said they preferred the parenthetical to read (Witness nods head affirmatively.) or (Witness shakes head negatively.) as that gives a definite answer. Some firms insist the reporter not make the decision as to what nods and shakes mean, simply inserting (Witness nods head.) or (Witness shakes head.).

Differing Pronunciations

If you are asked to read back during a deposition, should attorneys or witnesses have pronounced a word differently from your regular pronunciation of it, say it their way. Do not give the appearance of ever correcting the person, especially if the witness is a doctor or an expert. Many times the location of the school they attended governs their pronunciation of many words. Experts may feel you are trying to "upstage" them if you seem to correct them and may possibly harbor resentment. When people become angry, they go faster!

Ordinarily, the court reporter is the only person no one is angry at during depositions and court hearings. LET'S KEEP IT THAT WAY!

Certifying Questions

I shall never forget one day shortly after I began taking depositions when counsel were not getting along too well, and objections were being made frequently. Eventually one attorney told the witness (his client) not to answer a question. At this point the questioning lawyer, who had hired me for the afternoon, stated, "I think the judge is in his chambers here in the city today. Reporter, please certify the question, and we will find out whether this witness has to answer that question or not."

Suddenly, there I was in a small side office along with my notes, a strange typewriter, legal paper, and carbons, saying to myself, "Don't panic. Don't panic. Don't panic." Having repeated the magic words three times, the solution presented itself almost immediately.

After typing the venue, title, and case number, it was just a simple matter of preparing an affidavit describing the situation and presenting the question and following colloquy for presentation to the judge. A little later the attorneys returned with the decision that the judge had ruled the question must be answered by the witness, and we proceeded with our deposition.

Figure 24 will give an example of how to handle such a situation, should one ever happen to you. You may not ever be called upon to draw up a legal paper on the spur of the moment, but you can see how being an excellent typist and having an active mind can help in situations such as this. Many times, I have been asked to fill out bond forms or subpoenas at the end of the day by attorneys and judges, and such efficiency is appreciated by good will engendered (and sometimes by a hefty check!)

Don't be quick to say, "I can't do that," because exhibiting initiative establishes you as one of the team everyone finds indispensible.

Certification of a Question Usually Comes After a Deposition

Ordinarily it is not possible to have certification of a question prepared during the deposition as judges are not usually readily available to make a ruling. So, as you take a deposition, objections will be made from time to time, and certifications of questions will be requested. Indicate in your notes and on your information sheet what is asked for. When the deposition is typed up, make a separate certification of the required questions as shown in Figure 25 after completion of the transcription of the deposition.

Your Certification of Questions form should be inserted under the front cover of the deposition to be considered by the judge and ruled upon. If the judge's ruling requires the witness to answer the question or questions included in the certification, you may be called upon to report another deposition in the matter in the future.

Good Advice to the Fledgling Reporter

Nothing in your school training and short internship can quite prepare you for the give and take of opposing counsel when the winning of a lawsuit is at stake. Any unusual episodes tend to be very terrifying to a tyro unless your school has offered much four-voice practice and you have sat in on a good deal of actual reporting work. Therefore, as a student in the upper speeds, you should arrange for much practice time with experienced reporters and at any law school moot court mock trials that may be available.

There is a side advantage to doing extra practice with court reporters and on your own at mock trials. You will meet young lawyers and the judges who give their time to conduct these sessions, and they will see that you are serious about your profession and aim to become highly

FIGURE 24-A
Certification of Questions

```
 1    IN THE DISTRICT COURT OF DOUGLAS COUNTY, MINNESOTA
 2              FIFTH JUDICIAL DISTRICT
 3
 4   ANNA JUDITH PETERSON, ⋈
 5            Plaintiff, ⋈
 6                       ⋈      CIVIL NO. 696,137
 7        -vs-           ⋈
 8   NILES G. ROWAN,     ⋈
 9         Defendant.    ⋈
10            CERTIFICATION OF QUESTION
11      I, Neaton Correct, a stenotype reporter and Notary Public
12   in and for Douglas County, Minnesota, hereby certify that
13   pursuant to Notice dated January 10, 19--, duly served, the
14   deposition of ARTHUR ASHBY was taken before me commencing at
15   2:30 p.m., Monday, January 26, 19--, at the offices of
16   Jenkins & Barlow, Attorneys at Law, 419 Sycamore Street,
17   Linwood, Minnesota and that certain oral questions were
18   propounded and certain answers given; and certain questions
19   were propounded which were not answered, as follows:
20   Q   (By Mr. Stanton) Who, besides Nancy, could you name
21       by name as being Richard's closest friends?  Who are
22       his close classmates?
23           MR. MILLER:  That doesn't have anything to
24       do with this case.  You don't have to answer
25       that question, Arthur.
```

(continued at line 25)

```
25   Q   (By Mr. Stanton) Would you care to answer it?
```

FIGURE 24-B

```
 1           MR. MILLER:  I told him not to answer it,
 2   and he is going to do what I told him.  This is
 3   not a fishing expedition.  If you think it is a
 4   relevant question, you can have it certified.
 5           THE WITNESS:  Upon instructions from my
 6   counsel, I refuse to answer that question.
 7           MR. STANTON:  I think the Judge is in his
 8   chambers here today.  Mrs. Reporter, please
 9   certify the question, and we will find out whether
10   the witness has to answer or not."
11   WITNESS MY HAND AND SEAL OF OFFICE, this, the 26th day
12   of January, A. D. 19--.
13
14
15
16
17
18
19
20
21
22
23
24
25
```

```
     NEATON CORRECT, Notary Public
     Douglas County, Minnesota
     My Commission expires 6/30/--
```

FIGURE 25-A
Certification of Questions

```
 1    IN THE DISTRICT OCURT OF HARRIS COUNTY, TEXAS
 2              157TH JUDICIAL DISTIRCT
 3   HUBERT HAGOOD,                    :
 4              Plaintiff,             :
 5        -vs-                         :    CIVIL NO. 433,449
 6   MAGNOLIA PETROLEUM COMPANY,:
 7   ET AL.                           :
 8              Defendant.            :
 9              CERTIFICATION OF QUESTIONS
10    I, Ima Nifty Writer, a court reporter and Notary Public
11   in and for the County of Harris, State of Texas, do hereby
12   certify that on the 28th day of May, 19—, beginning at the
13   hour of 3:30 p.m., in the offices of Davis & Johnson,
14   Attorneys at Law, 421 Maple Street, Houston, Texas  77001,
15   there appeared before me one HUBERT HAGOOD for the purpose
16   of having his oral deposition taken.
17        Certain oral questions were propounded and certain
18   answers given, as shown in the transcript of the deposition
19   of HUBERT HAGOOD filed in the above-captioned cause, and
20   certain questions were propounded which were not answered,
21   as shown in the transcript of the deposition of HUBERT HAGOOD,
22   as follows:
23   Beginning at page 49, line 11:
24   Q  (By Mr. Harmon)  I just wondered, since you, apparently,
25   were there at that time.  Did it appear to you that it
```

FIGURE 25-B

```
 1   wasn't safe to be trying to unload the drums off to the
 2   boat from that platform there?
 3   A  Well --
 4   Q  I mean, did you think that he ought not to have been
 5   asking you to do the work in that way?
 6   A  Well, actually, I didn't feel it was my place to do it.
 7   Q  I realize that.
 8   A  Naturally, it was a little dangerous, it appeared at
 9   that time, but I guess to him and to me that was the
10   only way to do it.
11   Q  Did it appear to you then that that was a reasonably
12   safe way to do it?
13        MR. McDERMOTT:  Wait a minute.  You are going
14   into matters of opinion.  I think you ought to
15   interrogate him on facts.
16   Q  (By Mr. Harmon)  I want to know whether or not you
17   thought at that time it wasn't safe to be doing that.
18        MR. McDERMOTT:  I am going to instruct him
19   not to answer that.  That calls for an opinion
20   and his conclusion, and I don't think it's a
21   proper question.  If I am wrong, I am willing to
22   submit it to the Judge, but I don't think that
23   is a proper question.  I think this is to be a
24   factual deposition and not matters of opinion.  I
25   an perfectly willing, however, to submit it to
```

FIGURE 25-C

```
 1           Judge if you want an answer.
 2                MR. HARMON:  I would like an answer.  May we
 3           ask the reporter to certify it?
 4                MR. McDERMOTT:  Why, yes.  If the Judge thinks
 5           it's proper, he will surely answer.
 6    Beginning at page 56, line 24:
 7    Q    (By Mr. Harmon)  Do you feel that the place where you
 8           were doing your work was at least reasonably safe?
 9                MR. McDERMOTT:  That is, again, an opinion.  I
10           am going to instruct him not to answer.  Please
11           confine your questions to facts not opinions.
12                MR. HARMON:  I would just like to know whether
13           or not he thought at that time it was safe to be
14           trying to work there.
15                MR. McDERMOTT:  I still think it calls for an
16           opinion, and the jury will be called upon to
17           answer that question.  I am not going to let him
18           testify to it unless the Court says it is a proper
19           question.
20                MR. HARMON:  Certify the question, please.
21
22
23
24                ────────────────────────────
                  IMA NIFTY WRITER, Notary Public
                  Harris County, Texas
25                My Commission expires 6/30/__
```

proficient. Also, reporters you accompany will take stock of your performances and may offer you employment in their firm. One of my ex-students who did a number of mock trials while a student soon set up her own practice as a result of this, and today she drives her own Rolls Royce and lives in a townhouse in the best section of our city.

I always say it takes very little more to be great than to be average, and the rewards are certainly there for you!

PREPARE DILIGENTLY, AND THE FUTURE IS YOURS!

No Show!

Infrequently you will appear to take a deposition, and the witness will not appear. Sometimes neither the witness nor his or her attorney will show up. This is very disappointing to you since, as you left the office, everyone yelled the customary sendoff: "Get pages."

In the event this should happen to you, wait a reasonable amount of time, half an hour to an hour, and then return to your office and prepare a Certificate of Non-Attendance. In Louisiana, this is called a Proces-Verbal. The Certificate of Non-Attendance is filed with the proper clerk with the papers in the case.

Occasionally the attorney who hired you will dictate a statement to be filed with the clerk. Then, you will be paid for the page or two you transcribe and an appearance fee and transportation and meal expense if out-of-the-city travel was involved. Normally, in the city, you will collect only your appearance fee and transcript of the Certificate of Non-Attendance.

Figure 26 shows a form for preparing such a Certificate of Non-Attendance used in most jurisdictions.

Figure 27 is a copy of a Proces-Verbal used in Louisiana.

You may notice that the form at the top of Figure 27 sets up the style and venue in a order different from some other forms in this book. These forms are merely examples, and there are many different ways of setting up most legal papers and transcripts.

Of course, on the job you will follow what your firm or the judge considers the best method of setting up any document and their preferred wording of forms.

Concluding the Deposition

Make a notation of the time when the deposition finishes. Request any spellings and verifications you may need. Ask doctors and experts for copies of such things as curricula vitae and medical records which can save you hours of searching for new, unfamiliar, or possibly misheard terms. If experts have used complex chemical formulae, arithmetical expressions, and foreign terms, now is the time to check on them. Count your exhibits, and check them against your information sheet. Do not let any attorney leave the deposition room with any exhibits which are stated in the record to be entrusted to your care, even though you may have to detain such counsel to search his/her briefcase to turn over the missing evidence to you.

Obtaining the Billing Information

Ask each counsel present how many copies of the depositions he or she will require. Put this into your notes as they order, and also write it on your information sheet so there can be no later misunderstanding.

The attorney who hired you must pay for at least the original and one copy (two copies in some states by law if the reporter receives no other order for transcript). Ordinarily, the other non-hiring lawyer will order one copy, but if he or she represents an insurance company, a second copy may be ordered to transmit to them.

When you begin reporting work, check with reputable reporters as to how much to charge and what the customs are. Occasionally the attorneys will tell you to split the bill in half between them. If there are more attorneys, they will have you split it evenly among all of them. Be sure you take all this information down correctly.

When you have completed your business matters, pack up quickly, thank the lawyers, and take your leave. Do not hang around listening to their legal conversations or gossip. If you rode with one of the attorneys to an out-of-town assignment, go to the outer office and wait, leaving counsel alone to talk. Do not disrupt the work of the secretaries in the outer office. Busy yourself with a magazine, work a crossword puzzle, or read your notes and check your information sheet.

Attorneys may ask you to have lunch or dinner with them or to have a drink at the noon recess or at the conclusion of the day's take. Use your own good judgment. Never indulge in alcoholic beverages during the day before returning to an afternoon session, as this may cast doubts on your ability to secure a clear record. It is best not to mix business with pleasure, but certain occasions make it imperative that you join attorneys and judges for meals and at social gatherings. Just remember that it is easier to avoid embarrassing events than to live with them.

FIGURE 26-A
Certificate of Nonattendance

1	HENRY J. WALTERS IN THE DISTRICT COURT OF
2	*
3	Plaintiff, * MACON COUNTY, GEORGIA
4	-vs- * 142ND JUDICIAL DISTRICT
5	PRUDENTIAL INSURANCE COMPANY, *
6	DEFENDANT. *
7	
8	CERTIFICATE OF NONATTENDANCE
9	FOR THE
	DEPOSITION OF HENRY J. WALTERS
10	I, Paiges Plentee, a notary public in and for the
11	County of Macon, State of Georgia, do hereby certify that
12	a commission was issued out of the 142nd Judicial District
13	Court of Macon County, Georgia, to take the oral deposition
14	of Henry J. Walters on the 3rd day of March, 19___, at 10:00
15	a.m.,in the offices of Suemm & Winn, 8745 Grant Avenue,
16	Macon Georgia.
17	Pursuant to the aforementioned commission to take
18	oral deposition, a subpoena was issued on the 25th day of
19	February, 19___, over the official signature of Racke M. Upp,
20	notary public in and for Macon County, Georgia. The said
21	subpoena was served and executed the 26th day of February,
22	19___, by Speedy Service, a deputy sheriff in Macon County,
23	Georgia.
24	On the 3rd day of March, 19___, pursuant to the
25	said commission and subpoena, I was present in the offices of

FIGURE 26-B

1	Suemm & Winn, 8745 Grant Avenue, Macon, Georgia, at the
2	hour of 10:00 a.m., and did remain in said offices until
3	the hour of 10:45 a.m. on the said day. During the time
4	between 10:00 a.m. and 10:45 a.m., Henry J. Walters did
5	not appear to be deposed.
6	I further certify that the attached instruments
7	are the commission and subpoena referred to in the above
8	and foregoing certificate.
9	DATED: March 3, 19___.
10	
11	
12	
13	PAIGES PLENTEE, Notary Public
14	Macon County, Georgia
	My Commission expires: 1/2/___
15	
16	
17	
18	
19	
20	
21	
22	
23	
24	
25	

FIGURE 27
Proces-Verbal

```
1              IN THE CIVIL DISTRICT COURT

2             FOR THE PARISH  OF  ORLEANS

3                 STATE OF LOUISIANA

4   MARCELLA O. BRAY,   )
              Plaintiff,)
5        -vs-           )          CIVIL NO. 487-832-C
    ARIETTA S. OTIS     )
6   and BLUE CABS, INC.,)
            Defendants.)

7

8                   PROCES-VERBAL

9   BY MR. COMEAUX:

10       This is a deposition which was set for 3:00 p.m.,

11   today, April 6, 19_ _.  Mr. John A. Comeaux, representing

12   the plaintiff, Marcella O. Bray, was present.

13       Notice was sent by mail to counsel for defendant,

14   Arlo J. Pierce, by letter March 25, 19--.  Arietta S. Otis

15   was personally served March 26, 19--.  Neither Mr. Pierce

16   nor Mrs. Otis are here, although my watch reads 3:30 p.m.

17       This proces-verbal is being made for purposes of

18   invoking strictures of Article 1511 and following of the

19   Louisiana Code of Civil Procedure with respect to refusal

20   to make Discovery, and undersigned counsel will promptly

21   file the necessary motions.

22

23          _____

24       WITNESS my hand and official seal at New Orleans,
    Louisiana, this _____ day of April, 19--.
25

            _____
                    NOTARY PUBLIC
```

Transcribing the Deposition

Your next order of business is to return with your notes to your accustomed place of typing, dictating, or using CAT to get out your deposition or depositions.

The attorneys will tell you if you are preparing a rush job, but in any event, you should deliver all freelance work within seven days to two weeks—earlier if possible.

When trial time is close, never allow an unfiled original or notes in the case to lie on your desk, as attorneys will hold you liable and, at the least, refuse to pay you for the work and bear a grudge against you for impairing their case.

Chapter 10 *Preparing Your First Deposition*

You have just finished taking your first deposition, and now you are at your desk ready to do the most important thing: transcribe your first deposition transcript. The stack of notes seems to overwhelm you because you have been accustomed to transcribing five-minute takes in school for the most part. Your heart is doing flipflops because you are so afraid you will do something wrong. Your employer has undoubtedly told you to type or word process this first project to ascertain your spelling, word usage, and punctuation abilities, and see how you put the whole thing together; so you know a lot is riding on it.

As a student you have waited and prepared for this moment a long time, and you are certainly ready to start making some money! You eagerly approach this new adventure even though you face it with fear and trepidation.

Take It One Step at a Time

Reporters always place at the front or back of each transcript a page for Lawyer's Notes, or several of these pages if it is a long transcript. This is a convenience to attorneys, as they can jot down pages and lines of portions of the transcript pertinent to their case. Figure 28 is an example of such a page.

Get out your clearly marked notes from the information sheet. Use that vital information sheet and any notes you marked on the 3″ × 5″ pad on the top of your machine to prepare the title page, which will provide the first impression of your work. Remember, make no visible erasures and never use Liquid Paper or Ko-Rectape on errors.

The Title Page

The title page is not numbered. There are many possible forms for setting up title pages, but we will assume your firm centers each line of the venue (the jurisdiction the case is filed in). Type this in solid caps.

In the style or title (the box wherein the names of the parties appear), the proper names are usually in solid caps. The descriptive words, if any, are in the lower case, as JOHN JONES d/b/a SUPERIOR MOTORS.

Keep in mind you will have to vary the spacing on each title page in accordance with the information you have. For example, if you have several plaintiffs and/or several defendants, you

FIGURE 28

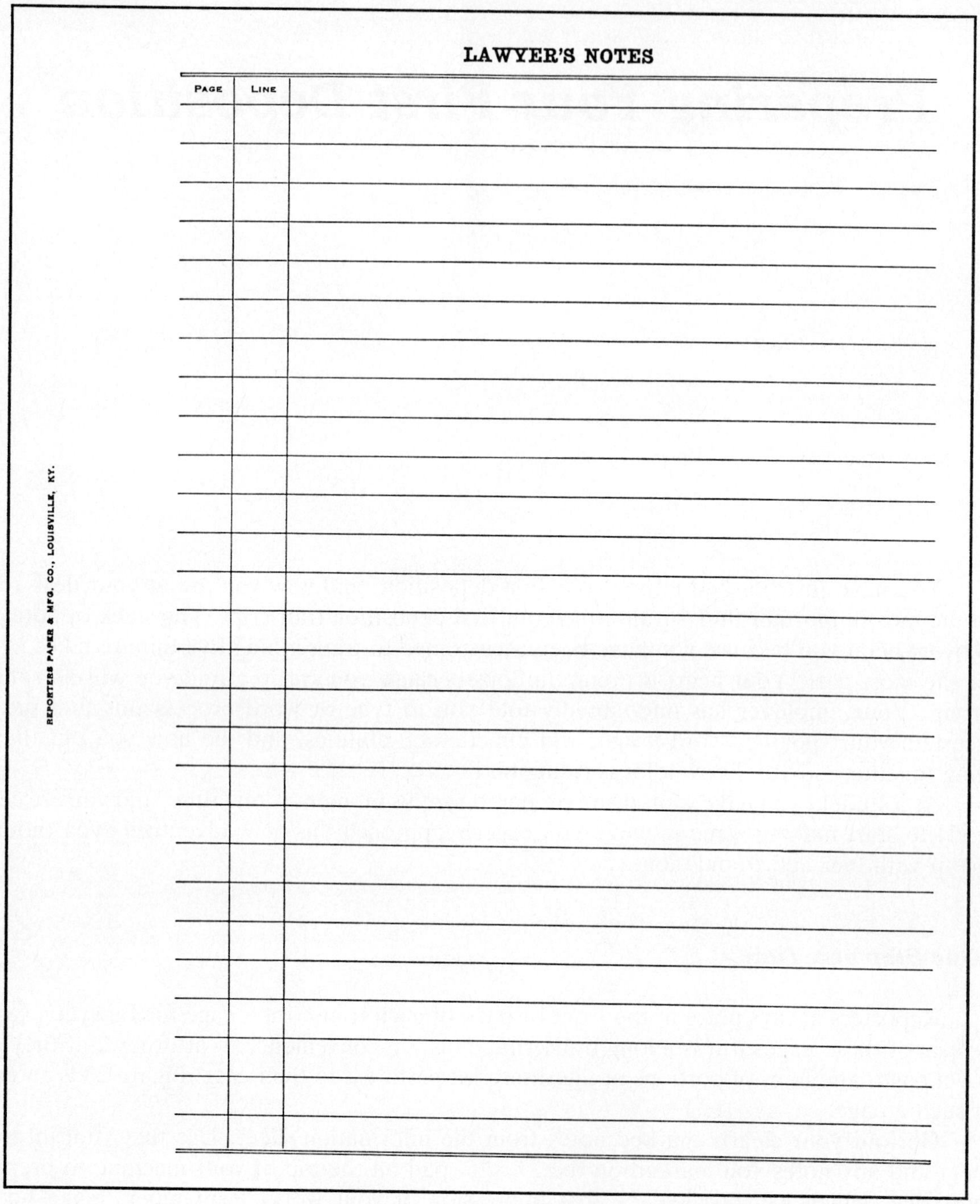
LAWYER'S NOTES

PAGE	LINE	

REPORTERS PAPER & MFG. CO., LOUISVILLE, KY.

will not leave as much space as you would if there were only one. The important thing to remember is: The title page is the first page that is seen, and it must have an attractive appearance.

Figure 29 is an example of a title page. Most of the better firms have a form book to give each new reporter setups for practically every situation, which is very helpful.

The Appearance Page

The next page of your deposition is the appearance page, which is numbered page 2 in the appropriate place if the title page was only one page. Do not place a period after any page number.

The word "APPEARANCES" should be centered, underlined, and typed in solid caps. The

FIGURE 29
Title Page

```
 1              IN THE SUPERIOR COURT

 2           FOR THE COUNTY OF CLAYTON

 3              STATE OF GEORGIA

 4

 5

 6

 7   LULU LOLLAPALOOZA,    )
                          )
 8          Plaintiff,    )
                          )
 9      -vs-              )          CIVIL FILE NO. 12,714
                          )
10   BORNE LOSER and      )
     IMA LOSER,           )
11                        )
            Defendants.   )

12

13            DEPOSITION OF RAZZLE DAZZLE

14

15        On the _____ day of _____, A.D., 19__,

16   beginning at _____ A. M. (or P. M.), in the offices of

17   (Name of firm, address, city, and state), before me,

18   (Your name), a stenotype reporter and notary public in

19   and for _____ County, (State), appeared (Name of

20   witness in solid caps), who, being by me first duly sworn,

21   gave his oral deposition in said cause pursuant to

22   agreement (or notice) of Counsel for the respective

23   parties as hereinafter set forth.

24

25
```

appearances of attorneys on behalf of the plaintiffs are always listed first, after which the appearances on behalf of the defendants are printed. If you have more than one plaintiff or more than one defendant, you must specify which plaintiff or defendant each attorney is representing.

It is customary to place the title "Esquire" after each male attorney's name. When you use "Esquire," you do not prefix a title, such as "Mr." before the lawyer's name. Esquire is usually abbreviated to "Esq." after names.

Should more than one attorney represent any party, be careful to show each one. Also, always list any other people who might be present at the deposition as adjusters and interested parties, such as a spouse, who are frequently in attendance at a deposition.

Be very careful to spell each attorney's name correctly and to list each address properly, complete with zip code. If an attorney is representing a firm, list the complete firm name, address, and indented five spaces below, type "By: WINNING NICELY, ESQ." Include attorneys' bar numbers where used.

Sometimes a very able attorney from another state will be present to assist in the trial or depositions in a case. He or she may not be able to try any of the case as he or she is not admitted to practice within that jurisdiction, so you will place "OF COUNSEL" after his or her listing.

Figure 30 shows a typical appearance page for the title page shown in Figure 29.

The Stipulations Page

Page 3 of your deposition transcript will be the stipulations page, which was discussed earlier.

FIGURE 30
Appearance Page

```
 1
 2
 3
 4
 5
 6                        A P P E A R A N C E S
 7
 8   REPRESENTING THE PLAINTIFF,
 9   LULU LOLLAPALOOZA:

10                        SEYMOUR DAMAGES, ESQUIRE
                          Attorney at Law
11                        Suite 2, Law Building
                          1412 Contentious Lane
12                        Macon, Georgia  12345

13   REPRESENTING THE DEFENDANTS,
     BORNE LOSER and IMA LOSER:
14
15                        PITCHING, CATCHING & THROWING
                          Attorneys at Law
16                        21 Defense Drive
                          Macon, Georgia  12345

17                           By:  INNE THAIR PITCHING, ESQUIRE
18
19   ALSO PRESENT:  MISS AZZIE SALLIE
20
21
22
23
24
25
```

A new page (normally page 4 unless the title page or stipulations have covered more than one page each) begins the setting up of the deposition witness. Figure 31 is an example of this setup.

Center the witness's name in solid capitals on line 1, place a comma after the name, and margin the rest of the introductory remarks concerning the witness, double-spaced, on the next lines as shown on Figure 31. Skip four lines and center in solid caps the word "EXAMINATION" and margin "BY MR. PITCHING:" in solid capitals, followed by a colon, and underline it also.

Then, proceed to margin your Q and A, paragraphing long questions or answers every four or five lines for ease of reading, since many depositions are read into the record in court by two attorneys taking the parts of questioner and witness at the time of trial.

FIGURE 31
Setting up of Deposition Witness

1	HARVEY W. WOOD,
2	called as a witness on behalf of the defendant, having been
3	first duly sworn, testified on his oath as follows:
4	
5	EXAMINATION
6	BY MR. SANDERS:
7	Q Would you please state your name, Mr. Wood, for the
8	record?
9	A Harvey W. Wood.
10	Q How old a man are you, Mr. Wood?
11	A I am 65.
12	Q Where do you presently live?
13	A Well, here and there.
14	Q Are you presently staying at your daughter's home,
15	Martha Winkler?
16	A For a while.
17	Q How long have you lived in Easton?
18	A We moved here in 1989.
19	Q You have lived here in Easton, Northampton County,
20	Pennsylvania, since 1989?
21	A That is right, 1989.
22	Q And you have never lived anyplace other than in
23	Northampton County since 1989?
24	A That is right.
25	Q All right. Mr. Wood, were you married to Edna Wood?

Ordinarily, in depositions, reporters do not designate whether the examinations of counsel are Direct Examination or Cross-Examination, as there are many legal questions here involving the calling of adverse witnesses and applications of various rules of statutes of the various states.

Colloquy

Colloquy is any spoken matter aside from Q and A, as when counsel talk to one another during a proceeding, or conversation occurs with the judge in court; or when counsel request that exhibits be marked or make objections; or when opposing counsel breaks in to ask some incidental question or makes a remark such as supplying figures from his file; and so on.

The NSRA format requires that colloquy material begin 15 spaces from the left-hand margin with carryover colloquy at the left-hand margin. Many firms prefer to indent colloquy more than Q and A in order that it may be readily seen, which is a much more attractive form. In any case, you will be guided by the rules and wishes of those by whom you are employed. However, NSRA is insisting its members follow their format guidelines entirely.

Figure 32 shows a page of testimony which includes colloquy.

When a freelance firm has its own format, this format must be followed by all reporters working therein.

Other Guidelines

Some other guidelines that will help you to produce attractive transcripts are found in the following paragraphs.

Type of Paper Required

Assignments not produced by computer-aided transcription (CAT) are normally typed on bond lined, numbered, erasable paper by transcribers for reporters in freelance firms. Many court documents are also produced on this type of paper. At the present time, practically all legal matters are placed on 8½ × 11 inch paper to secure uniformity and to make filing simpler and less expensive.

Care must be exercised to keep all typing within the ruled boundaries of each page.

CAT transcription, however, is becoming more universal all the time, and special computer transcription paper in fanfolded form is available and required for the accompanying CAT printer.

Binding of Freelance Transcripts

Interrogatories, statements, depositions, convention proceedings, and other freelance transcripts are normally bound at the side.

Paragraphing of Transcripts

Lengthy answers in testimony should be paragraphed about every four or five lines for ease in reading. Each time a speaker changes in quoted matter, a new paragraph should begin. Jury instructions, likewise, should be paragraphed frequently for improved appearance and comprehension. Very long sentences in jury instructions should be broken at such conjunctions as "and" and "but" for purposes of comprehension.

Figure 33 on page 100 shows a sample deposition exhibit index. On deposition indices it is only necessary to show the page at which the exhibit is marked for identification since there is no authority present to receive evidence until the Court rules at trial of the case in the courtroom.

You must be very careful to secure the exhibits the attorneys wish filed with the depositions

FIGURE 32
Sample Testimony with Colloquy

```
1   Q    Do you recall Kenneth Terry when he testified at a

2   prior deposition?

3              MRS. OWSLEY:  Please do not answer.  That

4   is wholly immaterial.

5              MR. KAHN:  Counsel, I can't help but

6   disagree with you.  It is material.

7   Q    (By Mr. Kahn)  I will ask you if you recall testifying,

8   and again in the Terry case, on the 5th of March, 1989, and

9   at that time you were asked:

10       "QUESTION:  Do you know of your own knowledge whether

11  or not prior to the time that Kenneth Terry got hurt on

12  the escalator that anyone wearing tennis shoes had ever had

13  their foot injured on this escalator?"  Do you recall being

14  asked that question?

15             MRS. OWSLEY:  Please do not answer that

16  question.

17  Q    I take it by your silence you are not going to

18  answer that question either.

19       Do you recall your answer to that question:

20       "ANSWER:  Yes, I know of one.  I didn't witness it

21  personally, but I know of it."

22       Do you recall that answer?

23             MRS. OWSLEY:  Please do not answer that

24  question either.

25  Q    I will ask you, and again the record should reflect
```

during the session before they leave. If counsel have agreed that the exhibits are not to accompany the deposition, the body of the deposition should also indicate that fact, and the exhibits will not be included within the deposition or its copies.

Some judges are now ruling that attorneys must retain deposition exhibits until trial because space for filing the voluminous materials is at a premium. You will have to check as to custom in these matters.

Copies of Original Exhibits

If the attorneys at a deposition stipulate that copies will be substituted for the original exhibits, that agreement will appear in the body of the deposition. It is then the reporter's duty to get the copies produced promptly and quickly return the original exhibits to counsel. Of course, a charge is made by the reporter for making copies.

FIGURE 33
Deposition Exhibit Index

```
                        INDEX OF
                   DEPOSITION EXHIBITS

PLAINTIFF'S                                          Page
EXHIBIT NO.

P-1          Profit & Loss Statement of Skinnem
             Good Company dated 2/28/__              36

P-2          Balance Sheet of Skinnem Good Company
             dated 2/28/__                           47

P-3          Check drawn on Astoria National Bank
             in amount of $10,500 dated 1/31/__      106




                                                      i
```

(lines numbered 1 through 25 down the left margin)

Numbering of Deposition Index Pages

Deposition index pages are numbered with lower case Roman numerals, the first page being marked "i" in the proper spot, and so on, since the reporter does not know how many pages an index will require sometimes until the transcript is complete. However, indexes are used more for court cases than in depositions.

Proofreader's Sheet

As you proofread transcript, fill out an error sheet indicating desired corrections as shown on Figure 34 and pull pages to be returned to the transcriber, placing them crosswise, to be corrected. Many reporters make small corrections themselves, particularly on rushes, but in the beginning insist that your transcriber make all corrections to insure that the operator learns the necessity for perfect pages. You can become more lenient later if you wish, but it is hard to tighten up on a typist and not have hard feelings if you do not start off right.

FIGURE 34
Proofreader's Sheet

PROOFREADER'S SHEET

Page No.	Line No.	SUGGESTED CORRECTION
14	16	Change pictoral to pectoral.
21	3	$50 instead of $40.
56	24	Capitalize Dr.
61	9	Change superspinatous to supraspinatous
85	7	Change ditb to debt.
126	1	Insert and between Tom Jerry
169	13	noticeable instead of noticable

Proofreading

After your deposition has been properly typed, your next task is careful proofreading of the transcript, first for context and next for wrong words, misspellings, typographicals, and the like. It is your job to be a blooper snooper!

At first, it is a good idea even to read your transcript backwards to pick up anything you might otherwise miss. Read through forward for context. Does everything hang together? Some attorneys do not ask questions in an orderly fashion, but if something seems missing or the jump to a new topic seems strange, go back to your notes to see if you have flipped two folds. That is where drawing a line through your notes will readily show you what happened.

On your second reading of the transcript, get down to business and catch all misspellings, transpositions, wrong words, faulty capitalizations, punctuation flaws, and poor corrections, keeping pulled sheets in order so they may be reinserted quickly.

Remember, if a page must be typed over by the transcriber because of the reporter's error, the reporter pays for the retyped page. If the error is due to the typist's poor performance, the page is redone for the reporter at no charge.

Check to be sure all parts of the deposition are present: title page; appearance page(s); stipulations; index or witnesses and exhibits, if required; all pages of testimony and colloquy; signature page; certificate; underlining; page and line numbers. The format should be considered to be sure it falls within the NSRA guidelines.

The transcript should be inspected for obvious errors, such as spacing, tab settings, paragraphing (for instance whenever a speaker changes), white space, proper margins (does the page look like a picture in a frame?), reader friendliness, and ease of reading where series of numbers and continuations occur. Frequently this can be done by holding the page at arm's length.

Read for meaning, perhaps reading aloud.

Read for content: Who? What? When? Where? How? Why?

Read the entire document again, possibly using tape recording.

Very carefully make all necessary corrections on every copy.

If you will use a straight edge as you proofread, it will help you find your place following interruptions and eliminate rereading.

Swap proofreading with someone else rather than proofreading your own work. You may not notice your own errors that have become habitual.

Use a proofreading checklist.

Scramble the parts of your proofreading formula from time to time. Read backwards, then frontwards sometimes. Check all the way through for misspellings once in awhile before reading the transcript. Look first for computer printouts that do not make sense; then reread for context and other errors. Vary your approach to proofreading every once in awhile to avoid becoming stale and missing obvious errors. Think what might happen if your parenthetical read (Afternoon sex with Judge Johnson) rather than (Afternoon session with Judge Johnson)! Proofread *very* carefully!

In most reporting offices your first transcripts will be read carefully by an experienced reporter before they are released. Write down criticisms, if any, for you must not make the same mistakes over and over. However, if you are sent out to perform on your own the first time and nobody supervises your work, do a great job. Remember: The fee paid to you and that paid to a reporter who has been working 25 years is the same.

In some firms all billing is done by office personnel, but if you bill clients, keep a copy with accounts receivable as the record of an unpaid bill. Should the bill remain unpaid at the end of 60 days, a copy can be made from the maintained copy to include with the letter requesting payment. The NSRA logo makes the billhead more attractive.

Computer Transcribed Depositions

Many of the better firms in the country still require new reporters to type or dictate all material for from three to six months to assess word knowledge, spelling ability, and punctuation skills. However, it is hoped that at a point not too far distant all reporters will be able to perform "real time," which means that the notes could be printed out with almost no errors simultaneously with the taking. That day has not yet come with most reporters, however.

Computer transcription will be taken up in quite some length later in this book, but at this point it should be pointed out that the dictionary must be scrupulously compiled, remembering that the more extensive the dictionary, the greater the production possibilities of the reporter. Many reporters proofread and mark the errors for a scopist to correct. This multiplies their productivity. Proofreading entails having a great sense of the way words flow together to avoid stupid errors and untranslates being overlooked. At the time Grace Kelly died, a reporter writing for closed captioning on television was evidently without a scopist that day, for printed on the screen were the words, "She said, 'My life is not all aviary tail.'" Of course, it should have been "a fairy tale." Also, you must be alert to catch such punctuation errors as sentences running together and improper designations. The drudgery of dictating will be missing with the computer usage, but your knowledge of the English language will be tested because the computer is a dumb beast, while that old-time transcriber often had a good head to help produce a perfect transcript.

Collection Procedures

Reporters are increasingly using collection agencies to secure payment of overdue accounts because a business cannot long endure if a number of bills are not paid. Firms should screen accounts carefully to avoid working for those who habitually do not pay their bills. Why should the reporter kill himself working twice as much while the attorney lives high on the money his rules of ethics say should be paid promptly? A threat to send the unpaid bill to the Bar Ethics Committee of the state has often secured quick payment, but the negative feelings that result make this a procedure to be used only when other measures have failed.

Keep in mind that insurance companies pay for statements and depositions on certain dates each month, so do not become edgy if these checks do not come in within 30 days or even 45. Insurance companies are very good about prompt payment to reporters.

Other Sources of Information Regarding Depositions

Lynn Brooks, a Dallas, Texas, freelance reporter, has prepared a booklet called *The Deposition*, which provides helpful information regarding taking, transcribing, and filing of depositions. This book is sold by NCRA, 118 Park Street, S.E., Vienna, VA, 22180.

The Federal Rules of Civil Procedure is published by West Publishing Company, St. Paul, MN. The State Rules of Civil Procedure are available in bookstores or from state bar associations, and these give the rules for taking depositions in each state. These should be consulted for each individual state's requirements. However, mere variance of form will never affect the validity and use of any deposition.

Chapter 11

Reading and Signing the Deposition and Making Corrections

Reading and Signing

Lawyers normally have discussed the reading and signing of the deposition in advance with their clients and have instructed them as to what to do in this regard.

Expert witnesses more frequently choose to read and sign their testimony than do laypersons because of the technical nature of their testimony and their experiences which may lead them to believe that the quality of court reporters may vary widely.

Many attorneys simply say "We will waive reading and signing," thus precluding any discussion on the matter. In some states the witness must personally state on the record that signature will be waived or requested. Be sure to follow the custom in your area.

Sometimes a witness will insist that he or she wants to read and sign the deposition even though the attorney may urge the witness not to because it slows up the process. In such cases, the reporter should say, "Do you want to go off the record to decide this and then place your decision on the record?" After five minutes of discussion goes by, the decision can easily be taken down. Reporters are in business for pages, but this immaterial discussion has nothing to do with the record and attorneys will appreciate your consideration.

You must get all your work out promptly, but be extra careful about depositions in cases you know are coming up shortly for court trial. Get the witnesses in to sign in plenty of time for you to bill, file the original of the deposition, and deliver copies before court time.

Procedures for Reading and Signing

The procedure for reading and signing the original of a deposition varies greatly from state to state. However, signing of the original deposition may be set before any notary public during regular business hours, which means signature may take place before a notary public other than the court reporter who took and transcribed the deposition.

Notification to Deponent to Read and Sign Deposition. A form letter should be prepared and sent to inform the witness's attorney that the original deposition is available in your office ready for the client to sign. Figure 35 on page 106 is a copy of such a letter. Should a second letter be required, Figure 36 on page 106 is a copy of another request.

Sending Deposition Elsewhere for Reading and Signing. Occasionally counsel will agree that you are to send the original of a deposition to the witness for signature when it has been

FIGURE 35
Form Letter Informing Witness That Original Deposition Is Ready

LIGHTNING DIGITS REPORTING SERVICE
1492 Accuracy Avenue
Newton, Maine 10574

Telephone: 384-5478

May 22, 19__

Mr. Ila Counsellen
123 Disputatious Boulevard
Newton, Maine 10574

In Re: Cornpone Investment Corporation
        v. Abner Yokum
        No. 614,384

Dear Mr. Counsellen:

The deposition of your client, Mr. Jubilation T. Cornpone, is now ready for signature as provided for in agreement between counsel at the taking of the deposition on May 20, 19__.

Will you please ask Mr. Cornpone to stop at our offices at his earliest convenience between the hours of 8:00 a.m. and 5:00 p.m., Monday through Friday, to sign the transcript of his testimony.

Thank you very much.

Yours very truly,

LIGHTNING DIGITS REPORTING
        SERVICE

_____
SPEEDY FINGERS

sf:ik
cc: Mr. Fighting Chance

FIGURE 36
Second Letter

LIGHTNING DIGITS REPORTING SERVICE
1492 Accuracy Avenue
Newton, Maine 10574

Telephone: 384-5478

June 6, 19__

Mr. Ila Counsellen
123 Disputatious Boulevard
Newton, Maine 10574

In Re: Cornpone Investment Corporation
        v. Abner Yokum
        No. 614,384
        Our Reference No. 64-102

Dear Mr. Counsellem:

The deposition of your client, Mr. Jubilation T. Cornpone, still remains in this office unsigned.

Will you please inform us what you want done with the original transcript, as it is our understanding that this case will be coming up for trial during the week of June 10, 19__?

Thank you for your immediate attention to this matter.

Yours very truly,

LIGHTNING DIGITS REPORTING
        SERVICE

_____
SPEEDY FINGERS

sfik
cc: Mr. Fighting Chance

completed, as in the case of a very busy doctor or an expert who travels a great deal and does not care to sacrifice time to appear at your office to sign the original.

In such a case the original of the deposition should be sent by certified mail, return receipt requested, and a letter such as Figure 37 should accompany the transcript. Of course, the reporter must retain a copy of the transmittal letter with the copies of the deposition and mailing receipt in his or her office and keep a tickler file to be sure the deposition is returned and filed in time with the proper court clerk.

Should the attorneys agree that the original is to be sent to the office of one of the counsel for signature, you will follow a similar procedure, wording your letter to correspond with the situation.

FIGURE 37
Letter Accompanying Original Deposition

```
                 STRICTLY VERBATIM & ASSOCIATES
                   Certified Shorthand Reporters
                    Legalistic Jargon Avenue
                   Butcherville, Florida  33745

                                     Telephone:   475-2345

              November 29, 1982


     I. L. Choppem, M.D.
     1459 Malpractice Lane
     Butcherville, Florida  33745

          In Re:  Marianne Maimed v. I. L. Choppem, M.D.
                  Civil No. 131,313

     Dear Dr. Choppem:

     Enclosed herewith is the original transcription of your
     deposition taken before the undersigned officer on November
     25, 1982, in order that you may read and subscribe to it.

     After reading the deposition, please sign it on page 121
     on the line provided.  Should you have any corrections to
     request, please do not make these on the typewritten pages
     of the transcript, but enter them on the sheet in the very
     front of the deposition that is entitled "Reference Sheet,"
     indicating thereon the page number, line number, and desired
     corrections, and reason for making same.  If you use this
     sheet for corrections, please date and sign it at the very
     bottom.

     After signing your deposition, please use the enclosed
     addressed envelope for returning it to this office.  The
     proper postage has already been affixed to this envelope.

     It is requested that you return the deposition so as to
     reach this office not later than December 31, 1982.

     Thank you very much for your cooperation in this matter.

                         Very truly yours,


                    By:  _____
                         Hunt N. Peck, Staff Reporter

     HNP:ir
     CC:  Ms. Liz Pending
          Suit N. Progress, Esq.

     Encl.
```

Filing the Original. Attorneys may stipulate that if the witness has not appeared by a certain number of days prior to the trial, the reporter shall file the original of the deposition; and it will have the same force and effect as though it were read and signed by the witness. The statutes also make provision for cases of this sort.

Using a Tickler File. A tickler file should be maintained of those interrogatories, statements, and depositions requiring action or signature, which should be checked weekly. Should the witness not appear within a reasonable time, a telephone call should be made to the law firm requesting signature of its client.

After repeated efforts have been made to secure signature on the original deposition and all have failed, the original should be properly filed with the proper court clerk, should trial date of the case become imminent, accompanied by a letter apprising the clerk of the fact that the document is being filed without signature. The reason therefor should accompany the deposition, and carbons of the letter should be sent to attorneys for both sides of the case.

Handling the Reading and Signing of Depositions

When a witness arrives to read and sign the original of the deposition, usher the deponent into a quiet area to read, instructing carefully as to the method to be used to designate changes, if any. Inform the witness that no questions or remarks of either counsel may be changed. Changes made in the deposition and procedures for handling them will be discussed later.

When the witness has finished reading the original and noting changes in the manner you have requested, ask him or her to sign before you or any notary in the office, being very sure the signature conforms to the way the witness's name appears in the opening of the deposition.

The Witness May Want to Change Everything

Sometimes, in spite of the fact that the witness should change only something that seems to have been down incorrectly, he or she will try to make the answers read in a way which would benefit his or her side of the case or that will explain answers in much more detail. Do not argue with the witness. Opposing counsel will like to see this self-serving deposition because this gives him or her a chance to tear the witness's testimony to shreds on cross-examination.

Certificate of Signing Witness

In some jurisdictions, a formal certificate of the witness may precede the signature. You will have to consult with a practicing reporter or study the Rules of Civil (or Criminal) Procedure for your state to discern if this is the requirement in your area. Figure 38 shows such a sample certificate.

Please note that the material in parentheses at the end of the certificate is omitted if no changes are made on the original of the deposition by the witness, as is usually the case. In some states no certificate is required preceding the witness's signature. (See Figure 39 on page 110.)

The Witness Who Refuses to Sign His or Her Deposition

Should a witness totally refuse to sign the deposition, notify the attorney who hired you and state the facts to him and dispose of the original and copies of the deposition as advised by counsel—usually by filing the original with a cover letter or certificate explaining the circumstances and sending carbons with a copy of the letter or certificate and proper billing to other attorneys involved.

FIGURE 38
Sample Certificate

```
 1              MR. QUESTIONING:  That is all the questions

 2   I have at this time.  Thank you.

 3              MR. HARDNOSE:  I have no questions at this

 4   time.

 5
     STATE OF MINNESOTA◊
 6                      ◊ss.      CERTIFICATE OF WITNESS
     COUNTY OF DEERWOOD◊
 7

 8         I, HEDGE N. EVADE, hereby certify that I have

 9   read the foregoing transcript of my deposition taken

10   February 3, 1982, at approximately 10:00 a.m., at Byron,

11   Minnesota, pursuant to the applicable Rules of Civil

12   Procedure, and that the foregoing 178 pages of transcript

13   are in conformity with my testimony given at that time,

14   (with the exception of any corrections made by me, in ink,

15   and initialled by me).

16

17                            _____
                              HEDGE N. EVADE
18   STATE OF MINNESOTA◊
                      ◊
19   COUNTY OF DEERWOOD◊

20         SUBSCRIBED AND SWORN to before me, the under-

21   signed authority on this the 8th day of February, 1982.

22

23                            _____
                              NEATLY WRITING
24                            Notary Public in and for
                              Deerwood County, Minnesota
25                            My Commission Expires 7/31/85
```

Deposition Corrections

No matter how careful a busy court reporter may be, occasionally gremlins cause an unde-tected error to go out on a transcript, and such things as "your analysis" for "urinalysis" or "curb" for "curve" will appear. Sometimes, too, a transcriber's or notereader's transposition or mishearing may be overlooked in proofreading, such as the common error of "now" for "not," which gives the opposite meaning, or "the Untied States" or "impcat" for "impact."

On the computer, properly programmed material will never be printed with any misspellings, but strange things may appear such as "Okay, you pansy," for the word "occupancy," which was written out as "O-K, U, PAN, SI" on your machine. Of course, that would never go undetected.

You must always take any errors in your stride, determining never to make the same one twice, but realizing it happens to every reporter occasionally. When a totally dishonest witness may insist that many things in a transcript are incorrect, stand on your record, for "this, too, shall

FIGURE 39
In many states, such as Texas, no certificate is required preceding the witness's signature. There, immediately following the last line of the deposition, the reporter adds the signature line, which must be on the same page as the end of the last testimony or colloquy. This is followed by the jurat of the notary public before whom it is signed.

```
                         MR. SMITHERS:  That's all.  Thank you.

                         THE WITNESS:  You're welcome.



                         _____
                         THE WITNESS
THE STATE OF TEXAS  §
                    §
COUNTY  OF  HARRIS  §

     SUBSCRIBED AND SWORN to before me, the undersigned authority,

on this the _____ day of _____, 19___.



                         _____
                         SARA N. DIPITY
                         Notary Public in and for
                         Harris County, T e x a s
                         My Commission Expires 7/31/


     BUT when the witness affirms, the jurat will read in every

instance:


THE STATE OF TEXAS  §
                    §
COUNTY  OF  HARRIS  §

     SUBSCRIBED AND AFFIRMED before me, the undersigned authority,

on this the _____ day of _____, 19___.



                         _____
                         GETTEM RIGHT
                         Notary Public in and for
                         Harris County, T e x a s
                         My Commission Expires 7/31/__

     Of course, neither the signature nor the jurat should appear
on the deposition if signature is waived.
```

pass away." It has happened before and will, no doubt, happen many times again. Above all, keep up your malpractice insurance at all times.

Honest Errors May Be Corrected on Depositions

Any deponent is permitted to correct any errors he or she claims are present in a reporter's transcript of his or her testimony. A person protesting a record will not be compelled to sign it. However, the Court has measures to deal with this situation.

Methods of Making Corrections

In some places corrections are made directly on the original deposition and initialled by the witness, but more frequently they are listed on a separate sheet provided the witness at the time of reading and signing, in order that the reporter may handle the matter properly.

In some jurisdictions the witness may add a statement at the end of the deposition listing claimed errors and reasons therefore and writing what the deponent considers to be correct answers. Figures 40A, 40B, and 40C represent a letter used when the original is sent to an attorney for securing signature of the client, a signature sheet for the witness, and a correction sheet for the listing of changes.

In some states the witness may cross out asserted objectionable matter and insert another version, initialling each change, before signing the original of the deposition.

Notify All Interested Parties of Changes

Be sure to notify all counsel, or all those who have ordered a copy, plus the court clerk, of any pertinent changes. This is usually done in the form of a certificate, the original of which is enclosed with the original copy of the deposition, preferably in the front, before the original is

FIGURE 40-A
Letter When Original Is Sent to An Attorney for Securing Signature of Client

```
                    GETTING ITT DOWNE & ASSOCIATES
                           Court Reporters
                            Verbatim Lane
                      Tranquility, Missouri  89006
                       Telephone (999) 999-9999

                           October 29, 19__

        Thomas Tryingwell, Esq.
        Tryingwell & Winning
        Attorneys at Law
        4837 Civil Practice Avenue
        Tranquility, Missouri  89006

            In Re:  Deposition of Larry Libelous
                    Civil No. 789-80 - Our Job No. 9,998

        Dear Mr. Tryingwell:

        In an effort to provide better service to all counsel of
        record, we have retained custody of the original deposition
        of Larry Libelous.

        Please have Larry Libelous read the deposition copy.  If
        there are changes to be made, please indicate on the enclosed
        sheet(s) the change, page number, line number, and reason
        for the change, using Number "1," "2," or "3" as the reason
        for the change.

        There is a line provided on each correction sheet for
        Larry Libelous's signature.

        Please have the witness sign each correction sheet.

        If there are no corrections, please have the witness sign
        the appropriate paragraph on the return form letter to
        Getting Itt Downe & Associates.

        Upon receipt of the signed correction sheet(s) and the
        appropriately-signed paragraph in the return form letter,
        we will then notify opposing counsel of any changes, affix
        the correction sheet(s) and signed return letter to the
        original deposition, and file the original with the Court.

        Thank you for your cooperation in this matter.

                           Very truly yours,


                           BY: _____
                               EZEE WRITER, CSR
                               Staff Reporter

        Encls.
```

FIGURE 40-C
Correction Form

If there are any corrections to your deposition, indicate them on this sheet of paper, giving the change, page number, line number, and reason for the change.

The reasons for making changes are:

(1) To clarify the record;
(2) To conform to the facts; or
(3) To correct major transcription errors.

Page number _____ Line number _____ Reason for change _____

Change _____ to _____

Page number _____ Line number _____ Reason for change _____

Change _____ to _____

Page number _____ Line number _____ Reason for change _____

Change _____ to _____

Page number _____ Line number _____ Reason for change _____

Change _____ to _____

Page number _____ Line number _____ Reason for change _____

Change _____ to _____

Page number _____ Line number _____ Reason for change _____

Change _____ to _____

Page number _____ Line number _____ Reason for change _____

Change _____ to _____

Page number _____ Line number _____ Reason for change _____

Change _____ to _____

_____
SIGNATURE OF DEPONENT

Figure _____ Correction Form

FIGURE 40-B
Signature Sheet

SIGNATURE SHEET

PLEASE SIGN THE APPROPRIATE PARAGRAPH WHEN
MAKING RETURN OF CORRECTION SHEETS TO
GETTING ITT DOWNE & ASSOCIATES

TO: GETTING ITT DOWNE & ASSOCIATES
Verbatim Lane
Tranquility, Missouri 89006

I have read a copy of my deposition.

Upon receipt of the enclosed signed sheet(s), you are hereby authorized to file the original of my deposition, as corrected.

SUBSCRIBED AND SWORN TO BEFORE ME on this the ____ day of _____, 198__.

_____
Notary Public in and for _____ County;
My Commission Expires: _____

* *

TO: GETTING ITT DOWNE & ASSOCIATES
Verbatim Lane
Tranquility, Missouri 89006

I have read a copy of my deposition.

Upon receipt of the enclosed signed sheet(s), you are hereby authorized to file the original of my deposition as transcribed.

SUBSCRIBED AND SWORN TO BEFORE ME on this the ____ day of _____, 198__.

_____
Notary Public in and for _____ County;
My Commission Expires: _____

FIGURE 41
Notification Form Used in Florida

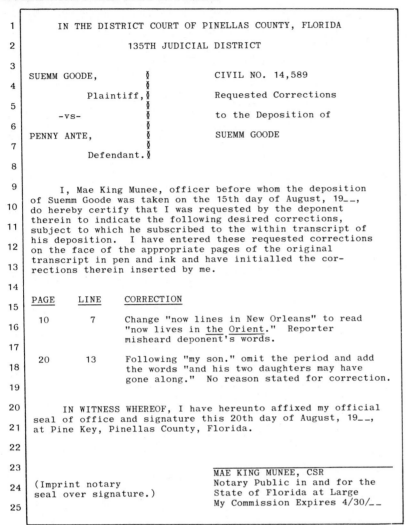

```
        IN THE DISTRICT COURT OF PINELLAS COUNTY, FLORIDA

               135TH JUDICIAL DISTRICT


SUEMM GOODE,          ◊        CIVIL NO. 14,589
                      ◊
        Plaintiff,    ◊        Requested Corrections
                      ◊
     -vs-             ◊        to the Deposition of
                      ◊
PENNY ANTE,           ◊        SUEMM GOODE
                      ◊
        Defendant.    ◊


     I, Mae King Munee, officer before whom the deposition
of Suemm Goode was taken on the 15th day of August, 19__,
do hereby certify that I was requested by the deponent
therein to indicate the following desired corrections,
subject to which he subscribed to the within transcript of
his deposition.  I have entered these requested corrections
on the face of the appropriate pages of the original
transcript in pen and ink and have initialled the cor-
rections therein inserted by me.


PAGE    LINE    CORRECTION

 10       7     Change "now lines in New Orleans" to read
                "now lives in the Orient."  Reporter
                misheard deponent's words.

 20      13     Following "my son." omit the period and add
                the words "and his two daughters may have
                gone along."  No reason stated for correction.


     IN WITNESS WHEREOF, I have hereunto affixed my official
seal of office and signature this 20th day of August, 19__,
at Pine Key, Pinellas County, Florida.



                              _____
                              MAE KING MUNEE, CSR
(Imprint notary               Notary Public in and for the
seal over signature.)         State of Florida at Large
                              My Commission Expires 4/30/__
```

filed. Figure 41 shows a notification form which is used in Florida. The notary seal is imprinted on this form.

Since quite some time is required to take care of any changes or corrections in a transcript, you should give every job your utmost care and attention to avoid being involved in this process.

You will, of course, be guided by the usages in your own jurisdiction as to how you will handle the matter of corrections on depositions.

Chapter 12

Final Steps In Preparing the Deposition

A reporter's certificate is always placed at the end of every deposition. The form of the required certificate is ordinarily set out in the rules of procedure governing each court.

Contents of the Reporter's Deposition Certificate

The reporter's certificate should set forth (1) that the respective parties had or had not appeared, (2) that the witness or witnesses were duly sworn, (3) that the testimony was reduced to shorthand writing by the officer or other disinterested person (not employed by or of kin to any party or counsel), (4) that the record was fully and accurately taken down and transcribed.

The reporter's certificate is a numbered page. In some states a list of all appearances by the parties and attorneys is made a part of such certificate. Wherever you report, secure a few sample deposition transcripts showing the exact form (or forms) for your state and study them. Figure 42 is a sample reporter's certificate which is adequate for use on any deposition because the law clearly states that diversity of form will make no difference in the validity of a transcript.

If you are signing your certificate as a notary public, imprint your notarial seal over your signature. You may then use a rubber stamp or insert beneath the signature information concerning your notary qualification as shown in Figure 42 on page 116. Many firms and individual reporters prepare forms for their applicable certificates on the computer, leaving blanks for the name of the witness or witnesses, page number, date, and other material required within their jurisdiction to be filled in as pertinent to each certificate.

You must be very careful to change the wording of your certificate if the witness is affirmed rather than sworn in order that the certificate will accurately depict what transpired.

Indexing the Deposition and Deposition Exhibits

Ordinarily each deposition is bound in its own cover, but, in a few metropolitan areas, if a number of reasonably short depositions are taken in one day, they are bound in one cover, and an index page is placed after the first appearance page, as shown in Figure 43 on page 116. This method is used to reduce the cost of a number of covers, title pages, stipulation pages, and certificates. The reason for this is that insurance companies look for ways to reduce costs associated with the many depositions they must take.

Some law firms and insurance companies hire employees whose job it is to check reporter's

FIGURE 42
Sample Reporter's Certificate

```
 1   THE STATE OF TEXAS )
 2   COUNTY  OF  HARRIS )
 3       I, Joe Reporter, a stenotype reporter and notary public
 4   in and for Harris County, Texas, hereby certify that the
 5   matters set forth in the caption to the foregoing deposition
 6   are true and correct; that the witness, JOANN A. WITNESS,
 7   appeared before me at the time and place set forth; that
 8   said witness was first duly sworn by me to tell the truth,
 9   the whole truth, and nothing but the truth, and thereupon
10   proceeded to testify in said cause; that the questions
11   of counsel and the answers of said witness were taken down
12   in machine shorthand by me and thereafter reduced to type-
13   writing under my direction; and that the foregoing 105 pages
14   comprise a true, complete, and correct transcript of the
15   testimony given and the proceedings had during the taking
16   of said deposition.
17       I further certify that I am not a relative or employee
18   or attorney or counsel of any of the parties hereto, nor
19   a relative or employee of such attorney or counsel; nor do
20   I have any interest in the outcome or events of the action.
21       WITNESS MY HAND AND SEAL OF OFFICE, this the ____ day of
22   _____, A.D., 198_-_.
23
24                           _____
25                           JOE REPORTER
                             Notary Public in and for
                             Harris County, Texas
                             My Commission Expires 3/31/-_
```

FIGURE 43
Index

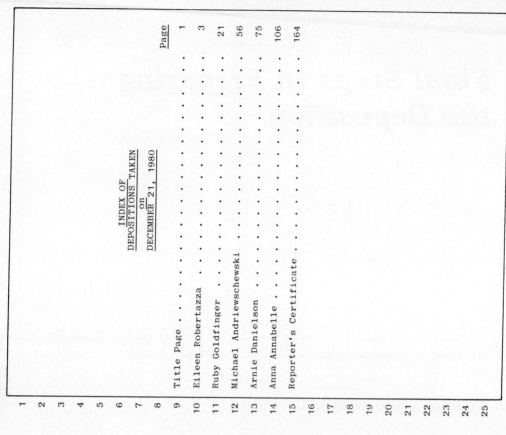

```
 1
 2
 3
 4
 5
 6                              INDEX OF
 7                         DEPOSITIONS TAKEN
                                 on
                           DECEMBER 21, 1980
 8                                                          Page
 9   Title Page . . . . . . . . . . . . . . . . . . .          1
10   Eileen Robertazza  . . . . . . . . . . . . . . .          3
11   Ruby Goldfinger  . . . . . . . . . . . . . . . .         21
12   Michael Andriewschewski  . . . . . . . . . . . .         56
13   Arnie Danielson  . . . . . . . . . . . . . . . .         75
14   Anna Annabelle . . . . . . . . . . . . . . . . .        106
15   Reporter's Certificate . . . . . . . . . . . . .        164
16
17
18
19
20
21
22
23
24
25
```

transcripts by counting words on pages to assure them that the reporter has not cheated by using excessive margins and short pages. In New Jersey, for example, if space remains on the question line of testimony, the answer is begun on that same line to ensure full pages of transcript.

Deposition Exhibits

Deposition exhibits are indexed as to the page where they are marked for identification by number and description. The originals of the exhibits are then placed at the end of the original deposition in correct order as marked, and copies of the exhibits are placed at the end of each copy in the same order as those in the original. Often the attorneys will keep all exhibits until the time of trial, and in marking and indexing exhibits the reporter must be careful not to confuse numbers which may have been placed on them during prior depositions with his or her markings.

Deposition Transcription Pointers

Once you have the speed so essential for a good reporter, and all the background you can acquire, success in court reporting depends a great deal on your being able to handle small details correctly and keeping your mind strictly on what you are doing, using lots of common sense all along the way.

Nowhere else is this so important as when you are producing any transcript. You will eventually be transcribing by computer, and you will have to be a meticulous and knowledgeable proofreader to recognize and correct conflicting words and strange material which results from combinations of strokes. However, the computer will never transcribe misspellings if it has been programmed properly, nor will it make typographical errors and transpose letters. Hopefully, you will be able to go straight from school onto a computer system, but this is not the case yet with many firms and courts. Also, a certain amount of experience in dictating to a transcriber is recommended because at times your computer will be down or circumstances will force you to resort to dictating; it will be a harrowing task if you have never done so. For these reasons, I am going to assume that you are producing your transcript in traditional ways during this chapter.

Mark Your Notes as You Transcribe or Dictate

As you transcribe or dictate material, always draw a line down the center of your notes as you go along. This practice will prevent your omitting material or transcribing the same part twice.

One reporter was called to the telephone. During her absence from her desk, someone flipped her notes, or she did it as she rose to go to the phone. She dictated the same 50 pages twice, and upon getting the transcript from her transcriber, she was chagrined to realize these pages had to be deleted and the rest of the deposition had to be renumbered, which meant retyping.

Of course, if she had had her mind on what she was doing, she would have soon realized that what she was dictating sounded familiar and would have checked it out. If she had been drawing a line through her dictated notes, she could not have made such a mistake at all.

When in Doubt, Check It Out

Dictate carefully or type painstakingly if you are preparing the transcript yourself, keeping your attention fixed strictly on what you are doing. The minute something does not make sense to you, consider whether there might be a word that sounds like what your notes say but might be altogether different. Consider what the context is around the strokes that printed, and think whether you misstroked.

Consult your dictionary, medical books, and technical references often to be sure you have everything right. When a lawyer "excepts" to a ruling, he or she does not "accept" it; in fact, it means quite the reverse. "Vile" and "vial" are two different words. "Awfully" is not spelled "auffly." When your notes read in a jury charge "Under our system of American jurisprudence, in cases of this kind, we separate as a team," think! A team does not separate and work effectively; so, no matter what you think you heard, change the word "separate" to "operate."

So, do not be too quick to assume your notes are always correct because sometimes in the middle of the afternoon what seemed like a certain word all morning turns out to be something quite different. There is nothing more exasperating to instructors or hiring agencies and judges than the words "But that's what I have in my notes." Attorneys and judges don't care what your notes say if they are not right. They care only about the finished product and your readback.

Never once in all my years of reporting did any lawyer or judge ever come over and say, "My, what beautiful notes." What you want them to say is, "What a beautiful transcript," or, "That reporter is great at readback."

Of course, it helps if you have noted all the unusual little things that occurred on your information sheet, but there is not always time as they happen. That is why it pays at the end of every deposition or hearing to sit down with your notes and your information sheet and jot down verifications.

Above all, be willing to learn and accept corrections without becoming defensive. No one likes to help someone who falls to pieces over every little criticism.

Use a Transcription Box

As you type your transcript, it is a good idea to use a transcription box. Transcript pages are laid crosswise, upside down, in order that they may be taken out quickly, right side up, and proofread. These handy aids can be found in some office stationery stores or may be custom made by any woodworker.

Errors on Carbon Copies

Admonish your typist that the carbons are often more important than the originals of reporters' transcripts. Many times the originals are simply filed, and the matter is settled on the basis of the attorneys' carbon copies. In such cases, the originals are never used in many cases, and a little error like "cut into" for "cut in two" could make a big difference. A transcriber may have been used to being a secretary where carbons are not always corrected carefully. He or she will want to make as much money as possible, not realizing the great importance of the carbon copies in reporting work until an explanation is given.

Signature Line Placement

Type the signature line to the right of center on the fourth line below the last line of a document unless it is necessary to "squeeze" material to get it all on a page.

Transcription Advice to Students

You must train yourself to do a good job on daily transcripts as, in the final analysis, it is your transcript upon which you will be judged to the greatest extent.

Do not rough draft your work first, as there will be no time for this out on the job. Follow the outline given below during your early transcription assignments to ensure turning out good work every time. After you have gained some experience in transcription, Step III. B may be omitted.

Three Steps to Transcription

I. Read notes through before transcribing.
    A. Look up unfamiliar words.
    B. Provide your own sufficiently detailed dictionary.
    C. Correct outlines.
    D. Include punctuation.

II. Type from your notes.
    A. Keep your eyes on your notes while transcribing.
    B. Correct errors detected while typing.
    C. Habitually type a space after each word. When you need to pause, you will not waste time looking from your notes to the typed copy to see if space has been left.

III. A. Correct all errors before removing paper from typewriter.
    B. Check your copy against your notes.

Numbering of Transcripts

The title page of a transcript or legal document is not numbered, but the second and all successive pages are numbered. The numbers are placed at the top right-hand corner just above the ruled horizontal line to the left of the vertical line or at the bottom in a comparable position outside the ruled line or at the center of the page according to the dictates of custom.

Numbering Index Pages

Since the index cannot be produced until the transcript is completed, it is numbered with lower-case Roman numbers: "i," "ii," "iii," "iv," and so on.

Typewriter Ribbon

If you have a sizable transcript to prepare, start with a new typewriter ribbon (unless your typewriter requires film ribbon) to avoid having the intensity of the print suddenly change in the middle of the transcript. However, type should never be allowed to become dim and even slightly illegible. All carbons must also always remain crisp and clear.

CAT transcribers should always be sure that the ribbons on their computer printers are dark and clear, as this is a frequent criticism of transcripts produced in this way.

Corrections

Liquid Paper and Taperaser are never used when correcting any reporting work. All erasures must be so skillfully done that no evidence remains. White chalk is handy to rub in to eradicate any traces of change. Should you be required at first to type your work, arm yourself with several grades of erasers and good carbon paper, for your product must be perfect. Word processors are now being used in many offices that do not have sufficient volume for CAT transcription, and the days of typed transcripts are undoubtedly numbered except in small jurisdictions with little transcript. However, on occasion even a totally CAT-oriented reporter may be forced to type a transcript, and perfection is what is required.

Before beginning any lengthy typed transcript, stack carbons with originals, carbons, and as many second sheets as will be required, laying stacks crosswise. Time will also be saved if you train transcribers to place finished work crosswise for easy proofreading.

Appearance Is Important

Margins and spacing may be varied somewhat to ensure proper placement of matter on the page and to maintain a fine overall appearance. This is particularly true of title pages, which are the first thing seen by the reader.

Remember that every legal paper should look like a fine picture on the page with proper framing provided by top, side, and bottom margins. No document should be flawed by apparent corrections or untidy appearance.

Personalized Transcript Paper

Many court reporters have their names, addresses, and phone numbers printed at the bottom of their numbered erasable bond transcription paper or CAT paper, note sheets, and cover bindings. This is convenient for attorneys who wish to call to discuss transcript matters or to schedule further work.

Preparation of Printed Forms

There are many printed forms attorneys use, such as leases, deeds, mortgages, notes of issue, and so on. You may occasionally be asked to prepare these forms. Sometimes forms such as these or government forms, such as Income Tax Form 1040's, do not line up perfectly because they are printed in different batches. It is a good idea to hold such forms up to the light to line them up exactly before typing to avoid poorly-spaced carbon copies.

However, very little of your work as a court reporter can be done using prepared forms.

Transcribing Legal Papers

Court reporters are often required to prepare court legal papers, such as Findings of Fact, Conclusions of Law, and Orders for Judgment. Occasionally ruled paper with marked side margins is used. Long 8½ × 13″ or 8½ × 14″ paper is not used much now, but bond paper is used for originals and onionskin for carbon copies.

A 2-inch margin is allowed at the top for binding, and a blue legal backing sheet is customarily used. The margins should be at least 1½ inches on the left and ½ inch on the right.

The first page, again, is not numbered, but each successive page is numbered at the center of the page about six to seven lines from the bottom. A hyphen is typed before and after the page number. Indentations on legal instruments may be either five or ten spaces. The last word on any page of transcript should never be hyphenated.

Most legal documents are double-spaced with land descriptions of any length and quoted matter indented and single-spaced. Frequent paragraphing is used for ease of reading. Some judges prefer a triple space between paragraphs of double-spaced instruments.

Judges and attorneys frequently require rough drafts of legal opinions, stipulations, and other legal material. If possible, triple space these so that insertions may be easily made. Also, make several copies to save yourself unnecessary work if the judge you work for likes to consider a number of changed versions before coming to a final conclusion.

Acknowledgments and Signatures

Acknowledgments and verifications on legal instruments are often single spaced to set them apart from the subject matter or in order to get an entire instrument on a page. Signatures are never placed on a page by themselves, and at least two lines of typing, and preferably three, should be at the end of each page or on the top of the next. Otherwise, the entire paragraph should be placed on the next page.

Titles of Cases

Titles in citations are underscored, as: <u>Alcott v. Pennsylvania R.R.</u>, 183 Atl. 2d (Pa. 1981).

National Shorthand Reporters Association Guidelines

The National Shorthand Reporters Association has set down clear guidelines as to format to be used by court reporters. These guidelines are as follows:

1. Use 25 typed lines on standard ruled, numbered 8½ × 11 inch paper.
2. Each line consists of 10 characters to the typed inch.
3. Left-hand margin is to be set at 1-3/4 inches.
4. Right-hand margin is to be set at 3/8 inch.
5. Each question and answer is to begin on a separate line.
6. Each question and answer is to begin at the left-hand margin with five spaces from the Q. or A. to the text.
7. Carryover Q. and A. lines begin at the left-hand margin.
8. Colloquy material begins 15 spaces from the left-hand margin with carryover colloquy starting at the left-hand margin.
9. Quoted material begins 10 spaces from the left-hand margin with carryover lines beginning 10 spaces from the left-hand margin.
10. Parentheticals and exhibit markings shall begin 15 spaces from the left-hand margin with carryover lines beginning 15 spaces from the left-hand margin.

Statutes Must Be Adhered To

The examples given in this book will follow the above guidelines where possible. However, in states in which the statutes require other formats, the required formats must be used. For instance, in New Jersey, if there should be space remaining on the same line as the question, the answer is begun on that line.

Chapter 13 **Billing and Delivery of Depositions**

Billing the Deposition

After you have proofread a deposition, made all corrections, used the burster and collator to sort a computer transcribed deposition, or sorted and collated a word processed or typed one, bound it neatly, and obtained the signature, if required, the most pleasurable part of the whole job, next to receiving and spending the money, is preparing the invoice.

Contents of Billhead

Your billhead should be neat, dignified, and complete. It should contain the firm name and its address and telephone number. Your Social Security number or Treasury I.D. number should appear on every bill sent out. Until it is supplied, many attorneys and insurance companies refuse to pay any statement which does not have this information.

Figure 44 on page 124, printed here by permission of Richard Smith, is a fine example of a proper billhead. This invoice consists of four parts bound together in books at the top. The first copy is white; the second copy, pink; the third copy, blue; and the fourth copy, yellow.

The first and second copies are sent with transcript copies to the attorney. Note that the second copy has printed at the bottom "PLEASE RETURN THIS COPY WITH REMIT-TANCE," as this helps to credit payment to the proper case in the firm's records. At the top appears "RE" for listing title of the case and its number. Provision is also made for the reporter's name. The third copy says "SECOND STATEMENT" at the bottom because it is sent out after 30 days have elapsed as a reminder. (Note businesslike charge for overdue bills.) Every firm must also set up a reserve of some type for bad debts, although good firms screen their accounts carefully to minimize losses through unpaid bills.

There are a number of computer programs available at the present time to facilitate the billing process, although they are expensive. You might like to develop such a program on your own for computer preparation of your invoices and followups.

Charges Vary According to Delivery Time

In billing, charges vary in accordance with delivery time requested by the attorneys, and the following will help you to understand the various terms used.

The term "daily delivery" has several connotations ranging from delivery the morning after the hearing to immediate copy.

FIGURE 44
Billhead

IN ACCOUNT WITH

REPORTER

RICHARD AND CASEY B. SMITH

CERTIFIED SHORTHAND REPORTERS

607-13 JAMES BLDG. • CHATTANOOGA, TENNESSEE 37402

TELEPHONE: AREA CODE 615
267-0989

(Reference: Martindale-Hubbell)

TO:

RE:

TREASURY ID No. 62-0518994

ATTENDANCE FEE:

TRANSCRIPT:

1½% CHARGE PER MONTH ON ALL ACCOUNTS OVER 30 DAYS OLD. THIS INVOICE REPRESENTS AN IMMEDIATE TRANSFER OF FUNDS FROM OUR AGENCY TO STAFF REPORTERS, TRANSCRIBERS, ETC. UPON DELIVERY OF TRANSCRIPTS TO YOU. YOUR PROMPT REMITTANCE WILL BE APPRECIATED.

(White Copy)

1½% CHARGE PER MONTH ON ALL ACCOUNTS OVER 30 DAYS OLD. THIS INVOICE REPRESENTS AN IMMEDIATE TRANSFER OF FUNDS FROM OUR AGENCY TO STAFF REPORTERS, TRANSCRIBERS, ETC. UPON DELIVERY OF TRANSCRIPTS TO YOU. YOUR PROMPT REMITTANCE WILL BE APPRECIATED.

PLEASE RETURN THIS COPY WITH REMITTANCE

(Pink Copy)

1½% CHARGE PER MONTH ON ALL ACCOUNTS OVER 30 DAYS OLD. THIS INVOICE REPRESENTS AN IMMEDIATE TRANSFER OF FUNDS FROM OUR AGENCY TO STAFF REPORTERS, TRANSCRIBERS, ETC. UPON DELIVERY OF TRANSCRIPTS TO YOU. YOUR PROMPT REMITTANCE WILL BE APPRECIATED.

SECOND STATEMENT

(Blue Copy)

1½% CHARGE PER MONTH ON ALL ACCOUNTS OVER 30 DAYS OLD. THIS INVOICE REPRESENTS AN IMMEDIATE TRANSFER OF FUNDS FROM OUR AGENCY TO STAFF REPORTERS, TRANSCRIBERS, ETC. UPON DELIVERY OF TRANSCRIPTS TO YOU. YOUR PROMPT REMITTANCE WILL BE APPRECIATED.

ACCOUNTS RECEIVABLE

(Yellow Copy)

1. Ordinary Copy: Delivery from five days to two weeks, depending upon the customer's stipulation. This is a routine delivery.

2. Expedited Copy: Delivery in three work days.

3. 24-hour Copy: Delivery within 24 hours after the conclusion of the hearing.

4. Daily Copy: Delivery by 9:00 A.M. of the day following the hearing.

5. Rush Copy: Delivery by 9:00 P.M. on the day of the hearing.

6. Split Rush Copy: Delivery of the morning session by 5:30 P.M., and the afternoon session by 9:00 P.M. of the day of the hearing.

7. Immediate Copy: Delivery of transcript as transcription is completed; usually one delivery per hour.

The table that follows, included by permission, is printed in the Form Book of Morgan J. Morey & Associates. It shows their method of charging for expedited copy.

Number of Pages Is Considered

The charge for expedited service varies according to the number of pages. In computing 1-day, 2-day, and 3-day delivery, count Saturdays, but not Sundays and holidays. A day is 24 hours, so a transcript taken at 10:00 A.M. Monday morning and finished by noon must be delivered before noon on Tuesday to qualify for a 1-day delivery. If not delivered until 3:00 P.M., the 2-day rate would apply.

If the deposition was concluded at 11:00 A.M. Friday and delivered by 11:00 A.M. Saturday, it would be 1-day; if delivered by 11:00 A.M. Monday, it would be 2-day delivery; if delivered by 3:00 P.M. Monday, it would be 3-day delivery.

Table of Charges for Expedited Copy

NUMBER OF PAGES	1-DAY	2-DAY	3-DAY	4-DAY	ORDINARY
1–25	+10%	—	—	—	—
26–50	+25%	+10%	—	—	—
51–75	+50%	+25%	+10%	—	—
76–100	+75%	+50%	+50%	+10%	—
100–upward	+100%	+75%	+50%	+25%	—

In order to charge for expedited transcript rates, a reporter must have a definite order for the specific delivery to be charged, and the lawyer must understand that an additional charge will be made. A differential (usually 10 percent) is charged per page for heavy technical or medical work.

The use of the previous terms gives reporters flexibility in setting price schedules. If a lawyer is just given the choice of ordinary or daily, the reporter is limited in the price he or she can charge. The circumstances will dictate how many of the terms the reporter will wish to discuss with the customer.

You should have a stamp made with the word "PAID" in large letters on it and a movable date below. Each second, or pink, copy of the invoice which is returned with remittance to your firm should be stamped "PAID" and mailed back with "Thank you" and your name signed on the face of it to add a personal touch.

The Highsmith Company, Inc., P.O. Box 25A, Highway 106 East, Fort Atkinson, WI, 53538, sells pre-inked, self-contained stamps that say "PAST DUE," and "PAID," among others. This company also sells a large variety of reporters' supplies, so it is a good idea to get their catalogue.

Keeping Good Business Records

All payments should be entered on the firm's records immediately, as clients become irritated when billed for something they have already paid for. Then, all checks should be deposited at once in the firm's business account, in chronological order, for reference in case of an IRS audit. Endorsements on checks should be made by rubber stamp, as shown, to save time.

PAY TO THE ORDER OF
UNITED BANK OF
HARMONY, IOWA
FOR DEPOSIT ONLY

Attendance and Transcript Fees Vary Widely

It is impossible to delineate in this book what to bill by way of attendance and transcript fees, as these change from time to time and vary widely from state to state, and even from firm to firm in any given city.

At one time state organizations used to print suggested rate scales annually for all reporters to follow, but this practice has been ruled illegal as restraint of trade. Attendance fees are almost universal when taking statements, as sometimes the reporter would earn nothing for a day's work when witnesses were unavailable. However, many places do not provide attendance fees on depositions. Reporters make up for this by charging a higher page rate, cover fees, or other extras.

Your firm will have worked all of this out before you begin work, and ordinarily all billing will be done by office personnel in any reasonably-sized firm. However, everything you know about such procedures will assist you.

Delivering the Copies and Filing the Original Deposition

Before transmitting any deposition, be sure the required signature of the witness is secured, or that proper arrangements have been made for filing the original in the event the witness has failed to appear within proper time to sign or the trial date is near.

Check to be sure all original deposition exhibits, if any, are bound into the back of the original deposition and copies are bound at the back of each copy.

Should there have been any certifications of questions or errata sheets, examine the original and all copies to satisfy yourself that they have been properly inserted under each front cover.

Finally assure yourself that all pages are in order and that you have signed the deposition reporter's certificate and placed your notary seal over your signature on the certificate, if this is required, including the expiration date of your notarial commission, if necessary.

Place the word "COSTS" and the amount thereof and the party who incurred them (plaintiff or defendant) on the cover of the original deposition on the right-hand side. Then, when the verdict is in, the costs will be available to the clerk of court to assess against the losing party.

Now you are ready to transmit the original and copies of the deposition to the clerk of court and the attorneys. Place the copies in manila envelopes which are appropriately addressed to counsel with your invoice clipped neatly to the top deposition copy cover.

If you have copies of depositions hand carried to the attorneys' offices, have the person receiving them sign a date receipt form which identifies the transcript by case title and number. Should you mail the copies, always send them by registered mail and request a return receipt for your protection. Private mail or delivery services, such as UPS, may also be used; they are usually faster than the U.S. Postal Service and often cheaper.

Seal your original deposition in a manila envelope and write upon it the style and number of the case, venue, and name of the witness or witnesses. Then sign, place your title below your signature, and place your notary seal over your signature if notarial commission is required to be reported in your locality.

Some states, such as Texas, have a certificate to be used on this envelope with an endorsement for the clerk of court. However, in Houston, Texas, many depositions are hand carried to the courthouse without any envelope, and I am sure this is the case in many other places. This is a bad practice, but it is the custom. Do everything right even though others do not follow proper procedures, for you will be blamed if anything goes wrong.

Seal your first envelope with case information on it within another larger manila envelope which you will direct to the clerk of court where the case is pending. If you must mail it, again, be sure to register the envelope and secure a return card. If it is hand carried, get a receipt. Then, if the original is misfiled, you will not be accused of not having delivered the deposition original.

Chapter 14

Court Organization

The structure of courts in the United States is complicated because two separate court systems—federal and state—operate side by side but independently of each other.

The federal court system was developed originally so the national government would not have to depend on state courts to carry out its laws. Eventually, federal courts came to have exclusive jurisdiction over criminal matters involving violation of federal laws.

The federal district courts (referred to also as United States District Courts) have exclusive jurisdiction in admiralty and maritime cases; bankruptcy matters and proceedings; actions arising out of patent or copyright laws; actions against ambassadors, consuls, vice consuls, or ministers; actions wherein the amount in controversy, exclusive of interest and costs, exceeds $10,000 between: (1) citizens of different states, (2) citizens of a state and foreign states or citizens or subjects, (3) citizens of different states, with foreign states or citizens or subjects as additional parties, or civil actions arising under the constitution, laws, or treaties of the United States; stockholders' derivative suits; eminent domain proceedings; actions for partition of lands wherein the United States is one of the tenants in common or joint tenants; any civil action whether or not of a local nature against defendants residing in different districts in the same state or involving property located in different districts.

Such matters as those of marriage, divorce, custody, probate proceedings, property disputes, and other criminal cases were reserved exclusively to state courts.

State courts and federal courts have concurrent jurisdiction over matters where there is diversity of citizenship (citizens of different states or of a state and foreign country) and where the amount in dispute is more than $10,000. In such a situation, if a lawsuit is filed in the federal court, the federal court applies state law.

Most actions are started in the lowest court authorized to hear the matter. If the parties are dissatisfied with the result, they appeal to the next highest court authorized to hear appeals; they can then appeal to an even higher court.

The United States Supreme Court

The United States Supreme Court is the highest court in the United States, and there is no appeal from its decisions. The Supreme Court consists of a chief justice and eight associate justices, any six of whom shall constitute a quorum. The power of the United States Supreme Court to review decisions of the state courts is limited to those which involve a federal question, but the Supreme Court has the power to declare unconstitutional any federal or state statute which is contrary to the United States Constitution.

The United States Supreme Court receives requests to hear more than 5,000 cases annually and dismisses nearly 90 percent of the appeals as unworthy of review.

The United States Supreme Court is the only court created by the United States Constitution. Its jurisdiction is varied and usually of an appellate nature. In most instances the United States Supreme Court may decide whether or not it will hear a particular case. Once there has been a decision in a trial court and in an appellate court, the losing party may petition the Supreme Court for a writ of certiorari (review). If the Supreme Court wishes to hear the case, it grants the writ.

There are some cases which the United States Supreme Court is obligated to hear, which come to them on appeal, bypassing the courts of appeal. There are also some instances in which the Supreme Court has original jurisdiction, as when states incur disputes over boundaries. Since it has original jurisdiction over disputes between states, it is a trial court in this instance.

Because the United States Supreme Court is the highest in the land, there is no right to appeal from its decision.

The United States Courts of Appeals

The United States is divided into 11 judicial circuits (10 judicial circuits, plus the District of Columbia judicial circuit), with a federal court of appeals in every circuit. These courts have no original jurisdiction. The Court of Appeals is the court of last resort in the federal court system, and cases may be appealed from the Courts of Appeals to the United States Supreme Court.

The United States District Courts (Federal Courts)

The United States is divided into judicial districts and the federal district courts are courts of record. Legal actions that involve an interest and a right of the government of the United States are tried in federal courts. All other litigation (less than international in scope) is tried in the state court system.

These courts are the trial courts of the federal court system and have original jurisdiction, exclusive of the state courts, in all criminal offenses against the United States. They have broad jurisdiction over civil actions arising under the U.S. Constitution and federal laws. They also have original jurisdiction of all civil actions wherein the contested matter exceeds the sum or value of $10,000, exclusive of interest and costs, which arise under the Constitution, laws, or treaties of the United States, plus those matters listed above.

There are special federal courts which include the Court of Claims, the Customs Court, and the Court of Customs and Patent Appeals, all of which are courts of record.

The State Court Systems

Each state has the authority to create its own courts, and these are by no means uniform. Most state court systems consist of a supreme court, or court of last resort; an intermediate appellate court, usually called the Court of Appeals; trial courts of regional jurisdiction where suits are commenced; and inferior (lower) courts, such as probate courts (called Surrogate's court in some states), and other specialized courts. Usually a case is originally brought and tried in a trial court and appealed to higher courts of appellate jurisdiction until it reaches the state's highest appellate court or, finally, the United States Supreme Court.

The states are divided into circuits, or districts, with a court for each, and all state courts operate independently. The courts in one state have no control over, or relation to, the courts of another state.

Most state supreme courts, or courts of last resort (not always called the Supreme Court), have appellate jurisdiction over all controversies arising in state trial courts unless the state has an intermediate court of appeals. There is only one supreme appellate court in each state. In

Oklahoma and Texas, the Criminal Court of Appeals are the courts of last resort in criminal cases. In 45 states the highest court is called the Supreme Court. In the remaining five states, the highest court is designated as follows:

Maine	Supreme Judicial Court
Maryland	Court of Appeals
Massachusetts	Supreme Judicial Court
New York	Court of Appeals
West Virginia	Supreme Court of Appeals

State Trial Courts

This tier of trial courts hears important matters—felony trials where the defendant may be sentenced to a long prison term, and civil suits that usually involve over $1,000. Such courts are generally located only at the county seat. In some states several counties share a single court, which normally sits in one and visits the other counties for short periods each year. Judges of these courts are always lawyers and normally serve for relatively long terms. All jury trials in state courts are heard in these courts, although most cases are heard by the judge alone or are settled out of court.

These superior courts are the highest state courts of original jurisdiction. In some states these courts are called circuit courts, district courts, or courts of common pleas. In New York, however, the highest state court of original jurisdiction is called the "Supreme Court." They have general jurisdiction over civil, criminal, and equity matters. Their jurisdiction often extends to two or more counties. They have appellate jurisdiction over cases originating in the lower courts, such as municipal, justice, and small claims courts, in addition to being the courts of original jurisdiction in the first instance. In some states their appellate jurisdiction extends to the probate courts.

In some states these courts have separate departments that have jurisdiction over special matters, such as matters of law or equity. They may have separate civil and criminal divisions. The state trial courts are courts of record.

State Lower Courts

Lower courts include those whose proceedings are directly subject to appeal review by a higher court, such as municipal courts, justice of the peace courts, small claims courts, city courts, traffic courts, police courts, justice courts, magistrate's courts, recorder's courts, village courts, mayor's courts, town courts, and so on.

All these lower courts have limited jurisdiction. In criminal cases they are generally restricted to misdemeanors, preliminary hearings, or inquiries in felony cases. In civil actions, their jurisdiction is over cases involving small amounts of money (in most places up to $5,000).

Generally speaking, lower courts are not courts of record, but in many jurisdictions examining trials are fully reported verbatim to bind defendants over to the superior court, and full-time reporters fill these positions in larger cities. In many instances in such hearings in those courts not of record, attorneys for defendants retain freelance reporters to take and transcribe the proceedings to assist in preparation for the case before the trial court.

Justice of the Peace Courts

Where the office of justice of the peace still exists, minor criminal and civil matters, such as traffic fines, local ordinance violations, and suits involving small amounts of money are handled. In many states these functions have been limited to minor matters, and a professional magistrate or judge has been installed to hear criminal and civil suits.

In most states courts of minor jurisdiction do not hold jury trials, but all matters that come before them are settled by the presiding officer alone. If a jury trial is requested and permitted by law, the case must be transferred to another court.

Jurisdiction

Jurisdiction is the authority or power of a court to hear a particular cause of action and to render a lawful and binding judgment against one or more defendants. Jurisdiction may be concurrent; that is, two or more courts may have jurisdiction over a particular cause of action, in which case the attorney may choose the best forum for the client's interests. A court must have jurisdiction over the subject matter of the litigation and over the person of the parties to hear a case and render a legal judgment.

Subject Matter Jurisdiction

Subject matter jurisdiction is limited by:

1. The nature of the case.
2. The amount involved.
3. The remedies the court can provide.
4. The location of property.
5. The identity of the litigants.

"Long Arm" Statutes

Most states have "long arm" statutes which give a court personal jurisdiction over nonresident defendants who commit civil wrongs in a state other than their resident state. These statutes provide personal jurisdiction in cases of automobile accidents in a foreign state, nonresident property owners, aircraft or ship operators, out-of-state corporations, and so on.

Venue

Venue is the place (city, county, district, or other geographical division) in which an action is to be heard and tried. Venue is determined by statute and usually lies where the cause of action occurred. Venue is designed for the convenience of the parties and, unlike subject matter jurisdiction, it may be waived. A defendant may request a change of venue if:

1. An impartial trial cannot be had.
2. Bias or prejudice of the judge or jury exists, if provided by statute.
3. Convenience of the parties and/or witnesses is better served.
4. It appears to be in the interest of justice.

Who May Sue?

Anybody can sue anybody else, but the important thing is whether or not the lawsuit has merit. Therefore, the parties must rely on a decision of a court to determine which party has taken the correct position. The person injured is the one who must sue, and that person must have the legal capacity to sue. A minor's legal affairs must be handled by a parent or a guardian.

In law, the word "person" may mean a company or a corporation, not only an individual. The litigants in a court case are called "parties," and the person who files the lawsuit is the plaintiff, sometimes known as the petitioner. The defendant is the party who is sued.

When a case is appealed, the party appealing is referred to as the appellant; the party against whom the appeal is filed is known as the respondent or appellee.

Pleadings

Written statements are made by each side of a lawsuit stating the various claims and defenses to be decided in court. These will include petitions, summonses, complaints, orders, motions, and affidavits, which, taken together, will be referred to as the pleadings. By the strictest definition of the word, only complaints and answers are pleadings.

Upon receiving the first pleading in a case, the clerk will open a new file and issue a docket, or case number. Fees are charged for filing papers with the court clerk, and, when these are paid, a paper is said to be "recorded."

A case is said to be "at issue" when the complaint and the answer have been filed. It is then said that "the issues have been joined," which means the parties have each presented their respective sides and are ready to proceed.

Default Judgment

After the complaint is filed, if the defendant chooses not to contest the action and enters no defense, after the time set by statute the defendant is held in default. The plaintiff, through his or her attorney, appears in court and receives a default judgment against the defendant.

Terms of Court

The law sets out the period of time during which the court sits to conduct business as a "term of court," which may be divided into "sessions." Usually terms are designated as "spring term" or "September term," relating to the time of year.

The Bar

There is a railing dividing the area where the attorneys, witnesses, court reporters, jury, and judge sit from the spectator's area. This railing is referred to as "the bar." When an attorney is licensed to practice, he may go beyond the railing into the privileged area, or is "admitted to the bar." "The Bar" refers to attorneys.

The Bench

The raised podium at the front of the courtroom behind which the judge sits is "the bench." During a trial, counsel may request permission to "approach the bench," meaning they wish to confer privately with the judge out of the hearing of the jury.

Court Chambers and Open and Closed Court

The judge may meet with attorneys and parties in his office, called his "chambers," for discussions outside the hearing of the jury (in camera) or for decisions of motions, etc. These sessions are usually more informal than open court hearings. Hearings conducted in the courtroom at which visitors may be present are "open," while those from which spectators are barred are called "closed." Juvenile hearings and adoptions are closed by virtue of the law.

Ex Parte Hearings and Order to Show Cause

A judge may sometimes sign an order without hearing from both sides of a case when immediate action must be taken to stop something injurious to person or property, such as issuing a restraining order. An ex parte order might result from application to the judge for continuance of a hearing date or more time to file a brief.

An order granted ex parte normally provides for a date and time for the opposing party to appear to present arguments against the order. This is designated as appearing to "show cause" why the order should not be granted.

Contempt of Court

When an individual refuses to obey either a written or oral order of the judge, the judge may find that person in contempt of court and levy a fine or impose a jail sentence or both.

Court Officers

The judge is the presiding officer of the court. His or her major duties are to preside over hearings and trials in a case and to rule on issues that come up during a hearing or trial. He instructs the jury on matters of law in jury trials. The clerk of court is the administrator of the court and is responsible for the clerical details of the case. The court clerk is the custodian of all public records in most jurisdictions and is ex-officio recorder of conveyances and mortgages, keeping records of sales and mortgages on property and other documents.

Each judge in a court of record normally has a court reporter unless a pooling system is used. The judge's court reporter may also function as a secretary and assistant to the judge. The reporter will sit in the court while it is in session and take and transcribe the records as required. The reporter may be responsible for the judge's calendar settings, file maintenance, and exhibits presented in lawsuits. Judges may also have law clerks, particularly in higher courts. The court reporter makes a verbatim record of all legal proceedings had before the court.

The bailiff is the peace officer of the court and is responsible for keeping order. He is also responsible for protection of everyone in the courtroom and for maintaining decorum during proceedings.

The sheriff or marshal is the executive officer of the court who serves summonses and citations and carries out court orders. The sheriff is a county officer, and the marshal is a federal officer. The marshal transports federal prisoners. Some lower state courts also have constables whose duties are the same as those of the sheriff. The sheriff not only deals with crime but plays an important part in civil proceedings, serving legal papers, making seizures to satisfy judgments, holding public auctions, and reporting back to the court regarding these matters.

Each attorney is an officer of the court and, as such, is obligated to uphold the dignity of the court and to abide by the rules of the court.

Assignment of Case Numbers

When a legal proceeding is filed with the clerk of court, the docket or case number is assigned in either numerical order or divided into various subject matters. Some courts use a method that keeps track of the number of lawsuits filed in a particular category for each year. Docket numbers may be referred to in different jurisdictions in pleadings as Civil No. _____, Criminal No. _____, Index No. _____, or Case No. _____.

Judgment

When a court issues a decision, it is said that the court "renders judgment." A judgment becomes a lien against the defendant until paid. In some states seizure of wages is not permitted. Once a judgment has been paid, it is said to have been "satisfied," and the clerk will record the cancellation when evidence of satisfaction is presented.

Findings of Fact, Conclusions of Law, and Order for Judgment

The court's decision in a non-jury case is referred to as a "finding." In briefs you will see wording such as "the Court found." Most courts give written reasons for judgment which set out the legal reasons for the decision. These are generally known as "Findings of Fact, Conclusions of Law, and Order for Judgment."

Chapter 15

The Official Reporter

Perhaps your mind is already made up that you want to be an official court reporter for a judge. One of the greatest jobs in the world can be that of an official reporter, if the official reporter has a good rapport with the judge. Official situations vary greatly, and there is probably a right spot for everyone so inclined.

Qualifying by Examination

Certified Shorthand Reporter (CSR) tests are given in 14 states. In a few of these states, civil service dictates who shall be chosen for positions. Appointments are made from a list, and eligible reporters work their way up the list. In these states, judges may come and judges may go, but the same reporter will remain unless removed for dereliction of duty. There may be testing for various levels of reporting, and advancement will come through testing and seniority.

Where the CSR test alone is used to qualify reporters, the judge will appoint an official of his or her choice from among those eligible. In a large city, should be judge retire, die, or be voted out of office, the new judge will possibly have a reporter he or she prefers. The reporter for the past judge will then have to secure other employment unless the new judge selects the incumbent reporter because of his or her reputation for excellent reporting ability.

In smaller cities, the judge will usually prefer to keep the same reporter. The judge knows that person has friends who may vote when the judge runs for re-election. The reporter also knows many things that will help brief an inexperienced judge on cases and pending situations.

Some states have certain certification tests which are given periodically, while others have no CSR or other certification requirement. In these states the judge has the exclusive power to appoint his or her court reporter. Frequently judges insist the reporter hold the NSRA Certificate of Proficiency as a hiring prerequisite.

In the United States District (federal) Courts, three years' experience is required, and $1,000 per year bonus is paid to holders of the NSRA Certificate of Merit.

Remuneration of an Official Reporter

Both men and women serve as official reporters. An officialship provides a good salary 12 months a year, a pension plan, insurance, and an annual paid vacation, although sometimes the official must vacation at the same time as the judge. The official court reporter is also paid for all legal holidays.

Should an officialship involve traveling, the reporter will receive remuneration for mileage, meals, and lodging while away from home and, occasionally, per diem if assigned to counties outside the regular district.

Transcripts for which the official reporter is paid on a folio basis for those provided the court and the attorneys represent extra compensation on top of the salary, which is liberal in most states. Also, in some areas officials do freelance deposition and statement work, which adds to their compensation.

Prestige of Being an Official Reporter

An offical court reporter holds a position of high respect in the community, and any judge with a highly competent reporter will value that person, be most considerate of him or her, and make the reporting job as pleasant as possible in order to retain such a jewel.

You, as an official reporter, will be very close to the judge, and the judge will share many confidences with you. Never discuss any matters having to do with your job outside the office, for any chance remark you might make could cause grave problems. Members of the press may come to you for information as to rulings the judge intends to make or as to what transpire during a closed-door session. Never furnish any information to them unless the judge has specifically told you to relay a news item to them. Always say, "You'll have to ask the judge about that."

Proper Decorum for Official Reporters

The official reporter's judge is entitled to the loyalty of his or her reporter. Never speak ill of the judge or allow others to do so in your presence.

You may be on a first-name basis with the judge, but do not call the judge by his or her first name in the presence of other people, whether in the courtroom or out socially. This presents a very unbusinesslike appearance to others and would be a very serious breach of courtesy in the courtroom where strict formality should prevail to lend dignity to the proceedings. On the telephone, say, "Judge Stanton would like to have the papers signed by next Monday," or "His (or Her) Honor has set your case ahead of the other civil cases on the calendar in accordance with your request."

You, as an official reporter, are an officer of the court, and it is good business also to address attorneys, court clerks, and other court officers formally. If you seem unduly friendly with any of these people, others may resent it, feeling that you are not acting totally impartially.

The best rule in regard to social affairs regarding court officers is to let your good sense be your guide. You cannot help knowing some people better than others. Informality may be fine on many social occasions; after you have been a court reporter for some time, you should be able to be at ease with court officials and courtroom personnel.

Preparation for the New Job

The new official should find out what the position will pay; what supplies and equipment will be furnished; what arrangements prevail regarding shared computers and scopists; if travel is involved and how reimbursement will be made; whether outside work will be permitted or required; and whether the judge will expect everything to be reported, including opening and closing statements, all jury impaneling, motions, in camera conferences, and the like. Come to an understanding with the judge about what to expect early in your tenure to avoid future problems.

Changing Status of Official Reporters

All students considering becoming official reporters should become proficient enough to be realtime writers in order to survive the push to supplant them with electronic equipment. The rapport that once existed between the judge and the official has eroded in many places, and some courts have instituted systems using swing reporters and reporter pools. Publicity regarding the vast amounts of money reporters make has raised animosity, as has publicity surrounding reporters who have been jailed for not preparing transcripts in a timely manner, and many officials have not kept up with demands of our present technological age.

All officials can ensure keeping their positions by becoming top notch professionals and being ready to work as realtime writers, but the burden is on them. As in everything else, the world will move along.

Qualifications of Officials

An official reporter must be competent to report and transcribe at a speed of 225–250 WPM on five-minute testimony takes, 200 WPM on five-minute jury charges, and 180 WPM on difficult literary material with less than 5 percent errors. The applicant must be a respected citizen with no criminal record, and a temperate individual whose behavior will never reflect upon the court. He or she must be punctual, efficient, and impartial at all times.

Cautions for the Official Reporter

The official reporter should not give advice to anyone concerning any matter in the court or which could end up in court. He or she should never purport to speak or act for the judge where judicial matters are involved. Unless specifically authorized, he or she should never exercise the court's discretion, as in excusing jurors or setting hearings. He or she should not discuss the merits of any case.

No official reporter should ever leave the impression with anyone that he or she could or would "talk to the judge" about a case or that he or she knows "what the judge is going to do." Neither should any official ever express an opinion as to how any case should be decided or what verdict a jury will return, thereby taking sides in a lawsuit.

No reporter should ever permit a lawyer to dictate anything into the record or change anything concerning any record out of the judge's presence.

The official reporter must be courteous and fair to the Bar and others, but not show favoritism. He or she should never improperly interpose himself or herself between the judge and others.

Court officials should never discuss publicly politics or religion and should avoid being identified with controversies that might reflect on the judge. If the official is an attorney, legal practice may not be done in the court wherein he or she serves as reporter.

No official reporter may ever neglect the work of the court in order to perform outside work. Of course, each official will be required to take all criminal proceedings, and each reporter must be responsible for seeing that all notes, records, tapes, cassettes, discs, and so on, are placed in a permanent file and maintained for the statutory period, then destroyed in a proper manner.

If any official reporter's employment is terminated, he or she must promptly transcribe and deliver all notes and records as required by the court.

Other Responsibilities of Officialship

The judge has the right to expect that his or her official will use the initiative to produce timely records and that all transcripts will be produced with accurate spellings and correct word usage and punctuation in an attractive format, complete in every way.

Transcript rates for official reporters are set clearly in each state's statutes, and the reporter may not overcharge for court transcripts. The salary of the court reporter is designed to compensate officials, who do not receive as much per transcript page as freelance reporters. The official reporter must not submit vouchers for payment of mileage, lodging, or food not provided for transcripts that are not delivered, as it is a felony to do so.

Chapter 16

The Official Reporter's Office

One day I was reporting on special assignment in a courthouse distant from my home county when the judge requested some immediate transcripts. As he took me into the reporter's office to use the County's typewriter, he said "You know, I often want to fire my reporter because he keeps such a messy office. The public gets a bad impression, too. I don't know how he ever finds anything, and he is always running out of supplies, which slows up his transcripts."

As I looked around, it was easy to see what he meant. Half-filled boxes of various types of transcript paper, stacks of unfiled notes, scraps of paper with telephone messages and notes on them, numerous pieces of correspondence, dirty coffee cups and fast food cartons, and waste paper were strewn all over the place. That demonstrated how much judges, attorneys, and the public notice a reporter's organization.

The Reporter's Desk

On top of your desk should be the telephone with pad and pencil or pen always beside it for taking messages and your rotating wheel or other index for frequently used phone numbers and addresses. Your computer, of course, belongs on your desk, and "In" and "Out" boxes should be there. If you still use dictating equipment, that should have its place on your desk.

Every well-equipped desk should have a desk calendar and an appointment book on top, readily visible, and good pens and pencils that really work. A pencil holder for colored pens, as well as extra pens and pencils, is also convenient. A proper desk lamp is necessary—in fact, most essential.

A rubber stamp rack is a must to hold the variety of stamps you need. Stamps saying "ORIGINAL," "COPY," "PAID," "RECEIVED," and "PAST DUE" are handy. Notary stamps, check endorsement stamps, exhibit stamps, and return address stamps are others you will require in the course of your reporting business.

Center Desk Drawer. In your center desk drawer belong pencils, several sizes of paper clips, perhaps some of different colors for color coding, labels, extra staples, clamps, typewriter erasers (if you still use a typewriter that is non-correcting), Scotch tape, twine, rubber bands of all sizes, scissors, stamp pads (stored upside down to keep the ink moist), a staple remover, and one more thing: cough drops or mints to soothe your throat if you dictate.

Side Desk Drawers. Your side top desk drawer should hold staplers, small reference books you use constantly (desk dictionary, word-division manual, personal telephone book directory, legal directory, legal secretary's handbook, and *Uniform System of Citation* (The Harvard Law Review Assn, Cambridge, MA)). You may keep an electric stapler at your work table, but having a hand stapler at your desk saves steps. Keep it out of sight, as staplers in open view seem to be borrowed and never returned more often than any other item except pencils and ballpoint pens.

Your side middle drawer should be partitioned with compartments for transcript paper, letterheads, carbons, envelopes, and billheads, all neatly arranged.

In the bottom side drawer, you should keep personal items and work in progress. It is a good idea for a woman reporter to keep an extra set of pantyhose on hand at all times in case runs pop up. A bottle of aspirin and a few makeup essentials, such as comb, emery boards, spot remover, nail polish, tissues, deodorant, hand lotion, lipstick, and towelettes should be kept in a leakproof pouch. A male reporter should keep tissues, a comb, a clothes brush, a shoeshine kit, deodorant, and such other personal items as he chooses in this spot.

In addition to a desk, every reporter's office must have a work table for sorting transcript and binding. An electric pencil sharpener, electric stapler, hole punch, paper cutter, and shredding wastebasket are helpful adjuncts to keep at this table.

The Proper Chair

A most important item for your office is your office chair. Since you must sit for long periods of time, secure a good posture chair. The one you select should have an adjustment permitting you to raise and lower the back rest or the entire seat so you can sit comfortably with your feet resting flat on the floor. Adjust your chair carefully to avoid fatigue, backache, and loss of efficiency.

Supply Cabinet

The reporter's supply cabinet should have all shelves clearly marked with similar items grouped together.

Shelves should be marked for shorthand machine paper, ink, and ribbons; transcript paper (ruled and numbered, 8½″ x 11″); bond paper and onionskin; ruled yellow legal pads; carbon paper; billheads; county claim forms; note sheets; covers; paper clips; wired tags; extra staples; erasers; pencils; ballpoint pens; Marks-A-Lot; Mystic tape; Scotch tape; numbering machine; cassettes and disks for computer or Stenorette tapes; manila envelopes of various sizes; letter and larger sized manila envelopes imprinted with your name and address; letterheads; typewriter or printer ribbons; copying machine supplies; type cleaner or rubbing alcohol to clean ink and platens; computer paper; a first aid kit; and any other items you regularly require in the course of your work.

Devise a System for Ordering Supplies

Mark on the label of each item on your supply cabinet shelves the quantity at which reordering should take place. Then, insert a colored card at the point at which the inventory of that particular article will need replenishing. On this card, mark the date and amount ordered, and soon you will be able to determine how much of each item you use. Reordering will thus be simplified.

Always maintain a good supply of each product so strikes, poor mail or delivery service, and items no longer supplied by a manufacturer will not cause problems.

Bookcases and Filing Cabinets

A large bookcase is essential for your reference library. Allow room for your library to expand, as it surely will if you are constantly improving your reporting performance. You should also keep copies of the *National Shorthand Reporter* on your bookshelves for ready reference.

You should have at least two file cabinets that lock because, although legal-sized papers are being phased out, there will still be some around for some time. With three cabinets you can maintain copies of transcripts of all sizes, as well as pertinent notices, manuals, and correspondence.

Storing Your Notes for Easy Retrieval

Space is required to file all shorthand notes. Perhaps your supply cabinet or file drawers will be adequate for this.

There are special cabinets now built for the purpose of storing notes. These are made of clear, high-impact plastic through which you can easily see to retrieve any wanted notes quickly.

Store your notes chronologically. Any time you remove notes for transcribing, insert a brightly colored card at the spot where the notes were removed because there might be more than one case taken on that particular pack of notes. This will keep you from feeling panic-stricken when you reach for a set of notes and find none in storage for a particular date.

Permanent Storage of Shorthand Notes

At the end of each year, the official reporter gathers notes for the past year, usually through November, in order to be able to refer to the most recent cases, and places the shorthand notes in a transfer storage file for transportation to the proper storage area in the courthouse for the statutory number of years (usually five years, although some states make no provision for ever destroying shorthand notes). You must check state statutes to ascertain how long your notes must be retained.

The Walls of the Official's Office

A large wall calendar with sizable blocks for each day will keep important dates in view and ensure meeting deadlines you enter on it. A map of your city and one of your state are also helpful for many quick references.

Your wall clock with large numbers will keep you on time for court and/or depositions. Clipboards hung on the wall will file chronologically such things as docket sheets, bulletins, and NSRA, local, and state reporting association information. A bulletin board is handy for thumb-tacking newspaper articles about cases that may come before you and other notices.

Make Good Use of Your Office

I highly recommend a good spring lock on the official's office door to help in the organization of work. This prevents counsel, jurors, old friends who visit the courthouse, witnesses, courthouse personnel, and others from barging in your office during daytime hours. There are many dangers in allowing your office to become a visiting spot. Ordinarily, the judge will have a buzzer system to summon you or an adjoining door through which he or she will communicate with you. It can be annoying for the judge to have to wait while you excuse yourself from visitors. Your office is a place of business.

Work hard when you work, and allow nothing to divert you. Then, you will find you will have time to enjoy the playtime you have so richly earned.

Schedule Your Time

Each day before starting work, make a list of the important things you plan to do that day. As far as possible, schedule your work on a daily, weekly, and monthly basis. Assign priorities to your work by planning ahead. Mark important due dates for transcripts, out-of-town court schedule dates, and other items on your large wall calendar, and then check these daily.

Above all, do not procrastinate. This will ruin your very best organization plans. That hard case transcript will become easier to put off the longer it remains undone.

The following hints may help you organize your day:

1. Since a reporter must have a flexible schedule, plan some emergency time into your day.

2. Try doing your routine jobs, such as filing, at a set time daily when you will not be called upon to do something else.

3. Verify spellings and make special notations on your information sheets immediately at the end of each day when the matter is fresh in your mind.

4. Make outgoing calls early in the morning when the person at the other end is less likely to be busy.

5. Set realistic deadlines for yourself.

6. Be sure lighting in your office is sufficient. If your overhead lighting is not adequate, secure a close-work lamp, which you should position so as to cut out shadows.

7. Use the telephone where possible instead of corresponding, except where you should keep a written confirmation of a matter.

8. Tape an extra ribbon to your machine for emergencies.

These are all small things, but they will help you become more efficient.

Plan Ahead. In organizing your work, it is a good idea to try to plan your next week before leaving the office for the weekend. Finish as much as you can before leaving for the weekend, and tidy up your office. It is easier to face a neat office at the start of the week.

Do your preferred work on Monday if you have no assignments scheduled. Ease into more difficult transcripts and work later in the week, if possible. Try to take care of all your personal matters over the weekend. A reporter's life cannot be scheduled as rigidly as that of some other workers, but wherever practicable, try to take care of matters in advance.

Use a Daybook. A daybook is a must if you are a reporter who travels outside the city. It can be used to record expenses and mileage in order that a claim voucher can be prepared. It is easy to forget when you bought lunches and other petty expense items which you need to verify at the end of the year for tax purposes. The daybook will serve as both a reminder in making up claim forms and as a good record for the Internal Revenue Service.

At the end of the year, if you are a reporter in a district composed of several counties, you may be required to apportion your salary over the various counties for pay purposes the next year. You will have to count the number of days spent in each county and divide your salary accordingly for the next year as shown in Figure 45. This form shows an order fixing salaries, which is then signed by the district judges involved. Of course, this order is ordinarily double-spaced. The order is filed with the affected county auditors of the district and used as a pay basis.

Use Form Books. One item which will improve your efficiency greatly is to maintain a form book in which you collect samples of transcripts, correspondence, vouchers, legal papers, jury charges, and so on. This book will be invaluable when new situations confront you. You will have a source to consult. It is also useful for scopists, proofreaders, or transcribers you may hire.

FIGURE 45
Apportionment Form
STATE OF MINNESOTA
TENTH JUDICIAL DISTRICT

ORDER FIXING SALARIES OF COURT REPORTERS AND APPORTIONMENT OF SAME TO THE TEN COUNTIES OF THE DISTRICT FOR THE YEAR OF 19--

WHEREAS, under and pursuant to Chapter 701, Session Laws of 19--, and Minnesota Statutes, 19--, Section 486.07, Judges of the District Court are empowered to fix and establish the salaries of their respective court reporters for the year 19-- at the sum of $3,160 per month each,

THEREFORE, IT IS ORDERED that I. M. Writing, of Blackduck, Minnesota; Ima Expert, of Detroit Lakes, Minnesota; and Accurate Pennibs, of Thief River Falls, Minnesota, court reporters of the Tenth Judicial District, and each of them, shall be paid the sum of $3,160 per month, commencing January 1, 19--, and ending December 31, 19--; and that the apportionment of said sum of $3,160 per month for each of said court reporters shall be distributed to the respective counties of the Tenth Judicial District of Minnesota as follows:

Blackduck County	$ 495.22
Rosemont County	422.56
Franklin County	390.30
Madison County	376.92
Irondale County	354.60
Grasslake County	280.96
Alvorado County	220.54
St. Louis County	260.27
Clark County	170.75
Loon County	<u>187.88</u>
TOTAL	$ <u>3,160.00</u>

Dated this 1st day of January, 19--.

_____

HEAVEE HANDE

_____

RULING DAILY

_____

LIGHTLY SENTENCING

Judges of the District Courts

Keep with this form book operating manuals for computers, typewriters, copying machines, bursters, collators, and other such equipment.

Organize Your Mail

Organization should extend to handling of the mail, particularly if you are the judge's secretary.

Handle the mail the first thing in the morning as soon as it comes into the office. Put a date and time stamp on everything you receive in the mail—envelope and contents—for appeal time requirements are rigid. Many times counsel will try to assert untruthfully that they did certain things within the proper time, so protect yourself.

Lay all envelopes flat on the desk to slit them, and be careful not to cut any contents. Staple each envelope to the correspondence it came in. Note in writing on the correspondence any enclosures that are missing. Stack correspondence in order of importance, screening it carefully.

If correspondence mentions certain files or cases, put the pertinent folders or other materials with the correspondence. If the letter refers to a certain document or paper, clip that item with the correspondence to the top of the file folder to save the judge's time.

Keep a tickler file of things you note must be complied with from correspondence. Mark important dates on your big wall calendar. Type a suggested reply for any correspondence you can answer and have it ready for the judge's signature if you feel he or she would appreciate this. Recap points in a long letter on a typed page whenever possible if you are the judge's secretary, as this will save him or her much time.

Handle Outgoing Mail Competently

A court reporter does a lot of mailing, so have a postage scale handy to avoid placing excess postage on correspondence. Use third- and fourth-class mail for forms and supplies to save money. Remember these mailings are slower than first-class mail, however. Use regular postage on mail addressed to a post office box, as special delivery to post office boxes gets there no faster than regular mail.

Certified mail should be used instead of registered mail whenever possible since this costs less and the sender still receives a receipt and notice of delivery for the mail.

One ounce of mail is about three sheets of bond paper plus an envelope, so consolidate mail wherever possible. Minimize enclosures, attachments, and carbon copies. Staples, paper clips, stamps, and such all add to the weight of items mailed; in some instances using lighter weight material for large mailings will save money. Also, check the accuracy of your postal scale. Be sure to mark large manila envelopes as "First Class" when mailing them as such, or they may be sent as slower third-class mail.

If you use a postage meter, remember that incorrectly metered envelopes and tapes can be redeemed at 90 percent of face value.

Organize Copying

When you make a limited number of copies on a copying machine, turn the original over and start with the back page and move forward to the first page. As the copies come from the machine, distribute them in appropriate piles. When the last copy is made, the copies will be in proper order.

Use Good Telephone Techniques

During training every student should think seriously about his or her telephone image, because one of the first places this skill may be required could be in securing a job. Many times the school will receive a telephone call offering employment to a beginning reporter. The placement officer will request a student nearing graduation to speak to the potential employer on the telephone for the purpose of setting up an interview or making arrangements to report to work. Often students stutter, stammer, and seem so unsure of their ability that they present a very negative impression. They talk indistinctly, appear scared, and mutter or murmur.

When a member of a hiring firm or a judge, speaking to a person being interviewed for a position, asks, "Do you feel you can do a good job for us?" the response should not be "I don't know," or "I hope so." This is the time to sell yourself and make that caller know you can do the job and that you want it. Be professional and mature. You should be ready for work, or you should not be asking for a job.

First Telephone Impressions Are Important. Once you are employed as a reporter, your telephone skill can establish you as a professional. Find out right away how to answer the telephone, using an appropriate greeting. Always identify yourself immediately thereafter so there is no doubt in the caller's mind as to whom he or she is speaking.

Get to know as much as you can in a short time about office routine and business matters so that if you should be left alone in the office you can provide telephone information intelligently.

If you are requested to take care of something, do it to the best of your ability. Do not ask someone who has been there longer to do it. This includes matters you are asked to handle by telephone. You learn by doing.

However, do not try to assume too much authority in the beginning. A person who arrives and tries to take over is often unpopular. If those who are more qualified to answer the telephone are present, let them do it. If you must answer in the absence of a more knowledgeable person, do your best, and tell the callers you will have someone call back with the information you cannot supply. Always take time to get correct spellings of names and phone numbers.

Taking Messages for Others. When you take a message for another, write down the spelling of the caller's name and the caller's phone number (including the area code), the time of the call (including the date), and the full message. Repeat the name, address, number, and message to the caller. Message forms secured at any stationery store are handy for this purpose.

Keep a pad and pencil handy beside the telephone at all times, and if the message is too lengthy for a form, type up a note, date it, show the time the call came in, and initial or sign it.

Put All Messages Where They Will Be Seen Immediately. Tape every message to the intended person's desk light or telephone so it cannot get lost. If you place a note about a call on the person's desk, papers or other items may be placed on top of it before that person returns and it may be lost and not taken care of properly. You could be blamed. Get every telephone message to the right person as promptly as possible.

Use a Telephone Log. Some judges and freelance firms log incoming and outgoing telephone calls. All incoming calls are marked on 8½" x 11" ruled sheets, and as soon as a call is noted by the intended person reporting in from an assignment, he or she checks it off. This method eliminates the need for 3" x 5" message forms and slips of paper and avoids lost messages. Outgoing calls are also listed on the log as to time, place, person, number called, and case involved so that proper charges may be made.

Immediately upon completion of long-distance calls, you should call the operator to secure the time and charges. Mark them on your calendar and on the company log. When the bill arrives, you will be able to check and assign responsibility for all calls easily.

Handling Telephone Calls for Others. Most judges want their calls screened so they will know who is on the line. Always ask "May I tell (him or her) who is calling?" unless specifically instructed always to put certain prominent attorneys or certain other individuals, such as a wife or husband, through to them immediately.

Learn to recognize voices, as this will help greatly in handling callers. Some callers will not state their names or the nature of their calls to anyone but the person they wish to contact. In this case, tell the callers when the desired person is expected in and offer to take their names and numbers.

Do not give the number of a reporter who is out on assignment, as reporters do not receive calls during assignments except for emergencies. An emergency might be that you accidentally locked your toddler in the bathroom before you left. He turned on the water in the bathtub and flooded the whole downstairs. Meanwhile, your spouse might be calling to tell you that through the keyhole they had observed that the child is now playing with a razor and a locksmith cannot be reached but you have a key in your purse. Anything less is not an emergency.

If you answer the telephone and the reporter or judge requested is away for a lengthy time, ask if there is anything you can do, but do not disclose the whereabouts of the individual unless you have been instructed to do so.

Again, if a reporter is reporting depositions in your deposition room, do not interrupt the deposition for telephone calls. Carefully take the message and give it to the reporter at the end of the deposition. If you can estimate the time he or she will be free, give the caller this information.

Do Not Forget When You Put Someone on Hold! Sometimes a call may be made for a person who is on another line or momentarily tied up. Ask the caller if he or she wishes to hold the line. If the person called is not soon available, get back to the caller and explain the delay. Keep checking back every few minutes so the caller does not feel he or she is hanging there unnecessarily and that no one cares. Never, never forget that you have someone on hold on the line.

Develop the Right Tool for Telephoning: Your Voice

You must develop a pleasant voice: well-modulated, clear, distinct, and loud enough to be understood easily at all times. Your telephone voice and usage of the English language will cause the person on the other end of the line to judge the efficiency and competence of your office, so think and give intelligent, courteous responses at all times. "Please" and "thank you" should be used wherever possible since everybody likes to hear these words.

Keep Your Personal Life Out of the Office

Do not tie up office or courthouse phones with your personal calls except in emergencies. There are times when late hearings, deliberating juries, and extended depositions will justify personal calls. You may be working long hours on rush jobs and simply have to use the business telephone to transact some personal business at your office. You should not, however, carry on long, extended personal calls on a business telephone.

Secure a Telephone Credit Card

A telephone credit card is essential if your work involves much travel and telephoning back and forth to your office, home, and attorneys. These items are particularly handy in those instances where an individual cannot secure change for pay telephones and in cases of emergency.

Outline Lengthy Phone Calls before Dialing

When you have business calls to make which require that you cover several points, write down the topics you must discuss in advance to avoid unnecessary conversation and wasted toll call costs.

Answer the Telephone Promptly

Always answer your telephone at the first ring if possible, as it is most annoying to a caller to be kept waiting and to those in your office who must hear the repeated ringing. Then, too, an attorney at the other end may be trying to get through to set depositions. If so, he or she may simply dial another firm. That competitor may get the work and, perhaps, the client.

Remember, Time Zones Differ

When you telephone long distance numbers, keep in mind differences in time zones. If you do not take time differences into consideration, you may create enemies.

Respect Others' Privacy

Do not give information to anyone who is not known to you regarding anyone's whereabouts, telephone number, address, business, or reporting work. If you are the judge's reporter, give no information to newspaper people or outside parties at any time over the telephone, or face to face, unless you have been instructed to do so by the judge.

Learn to Arrange All Types of Calls

A court reporter must know how to place all kinds of calls, from station-to-station to conference calls.

The number to call for local directory assistance is 1-411. For information for towns and cities within your own area code, call 1-555-1212. For information on numbers outside your area code, dial 1-area code-1212. You can often save money by finding out if a company or a government agency has a toll-free line. Dial 1-800-555-1212 to secure this information. Learn to dial calls by direct long distance to save money and learn how to make all types of travel reservations by telephone.

If the judge asks you to put through a call to a certain person for him or her, make sure the judge is on the line or close at hand when you have reached the other person; it is rude to subject anyone to lengthy waits under such circumstances.

Use a Desk Telephone Directory

Your desk telephone directory can be a real timesaver. The handiest ones are open semi-circular alphabetical card files which can be flipped to the correct letter in an instant. Some reporters prefer a book-type system of keeping their most-used numbers. Today, there are hand held calculators that can have most-used numbers programmed into them.

Your personal telephone directory should contain names, addresses, and telephone numbers of attorneys; judges; probation officers; clerks of court; welfare workers; vendors of office supplies; repairpeople for all types of machines; the judge's wife or husband; reservation clerks for airlines; officers of Bar and judicial associations; NCRA; home and office phone numbers of other reporters, as well as yours and the judge's if you are an official; local and state reporting organizations; doctors; dentists; banks; and insurance dealers and adjusters. It is also handy to list in your personal desk telephone directory the numbers for the weather and time of day.

The judge's reporter will find it helpful to list such things as his or her social security number, birthdays, anniversaries, and special occasions he or she might like to be reminded of.

Extension System Telephones

If your office is served by an extension system of telephones, when you place an outside call, always listen before dialing when you pick up the telephone to be very sure the extension is not in use.

General Telephoning Tips

After you dial any number, wait at least ten rings or one full minute for an answer. Nothing is more annoying than to get to the instrument only to have it stop ringing as you pick it up!

Dial very, very carefully. When you must have the operator secure a number for you, speak distinctly to avoid getting a wrong number. If you should reach a wrong number, be polite to the person called in error. If you detect a strange voice in answer to your call, ask, "Is this 234-5678?" Apologize if you have a wrong number, and consult the directory again. Call the operator for help if the number seems to correspond with what you have called.

Sometimes you will receive a wrong number call. Be courteous to the person calling no matter how busy you are. Say pleasantly, "I am sorry. There is no Elmer Zanisziewsklitski here. Were you calling 741-3246?" This technique will prevent the person's dialing you a second time.

Use Names and Titles of People. It is a form of flattery that builds ego to call people by their own names and any titles they possess, for there is no one who is not enamored of the sound of his or her own name. Get to know those you have frequent contacts with so you can greet them by name and title at the start of telephone conversations. Use their names and titles at intervals during calls, but not to the point of affectation.

In business calls, do not call judges, attorneys, or other business people by first names until you are well established with them, as this might label you as assuming and unprofessional.

Learn to Handle Information Searches. When you have to spend quite some time looking up information requested by callers or checking records of cases, explain why you have to leave the telephone. Ask if you may call back instead of letting the person at the other end of the wire wait there for a period of time. Be careful how you lay the receiver on the desk as you leave to secure the needed facts.

Always Keep Your Lines of Communication Open. When you leave your office, always notify the person who takes incoming calls where you will be, how long you expect to be there, and when you expect to be back. Get an answering service or home answering device if you transact matters at home if someone is not present to handle your business matters. An answering service or device is essential if you run a one-person office or travel extensively. Above all, if you use a home telephone for business matters, get a separate number for the family and children to use.

Display Courtesy When Others Are on the Telephone. At times you may be typing or printing out when an associate or the judge will answer a telephone near you. Cease doing noisy work unless you are doing a rush job or have a backlog that does not allow you to waste even a minute. However, if you pay workers by the hour, instruct them to continue to work under all circumstances unless you tell them to stop for reasons of economy.

When there is a great deal of noise outside and another person is on the telephone, close doors or windows that may be open to block out as much noise as possible. Be polite when you must cut off a wordy conversation by saying, "Thank you for your help. Goodbye." However, do not give any person the impression that you are cutting them off or being abrupt or curt with them.

If a person you call on the telephone is out, suggest a convenient time for a return call. Then, be in your office at that time to take the call when it is returned.

Do Not Quote Prices by Telephone. Never quote a price to anyone for work over the telephone unless you immediately type a confirming letter so there can be no later disagreement.

When my husband was a very new official, he received a telephone call from an attorney requesting a price for a transcript. He quoted $550 as the cost, and the attorney wrote a letter ordering the transcript, not mentioning the cost. When the lawyer looked at the bill upon delivery of the transcript, he insisted the price quoted was $300.

It had a reasonably happy ending because the judge called both men into his chambers at the next hearing that attorney had before him. He said, "How long have you been a lawyer?" to which the man admitted to over 20 years. Then the judge said, "Then you certainly know no case lasting that long could cost under $500, and I expect you to pay my reporter in full for his bill before you attempt to try another case before me because I know this reporter well enough to take his word."

The attorney grumbled a bit and wrote out a check. However, he held a grudge for some time. This situation could have been avoided.

Put a Smile in Your Voice and Win Business. Your telephone personality will give callers many first, middle, and last impressions, so put a smile in your voice, be sincere and friendly, and be efficient. Determine that each and every telephone call you make or receive will lead to many, many more calls asking your firm or you to do more of your excellent work.

Reporting by Telephone

You may be requested to take in shorthand telephone statements between two people or conferences carried on among several parties over the telephone. Even depositions are taken by telephone. There is an attachment for the telephone so both your hands may be free, and there are new speaker phones which project the spoken voice, both of which allow you to listen and write at the same time. Type the matter taken just as any other transcript, and make your certificate conform to the situation. Conferences, of course, are held by telephone by many companies these days to save travel expenses; and these, too, are typed in regular form.

Telephone Books are Great Reference Volumes

Telephone directories, both residence and yellow pages, will provide you with much necessary information—ZIP codes for your state on a map in the front of the directory, postage rates for different classes and weights of domestic and foreign mail, time zones, sample long-distance rates, emergency numbers, information on where to secure any product or service, and numbers to call for information. You can check spellings of names and addresses and occupations and much more, so collect all the telephone books you can.

Use Safety

Safety in your office will affect your efficiency:

1. Keep wastebaskets where persons cannot step in them or fall over them. Do not leave file and desk drawers open or telephone wires and extension cords where anyone can trip over them.

2. Don't climb on chairs with casters to secure materials from bookshelves or lean too far back in a swivel chair. Hold handrails on steps, and don't run down steps.

3. Do not place very heavy objects on top of a file cabinet, as they may topple. Arrange supply cabinets so things don't fall off when you remove items from the shelves.

4. If you handle or sort lots of paper, wear a fingerguard and pick up paper at the corners to avoid paper cuts.

5. Use a moistener to seal envelopes to avoid cutting your tongue.

6. Keep lighted cigarettes away from wastebaskets to avoid fires. Be careful to put out all cigarettes and confine them to an ash tray which is not near anything combustible. Better yet, do not allow smoking in your office.

7. Do not carry pens, pencils, or scissors with the points outward. Fold the legs on your tripod while carrying your machine. Store sharp objects such as pins, needles, nails, and razor blades so they cannot damage anyone.

8. Do not plug or unplug electric machinery with wet hands.

9. Turn a light on immediately upon entering a dark room so you do not trip over misplaced chairs or other objects.

10. Do not place heavy books near the edge of table or desk to fall on your foot or your machine.

Tab Your Directories

Place index tabs on your large city telephone directories and legal directories. Indexing these frequently used sections can save you time when you have to look up names, addresses, and numbers. You can flip the book open to the proper place quickly.

Prepare a Reporter's Survival Kit

Every reporter should keep a survival kit in a top drawer of his or her desk. This should contain names and addresses of people who can transcribe notes in case of lengthy illness, disability, or death. It should also include the system of writing and computer tips on special topics and the school the reporter attended, plus unusual brief forms made up by the reporter. This should include information about the reporter's insurance, pension plan, annuities, property, securities, stocks and bonds, will (particularly where it is located), and other data which might be of help to others in an emergency.

Chapter 17

The Role of the Court Reporter in Pretrial Matters

Pretrial Conferences

Pretrial conferences are held in courts of record (those having a regularly assigned court reporter) to decrease the backlog of cases through settlements.

Once the court calendar is printed, a day is set down for pretrial conferences. On that day the lawyers representing both sides of each case, or their representatives, appear after receiving notice from the clerk, bringing all proof necessary to make out a prima facie case. In personal injury cases, a plaintiff's attorney is expected to bring all bills and proofs of damages, plus medical reports in triplicate so the court and opposing counsel will be informed as to extent of injuries, claims, and permanency of injuries.

The Court Reporter at a Pretrial Conference

The court reporter is usually required to record important parts of the pretrial conferences. Some judges ask that the court reporter be present to report each and every matter to be discussed and to write up a summary of each case for the court's consideration and information.

The court clerk also maintains a record of what transpired during these conferences and marks off the calendar those cases which are settled, stricken, or ordered continued by the judge.

It usually takes about a half hour to complete each pretrial matter. A number of stipulations are often dictated. The reporter must take these and transcribe them for the records, although the judge often directs counsel to prepare stipulations and motions in typewritten form and present them for his or her signature within a stated time.

The judge may order depositions taken by one or both parties to a lawsuit at the pretrial conference.

Delaying Tactics May Be Used by Attorneys. Many attorneys come to the pretrial conference held in a case to move for continuance. The trial judge must consider the reasons for such requests and decide whether dilatory tactics are being used, denying continuance when delay of the trial is not merited.

Pretrial Order. Figure 46 on page 154 shows a typical Pretrial Order, which is normally placed on a legal-sized page to allow room for disposition to be entered. The court reporter is frequently required to fill in these forms for the court.

FIGURE 46
Pretrial Order

PRETRIAL ORDER

Pretried by Judge _____
(Type Name)

on (date) _____

N O T E
First determine if the case is to be transferred to the County District Court as provided in Rule 4:3-4.

PRETRIAL CONFERENCE PROCEDURE

Recite specifically ALL of the following items, in sequence, identifying each subject by the numeral assigned below. If no statement is to be made upon a subject, type "NONE" after the identifying number.

1. A concise descriptive statement of the nature of the action.
2. The factual contention of plaintiff as to liability of defendant.
3. The factual contention of defendant as to non-liability and affirmative defenses.
4. The admissions or stipulations of the parties with respect to the cause of action pleaded.
5. All claims as to damages and the extent of the injury, and admissions or stipulations with respect thereto.
6. Any amendments to the pleading made at the conference or fixing the time within which amended pleadings shall be filed.
7. A specification of the legal issues raised by the pleadings, as amended to be determined at the trial.
8. A specification of the legal issues raised by the pleadings but now abandoned.

9. A list of exhibits marked in evidence by consent.
10. If leave is granted for further discovery by way of additional interrogatories, depositions or otherwise, state such fact and any time limit for completion thereof. Such leave at this stage is undesirable, and should be granted only in the most exceptional cases.
11. Any limitation on the number of expert witnesses.
12. Any directions for the filing of briefs.
13. State the order of opening and closing to jury, when a consolidated action or an action including third-party suit, counterclaim, cross-claim, or where there are several plaintiffs or defendants separately represented by counsel.
14. Any other matters which have been agreed upon to expedite disposition of the matter.
15. Estimated length of trial.
16. Weekly call or trial date.

_____ COURT, _____ COUNTY, _____ DIVISION

Docket No. _____

Plaintiff

vs.   Calendar No. _____

Defendant

The parties to this action, by their attorneys, having appeared before the Court at a pretrial conference on the above date, the following action was taken:

1.

Chapter 18

Grand Jury, Preliminary Examinations, and Coroner's Inquests

As an official or freelance reporter, you may be asked to report grand jury proceedings or preliminary examination hearings at some time in your career. These proceedings are held to determine whether a person should be held for hearing on criminal charges in a trial court.

Grand Jury Proceedings

When a grand jury decides there is conclusive evidence of guilt sufficient to try an individual, an indictment is issued.

Grand jury hearings are secret.

A felony case may also be brought to trial upon the filing of an information by the District Attorney, but no reported hearing is held in these cases.

Function and Composition of the Grand Jury

A grand jury is selected from the citizenry for the purpose of investigating and determining whether there is sufficient evidence to charge a person with a criminal offense by means of an indictment and bringing that person before the trial court.

The number making up a grand jury varies, but it is usually 23 jurors with 12 to 16 members required for a quorum. In large cities, several grand juries may be meeting at any given time. In some places, a grand jury is chosen for an entire term of court, whereas in highly metropolitan areas a given grand jury may serve for only one month. Grand jury members may be held over to complete any cases not finished at the end of their term.

The grand jury members consider all business brought before them by an elected public officer, who may be called the prosecutor, the prosecuting attorney, the state's attorney, the city attorney, or the county attorney.

Procedure of Grand Jury

The presiding judge administers the oath to the grand jury members in the courtroom and appoints one of their members as foreman, or presiding officer, during their deliberations. The grand jury is then instructed as to the law and their duties and responsibilities by the judge, which is the reverse order of that followed in the trial courts. The court reporter normally reports the charge, but it is not usually transcribed.

Following the judge's charge, the jurors are taken to the grand jury room by the bailiff (in state court) or deputy marshal (in federal court) to hear the testimony regarding the cases in which indictments are sought by the presiding official. Upon entering the grand jury room, the reporter is sworn as the official reporter and sworn to secrecy by the secretary of the grand jury.

Grand jurors are either seated at long tables with the witness seated beside the reporter or in a horseshoe with the reporter placed between the heels of the horseshoe close to the door. The foreman usually sits at the head of the horseshoe.

After the reporter has been sworn by the secretary of the grand jury, the prosecuting officer makes a brief statement about the case and the witness or witnesses to be presented. The reporter takes this stenographically but does not transcribe such matter.

The foreman of the grand jury calls the witnesses by summoning the clerk from the outer room by buzzer or bell to present each witness. The foreman or clerk will swear the witness, using a Bible if required, as in New Jersey and New York. Then the prosecuting officer will ask a number of questions regarding the matter under consideration, after which the grand jurors will question the witness.

Readbacks may be requested when grand jurors do not understand testimony or when they wish to have a point reviewed to assist them with further questioning.

When each witness is excused, it may be the custom for the reporter to leave the room with the witness so discussion may occur secretly. In some places, however, it is customary for the presiding officer merely to say "Off the record," and allow the reporter to remain seated to save time. Sometimes the court reporter will be called back in during deliberations of the grand jury to read testimony in part or in whole of any or all of the witnesses called for questioning.

Grand jury proceedings can be very formal occasions in cities where the presiding officer begins the questioning, which is followed by questioning by the grand jury members. Or, they can be informal meetings in small places where jurors' questions are scattered all through the testimony.

Questions by the Grand Jurors

When all the questioning by the grand jury members follows questioning of the prosecuting official, many reporters margin the words:
BY THE GRAND JURY:
When questioning by the jurors is scattered within the interrogation by the presiding officer, it is satisfactory to preface the questions in the transcript as follows:

A Grand Juror: You said you paid him $75, or agreed to pay him?

The Witness: Yes, sir.

Reporter's Transcript

At the end of a grand jury session, the reporter should request the exhibits and documents referred to during the proceedings to use for assistance in transcribing. He or she should also determine at this time how many copies are needed and by whom.

The defendant may apply to the judge of the court in which an indictment is presented to have a copy of the transcript of the grand jury record. The reporter charges the statutory rate for such a transcript. An example of a page of grand jury transcript is shown in Figure 47.

Justice Reporters

In some large cities, the prosecutor's office hires a number of reporters, who come under the classification of "Justice Reporter," and they are either pooled or assigned to a certain examiner for a given term. In the U.S. District Court, they are often hired on a contract basis by the United

FIGURE 47
A Page of Grand Jury Transcript

```
1   Q    Did you have access to this information or not, or

2   did Mr. Carr keep that information to himself?

3   A    At one time we had a running account of the bank

4   deposit for the payroll account; but, of course, during

5   the last few days there wasn't any.

6             MR. FREESE:  Are there any further questions

7   of this witness?

8   BY THE GRAND JURY:

9   Q    Is the payroll week ended on a Saturday?

10  A    Yes.

11  Q    In other words, there was a work week, but they did

12  not get paid until the following week?

13  A    That's right.

14  Q    Both of these banks have a service charge for checks

15  returned.  Were those charges made for these returned checks?

16  A    Yes.

17  BY MR. FREESE:  Tell us how much Bob Carr was paid for his

18  salary.

19  A    I think it was $150 a week.

20            A GRAND JUROR:  Was Bob Carr authorized

21  to sign checks of the corporation?

22            THE WITNESS:  Not to my knowledge.

23            A GRAND JUROR:  Who did the typing of the

24  information on the checks?

25            THE WITNESS:  Most of it was done by hand.
```

States Attorney. The method of payment under these circumstances varies widely, being on a per diem basis in some instances and salary basis in others.

Preliminary Examination

A justice of the peace, a judge, or a magistrate presides over Preliminary Examinations, which are hearings held to decide either that sufficient evidence exists to order an accused person held for trial in a higher court within the jurisdiction or that the person should be ordered dismissed.

If sufficient evidence is presented by the prosecution in a preliminary hearing to make it seem that there is probable cause to believe that the person who is the subject of the hearing committed the alleged crime, he or she is bound over to face trial.

There is no jury present during a Preliminary Examination. In large municipal courts, assigned reporters regularly take and transcribe these proceedings.

Preliminary Examination Procedure

Preliminary Examinations follow regular trial procedures as far as direct and cross-examination of the prosecution's witnesses, and the defendant seldom presents any witnesses.

FIGURE 48-A
Appearances

```
 1                          No. 366,890
                           No. 366,891
 2

 3   THE STATE OF TEXAS)              IN THE JUSTICE COURT
                       )
 4      -vs-           )          PRECINCT  NO.  O N E
                       )
 5   MICHAEL W. LEE and)          HARRIS COUNTY, TEXAS
     ELMER A. LEE      )
 6

 7                   A P P E A R A N C E S

 8   FOR THE STATE OF TEXAS:

 9              NATHAN MORTENSON, ESQUIRE
               Assistant District Attorney
10             Harris County, Texas

11   FOR THE DEFENDANTS:

12             HARVEY ATKINSON, ESQUIRE
               Attorney at Law
13             429 Vining Street
               Houston, Texas  77009
14
               PRELIMINARY EXAMINATION
15

16             At an examining trial held on the 12th day

17   of December, A.D. 19__, in Houston, Texas, before the

18   Honorably Harry A. Irwin, Justice of the Peace, the following

19   proceedings were had and testimony adduced:

20                     H. R. WILSON

21   was called as a witness by the State and, having been first

22   duly sworn by the Court, testified as follows:

23                   DIRECT EXAMINATION

24   BY MR. MORTENSON:

25   Q    State your name, please, sir.
```

Ordinarily there is no opening statement from either side, and no jury instructions are given. Occasionally defense counsel may make what may be termed a short closing argument in behalf of his client.

At the end of the testimony, if the defendant is ordered held over to a higher court, the presiding officer will read a form holding order naming the offense, the defendant, and bail assessment. This order is kept in the file and may be secured by the reporter to compare with the shorthand notes, as such papers are usually read very rapidly when there are a number of cases to be read.

Typical Preliminary Examination Transcripts are found in Figures 48-A-G.

FIGURE 48-B

1   A   H. R. Wilson.

2   Q   How are you employed, Mr. Wilson?

3   A   Houston Police Department.

4   Q   And were you so employed on November 2nd of this year?

5   A   Yes, I was.

6   Q   About that time, on that date, did you meet two brothers

7   named Michael Wayne Lee and Elmer A. Lee?

8   A   Yes, sir, I did.

9   Q   Do you recognize those men in Court today?

10   A   Yes, sir. The gentlemen at the end of the table

11   (indicating).

12   Q   All right. Where was it you met these men, Officer?

13   A   It was in the 5600 block of Yale.

14   Q   And what was the occasion on which you met them?

15   A   We were on routine patrol. We observed their vehicle

16   northbound on Yale Street, and it appeared to have expired

17   dealer's tags.

18   Q   You stopped them and talked to them about the tags?

19   A   Yes, sir.

20   Q   Did anything unusual happen while you were talking?

21   A   Yes, sir. As I approached the right side, one of the

22   defendants appeared to be stuffing a paper bag under his

23   seat.

24   Q   Under the seat that he was sitting on?

25   A   Yes, sir.

FIGURE 48-C

1   Q   Would that be the passenger or the driver?

2   A   Passenger.

3   Q   Which one was the passenger?

4   A   The gentleman in the brown coat.

5   Q   That's Michael Lee?

6   A   Yes, sir.

7   Q   Did you make a search of the vehicle?

8   A   Yes, sir, I did.

9   Q   And what, if anything, did you find?

10   A   I found inside the paper bag four plastic baggies

11 containing a green, plant-like substance which, in my opinion,

12 was marijuana.

13   Q   Did you place the defendants under arrest?

14   A   Yes, sir.

15   Q   Did you find anything else?

16   A   We found one glass pipe in the console of the vehicle.

17   Q   What kind of car was this?

18   A   If I'm not mistaken, a 1990 Chevrolet.

19   Q   You didn't charge them with paraphernalia or anything?

20   A   No, sir.

21   Q   Just marijuana?

22   A   Yes, sir.

23   Q   And you charged them with the marijuana that you found

24 under the seat of Michael Lee?

25   A   That's correct.

FIGURE 48-D

1 Q   Did you search their persons?

2 A   Yes, sir, I did.

3 Q   Did you find anything on their persons?

4 A   We placed Michael Lee in the vehicle after I found

5 the marijana in the bag. He stated to me, "I have one bag

6 in my pocket."

7 Q   Did you check this out?

8 A   He handed it to me.

9 Q   Did you find anything on Elmer?

10 A   No, sir.

11 Q   Did you find any evidence to connect Elmer Lee any

12 closer than you've already testified?

13 A   Yes, sir. He stated that he and his brother had

14 bought the marijuana together.

15 Q   Elmer did?

16 A   Yes, sir.

17   MR. MORTENSON: Pass the witness.

18   CROSS-EXAMINATION

19 BY MR. ATKINSON:

20 Q   Officer, with regard to the tags, how did you determine

21 that they were probably outdated?

22 A   They were faded and were too faint; you could barely

23 read the numbers.

24 Q   When you got out of the car, did you check that

25 first?

FIGURE 48-E

```
 1   A     My partner did.

 2   Q     Were they outdated?

 3   A     No, they were not.

 4   Q     Had you already gotten to the side of the car?

 5   A     Yes, sir, I had.

 6   Q     In other words, when you got out, it was your main

 7   objective to go check the dealer's tags, or was it to

 8   check the occupants?

 9   A     To approach the car, as the passenger of the vehicle

10   was making several movements.

11   Q     He started making these movements before you got out?

12   A     Yes, sir.

13   Q     Is it true, Officer, that the statement was made out

14   there by Michael Lee that he possessed the marijuana and not

15   his brother?

16   A     No.  That's not true.

17   Q     You didn't find any marijuana, as you've earlier

18   testified, on Elmer Lee?

19   A     That's correct.

20   Q     Did either of the boys offer any resistance?

21   A     No, sir.

22   Q     They were courteous and polite, were they?

23   A     That's true.

24   Q     Evidently you didn't have to conduct a search?   They

25   went ahead and gave the marijuana to you?
```

FIGURE 48-F

1   A   That's correct. I patted them down as they got out

2   of the car for weapons.

3   Q   Did you take them to the Houston Police Department?

4   A   Yes, sir.

5   Q   Did you search the boys there?

6   A   Yes, sir, we did. Upon placing them in jail, we

7   searched them.

8   Q   The marijuana that you had previously found was the

9   only marijuana found; is that correct?

10 A   That's correct.

11 Q   And all of this was under the right-hand side where

12 Michael had been sitting?

13 A   Four baggies were, and one was in his pocket.

14 Q   And Elmer didn't have any in his pocket?

15 A   No, sir.

16   MR. ATKINSON: That's all.

17   THE COURT: I find probable cause, and they

18 will be bound over.

19   (Whereupon, at 2:55 p.m., Court was in

20   recess in this matter.)

21

22

23

24

25

FIGURE 48-G

```
 1                              NO.  366,890
                                NO.  366,891
 2

 3   THE STATE OF TEXAS ⁜              IN THE JUSTICE COURT
                         ⁜
 4      -vs-             ⁜              PRECINCT  NO.   O N E
                         ⁜
 5   MICHAEL W. LEE and ⁜               HARRIS COUNTY, TEXAS
     ELMER A. LEE        ⁜
 6

 7

 8

 9              I, Justin Accurate, Official Court Reporter,

10   hereby certify that the foregoing _____ pages comprise a

11   true, complete and correct transcript of the proceedings

12   had at the Preliminary Examination in the above-styled

13   and numbered cause had in said Court on the date stated

14   above and recorded in machine shorthand by me.

15              WITNESS MY HAND this the ___ day of December,

16   A.D. 19__.

17

18                              _____
                                JUSTIN ACCURATE
19                              Official Court Reporter

20

21

22

23

24

25
```

Coroner's Inquests

Reporters are also called upon to report coroner's inquests, which are examinations to determine the cause of death. The coroner, the jury, witnesses, a defense attorney or attorneys of other interested parties, and perhaps the district attorney will be present. However, no corpse will be there. The principal witness will usually be the doctor who performed the autopsy.

A reporter who takes coroner's inquests must have a good knowledge of medical terms, although it is possible for the reporter to secure a copy of the written report for reference.

Chapter 19 *Jury Selection*

The official reporter should check with the judge as to just what he or she will be required to report prior to trial. In some jurisdictions it is mandatory for the court reporter to report everything. Fortunately, in most others, the judge calls him or her in when required. In capital cases the official reports everything from the impaneling of the jury on, including all motions, arguments and ruling on motions, opening statements, final arguments, jury instructions, and verdict.

Occasionally a lawyer will anticipate possible error in voir dire that is not normally reported and will request the reporter to take it. Customarily, that attorney is billed per diem and the statutory page rate for the transcript in such event. It is good for the reporter to warm up by taking the voir dire even when not required to record it in shorthand, but if you do so, take it in earnest because you may be asked to transcribe it. It does save time if you always take the voir dire because when objections are made to questions, answers, or handling of the matter by the judge, any of which may afford grounds for appeal of the case, you have to back up the proceedings to make a record if you have not been taking the voir dire.

General Questioning in Courtroom

Before the attorneys begin questioning the venire, they often make a few introductory remarks before their interrogation. These remarks are not the opening statements of the attorneys. Sometimes the entire venire will be seated out in the courtroom and questions will be asked of the whole group with responses from one or a few prospective jurors being given. In this case, the reporter often has no way of identifying the particular jurors unless the attorney calls them by name or if the reporter knows them, as he or she would in a smaller county seat. Voir dire means "to speak the truth." It is easier when taking voir dire examinations of the jury simply to designate the person speaking as "A Prospective Juror," but many counsel representing defendants want more than that, and in capital cases that will certainly not be sufficient. One solution is to refer to each by number; for example, "Prospective Juror No. 3," or "P.J. 3," and refer to the list later for identification. If this is too cumbersome, the voir dire may simply be recorded as Q and A in ordinary cases, which eliminates the necessity of identifying the prospective jurors, especially when the court or counsel address them by name.

As the selected jurors are seated in the jury box, secure the name of each juror. Have with you a diagram of 12 seats, and mark the names in the proper boxes. It helps always to have copies of the jury list with you to keep track of those challenged and those selected.

Generally speaking, as each juror is called to the jury box to be examined, the clerk will read his name and address. As he does so, each attorney and the court have in front of them a big sheet of paper with at least 18 squares. As the first person is called, his or her name and address is written in Square No. 1. As the interrogation proceeds, the person's occupation and other salient points are filled in.

Usually, before interrogation begins, the first 18 chairs are filled. If a juror, such as Prospective Juror No. 3, Mr. Jones, says he is related to the plaintiff and does not think he can serve, the court will excuse him, and he will leave the box. Everyone then draws a line through his name, one more name is selected, and that person takes Seat No. 3. As others are dismissed, the same procedure is followed. Jurors excused for such reasons are "challenged for cause."

Finally, attorneys on each side exercise what is called in law their "peremptory challenges," for which no reasons need be given. The attorneys strike potential jurors alternately, and as their names are stricken, those persons step down from the jury box which holds 12, and the Court will assign the remaining six by name to certain seats.

The reporter uses the same type sheet as the court and counsel. As any name is called, he or she uses the same procedure as they do, writing in the proper box the person's name. When someone steps down, the reporter strikes the name by drawing a line through it on the sheet. Then, throughout the entire voir dire examination and the rest of the trial, anytime a juror speaks up, the reporter simply glances at his chart, notes the name of the juror sitting there, and indicates it in his notes.

In the excitement of getting a jury in a hurry and, thus, getting on with the business of trying the case, attorneys often question prospective jurors without ever using their names. Glance down at your chart, and you will have the name every time. To save time, attorneys also ask what is called a "shotgun question" such as: "If any member of the panel has ever had an accident, will you please raise your hand?" About six hands will go up all over the jury box. You will be lucky to note seat numbers, let alone the names, but do not panic. The attorney will come right back and interrogate them one by one, and you have the names on your chart.

Importance of Precise Reporting

Many times after a verdict comes in, counsel on either side has the right to subpoena the whole jury to return to court. There, questions are asked as to what transpired in the jury room, and the attorneys will have had the official transcribe all the voir dire examination showing their answers to questions before being accepted for jury duty.

They sometimes find jurors were not quite honest in their answers or failed to divulge something that might have had an impact on their acceptance as a juror. The court rules on whether such answers were vital and on whether the jury discussions were proper. In some cases the court may grant the losing party a new trial as a consequence of what the voir dire transcript revealed. For this reason, it is important to get the proper name affixed to what was said.

As has been pointed out before, judges and reporters work together as a very efficient team. Reporters learn how the judges operate, what they like and dislike. Judges also learn how to make life easier for their reporters, and they will cooperate fully.

If you have a good working relationship with the judge, suggest to him or her, before voir dire examination starts, that it would enable you to make a much better record if he or she would call each prospective juror one by one to the witness stand and let him or her testify as to his or her qualifications. If the judge will go along with your idea, reporting the voir dire will be easy. This procedure does not in any way hold up the jury selection.

If you were not required to be present during voir dire examination or any other matter, be sure to indicate in your notes that you were not. The judge's trial docket on the bench in which he keeps a running account of the trial will then show that the jury was impaneled and sworn and that each side made its opening statements, and so on.

Questioning in the Various Court Levels

In the U.S. District Courts (federal courts), it is customary for the attorneys to prepare lists of questions they want asked on voir dire. Then the judge conducts the jury voir dire, allowing the attorney to make additional inquiry or to submit further questions.

In the State District Courts, Circuit Courts, and County Courts, it is usual for the lawyers to do the voir dire questioning. In that event, the attorneys will have found out all they could about the veniremen and venirewomen and will have prepared their questions well in advance of every case.

Selection of Alternate Jurors

Alternate jurors are selected in the same manner as the 12 original jurors from the panel. An alternate juror is essential in long, important cases to prevent disqualification of a juror because of illness or accident being unable to serve. Alternate jurors sit in the front row of the spectator's section of the courtroom.

Challenges to the Prospective Jurors

Two types of challenges may be made to a prospective juror: (1) peremptory challenge and (2) challenge for cause. Each party is allowed an unlimited number of challenges for cause, which are challenges for which some reason is stated. Each side is entitled to a certain number of peremptory challenges for which they need to give no reason. If there are several parties, the court may allow additional peremptory challenges.

Peremptory challenges should be exercised immediately, but attorneys often wait to dismiss a juror, fearing the effect this will have on others on the panel. However, challenges for cause are normally made at the time the cause becomes apparent. The judge will then rule on the challenge.

If the judge overrules the challenge for cause, the objecting attorney usually must exercise a peremptory challenge to prevent having a prejudiced juror on the jury panel. The reporter should keep track of peremptory challenges and challenges for cause and chart the jury as it is seated. Put a "P" over the peremptories on your list and a "C" over those excused for cause.

Attorneys may make objection to the entire venire. This is called a challenge to the array. I once reported a case wherein an American Indian was being tried for crime, and the attorney representing him proved no Indian had ever served on a jury in that county; therefore, his rights were not guaranteed. The names of some Indians, in proportion to their number in the general population, were placed in the jury wheel, and a new panel was drawn before whom the trial was held.

Sequestration of the Jury

After the jury is sworn, if the court reporter is not regularly assigned to the court, the judge may administer an oath to the court reporter. Jurors are usually allowed to pursue their normal outside activities when court has adjourned for the day, but the judge may confine a trial jury to hotel rooms overnight in capital cases or when other reasons may justify such action.

Recess Admonishment to Jury Panel

At each recess period for lunch or overnight, the judge will instruct the jury somewhat in the following fashion:

Example
"Members of the jury, we are about to recess at this time for lunch (or until tomorrow morning). You are instructed not to discuss this case among yourselves nor

with anyone else, nor permit anyone to discuss it or any phase of it in your presence. If anyone should attempt to violate my rule regarding this, please report it to the court. Neither should you read anything in the newspapers regarding this case or watch anything about it on TV until your verdict has been handed to this Court."

Miscellaneous Information

Chapter 9, *Goldstein's Trial Technique*, Volume 1, provides good background material regarding jury selection. A number of standard questions asked in civil and criminal cases are included, starting with Section 9.80.

Chapter 20 *Arraignments and Sentences*

Types of Pleas

The hearing at which a person accused of a crime is brought before the Court to enter a plea to charges contained in the counts of an indictment is called an arraignment.

The accused may plead "guilty," "not guilty," or (where permitted) "nolo contendere," which means "no contest." In a plea of nolo contendere, the defendant indirectly admits guilt and throws himself or herself on the mercy of the court. Should any defendant stand mute at arraignment, the court will enter a plea of "not guilty."

When a defendant enters a guilty plea and is adjudged guilty by the court, sentence may be pronounced immediately or the case may be set for later hearing and a presentence investigation may be ordered to allow probation if merited by the accused's background and lack of criminal record.

Many defendants "cop a plea" (plead guilty), or plead nolo contendere, feeling that the judge will give a lighter sentence than a jury would because of the saving of taxpayers' dollars spent to try the case, and in consideration of the defendant's honesty.

The Official Transcribes All Pleas and Sentences

As official reporter for a judge officiating over criminal matters, you will be responsible for taking in shorthand and transcribing pleas and the sentences meted out by the court.

Today, plea and sentence transcripts are prepared on 8½″ × 11″ ruled and numbered paper, which will have a line an inch and a quarter from the left edge of the paper and 3/8 of an inch from the right edge of the paper. About two spaces should be left on each side of the ruled margin, and all typing should be kept within the lined edges. Originals of arraignments, rearraignments, and sentences are filed with the proper clerks of court, and copies are provided the attorneys involved.

On occasion it will be necessary to type sentences immediately at the close of a hearing so that the transcript may be available upon commitment. It may seem difficult for you to turn out a rush transcript while the prisoner sits in your office, perhaps handcuffed to the sheriff or deputy waiting to transport him or her to the penitentiary. Here, however, is an opportunity to show your excellent transcription skills. Take your time and carefully proofread each page before you remove it from the typewriter and again at the end of the whole transcript. Keep your mind strictly on what you are doing, and do not engage in conversation with the people waiting or anyone else while preparing such a transcript.

Format of Pleas and Sentences

Transcripts of pleas and sentences are normally set up as colloquy unless a prolonged examination by the court takes place, in which place you may head that portion "EXAMINATION BY THE COURT:". Whenever the defendant speaks, the remarks are prefaced by "THE DEFENDANT:" instead of the name. The letters are typed in solid caps, followed by a colon. When counsel speak, their remarks are prefaced by their names in solid caps, as "MR. SMITH:" as in any other colloquy.

When the judge of any court speaks, designate his or her words by "THE COURT:", and others who interject any remarks, answers, or information are indicated by title in solid caps followed by a colon, as "DEPUTY COURTROOM CLERK:", "PROBATION OFFICER:", and so on.

Title Page of Pleas and Sentences. The title page lists venue, indictment or information number, style of the case, and designation of the case, as ARRAIGNMENT, REARRAIGNMENT, or SENTENCE. Under the title box, the location and date are typed. The judge presiding is listed, and the appearances of counsel are placed on the title page. The reporter's name and title is shown at the bottom right-hand side of the title page.

Reporter's Certificate. At the end of each such transcript, the reporter appends the proper certificate. A notary seal need not be impressed over the signature of an official reporter because the official's authority is not secured through that office.

Sentences

The reporter must listen carefully to be sure whether the sentence is served concurrently or consecutively in the event there are several charges (counts to the indictment) because concurrent sentences are served at the same time, while consecutive sentences are served one after another.

The Penal Code for each state lists possible sentences for each offense. You may have to do checking there because sentences seem to be given rapidly, and you must be totally accurate in taking the term, as people's lives and liberty are affected by your transcripts of these matters. Of course, the courtroom clerk and the judge also take notes, but do not depend upon someone else to have these things right as this is your job. You are the protector of the record!

An example of a typical sentence is shown in Figures 49A–F. Always remember the form may vary somewhat in your jurisdiction and study carefully such a sample form before transcribing your arraignments and sentences out on the job.

It should be noted here that the certificate on matters heard in the United States District Courts (Federal Courts) is placed on the title page of the matter as shown on Figure 50.

FIGURE 49-A
Sentence

```
 1              COUNTY COURT OF NEW JERSEY
 2              LAW DIVISION : JUSTICE COUNTY
 3              INDICTMENT NO. I 173 M 80
 4   STATE OF NEW JERSEY,          :
 5        Complainant,             :
 6             -vs-                :       S E N T E N C E
 7   ANGELO CAGGIATORE,            :
 8        Defendant.               :
 9   -----------------   Litigationville, New Jersey
10                       Thursday, August 31, 19--
11   B E F O R E:
12        HONORABLE SHOWING MERCIE
13        Judge, County Court
14
15   A P P E A R A N C E S:
16        I, WRACKEM UPP, ESQUIRE,
17        Procesutor, Justice County, New Jersey.
18        HABEAS CORPUS, ESQUIRE,
19        Attorney for the Defendant.
20
21
22
23
24                     TURNEM OUTTE ACCURATELY
25                     Official Court Reporter
```

FIGURE 49-B

```
 1       THE COURT:   State of New Jersey
 2   versus Angelo Caggiatore.
 3       Mr. Caggiatore, do you have the
 4   services of an assigned counsel?
 5       THE DEFENDANT:   That is right, your
 6   Honor.
 7       THE COURT:   Who is he?
 8       THE DEFENDANT:   Mr. Corpus, your
 9   Honor.
10       THE COURT:   Are you satisfied with
11   the advice he has given you?
12       THE DEFENDANT:   Are you talking to
13   me?
14       THE COURT:   Yes.
15       THE DEFENDANT:   Yes, sir.
16       THE COURT:   You, of course, have had
17   explained to you your rights as to trial by
18   jury, have you not?
19       THE DEFENDANT:   Yes, sir.
20       THE COURT:   And you have previously
21   waived your right of trial by jury?
22       THE DEFENDNAT:   Yes, sir.
23       THE COURT:   I will give you the
24   right of trial by jury if you desire it now.
25   Do you want it?
```

FIGURE 49-C

```
 1          THE DEFENDANT:  Sure.
 2          THE COURT:  Do you now want to have
 3    your case tried by the jury?
 4          THE DEFENDANT:  I am pretty sure I
 5    do.
 6          THE COURT:  I would suggest that we
 7    take a recess and you talk to your counsel.
 8          (Recess taken.)
 9          THE COURT:  You are having a tough
10    time understanding me; is that right?
11          THE DEFENDANT:  Yes, sir.
12          THE COURT:  Do you want me to have
13    this matter brought on before a jury?
14          THE DEFENDANT:  Well, I would like
15    to get it over with today, if I could.
16          THE COURT:  Has your attorney
17    explained everything to you?
18          THE DEFENDANT:  Yes, sir.
19          THE COURT:  Are you satisfied with
20    the services which this attorney assigned by
21    the Court has rendered to you?
22          THE DEFENDANT:  Yes, sir.
23          THE COURT:  Mr. Caggiatore, I have
24    a report from the New Jersey State Diag-
25    nostic Center.
```

FIGURE 49-D

```
 1          The sentence of this Court is that
 2    you, Angelo Caggiatore, be confined to New
 3    Jersey State Prison for a term of not less
 4    than one year and not more than two years.
 5          The sentence is hereby suspended,
 6    and you are hereby placed on probation for
 7    a period of three years.
 8          This action is subject to your
 9    agreeing to comply and your compliance with
10    the standard conditions of probation which
11    have been adopted by this Court and which
12    are on file with the Clerk of the Court,
13    and also with the special conditions of
14    probation which may be ordered by this Court
15    now or in the future.  A copy of the rules
16    and regulations of the Probation Office will
17    be provided you by the Probation Department
18    following this hearing.
19          In your case, the following special
20    conditions are imposed:
21          That you attend the Justice County
22    Guidance Clinic for treatment, and you are
23    to attend the Justice County Guidance Clinic
24    as such time or times as they will call you.
25          The Probation Officer will explain
```

FIGURE 49-F
Reporter's Certificate

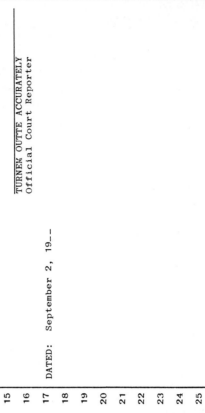

```
 1
 2
 3
 4
 5
 6
 7              REPORTER'S CERTIFICATE
 8
 9      I, TURNEM OUTTE ACCURATELY, an Official Stenographic
10  Reporter for the County of Justice, State of New Jersey, do
11  hereby certify that the foregoing is a true and accurate
12  transcript of the proceedings as taken stenographically by
13  me at the time and place aforementioned.
14
15
16                      TURNEM OUTTE ACCURATELY
17  DATED:   September 2, 19__        Official Court Reporter
18
19
20
21
22
23
24
25
```

FIGURE 49-E

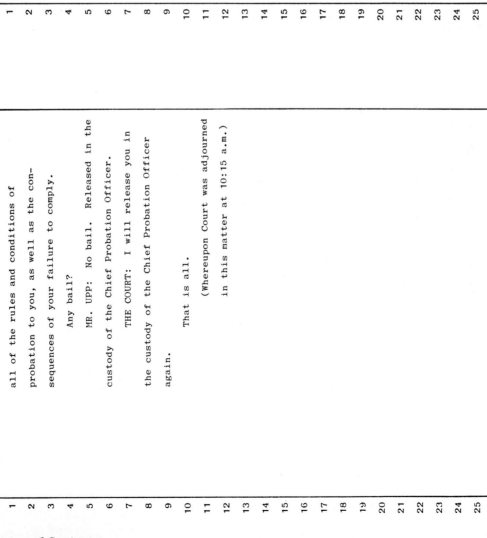

```
 1  all of the rules and conditions of
 2  probation to you, as well as the con-
 3  sequences of your failure to comply.
 4      Any bail?
 5      MR. UPP:  No bail.  Released in the
 6  custody of the Chief Probation Officer.
 7      THE COURT:  I will release you in
 8  the custody of the Chief Probation Officer
 9  again.
10      That is all.
11      (Whereupon Court was adjourned
12       in this matter at 10:15 a.m.)
13
14
15
16
17
18
19
20
21
22
23
24
25
```

FIGURE 50
Sentence Title Page

```
 1          IN THE DISTRICT COURT OF THE UNITED STATES

 2             FOR THE SOUTHERN DISTRICT OF TEXAS

 3                    GALVESTON DIVISION

 4

 5   UNITED STATES OF AMERICA)
                            )
 6          -vs-            )        CRIMINAL NO. G-82-1
                            )
 7   WILLIAM HARVEY WOODSON, )
     HAROLD OTIS SMATHERS,  )
 8   OSCAR HARRISON, ELBERT )
     GROVES, and MARK MILTON )
 9
                            SENTENCING
10

11       BE IT REMEMBERED that beginning or commencing at

12   1:25 p.m. on the 5th day of March, 19__, at Galveston, Texas,

13   the above-entitled matter came on for hearing before the

14   Honorable John Johnson, United States District Judge, and

15   the following proceedings were had.

16       I HEREBY CERTIFY that all oral proceedings were

17   reduced to writing by me by means of machine shorthand and

18   were thereafter placed in typewritten from under my direc-

19   tion, and that the following pages represent a full, true,

20   and correct transcript of my Stenotype notes.

21

22

23                        RIGHT THERE WRITING
                          Official Court Reporter
24                        Room 892, Post Office Building
                          and United States Courthouse
25                        Galveston, Texas  77550
```

Chapter 21

Reporting Motions

Types of Motions

Some judges hold a regularly scheduled Motion Day for general motions, at which time the reporter is required to be present and record all proceedings in shorthand. Other judges keep their own notes of all except the most important motions presented outside of regular court sessions.

Motions may range from those addressed to the most simple topics, such as continuance of a case, to highly technical matters where the court reporter reports material totally foreign to his or her knowledge. There are, however, a number of motions that are often made; knowledge of some of these is a help to the reporter.

Motion in Limine

Motions in limine are made at the outset of a trial in an attempt to suppress damaging or inadmissible evidence the other side may want to use. Such motions ask the court to prevent opposing parties, their counsel, and their witnesses from presenting some evidence until its admissibility is decided upon outside the hearing of the jury.

Motion for a Bill of Particulars

A defendant's attorney frequently makes a motion for a bill of particulars when the plaintiff in a civil or criminal case has claimed the cause of action in a vague, general, or indefinite manner.

Motion to have Claimant Medically Examined

Defense attorneys often make a motion to have a claimant examined by an impartial medical expert in a personal injury case because many cases can be settled as a result of such an examination or, at least, if the case is not settled, defendant's counsel can prepare adequately to refute the medical testimony if the motion is granted.

Motion for Change of Venue and Motion to Disqualify a Judge

Motions for a change of venue are routine when a case has had widespread publicity and it does not appear a defendant can secure a fair trial in the place of original jurisdiction. Now and then an attorney representing a client will make a motion that the judge appointed to sit on a certain case be disqualified because of suspected bias or prejudice.

Motion for Continuance of Case

Be prepared to take many motions made by lawyers requesting continuances of cases due to substitution of counsel, unavailability of witnesses, military service of parties or witnesses, absence of material evidence which can be procured in the future if continuance is granted, and so on. Sometimes continuances are set by the court's own motion.

Motion for Amendment of Pleadings

Counsel may make motions for amendment of the pleadings including addition or deletion or parties to an action or severance of defendants from jointly tried cases.

Motion for Summary Judgment

If, during preparation of a case, it becomes apparent to either party that there is no real issue of fact to be decided at trial, a motion for summary judgment may be made requesting the court to grant judgment in favor of the party filing the motion. It is usually accompanied by affidavits or answers to discovery stating undisputed facts which entitle the party to a judgment in his or her favor. The party filing such a motion has the burden of proving there is no genuine issue of fact in dispute, and the opposing party has time to respond. The court usually holds a hearing on such a motion, and if the court determines there is no fact issue, judgment is granted for the moving party. If the motion is not granted, the case is then tried on its merits.

Motion to Dismiss for Want of Jurisdiction

This is a defendant's motion to dismiss the case because he or she feels the court does not have authority to hear or decide the case.

Motion to Dismiss for Lack of Prosecution

A defendant's motion to dismiss for lack of prosecution may be made after a case has been on file for a long period of time with no action on the part of the plaintiff's attorney to prepare it for trial.

Motion for Nonsuit

This is a plaintiff's motion which requests the court to dismiss the case either with prejudice or without prejudice. In some jurisdictions it is called a voluntary dismissal. When such a motion is granted without prejudice, the plaintiff may later refile the same action; but if the case is dismissed with prejudice, the plaintiff cannot again file the same cause of action. In federal court, this motion is called a motion for dismissal pursuant to Rule 41 of the Federal Rules of Civil Procedure.

Motion for Protective Order

This is a motion filed in response to some action by the opposing side asking the court to take some action. For instance, such a motion can be filed regarding a notice to take a deposition if the distance involved in travel or shortness of time of the notice makes it difficult or impossible for deponent or attorney to appear at the time and place of the deposition. It may also be used when interrogatories are oppressive or when requests for production are unduly burdensome.

Motion to Compel

This motion is filed to require the opposing party to perform some act, such as to answer interrogatories or produce documents in accordance with a motion for production. If this motion is not responded to or action performed, it is set for hearing, and the court may impose sanctions, including an order that the act be performed. If the order is not obeyed, the disobedient attorney may be held in contempt of court or his or her pleadings may be wholly or partially stricken or removed by the court, and money penalties may be assessed.

Counsel may make a motion at any time before a case comes on before the court requiring a party to produce at trial such items as medical reports, hospital records, letters, correspondence, documents, plats, charts, diagrams, sketches, surveys, insurance policies, photographs, accounting records, and testimony from previous trials.

Motions are also made to secure a list of planned witnesses, production of confessions, transcripts of grand jury testimony, police reports, and statements of witnesses. Likewise, motions are made to suppress materials contained in an illegal search and seizure, confessions illegally secured, and other improper evidence.

Motion for Writ of Habeas Corpus

A common motion is made for a Writ of Habeas Corpus inquiring into the reason for detention of a defendant and securing release if the holding is illegal.

Motion to Dismiss Complaint

At the end of a plaintiff's case, and again at the end of the entire case, a motion is routinely made in many cases to dismiss the complaint or for judgment to be had based upon such arguments as (1) that the plaintiff has wholly failed to establish negligence on the part of the defendant, (2) that contributory negligence was exhibited on the part of the plaintiff, (3) that the accident complained of was not the proximate cause of injuries alleged, (4) that the evidence is insufficient to base the complaint upon, (5) that the indictment is incorrectly worded, and so on. These motions are denied by the court in almost every instance.

Motion for Mistrial

Motions for a mistrial occur (1) when counsel is guilty of misconduct, (2) when a juror becomes ill and no alternate was appointed or due to inability of a material witness or party to continue on the witness stand, or (3) when other misconduct occurs. Mention of insurance will cause a motion for mistrial. (See Figure 51A, 51B, and 51C on pages 178 through 180.)

Motion to View Premises

During trials request may be made by counsel to have the jury view an alleged arson scene or hazardous intersection where a collision occurred or other premises, when the ends of justice may be thus served.

Motion for a New Trial

After a case has been tried, and the verdict is in, it is customary for defense counsel to make motions requesting a new trial and/or, in the alternative, setting aside the verdict in the matter as excessive or not supported by the facts. These motions are almost universally denied unless the judge is convinced that a gross miscarriage of justice has prevailed. (See Figure 52 on page 181.)

FIGURE 51-A
Motion for A Mistrial

1   NO. 837,458

2   WILLIAM J. McNAMARA, +   IN THE DISTRICT COURT OF
                          +
3   Plaintiff, +   HARRIS COUNTY, T E X A S
                          +
4   -vs-   +   174TH   JUDICIAL DISTRICT
                          +
5   JOHNSON CORPORATION, +
                          +
6   Defendant. +

7

              DEFENDANT'S MOTION FOR MISTRIAL
8

9   Comes now defendant at approximately 10:00 a.m.

10   on the morning of Wednesday, the 22nd of October, 19_ _,

11   and following receipt from the jury of their third note

12   indicating irreconcilable conflict, respectfully moves the

13   Court to discharge the jury herein and respectfully states

14   that in the light of the statements contained in the three

15   notes that have previously been sent in by the jury, the

16   first one having been sent in at approximately 2:50 p.m.

17   on Tuesday afternoon, in which the jury indicated they

18   were eleven to one on Issue No. 6 and unable to resolve

19   that issue (reference hereby being made to the first note

20   for its contents); thereafter the jury, at approximately

21   4:15 p.m. on Tuesday afternoon, sent in their second note

22   stating that they were eleven to one on Issue No. 7 and

23   ten to two on Issue No. 12, and stating that they had

24   considered the evidence and had repeatedly been over the

25   Court's instructions, and they could not seem to resolve

FIGURE 51-B

1 the issues (reference being made to such note of the jury

2 for its full contents); and the jury having now sent in

3 their third note to the Court on Wednesday morning at

4 approximately 9:45 a.m., in which they advise that they

5 are still eleven to one on Issue No. 7 and ten to two on

6 Issue No. 12 and advise that they have considered all the

7 evidence and have been over the Court's instructions many

8 times and are unable to resolve the issues (reference

9 hereby being made to the contents of such third note from

10 the jury for the contents thereof); and the jury having

11 started their deliberations at 10:00 a.m. on the morning

12 of Tuesday, after having briefly retired following the

13 submission of arguments on Monday afternoon, and having

14 deliberated all day Tuesday, and now being in their second

15 day of deliberations; and in the light of the clear and

16 unequivocal statements that there is a conflict or impasse

17 in the jury as to Issue No. 7 and Issue No. 12, which

18 cannot be resolved although they have reviewed the evidence

19 and the Court's charge many times in an attempt to do so,

20 it is respectfully urged and submitted to the Court

21 that any further requirement that such jury deliberate

22 or any further instructions that they continue to do so

23 would, in effect, constitute coercion of the jury and an

24 indication of a compulsion that they must resolve such

25 conflict even though they have clearly indicated on

FIGURE 51-C

1 three occasions that they cannot do so.

2   WHEREFORE, defendant respectfully moves the Court to

3 discharge the jury herein and not compel them to remain in

4 deliberation when they have made it clear on three separate

5 occasions that they cannot resolve such differences after

6 repeated efforts and studies of the evidence and the Court's

7 charge.

8

9

10

11

12

13

14

15

16

17

18

19

20

21

22

23

24

25

FIGURE 52-A
Motion for A Judgment N.O.V. N.O.V = non obstante vere-
dicto (notwithstanding the verdict)

1	UNITED STATES DISTRICT COURT
2	SOUTHERN DISTRICT OF TEXAS
3	
4	JAMES A. HILL, ET AL. ◊
5	◊ Plaintiffs, ◊
6	◊ -vs- ◊ C. A. No. 81-H-2478
7	◊ BEECH AIRCRAFT COMPANY, ◊
	A CORPORATION, ◊
8	◊ Defendant. ◊
9	
10	DEFENDANT'S MOTION FOR JUDGMENT N.O.V.
	OR ALTERNATIVELY FOR A NEW TRIAL
11	
12	TO THE HONORABLE JUDGE OF SAID COURT:
13	Comes now defendant, Beech Aircraft Corporation,
14	and files this Motion for a Judgment Notwithstanding the
15	Verdict or in the alternative for a new trial, pursuant
16	to Rules 50 and 59 of the Federal Rules of Civil Procedure;
17	and in support thereof would show as follows:
18	I.
19	There was no credible evidence to support the jury's
20	finding of a defect in the fuel cell in question. In fact,
21	there was no evidence of any kind to the effect that the
22	fuel cell in question was unreasonably dangerous if the
23	aircraft was flown according to the proper warnings and
24	instructions contained in the flight manual therefor. The
25	facts developed during the trial were so strongly and

FIGURE 52-B

```
 1   overwhelmingly in favor of defendant on this issue that
 2   reasonable men should not arrive at a verdict of "defect"
 3   in this case.  Under those circumstances, a judgment in
 4   favor of the defendant notwithstanding the jury verdict
 5   should be entered herein.
 6                           II.
 7        There was no credible evidence to support a finding
 8   that the design of the fuel cells in question was the cause
 9   of the accident in this case.  The only evidence introduced
10   on this issue which specifically related to the facts of
11   this case demonstrated that the fuel in the fuel cells will
12   not unport under the flight conditions as testified to by
13   the pilot.  Under these circumstances, the evidence is of
14   such quality and weight that reasonable and fair minded men
15   in the exercise of impartial judgment could only reach the
16   conclusion that a defect as alleged by plaintiffs was not
17   the cause of this accident, and the Court should enter a
18   judgment notwithstanding the verdict of the jury hereon.
19                           III.
20        Even if the Court were to find that there was sufficient
21   evidence in the record to permit an inference to support the
22   jury's findings, the verdict is against the clear weight
23   and preponderance of the evidence and would result in a
24   miscarriage of justice if permitted to stand.  Under these
25   circumstances, the Court should grant a new trial on the
```

Motions Often Heard in Camera or Outside Hearing of Jury

Many motions and lengthy arguments upon them are presented during recesses or in chambers before court sessions outside the presence and hearing of the jury members.

The court reporter must be very careful to show this fact in the transcript by a proper parenthetical because a mistrial or overturning of a verdict could result from having the jury shown as present at such times.

Reporting Argument on Motions

My good friend Dick Mowers has supplied some fine advice regarding reporting of argument on motions which I will pass on to you here:

"When reporting argument on motions, use the same cardinal rule which applies to anything that is read in court or during a deposition from a document: TRY TO GET THE DOCUMENT.

"Generally speaking, in arguing a motion, each attorney has prepared well in advance of trial what he calls a Trial Brief. This contains all the legal propositions and case citations that can possibly come up during the trial.

FIGURE 52-C

```
 1  issues of defect and causation, as well as the defensive
 2  issue asserted thereto.
 3      Wherefore, premises considered, defendant urges this
 4  Court to grant its motion for a judgment notwithstanding
 5  the verdict or in the alternative to grant a new trial in
 6  the above case.
 7
 8
 9
10
11
12
13
14
15
16
17
18
19
20
21
22
23
24
25
```

"Sometimes the court has received copies from each attorney in advance of the trial. In arguing other motions at other times, the good attorneys will always have prepared a brief on the law supporting their contentions. The court will have these in his office, also.

"Getting whatever is read from is so much quicker than trying to dig it up months later when you are getting out the transcript." To which I say, "Amen!"

Chapter 22

The Official Reporter's Worksheet

No reporter should ever enter a hearing room or courtroom without a proper worksheet to record the essential information required to produce the transcript should one be required. Figure 53 shows a type of worksheet used by many official reporters, although many others have been developed. You may prefer to prepare one to suit your own purposes after you have been reporting for some time.

You should never enter your Courtroom Procedures class or internship assignment without a worksheet because it is essential that you learn to get down all information in an orderly fashion before you work in a courtroom.

Contents of a Worksheet

The official reporter's worksheet provides a place for the clerk of court's file number regarding the case at hand, date the reporter took the matter, term of court, judge before whom the matter was heard, title and venue of the case, appearances of counsel for both sides, exhibits, witness listing, and arbitrary abbreviations, such as "H-RT" for "Houston Rapid Transit." This last item may not seem too important the day the matter is reported, but six months or a year later when the reporter receives an order for transcript, this information may be vital.

The back of the worksheet may also be used for arbitraries, extra appearances, and words the reporter verifies with witnesses and counsel during the take, at recesses, and at the end of each day. It also should contain any unusual words, correctly spelled, that the reporter writes down while dictating to a transcriber, if such is still done. On the back of the information sheet, information may also be listed regarding interested parties sitting at counsel table, such as the government agent in Federal Court drug cases, welfare workers, insurance company representatives, and so on.

Securing Information for the Worksheet

Sometimes you will be aware of information for part of the worksheet in advance because of your close association with the clerk and the judge. Always be in the courtroom at least 15 minutes early to secure and fill in any information you can and to get set up ready to write.

The judge should keep an orderly court and announce the style of the case at the start of the session and have attorneys state their appearances. You should always know the venue.

Take the appearances very carefully because substitute counsel are often sent in to replace another firm member. Write all this in your notes and transfer it at an appropriate time to your worksheet.

FIGURE 53
Worksheet

WORKSHEET

No._____ Date_____ Term_____ Judge_____
Title_____
_____
_____
_____

APPEARANCES

Plaintiff   Defendant
_____   _____
_____   _____
_____   _____
_____   _____

EXHIBITS

Plaintiff	Ident.	Evd.	Defendant	Ident.	Evd.
P-1			D-1		
P-2			D-2		
P-3			D-3		
P-4			D-4		
P-5			D-5		
P-6			D-6		
P-7			D-7		
P-8			D-8		
P-9			D-9		
P-10			D-10		
P-11			D-11		
P-12			D-12		

WITNESSES

Plaintiff	Direct	Cross	Red.	Rec.	Defendant	Direct	Cross	Red.	Rec.
1.					1.				
2.					2.				
3.					3.				
4.					4.				
5.					5.				
6.					6.				
7.					7.				
8.					8.				
9.					9.				
10.					10.				
11.					11.				
12.					12.				
13.					13.				
14.					14.				
15.					15.				

Arbitrary Abbreviations and Spellings:

File Worksheet with Notes and Case Lists

At the end of each hearing, wrap the worksheet about the shorthand notes of the proceeding and secure it with elastic bands. Write the date, case title, venue, and number of packs of notes enclosed therein on top of the covering worksheet. Place all computer cassettes and disks with this. Place in large letters the date on ends of the pack or packs of notes enfolded therein for easy location of required notes for transcription or reference in chronologically filed stacks.

Worksheets are often placed on legal-sized paper to accommodate all notations. It is well to take several with you into the courtroom to be prepared for extra long cases or several matters which occur within a given session.

In busy courts, such as criminal court in a metropolitan city, where you may take many arraignments, pleas, and sentences in a day, or in domestic relations court where many matrimonial matters come up in a session, the clerk of court provides the reporter with the case list (docket sheet) for the day. The reporter marks the ones not heard and beside them numbers the order in which those heard occur. These case lists show case number, name, and expected appearances, but these, again, may be changed by the firm concerned.

One of these case lists is wrapped around the reporter's notes with the worksheets for larger cases, and the extra copy is placed on a wall clipboard or in a file for ready reference should transcript be ordered of any of the small matters. Attorneys ordering transcripts in any of the minor suits furnish date of trial, and the reporter pulls notes for the day to provide a transcript. Should you work in this situation, be sure to put a brightly colored card where you remove notes as suggested before.

If you are called upon to report a portion of a case another reporter has worked on, secure copies of the information sheets the former reporter kept and any docket sheets or other forms, which preceded your tenure. It would be a nice courtesy for you to do the same for other reporters.

To save time, a large number of information sheets should be printed up and a good stock maintained at all times.

Chapter 23 *Reporting During the Trial*

After the jury has been impaneled and sworn, the attorneys for both sides of the case may make an opening statement to the jury, which is really a sales talk outlining their theory of the case and telling what they expect the evidence to show.

The reporter is not allowed to interrupt counsel during their opening statements, which sometimes tends to present a problem because counsel walk about, sometimes becoming very confidential with the jury, turning their backs on the reporter, other counsel, and the court.

Before the opening statements, many reporters move their chairs next to the jury box in order to hear better. This is also done during summations at the end of the case. You must always insist on sitting where you can hear clearly everything that transpires.

Plaintiff's attorney is afforded the first opportunity to speak to the jury. If he or she feels the facts are strongly in favor of his or her client, the making of an opening statement may be waived.

Next, the attorney for the defendant may make an opening statement, or he or she may waive the privilege and elect to make a statement at the close of plaintiff's case in chief before presenting his or her direct evidence.

If there is more than one defendant, each counsel will be given a chance to make an opening statement on behalf of his or her client. The amount of time allotted to each opening statement may be set in advance by agreement of court and counsel.

More and more judges are requiring officials to report opening statements, although these are included only in transcripts of first-degree felonies unless requested by ordering counsel to be included in the transcript of the statement of facts.

Opening statements, again, are a good way for the reporter to "warm up," and, again, if objections are made, the reporter does not have to back everyone up and have the objectionable portion restated in order to have a complete record.

A common objection made during opening statements is that the remarks of counsel are inflammatory in nature and calculated to inflame and prejudice the jury.

During opening statements lawyers will make gestures and demonstrations toward the jury, and they often present figures and charts on large pads of paper on an easel or show enlarged diagrams or photographs and models to present points. Try to copy these charts and figures as they are often helpful later in getting out the transcript.

If the defendant's attorney has a good strong case, a good opening statement will often weigh heavily in his favor.

Attorneys may tell the jury in their opening statements that the judge will instruct them in a certain way concerning the law later on in the case, but what an attorney says about the law does not govern. Opening statements of the attorneys are not evidence, and trial lawyers usually make no attempt to discuss the law in any detail during the opening statements.

Opening Statements in Nonjury Cases

Many cases which are technical in nature are tried directly by the court with no jury because the average layperson could not follow the facts sufficiently to render a proper verdict.

In nonjury cases, opening statements are particularly important because the judge may not have had a great deal of time to study the case, and the opening statements will give him or her a better perspective of the case.

Transcription Format of Opening Statements

If the official is requested to record and transcribe the opening statements, per diem and page rates are normally charged for this service according to the custom in the reporter's locality.

Many reporters use wider margins in transcribing solid material such as opening statements, but since they seem to flow along, it seems preferable to give a full page of transcript to attorneys on all transcripts as this engenders good will. A few pages are involved at best. An example of an opening statement transcript is shown in Figure 54A through Figure 54E.

Parenthetical Expressions Regarding Opening Statements

When opening statements are not ordered in a transcript an appropriate parenthetical expression should be placed in the transcript:

> (Mr. Cliffhanger made an opening statement
> on behalf of the plaintiff.)
> (Mr. Cringing waived making an opening
> statement on behalf of the defendant.)
> (Mr. Cautious reserved making an opening
> statement on behalf of the respondent.)

Trial

After selection of a jury, preliminary motions, and the opening statements have been disposed of in a civil or criminal trial, the plaintiff's attorney will present, in order, all witnesses on whom he or she will rely to establish the facts of his or her case and all physical evidence (exhibits) which support the allegations.

The exhibits will ordinarily first be identified by the witness. Then, they are offered in evidence when they have been authenticated by testimony of a witness or witnesses, although sometimes exhibits are identified, offered, and received at the same time. Many exhibits may be identified but never received into evidence.

Setting up the Witness

At the beginning of each witness's testimony, the transcript heading is set up as follows. It is important to show by whom the witness was called.

FIGURE 54-A
Opening Statement

```
 1              OPENING STATEMENT

 2               BY MR. DUVALL

 3

 4       May it please the Court, Counsel for the defendants,

 5   ladies and gentlemen of the jury, the Government and

 6   Grand Jurors for the Southern District have indicted these

 7   three people who are on trial today.

 8       There is one Count of Conspiracy and there are two

 9   Counts of Possession of Marihuana, Possessing Marihuana

10   with Intent to Distribute.  There are two Counts against

11   one of the defendants, Juan De Dios Garza, for Possession

12   of Marihuana.

13       To the Indictment, the defendants have each plead

14   not guilty, which puts the burden upon the Government to

15   prove its case to you beyond a reasonable doubt.  Each of

16   these essential elements of the Government's case must be

17   proved to you beyond a reasonable doubt.

18       The Conspiracy Count:  At the heart of the conspiracy

19   is an agreement.  Two or more people must get together and

20   agree to do something to violate the laws of the United

21   States.

22       In addition to the agreement to go out and do something,

23   they have to do something in furtherance of that agreement.

24   In other words, talking is not enough.  They have to

25   actually go out and do something in furtherance of it.
```

Example

I. SAWE ITT,

a witness called on behalf of the defendant, having been first duly sworn by the Clerk of Court, was examined and testified on his oath as follows:

DIRECT EXAMINATION

BY MR. SICKIMM:

Q: What is your full name?

A: I. Sawe Itt.

Setting Up Witness Appearing in His or Her Own Behalf

If the witness who is to testify is either a plaintiff or a defendant in the case, the heading may read as follows:

FIGURE 54-B

```
 1      Now, the thing that they have to do does not have
 2   to be illegal in itself.  The thing that they do in
 3   furtherance of the conspiracy --
 4              MR. ALFARO:  Just a minute.  Would your
 5   Honor instruct the jury on the law?  I think this is beyond
 6   the realm of an opening statement.
 7              THE COURT:  I will tell them.
 8      Go ahead.
 9              MR. DUVALL:  So, the burden is upon us
10   to show there was a conspiracy and that there were some
11   overt acts committed in furtherance of that conspiracy.
12      Now, it is not necessary, of course, as the Judge
13   will instruct you at the close of the case, for the
14   Government to prove every overt act of the Indictment, so
15   long as there has been an overt act.  The overt act that
16   you find may not even be named in the Indictment.
17      If you find that there has been an overt act, of
18   course, the Government has met its burden of proof.
19      The agreement that we are talking about does not have
20   to be a formal agreement, a contract that they made.  You do
21   not have to all gather around and sign a piece of paper
22   and say, "Each of us is going to violate the law."  The
23   agreement can be inferred from the acts of the defendants.
24   They met and certain acts followed.  When two or more are
25   joined to form a conspiracy, then one of those two can go
```

Example

REE SISTING,

called as a witness on her own behalf, having been first duly sworn by the Clerk of Court, was examined and testified on her oath as follows:

<u>DIRECT EXAMINATION</u>

<u>BY MR. QUASH:</u>

Q: What is your full name, please?

A: Ree Sisting.

Order of Examination

Each witness brought forward by the plaintiff is first questioned by plaintiff's counsel on direct examination and is then cross-examined by defense counsel. The direct examination and cross-examination are followed by redirect examination and recross-examination should further questioning be deemed necessary by counsel, and repeat examinations are then titled FURTHER REDIRECT EXAMINATION and FURTHER RECROSS-EXAMINATION.

FIGURE 54-C

```
1   out and other members can be brought into the conspiracy.
2   In other words, all of the members of the conspiracy don't have
3   to know each other, and they do not have to have all sat
4   down together at one time, at one place, and reached an
5   agreement.
6        In this particular case, the Government expects to
7   prove -- and I will go over the witnesses very briefly
8   with you -- we expect to prove by the testimony of two
9   unindicted co-conspirators that we readily admit to you that
10  they were knowingly involved in this marihuana transaction
11  themselves.  We wish that we could bring you Sunday School
12  teachers and outstanding citizens from the community to
13  testify in cases like this --
14              MR. ALFARO:  I object, your Honor.
15              THE COURT:  Sustained.  Don't argue it now.
16  That is argument, and you can argue that later.  Just tell
17  them what you expect to prove.
18              MR. DUVALL:  We will bring before you as our
19  first witness Lloyd George Griffith from Florida, who came to
20  Texas to buy some marihuana, he and a man named Manuel
21  Alcorta.  They stayed in the Edinburg and McAllen area.
22  Alcorta made some contacts.  They went to Rio Grande City,
23  or in the vicinity of Rio Grande City, to a little community
24  called Alto Bonito and made an agreement to purchase some
25  marihuana.  They wanted to buy about 200 pounds.
```

Interrupted Testimony of Witness. The testimony of a witness may be interrupted by the hearing of the Court of another unrelated short matter or by a lunch break or by adjournment. In such a case, set the witness up again as follows:

Example

URA MEANTOMEE,

resumed the witness stand and testified further on her oath as follows:

<u>DIRECT EXAMINATION</u> (Continued)

Parentheticals Excusing Witness. When the questioning of a witness has been completed, the following parentheticals should be inserted in the transcript, depending upon whether the witness has been excused or merely interrupted:

(Witness excused.)
(Witness temporarily excused.)

Voir Dire Examination of Witness. During examination of a witness, opposing counsel may ask to conduct voir dire examination to establish competency or qualification of the witness to

FIGURE 54-D

```
1        Contact was made with Mr. Flores -- he is one of the
2   defendants in this case -- and Flores made the arrange-
3   ments with the first contact.  He didn't have it.
4        They went to Juan De Dios Garza, another defendant
5   in this case, and he had the marihuana.
6        The middleman in the case was Jose Gilberto Munoz,
7   another unindicted co-conspirator, who will testify in the
8   case.  He was the middleman between Griffith and Juan
9   De Dios.
10       The deal was set up.  They took the pickup that they
11  were riding in from Florida and went to Alta Bonito and
12  they locked at a sample of the marihuana.  They saved the
13  sample, and they want to Juan De Dios Garza's home, where
14  the marihuana was loaded in a false compartment of the
15  pickup truck; and the defendant, Juan De Dios Garza, helped
16  load the marihuana in that pickup.
17       They left those premises and were headed north on
18  281 south of the Falfurrias checkpoint of the Border Patrol
19  where there was a check of the vehicle because of the odor
20  of marihuana which was observed.  They saw the false com-
21  partment in the truck, as a result of which Mr. Griffith
22  and his friend were arrested.
23       Mr. Griffith, at that point, became a cooperating
24  individual for the Government.  He told them fully and
25  freely all that had transpired.
```

testify concerning some subject or exhibit to prevent improper evidence from being placed on the record. You will set this up as follows:

Example

VOIR DIRE EXAMINATION

BY MR. HEARTENSOUL:

Plaintiff's Case in Chief Concluded. When all plaintiff's witnesses regarding the case in chief have been examined by both sides, the plaintiff will make the announcement "The plaintiff rests." It is very important that this fact be noted in the reporter's record.

As soon as the plaintiff rests, in many instances, a motion to dismiss the case is made by defendant's attorney, which motion is usually denied by the court. An example follows:

MR. TRYFULLY: The plaintiff rests.

MR. PUSHEM: At this time we move to dismiss the complaint on the grounds that the plaintiff has failed to establish her cause of action and that the plaintiff has failed to prove freedom from contributory negligence on her part and that the plaintiff has absolutely failed to prove any negligence whatsoever on the part of the defendant.

FIGURE 54-E

```
 1        He met with Mr. Ralph Mortis, an agent of the TDEA
 2    and the unindicted co-conspirator, Griffith, and he went
 3    to all of the various locations and he pointed them out,
 4    and the investigation continued from that point.
 5        We will have testimony about many meetings between
 6    the various parties showing the connection, and when all
 7    the evidence is in, I am sure your verdict will be "Guilty
 8    as charged."
 9        Thank you.
10
11
12
13
14
15
16
17
18
19
20
21
22
23
24
25
```

At this point, the jury may be excused, and lengthy argument may ensue regarding this motion.

In some states, if the judge makes a ruling unsatisfactory to counsel making a motion or an objection, it is necessary for that attorney to take exception on the record to preserve his or her record in the event of appeal being taken on that point.

If the complaint is dismissed at this point, the case is ended; and the defendant will need to present no evidence.

The Defendant Now Presents His or Her Evidence

Assuming the judge denies the motion to dismiss the case, the defendant will now present all witnesses and tangible evidence (exhibits) to support his or her case. At this time the defendant will produce evidence not only to deny the plaintiff's claim, but also in support of any affirmative defenses which defendant has pleaded. If defense counsel has not presented an opening statement at the beginning of the case, he or she may do so at this time or may waive it altogether.

The witnesses presented by defendant's attorney are called on direct examination by the defense and cross-examination by plaintiff's counsel. The same is true of redirect examination by defendant's attorney and recross-examination by plaintiff's lawyer.

When defense counsel has completed presentation of his or her proof, the statement "The defendant rests" follows.

Case in Rebuttal

At this point, plaintiff may now present his or her case in rebuttal. Rebuttal is confined to presenting testimony to refute evidence of the defendant unless the court grants permission to present witnesses to support the allegations of the complaint. The plaintiff may call new witnesses or those who have testified previously on direct examination. Defense counsel may then cross-examine, and redirect and recross-examination may follow.

When the plaintiff's case in rebuttal is finished, he or she closes his or her case. If new points are brought out by plaintiff's rebuttal evidence, the defendant may present evidence in rejoinder; otherwise, he or she closes his or her case immediately.

Motion to Dismiss May Follow Close of Evidence

Finally the case is finished, and both sides have announced that they rest. At this point, defendant's attorney may make another motion to dismiss the case, which is invariably denied by the court, and exception is taken by defense attorney if that is the custom in the jurisdiction.

If the judge dismisses the complaint at this time, the case is ended; plaintiff would note his or her exception and request time to prepare the case on appeal.

Testimony by Deposition

Testimony may be adduced at a trial by having depositions read into the record by counsel taking the questions and answers. Should this happen, the reporter may be furnished a copy of the deposition, and the court may tell the reporter to take only any objections and rulings concerning this material. When objections or colloquy occur, the reporter writes the material before the objection, all ensuing colloquy, and the judge's ruling. Then, appropriate parentheticals are placed in the record upon transcription of the matter. If no copy of the deposition is furnished the reporter, at the judge's discretion the reporter may or may not be requested to take the reading of the deposition in shorthand.

If no objections are registered to any of the deposition material read, the transcript parenthetical may simply read:

> (The deposition of Dr. Cuttem Upp was read
> by counsel in open court.)

Bench Conferences

The reporter may be called to the bench to take material outside the hearing of the jury. It is important that such matter be included in the record and that the reporter include everything said in such a conference.

One reporter was walking away from the bench when an attorney made what he considered to be a flippant, extraneous remark. He did not record it or include it in the transcript. Upon delivery of the transcript, the attorney challenged the record as incomplete. When in doubt, ask the attorney or the court "Is that on the record?" Never assume counsel does not intend any spoken utterance to be included in the record.

Should you ever inadvertently omit a bench conference from the record and realize it when you find the notes at the end of your shorthand tapes, it is not necessary to retype the transcript to insert this material. Simply complete the page leading up to the bench conference at the proper breaking line. Then, type the pages for the bench conference and number them, for instance,

460-a, 460-b, 460-c, and so on, or if there are many, many pages, number them 460-1, 460-2, 460-3, etc. Do not forget to add these extra pages in your billing.

Most court reporters keep a second machine on a Hi-Boy Tripod at the bench to save time in going up to take bench conferences and such matters as exceptions to charges, motions, and the like. If this is your custom, be sure this machine, like the one you customarily use, is always well oiled and inked and in good, quiet working condition, as attorneys or the judge will take great exception to the disconcerting effect of a noisy machine.

Send your machine for maintenance annually, and always keep a spare machine for emergencies. If you use a second machine to report at the bench or sidebar, be very careful to mark this material and insert it at the proper spot in the transcript.

Jury Visits

The court, on motion of counsel, may direct that the jury be escorted by court officers to inspect the locality of an alleged accident or crime or to view a large piece of heavy equipment about which there is controversy. The court reporter may be taken along to report matter at the scene.

After arrival at the locality and during inspection of whatever is in question, the court is in session, and all material may be requested to be reported and included in the transcript of the trial.

Official Transcript

Occasionally counsel may want an immediate transcript of proceedings in a matter, and the official may not be in a position to provide daily copy, although this can seldom be said in these days of Computer-Aided-Transcription because reporters are getting closer to providing realtime transcript alone. However, the court reporter may find a time when counsel will have brought with them a freelance reporter to provide such a service. In such cases the official reporter's transcript is the official transcript of the case.

Closing Arguments

After both sides have finally rested in a court case, summation to the jury, also called closing statements or final arguments, takes place on behalf of the parties on both sides of the lawsuit. Final arguments may be brief, although in big cases or when there are a number of parties involved, final arguments may not be completed in one day's session.

The summations may be very difficult to report because the reporter does not interrupt the attorneys, who may become excited and very vocal in interpreting to the court and jury what they feel the evidence has proven. The final arguments will include analysis of the evidence and discussion as to credibility of witnesses and application of the rules of law that will be given by the judge in his or her charge to the jury.

Again, the reporter may not be required to report most closing arguments, but a beginning reporter should make sure what the judge wishes in this regard, as the trend is more and more to have the reporter record everything which occurs from the very start of a case in order that no time is lost when objections are made. Occasionally, an attorney who made an objectionable remark will refuse to repeat it, and the court and/or opposing counsel will supply the substance of the statement for the reporter. Here, again, the reporter can often sense when an objection is about to ensue and should start writing at that point if in the courtroom to prevent wasted court time.

Many experienced trial attorneys keep final argument to a minimum unless the case is very complicated, feeling that the jury may become weary and bored and react negatively to their side of the case as a result.

In cases tried by the court alone, the final arguments are more often requested to be reported and transcribed, and these are frequently more complicated and longer because of the more technical nature of the many cases tried to the court alone. Some judges restrict the time for final argument, but many judges will not. Usually the court will ask the attorneys outside the presence of the jury how long they would like for presentation of their summaries, and a limit will be set in conformance with their expressions regarding this.

Normally, the plaintiff's attorney will argue first and have rebuttal. If there is a counterclaim, the procedure will be: opening final argument by plaintiff, opening final argument by defendant, rebuttal by plaintiff, and rebuttal by defendant.

During final arguments counsel may use large pads of paper on an easel or the blackboard for presentations to illustrate points to the jury, particularly when comparisons of figures are involved. Some of the references to these may be very vague, but it is not up to the reporter to make the record for counsel. I always try to jot down on a pad anything on the board or these sheets if they are not photographed or introduced as exhibits, even if I have to remain during recesses or at the end of the day. They can sometimes be a real help in transcription.

Proper parentheticals will indicate in the record what happened during such exhibitions. Figure 55A through C shows an example of a brief closing argument.

FIGURE 55-A
Closing Argument

```
 1                    CLOSING ARGUMENT
                        BY MR. WALTERS
 2

 3       We will soon leave this case to the jury.

 4       Now, we have introduced evidence about the owner,

 5  how she has lived for many, many years in town, has been

 6  in the theater business, has never had any other trouble

 7  at all in the operation of her theaters.

 8       You see, you sort of have to look at it from the

 9  situation that she is in.  She is sitting there either

10  working on her knitting, taking in money from tickets, the

11  things you do to busy yourself if you are a person that's

12  active, just keeping doing something while you are waiting;

13  no complaints from anybody.  She never saw the movie.  She

14  never knew anything about the movie.  So far as obscenities

15  are concerned, if there were obscenities, she never saw them.

16  Do you feel that she should be convicted under this act?

17       We have what we call material allegations, and the

18  Judge will tell you what those material allegations are

19  in this complaint.  Material allegations are that if the

20  act was committed, it was committed, if at all, on or about

21  May 25, 1982; and, of course, nobody is arguing about that.

22  Two, that the crime was committed in Hill County; that's

23  the second allegation.  Three, that the defendant did

24  knowingly disseminate the movie specified in the indictment.

25       Well, there is no question she knew "Southern Comforts"
```

FIGURE 55-B

1 was running. She was selling tickets to it. Four, that

2 the movie was obscene. Five, that she knew that it was

3 obscene. Well, I think that's where there is going to be a

4 great deal of problem for there is no evidence at all for

5 the jury to find that this lady knew that this movie was

6 obscene, if it was obscene, because she had never seen it.

7 She had been told that it was a GP to a shaky R. She

8 had put up the sign and, actually, the sign was there because

9 of "Where's Papa?" another movie which was seized at the same

10 time and the Court found not to be obscene. Those signs were

11 there; but, as the District Attorney has indicated, those

12 signs were not really important.

13 The real question here is: Did this lady know at the

14 time this movie was being shown that it was obscene?

15 There is no evidence in this case whatsoever. You have

16 heard a person who has known her for a number of years testify

17 about her character and her reputation for truth and veracity

18 in the community.

19 Look at this one long and hard, folks. I don't have a

20 chance to talk to the jury again, but the State has to prove

21 its case beyond a reasonable doubt. They get to talk to

22 you again, but watch the way he faces his argument to you.

23 He is supposed to discuss just these things that I have

24 discussed; that's all he is supposed to discuss. He gets

25 an attempt to rebut my argument.

FIGURE 55-C

```
 1       His first argument is supposed to be an argument to

 2   you to discuss the evidence with you.  His second argument

 3   is supposed to be merely to rebut what I have said to the

 4   jury.  Now, hold him to that and don't allow emotion,

 5   prejudice, or any of those things to cloud your judgment in

 6   this case.

 7       Thank you.

 8

 9

10

11

12

13

14

15

16

17

18

19

20

21

22

23

24

25
```

Chapter 24

Handling Parenthetical Expressions in the Record

The court reporter can be compared to a photographer. You might ask "What possible relation can there be between those two?" Well, like a photographer, you are going to be producing by your transcript a picture of everything important that transpired during any proceeding you report.

Have you ever watched children with their first cameras? They go about snapping everything and anything, cutting off the heads or feet of the central figure and blurring fine scenes with quick, unsteady little hands.

Then, there are the great photographers who carefully plan the background, consider the lighting from every angle, advise the subject on clothing and perfect makeup, and use a world of experience to take a portrait that could well hang beside any Rembrandt on the wall.

Your transcript tells what kind of reporter you are, for there are finished records and then there are unfinished records. Transcripts reflect every grade of reporter. Make your transcripts reflect quality.

Not everything in the record will be just words. A complete transcript of any proceeding contains not only the verbatim record of the spoken words, but also such parenthetical notations as are necessary to round out a total representation of what happened. These entries are just as essential to the record as any other part of the transcript, and sometimes more so. The following paragraphs list various parentheticals that should be included in transcripts and describe how they should be indicated.

Presence of the Defendant

In one case the reporter did not show in the typed record that the defendant was personally present during a phase of his criminal trial. When the felon started studying law during his stay in the penitentiary, he discovered this omission and was granted a new trial. In that next trial, since a key witness was no longer to be found, the defendant was released.

Be very careful about placing this notation at the beginning of a criminal case transcript where applicable. It should be indented 15 spaces with a second line, if required, also indented 15 spaces. It should read as follows:

> (The defendant was personally present,
> together with his counsel.)

Your record should also show the matter was in open court, if such was the case:

(In open court.)

Voir Dire Parenthetical

When a jury trial is required, the jury panel is sworn before the voir dire examination is conducted to qualify "twelve good men and true."

The oath given by the clerk of court is "You, and each of you, do solemnly swear that you will well and truly answer such questions as may be asked of you touching upon your qualifications to serve as trial jurors in the case now pending before this Court, so help you God." You should type in your transcript:

(The jurors were duly sworn for voir
dire examination.)

Later, 12 jurors are selected, plus two alternates in large cases, so the case need not be retried should any juror become incapacitated. The alternates sit in a front row and are excused at the end of the trial when it becomes evident their services will not be required. The clerk of court swears the jury panel as follows: "You, and each of you, do solemnly swear that you will well and truly try the cause now pending before this Court and a true verdict render therein according to the evidence and the instructions of the Court, so help you God."

The proper parenthetical will read:

(The jurors were duly sworn to try this case.)
(Two alternate jurors were sworn.)

Unless the voir dire is required to be transcribed in your record, you will start the transcript of a jury case as follows:

(A jury was duly impaneled and sworn.)

Invoking the Rule

At any time during the trial of a case, either party may ask for sequestration of the witnesses (in many places called "Invoking the Rule"), at which time the witnesses will be sequestered and not allowed in the courtroom to hear what other witnesses may testify. This rule is invoked to prevent witnesses from changing their testimony because of what they hear others testify.

Your notation will read:

(The Rule was invoked, and the Court
instructed the witnesses as follows:)

or

(The Rule having been invoked, the Court
gave the following instructions:)

or, in some locations:

(The witnesses having been ordered
sequestered, the Court gave the
following instructions:)

After the Court's instructions to the witnesses explaining what it means to invoke the Rule or sequester the witnesses, you will note:

(The witnesses left the courtroom.)

Reading of the Indictment

In a criminal case, when the defendant does not waive the reading of the indictment, the parenthetical will read:

(The indictment was read.)

At an arraignment where the indictment is read and the defendant enters a plea, if you are not required in your jurisdiction to transcribe all of the proceedings, your expression will be:

(The indictment was read and the defendant
entered his plea of not guilty (or guilty).)

Should the defendant waive the reading of the indictment, you will insert:

(The defendant waived the reading of the indictment
and entered his plea of guilty (or not guilty).)

Opening and Closing Statements

Counsel on each side of a case are entitled to make opening statements detailing what they intend to prove and closing statements summing up what they believe the evidence has shown relative to their sides of the case.

Should opening and closing statement transcription be ordered as a part of the transcript, transcribe them in their entirety. However, it is common for a lawyer who orders an appeal transcript to omit these unless they are germane to the appeal.

If the opening statements and closing arguments are to be omitted from the case transcript, a notation is placed in the record:

(Mr. Ransom made an opening statement on behalf
of the plaintiff.)—or Government, or State,
or Petitioner, etc.
(Mr. Ibsen made an opening statement on behalf
of the defendant.)

and

(Mr. Ibsen made a closing statement on behalf
of the defendant.)
(Mr. Ransom made a closing statement on behalf
of the plaintiff.)—or Government, or State,
or Petitioner, etc.

Bench Conferences

One of the nightmares of many an official reporter's life is the calling of bench conferences, supposedly outside the hearing of the jury.

One of the attorneys will say "May we approach the bench, Your Honor?" The judge will grant permission, and the lawyers approach the bench. To save time, you should arrange a signal between you and the judge whereby he or she informs you to come up to record these discussions.

As stated before, most reporters keep a second machine on a Hi-Boy tripod at the bench so they can write while standing there, since the closer the reporter is to the semi-whispered conferences, the easier it is to hear. Always mark your notes at your reporter's table to be sure you have clearly indicated where bench conferences are to be inserted and mark your information sheet, and be sure you keep your bench conference machine notes with the day's take to avoid leaving them out of the final transcript.

You must strain your ears to catch every word. During these sessions counsel often forget about the reporter, turn their backs, go behind the judge to get books from the bookcase to prove points, and lean over the bench while referring to points of law they have been studying for the past six months.

Do not give up. Reporters have always managed to record these sessions, and you can, too, by paying close attention. Do not be afraid to ask to have something repeated when absolutely necessary, if you feel a vital point may be slipping away. Catch the attorneys at recess, if necessary, to verify notes; but be sure the following parenthetical remark appears in your record:

> (Conference at the bench without the hearing
> of the jury, as follows:)

or

> (The following proceedings were had at the bench
> by Court and counsel out of the hearing of the
> jury:)
>   THE COURT: State your motion.
>   MR. BERLITZ: I move to strike the testimony
> on this point for the simple reason, etc., etc.
>   THE COURT: Overruled.

Following this, the parenthetical will read:

> (Thereupon, the following proceedings continued
> within the hearing of the jury.)

or

> (The following took place within the presence and
> hearing of the jury.)

Reported and off-the-record conferences are frequently held at the side bar or at the bench. The proper notations for such conferences are:

> (Conference at the side bar between counsel
> and the Court.)

or

> (Conference at the bench between counsel and
> the Court.)

Jury-Related Parentheticals During Trial

It is vital for the reporter to note where the jury is at all times. A number of conferences, motions, voir dire questionings by the Court and counsel, colloquy discussions as to legal points and admissibility of evidence, considerations of requested jury instructions, and so on, require hearings outside open court. Many of these items must be recorded by the court reporter, but uld be grounds for appeal should the jury be present during the discussion.

Your record should contain proper parentheticals, where pertinent, at the start of each session and at such times throughout the hearing as required. Examples follow:

(The following took place within the presence
and hearing of the jury.)

or

(The following took place without the presence
and hearing of the jury.)

or

(The jury left the courtroom, after which the
following proceedings were had:)

or

(The jury returned to the courtroom, after which
the following proceedings were had:)

If the judges anticipate that colloquy (which is a word meaning discussion between Court and counsel or between counsel from opposing sides) on legal points will be lengthy, or sometimes, if they wish to speak out to counsel without harming their image before the jury, they will send the jury to the jury room, accompanied by the bailiff (or marshal) and matron. This will simplify your getting the record, but be sure to put the proper notation in the transcript.

(The jury left the courtroom.)

When the jury returns and they resume their seats in the jury box, indicate this by inserting:

(The jury returned to the courtroom, after which
the following proceedings were had before the
Court and jury.)

Sometimes the judge will hear legal arguments toward the end of the day or will wish to discuss points of law with counsel which will be reported on the record but outside the hearing of the jury. Your parenthetical should read:

(The jury was excused for the day, after which
the following proceedings were had before the
Court in this matter:)

Your life would be so much easier if every trial began and went right through without interruption, but sometimes the jury is excused and naturalization proceedings, pleas, sentences, and other small matters are taken up by the Court in their absence, which complicates your notekeeping and adds to the burden of taking long cases. Show these in your transcript as follows:

> (The jury was excused, and another matter was
> heard before the Court.)

If the jury is still deliberating at or about 6:00 P.M., the Court will usually send them to dinner. Your parenthetical remark will read:

> (At 6:15 P.M., the jurors were escorted to
> dinner, after which they returned to the jury
> room and continued deliberating.)

Sometimes the jury will send a note in requesting further clarification by the Court. They will be ushered into the courtroom for this. Your record should reflect:

> (In open court, jury present.)

When they again retire to deliberate after the explanation by the judge, the parenthetical will be as follows:

> (At 5:45 P.M., the jury returned to the courtroom.
> The jury roll was called, and all members were present.)

If there are no intervening episodes between the retiring of the jury to deliberate and the rendering of the verdict, your parenthetical expression should be condensed into one statement:

> (Thereupon, the jury retired to the jury room to
> consider their verdict. Thereafter, and (on the
> same day) (on the 10th day of June, 19—), the
> jury returned into court at 9:00 A.M., and the
> following proceedings were had:)

Polling the Jury

The reporter will record the colloquy surrounding the verdict and, should the defense counsel request polling of the jury, the reporter may transcribe the entire polling if required by the Court to do so, but usually the following parenthetical is inserted:

> (Each juror, upon being asked by the Court, "Is
> that your verdict?" answered in the affirmative.)

Excusing the Jury

At the end of each jury case, the Court will thank the jury, with appropriate remarks as to when they should report for further service, what a fine jury they have been, how they have contributed to our democratic process, and so on, none of which is material, perhaps, but it does leave a good impression with those who served, and that is helpful on Election Day. The jury is then excused. Show the departure of the jury in your record.

> (Jury excused.)

If this is the last case of the term, and the judge tells the jury they need not report back again, the notation would be:

> (Jury dismissed.)

In Chambers Hearings

Many matters are heard in the judge's chambers. These in camera hearings are fully as important as any others, and often much more so. Be sure to insert the vital parentheticals:

> (The following proceedings were had in chambers.)

or

> (The following proceedings were had in chambers,
> the defendant being personally present.)

Identifying Recesses

Joy reigns in the reporter's heart at such words from the judge during lengthy sessions, usually midmorning or midafternoon, as "We will take a 15-minute recess." For these short breaks, the following notation will suffice:

> (A recess was taken, after which the following
> proceedings were had:)

or simply

> (Recess taken.)

Proceedings may take place during recess which are reported, and the proper notation should be inserted.

> (Recess.)
> (Jury not present.)
>
> MR. MATTHEWS: If Your Honor please, while
> the jury is not present, in light of the evidence
> which has just been presented, I feel that further
> trial of my client as a joint perpetrator is
> unwarranted. I move at this time for separation
> of the cases in order that the ends of justice
> may be served. (Etc., etc.)

For the noon recess, include the time in your parenthetical remark:

> (At 12:30 P.M., a recess was taken for the noon
> hour, after which the following proceedings
> were had:)

In some jurisdictions the following notation is used at the end of a day's proceedings when the trial lasts more than one day:

(On Tuesday, March 22, 19—, at 5:30 P.M., Court
was recessed until Wednesday, March 23, 19—, at
9:30 A.M., and after such recess the following
proceedings were had before the Court (and jury).)

However, the trend is toward brief notes, and the typical adjournment note at the end of the day is:

(Thereupon, the proceedings were adjourned at
5:00 P.M.. to the following day, June 9, 19—,
at 9:00 A.M.)

or

(At 5:30 P.M., Court was adjourned to the following
day, May 16, 19—, at 9:30 A.M.)

Of course, the times are arbitrary. If you are on line 25, and there is no late hour indicated (meaning that the reporter was not working during the noon hour or working overtime in the evening), simply eliminate the carryover line to the next page, which would be the only line on that page, and put:

(Noon recess taken.)

or, at the end of the day:

(Court adjourned.)

Following a recess, a witness who has not completed his or her testimony may be required to resume the stand to testify. Your record should appear as follows:

(After a short recess, the witness resumed the
stand, and the following proceedings were had
within the presence and hearing of the jury.)

Whereupon, you will set up your hearing again, followed by

DIRECT EXAMINATION (Cont'd.)

BY MR. GREEN:

Q: Now, we have discussed this overpayment of $60—is that the correct amount?

A: Yes, sir. (Etc., etc.)

Off-the-Record Discussions

During depositions and court cases, frequent off-the-record discussions are held. These, of course, are not taken in shorthand by the court reporter, although you should be alert to record material when it becomes apparent they have forgotten that you have been advised that they are off the record. When in doubt, ask. Where there is off-the-record discussion, put in your record:

> (An off-the-record discussion was held.)

or

> (Discussion off the record.)

Exhibit-Related Parentheticals

In a federal court (United States District Court) the exhibits are marked and retained by the clerk of court. In depositions, the reporter marks an exhibit only for identification, usually noting that it is a deposition marking. If there are deposition or court exhibits of several parties, they are so designated by the reporter.

In many State District Courts, Circuit Courts, County Courts, and Municipal Courts, the reporter will be responsible for marking and, perhaps, retaining the exhibits. Be sure to put in your transcribed record correct parenthetical expressions, substituting "State's Exhibit" or "Government's Exhibit" in criminal cases and other such applicable identifications as "Appellant's Exhibit," "Respondent's Exhibit," and so on, where required.

> (Plaintiff's Exhibit No. 1, a lease dated
> May 1, 19—, was marked for identification.)
> (The following exhibits were marked for
> identification: Plaintiff's Exhibit No. 16,
> a check dated June 30, 19—, and Plaintiff's
> Exhibit No. 17, an envelope addressed to the
> Martin Company, postmarked June 30, 19—.)
> (Defendant's Exhibit No. 32, a ledger sheet of
> the May Company, was received in evidence, and a
> copy of same appears in this record at the
> page shown in the index.)
> (The following exhibits were received in
> evidence: (List and describe.).)

Sometimes photostatic copies or photocopies are substituted by agreement for original exhibits. A proper notation should be made as follows:

> (The original of Plaintiff's Exhibit No. 4, a
> divorce decree dated August 16, 19—, was
> withdrawn by agreement, and a copy of same was
> substituted and identified as Plaintiff's
> Exhibit No. 4-a.)

When exhibits are handed to the jury for their examination, an appropriate parenthetical should so indicate:

> (Defendant's Exhibit No. 19, a photograph of the
> intersection involved in the accident, was
> circulated among the jurors for their examination.)
> (Plaintiff's Exhibits 1 and 2, accident
> photographs, were handed to the jury.)

or simply

> (The exhibits were handed to the jury.)

Sometimes a large number of exhibits will be marked for identification or received in evidence at one time, and an entire listing of the contents would not be made, as:

> (Government Exhibits 12 through 64, marked for
> identification, were received in evidence.)

Actions of Participants

At times parenthetical expressions regarding actions of counsel such as the following are needed.

> (Counsel confer briefly.)
> (Counsel examines exhibit.)
> (Counsel hands exhibit to the witness.)—or
> to the Court, or to opposing counsel.
> (Counsel reads document.)
> (Counsel hands document to the Court.)—or
> other person, such as counsel.
> (Mr. Reynolds read to the jury from Defendant's
> Exhibit No. 1 as follows:)

When a witness is asked to mark an "X" on a map or plat or some similar request:

> (The witness complies.)
> (The witness indicated on the map.)

Frequently, the witness is asked to step down from the witness stand to illustrate some point on a map, chart, blackboard, or for some other similar purpose:

> (The witness left the stand and went to the
> blackboard.)
> (The witness left the stand and stepped over to
> the plat.)

After questioning of the witness away from the stand is completed and he or she takes his or her seat, the following notation should be entered in the record:

> (The witness returned to the stand.)

Parentheticals to Indicate Use of Motion Pictures and Slides

Motion pictures and color slides are often presented during the course of a trial, necessitating the use of projectors and screens. Place the proper entry in your transcript:

> (A slide projector and screen) (motion picture
> projector and screen) were set up in the courtroom,
> and Plaintiff's Exhibit No. 5 was projected for
> the Court and jury.)

Witness-Related Parentheticals

When a witness's testimony is suspended to permit the examination of another witness, the parenthetical expression should read:

> (Witness temporarily excused.)

When a witness completes his or her testimony, your notation may read:

(Witness excused.)

or

(The witness left the stand.)

When a witness who was called under the Rule was excused, the proper parenthetical is:

(The witness left the courtroom.)

Descriptive One-Word Parentheticals

Some descriptive parenthetical expressions often used are:

(Reading.)
(Indicating.)
(Pointing.)
(Marking.)
(Demonstrating.)
(Drawing.)
(Exhibiting.)
(Writing.)
(Humming.)
(Examining.)

Proper Use of Parentheticals

Since your parentheticals could easily become conclusions of the reporter, limit them to those required to prevent confusion. It is up to the attorneys to make their record. If a lawyer asks the witness "Where does it hurt you?" and the witness replies "Right here," you will transcribe:

Q: Where does it hurt you?

A: Right here (Indicating.)

Do *not* add interpretations or your conclusions such as the following:

A: Right here (Indicating the occipital region of the head.).

After all, your occipital might be someone else's idea of the parietal region. The same is true of dimensions. If you insert (Indicating 6 inches.) the witness may mean a foot. One attorney may think she is spreading her hands 3 inches, and to the other lawyer, that may indicate 8 inches. It is up to the examiner to clarify the record by asking qualifying questions, such as:

Q: Are you pointing to the back of your head, to what I call the occipital region of the skull?

A: Yes, sir.

or

Q: Would you say you are indicating a distance of about 6 inches, sir?

A: I would say closer to 8 inches.

When the witness or counsel is pointing at a map or chart for a few minutes, do not keep writing "(Indicating.)" or "(Pointing.)" all the time in your notes—only if a person points once to something. Likewise in your transcripts, do not overdo the use of parentheticals.

Attorneys like to add drama to their presentations to the jury, and they will ask witnesses to demonstrate actions and happenings. Where necessary for clarifications, use the parenthetical

(Demonstrating.)

Sometimes the witness will make no reply, but will physically comply with the question. Examples of this follow:

Q: Where did you go next?

A: (No audible response.)

Q: Where does your head hurt you now?

A: (The witness indicated.)

Q: Step down from the stand and mark an "X" on this plat where the car you hit was in the intersection at the time of impact.

A: (The witness complies.)

Q: Did you participate in this riot?

A: (Witness nods head.)

Q: Were you present when John Marks killed this girl?

A: (Witness shakes head.)

Again, it is up to the lawyer to amplify on these "nods" and "shakes." It is really not within your province to put such things as (Witness nods head affirmatively.) or (Witness shakes head negatively.), although some reporters in courts and in very good firms do this. If you work for a firm which prefers these forms, do things their way, by all means. To me, a nod means "Yes," and a shake means "No." If I cannot tell which it is, I simply ask "Is that 'yes'?" and the questioning attorney will clarify it. In fact, at that point, one of the attorneys present will usually instruct the witness concering furture answers, thus assisting you greatly.

Identify the Examiner after Lengthy Colloquy

Following long colloquy, particularly that which continues to the next page, indicate which counsel is questioning for clarity of the record. However, do not do this after each brief objection.

Q: (By Mr. Hardart) Now, I will ask you that question once more. Were you present during the signing of Mr. Lee's will?

A: Yes, sir.

Parentheticals in Interpreted Proceedings

Non-English-speaking witnesses testify through an interpreter, who is sworn first by the clerk, as follows: "You do solemnly swear that you will well and truly interpret for Siro E. Guitierrez-Monterez Spanish into English and English into Spanish in the cause now pending before this Court, so help you God?" The clerk then administers the oath to the witness through the interpreter. Your record will show:

(Jose Jiminez Gonzales was sworn as the Spanish
interpreter by the clerk of court. The witness
was duly sworn through the Spanish interpreter.)

At times, a witness testifying through an interpreter will answer in English. Some reporters put an asterisk before each numbered line in which the witness responds in English; and at the foot of the page, they place an asterisk followed by the words, "Answers of the witness in English."

Other reporters denote this by use of the parenthetical phrase (in English.). Then, when the witness lapses into his or her native language, and the testimony is again taken through the interpreter they insert the parenthetical (Through the interpreter.), as shown below:

Q: Have you ever been involved in any other maritime accidents?

A: (In English.) Five times.
       (Through the interpreter) I slipped on the dunnage in a stow twice, was in a chain fall accident once, and fell myself twice.

Depositions Read into the Record

Depositions are read into the record, usually by two attorneys from the firm taking the parts, when certain witnesses are unavailable or deceased. Ordinarily, the reporter follows the reading and notes interruptions, objections, colloquy, or rulings as they may occur. If the attorneys indicate they want the entire reading in the record, of course the judge will instruct the reporter to report and transcribe all of it. When the reporter is told not to transcribe reading of the depositions, but merely to note parenthetically the fact that they were read, plus all objections, colloquy, and rulings, your entry will look like the following:

(Mr. Jellybelly read to the jury from page 4, line 9,
to page 56, line 2, of the deposition of Seymour
Doolittle.)
       MR. KNOWITALL: That last question is objected
to as immaterial to the issues in this case.
       THE COURT: Sustained.
(Mr. Jellybelly continued reading from page 56, line 3,
to page 102, line 14.)

When a deposition is simply read in full to the Court and/or jury, use the following parenthetical:

(Mr. Winning read the deposition of I. M. Reddy
to the jury.)

or

(Mr. Winning and Mr. Cunning read to the jury the
direct examination from the deposition of Dr.
Cutemm N. Cutemm.)

Readbacks are requested during depositions and hearings to a great extent. In court, always glance at the judge for his or her consent to the reading. Some judges insist that all requests for readbacks be made by the attorneys directly to them; and they, in turn, direct the reporter to read. Remember, the judge is in charge of all hearings before him or her, and whatever you do should lend dignity to the office; so, do clear with the judge how he or she would like to handle readbacks.

Your parenthetical regarding a readback should be as brief as possible, consistent with clarity.

(The last question was read by the reporter.)

or simply

(Question read.)
(The answer was read back by the reporter.)

or simply

(Answer read.)
(The last question and answer were read.)
(The last three questions and answers were read.)
(Record read.)

When a portion of the record remote from the present questioning is read back, definite reference to the material read must be made in the transcript in order that there will be no misunderstanding on the part of anyone as to what transpired:

(The question was read by the reporter as follows:
"What did you see on the second occasion that you
encountered the defendant on the night of May
24, 19—?")
(The first six questions and answers contained in
the direct testimony of Alle N. Funn were read
back by the reporter.)

Sometimes the reporter will be requested to read back objections or rulings, in which case the record will read:

(The objection was read by the reporter.)

or

(The ruling of the Court was read back by the reporter.)

Readbacks to the Jury

At the end of a jury case, the judge will send the jury to a jury room to deliberate and arrive at a verdict. If marshals are sworn (in Federal Court), you will insert:

(Two marshals were duly sworn.)

Your transcribed record will also show:

> (At 3:30 P.M., the jury retired to deliberate
> upon a verdict.)

or

> (At 3:30 P.M. the jury retired to commence their
> deliberations.)

When you read all or a portion of a witness's testimony to the jury during its deliberations, you will omit from your reading the following: (1) objections and rulings; (2) questions to which objections have been sustained; and/or (3) questions and answers ordered stricken. It will help greatly in reading to the jury if you have carefully indexed witnesses as the trial proceeded. Numbered pads are highly recommended because of this.

Proper insertions to show what happened during such readbacks are:

> (The testimony of Ima Witness was read to the jury
> by the reporter.)
> (The cross-examination of Mercy Ponnus was read to
> the jury by the reporter.)
> (Portions of the testimony of Ura Lyre were read
> to the jury by the reporter.)
> (Record read.)

If you have transcribed the testimony read to the jury previously, as would be the case in a daily copy, you may indicate what was read as follows:

> (The reporter read to the jury from the transcript
> of May 3, 19—, page 2, line 3, through page 28,
> line 14, inclusive.)

Each note from the jury should be marked as a separate court exhibit. Requests for the reporter to read will be made by a note signed by the foreperson of the jury:

> (A note from the jury was marked as Court Exhibit
> No. 1.)

Verifying the Spelling of a Name

Occasionally, you will be unable to verify the spelling of a name or unusual term. It is customary to put after such transcribed terms "(Spelled phonetically.)" This is not to be used as an excuse not to research names or terms, but is only for immaterial terms and the like that you have searched diligently for. There are times when the witness will say, "His name is Boris Vanitschlewski." When asked for the spelling, the witness will have no idea how to spell it, the attorneys will have no record, nor will the clerk's file reveal it. If it does not appear in any directory or phone book, etc., you will transcribe:

> *A*: His name is Boris Vanitschlewski (Spelled
> phonetically.).

Attorneys will misstate dates or amounts on occasion, or witnesses will unintentionally say a wrong word or amount; and you will know that if you transcribe it the way they stated it, the reader of the transcript will believe it was your error.

It is the practice to put after such expressions "(sic)," which indicates the reporter noted that it was incorrect, but that is really what was said. For instance, counsel may say, "When our Constitution was framed in 1877," meaning to say, "1777." You will type: "When our Constitution was framed in 1877 (sic) . . ."

Seldom-Used Parentheticals

There is one other type of parenthetical which should be mentioned, since you may be called upon to use these during the course of your career. These seldom, if ever, appear in court and deposition work, but are restricted almost entirely to transcripts of addresses, speeches, convention proceedings, conferences, and meetings. These parenthetical expressions consist of a word or phrase immediately following a transcribed sentence, but within a paragraph.

The most frequently used words of this nature are (Laughter.) and (Applause.). For example: "I am very happy to announce the winner of the sales contest, Harry Bascomb (Applause.)."

"When I was in school, I was known as the 'knucklehead of the year,' but now I am simply known as 'Mr. Hardknuckles.' At least, that is a shift in direction that will get something done (Laughter.)."

You will find that other parenthetical remarks will be required from time to time to suit particular circumstances. With common sense and a little forethought, you will be able to devise these as required, keeping in mind that each parenthetical comment should be clear, concise, and essential to the understanding of what transpired during the hearing.

Be alert, and you will soon find that you are easily inserting in your notes all the illustrative or explanatory descriptions to explain happenings and gestures witnesses, counsel, and the Court employ to make your transcript a truly complete record.

Chapter 25 *Exhibits*

Exhibits are material items of physical evidence introduced by attorneys to corroborate and confirm oral testimony.

Deposition Exhibits

Exhibits are marked for identification only during depositions since there is no one present during a deposition to rule upon their admissibility. Exhibits marked for identification during a deposition may or may not be introduced during the trial of a case.

Courtroom Exhibits

Generally, most of the exhibits in a case are identified and received into evidence in court during the direct case of the party bringing suit. The exhibits are offered in court first for identification and shown to opposing counsel and the Court. Objections and rulings are made, after which questioning proceeds regarding the exhibit. Then, the exhibit is offered in evidence. Objections, if any, are made once more, and the exhibit is either received or refused.

Objections made to courtroom exhibits frequently require recesses so that in-chambers offers of proof and discussion may follow, and the jury may be retired or excused for this purpose. The court reporter must be careful to show in the record that the jury is not present at such times.

Disposition of Deposition Exhibits

During depositions, exhibits are marked by the court reporter when requested by attorneys to do so. The attorney providing the exhibit will inform the reporter to retain the exhibit and file it as a part of the deposition original at times. If the exhibit is made a part of the deposition, it is customary to place the original exhibit at the back of the original of the deposition and to make copies for placement at the back of the attorneys' copies. The reporter charges the customary fee for this service.

What Constitutes an Exhibit?

Physical evidence may include guns, bullets, medical records, marriage certificates, soil and quicksand samples, tapes or slides, films, stamps, charred rugs and furniture in arson cases, chemicals, X-rays, statements, confessions, clothing, hospital records, drugs, machinery, accounting records, mortality tables, city ordinances, bloodstained items, blood samples, letters—the list is endless.

Exhibit Supplies

A reporter must have certain supplies at hand to mark exhibits. The following is a list of the essentials:

1. Exhibit stamp.
2. Well-inked stamp pad.
3. Ballpoint pen.
4. Small and large paper clips.
5. Stapler and staples.
6. White china marking pencil or wax pencil for marking X-rays and photostats.
7. Black or red china pencil to mark other exhibits.
8. Wired cardboard tags or tags with string attached.
9. An assortment of envelopes for those items you are not allowed to mark, such as X-rays, photographs, stamps, plats, etc.
10. A small penknife for creating a hole in which to attach a tag.
11. Gummed labels that are large enough to accommodate your exhibit stamp and others for small objects.

Pengad Co., Bayonne, NJ, and The Highsmith Co., Inc., P.O. Box 25A, Highway 106 East, Fort Atkinson, WI 53538, and Stenograph Corp., 1500 Bishop Court, Mount Pleasant, IL, specialize in reporters' supplies. They offer a wide supply of labels in different colors, both plain and already marked "Defendant's Exhibit," "Plaintiff's Exhibit," "State's Exhibit," "Appellant's Exhibit," "Respondent's Exhibit," "Government's Exhibit," etc. These gummed labels can be used to handle practically every conceivable situation.

FIGURE 56
Examples of Color-Coded Exhibit Labels

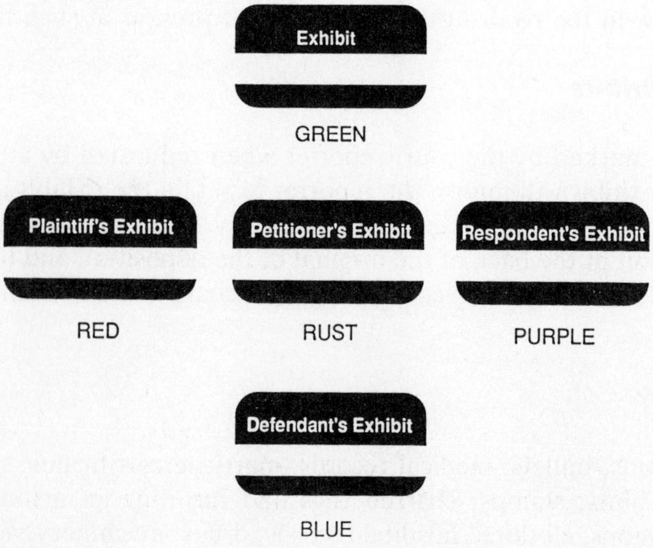

Exhibit

GREEN

Plaintiff's Exhibit

RED

Petitioner's Exhibit

RUST

Respondent's Exhibit

PURPLE

Defendant's Exhibit

BLUE

When a reporter uses these color-coded labels, it takes only seconds before each recess or adjournment to glance at an information sheet and count the exhibits listed for each side and then count the corresponding physical exhibits that have distinctively colored labels.

Exhibit Information

The reporter includes three things in marking any physical evidence: the exhibit number, the reporter's name or initials, and the date. The reporter also indicates whether the exhibit is marked for identification or placed in evidence.

Sometimes such designations as "Defendant Latham's Deposition Exhibit No. 4" will be requested by an attorney to designate a certain party of several named.

Generally speaking, the proper place to mark each exhibit is in the upper right-hand corner, but custom decrees it shall be marked at the bottom right-hand corner or other place in some locales.

Be very careful in marking exhibits not to cover any writing or material part. Photographs should be marked at the right-hand corner at the top on the back unless otherwise decreed.

X rays should be held to the light before marking with a white wax pencil or affixing a label to be sure nothing important is covered. One word of warning: Sometimes labels will not hold well on X rays and other shiny-surfaced items, so be guided accordingly. Some doctors will not allow markings to be made on their X rays or medical records, in which case you must place these items in a manila envelope and mark the outside of the envelope.

Multipage Exhibits

If an exhibit consists of more than one page, count the number of pages and place this information with your exhibit marking information on the envelope and your information sheet. If possible, mark each sheet of a multipage exhibit D-1-1, D-1-2, D-1-3, and so on.

Multiunit Exhibits

Check carefully as to an attorney's preference when you mark exhibits consisting of more than one page or more than one article as to how it will be most identifiable and useful to him or her.

In a rape case a beginning reporter had a number of items of clothing to mark. She put them all in one bag and marked the bag as one exhibit during a phase of the case. Throughout the trial the attorneys pulled out one item when they were talking about another item. The testimony would have been hilarious except for the fact that rape conviction carries a life sentence or the death penalty in some places. Always use common sense!

Specific Requests

When lawyers distinctly inform you how they want exhibits marked, it is their case. Do not argue with them unless you know the number they are giving you is a duplicate or out of sequence or otherwise obviously wrong. In such a case, be very courteous about the matter, but get it resolved right then.

Letter Markings Versus Number Markings

The custom once was to number plaintiffs' exhibits and letter defendants' exhibits. This method works reasonably well if there are few exhibits, although some letters sound very much alike. You may find when you check the exhibits against your notes what you thought was an "M" was an "N," or that "B," "G," and "V" were misheard.

In the federal courts the exhibits are marked by the court clerk and may precede your record in going up to the Court of Appeals. Unless you check them at the time of taking, you may not know until you are informed such an error occurred.

The other problem with using letter identifications for exhibits appears when you have used up 26 letters. The 27th exhibit becomes "AA." After 52 exhibits, the 53rd exhibit becomes "AAA," and so on. Picture what happens in a case containing 500 exhibits! Counsel invariably refer to Defendant's Exhibit A, meaning AAA, or vice versa, which causes your exhibits not to match up when you are transcribing a record.

A Better Method of Marking Courtroom Exhibits

When attorneys ask you to mark an exhibit, if possible, use the following system: P-1 to P-5,000, if necessary, for plaintiff's exhibits; D-1 to any number for defendant's exhibits; S-1 to S-7,500, if necessary for state's exhibits; R-1 to any number for respondent's exhibits; PE-1 to any number for petitioner's exhibits; and so on.

Exhibit Stamps

The specific form of exhibit stamp I particularly favor looks like this:

        _____ ID. _____ EVD.
        *Movable Date
        Mary H. Knapp, CSR
        Court Reporter

*The date is turned by a wheel on top of the handle.

This particular exhibit stamp provides for marking exhibits both as to identification and in evidence, so you can tell the status of each exhibit at a glance.

You should have your rubber exhibit stamp made with type as small as possible consistent with legibility so that it can be used on most exhibits, as an exhibit stamp saves much time. You may prefer a different form of stamp, for reporters have a multitude of preferences in this regard.

If a stamp cannot be used on an exhibit due to the size of the exhibit or for fear of destroying important matter, simply write on the exhibit the number, your initials, the date, and "for id." in ink. Then, simply draw a line through "for id." on your handwritten marking when the physical evidence is received, and this will tell you the exhibit is now in evidence. Be sure to mark your notes and information sheet accordingly.

Some Procedures to Follow

Premark Exhibits Whenever Possible

It has been previously suggested that you premark exhibits in advance when you realize there will be a large number in a case. Making up a careful list of what each exhibit is will save much time in taking the matter and in compiling the exhibit index at a later time.

Check and Doublecheck

When attorneys read from exhibits, as they frequently do, always check the exhibit against your notes, as there is always the possibility of mishearing. Occasionally intentional or unintentional misreadings do occur.

Storing Exhibits

Take all exhibits you receive in any proceedings to your office. If they are bulky, store them in a fireproof vault or cabinet. Place the others in a large envelope, labeling it with case title, venue, date taken, and so on. File them chronologically until they are copied and used for the proper purpose. Then return the exhibits to the proper party, always securing a receipt.

Substituting Copies for Original Exhibits

Counsel often stipulate on the record that photocopies may be substituted for original exhibits to free business records and items needed for other purposes. Be careful to do a good, clear job of copying and return these originals very promptly, securing a receipt in every instance when you give them back or mail them to the specified person. The photostatic copies should then be marked as exhibits and included with the record.

Writing about Exhibits in the Dark

Many times after you have marked films, slides, X rays, and microfilm, these will be shown in the courtroom using projectors or view boxes. When this happens, you must write comments in the semi-darkness or take testimony simultaneously. Be sure to place the proper notations in your machine shorthand notes in the interest of a clear record.

The handling of physical evidence (exhibits) by the court reporter is a grave responsibility where this duty falls to his or her lot. Procedures regarding exhibits vary greatly from court to court and jurisdiction to jurisdiction.

Marking of Exhibits

In the United States District Courts (federal courts), the exhibits are marked and maintained by the clerk of court and often precede the reporter's transcript up to the appeals court. In the state district courts and county courts, the reporter usually marks the exhibits and may be required to keep control over them until the case is disposed of, returning them finally to the counsel who presented them during the case. In most of these courts, however, the exhibits are maintained by the clerk of court and transmitted by him or her to the proper appellate court with the other records. Later they are returned to the attorneys by the clerk of court when the matter has been finally settled.

In courts not of record, the judge or clerk may mark the exhibits and retain them, even though an attorney may have brought a reporter for the purpose of securing a record to study for an accompanying civil case or for purposes of appeal. The new reporter simply must learn for himself or herself from experienced reporters what the procedures are in a given locality.

Re-Marking Exhibits at Trial

One thing that may lead to confusion regarding exhibits is the fact that many of those offered during trial have already been marked as exhibits during the taking of depositions. Counsel often read from the wrong markings due to this, and the court and the clerk and the reporter must be alert to avoid total confusion in the record.

In some places, letters are used as markings for exhibits in depositions, and numbers are used when the exhibits are marked during a court trial. Then, if the attorney in court is about to show a witness an exhibit, saying "I show you, Mr. Witness, what the reporter has marked Plaintiff's Exhibit A," the reporter knows that is the deposition marking and asks counsel to have the exhibit marked as a trial exhibit. This excellent suggestion was given me by Mr. Dick Mowers, who also informed me that if the plaintiff introduces 20 exhibits, the first one by the defendant is marked simply Exhibit 21, and so on, in their courts. This method would certainly facilitate the checking of exhibits at recesses and adjournments.

Marking Exhibits at Pretrial Hearing

Many times trial exhibits are now marked at the Pretrial Hearing, at which time the reporter lists them on a worksheet and identifies them by description. In some places, the known exhibits are offered and received into evidence at that time, often with no objection from either side.

If the trial exhibits are marked and received at the Pretrial Hearing, they are already in evidence before the trial begins. You can use your worksheet from the Pretrial Hearing for the trial, thus saving a great deal of time.

Marking Exhibits in Advance of Trial

Any time you know there will be numerous exhibits in a case, try to have the attorneys bring them in to be marked and listed as to descriptions by you on a day before the trial begins to save time. Some attorneys bring in their exhibits already marked in sequence, requiring the official court reporter only to date and initial them.

Procedures for Marking Exhibits

You must have at hand all the essentials for marking exhibits previously described. In court, you may be handed an exhibit to mark while counsel is still talking. Be sure to get all his or her remarks and all answers, rulings, and so on, before you accept the exhibit to be marked. Then, hold the exhibit so counsel cannot take it until you have completed all your work with it.

Mark in your notes what exhibit it is and whether it is identified or received. Mark the exhibit off on your information sheet. Then, stamp the exhibit with your exhibit stamp or place a Pengad label on it, and be sure to include the designation of the exhibit by letter or number (whichever you use), the date, and your initials or your name.

Now, you can let go of the exhibit. Remember, as soon as you do, counsel will begin to discuss that exhibit immediately. I always make an arrangement with the judge that as I finish marking an exhibit, I turn to my machine and I say "Your Honor, I have just marked for identification Plaintiff's Exhibit No. 23," and I hand the exhibit to the attorney presenting it. If there should be any error or problem or misunderstanding concerning the exhibit at that time, it can be easily caught, as the court and the court clerk also keep lists of the exhibits. This also gives the reporter a chance to get in writing position before counsel starts to speak.

Occasionally, a lawyer will remark "While you are marking those exhibits, I will just ask a few questions." Courteously remind counsel that you cannot make the record while you are marking the exhibits and ask him or her to wait until you complete this chore.

The place of marking trial exhibits varies. In some places exhibits are marked in the upper right-hand corner. In other places, the trial exhibits are marked in the lower right-hand corner, since this is not where deposition markings usually have been made.

The reporter's marking of an exhibit includes the number of the exhibit, the date, and the reporter's initial or name, as:

S-1

MHK

5–16—

This marking in the proper location would be understood to mean that the exhibit is the first State's Exhibit marked by Mary H. Knapp on May 16 of whatever year.

Of course, your exhibit stamp will save time in many instances when used. Some reporters do not use labels when they can mark directly on paper, as labels can be removed easily; and, should no mark remain, evidence could be obliterated. Bullets and small items, such as stamps, may be placed in envelopes which are then marked for identification.

Do watch for ink smearing, particularly on the back of photographs. Some reporters mark photographs on the front so that if copies are made, the exhibit marking will be visible, but it is very hard to mark on such a shiny surface.

Re-mark exhibits if markings become illegible. When deciding where to mark exhibits, watch for previous markings by officers, chemists, and so on. Do not cover initials that have been scratched on such items as guns or those inked in. Find a clean spot for your marking. Hold X rays to the light to ascertain where markings should be made. If a doctor insists that no markings be placed on the X ray, mark the large manila envelope you place the X ray in.

Marking Papers that Are Clipped Together. Be sure papers in one exhibit are stapled together before you mark them as one exhibit. Ask the district attorney or other officer to staple them if they are just papers clipped together. Then count the pages and make a notation as to how many pages are contained in the one exhibit. It is a good idea to mark each sheet, as P-26-1, P-26-2, P-26-3, and so on to prevent any sheets being taken out and others inserted.

Marking Envelopes or Bags Containing Various Items of Evidence. If an evidence envelope or bag and its contents are introduced as one exhibit, mark the envelope or bag as 1-a, and then the contents individually as 1-b, 1-c, 1-d, and so on, describing each item on your worksheet carefully. When the contents are taken out and scattered, you will know where they belong.

Marking Substitutions for Original Exhibits. When an original is introduced as an exhibit, mark it as S-8, for example. Then, if the original is withdrawn and a copy is substituted in the record, mark that S-8-a. Be sure to indicate on your worksheet what happened.

Marking Blackboard Drawings as Exhibits. If you are asked to mark a blackboard drawing as an exhibit, mark it as you would any other exhibit, with a chalk mark in the proper place for your locality. If it is received in evidence, be sure the attorney offering it gets this verbally on the record and that a photograph thereof will be substituted.

Usually, the Sheriff's Department takes the photographs in a criminal case with the bailiff making the arrangements should this ever occur. In a civil case, the arrangements and stipulations will be arranged between counsel and the Court.

Marking Bulky Items as Exhibits. For bulky narcotics, burglar tools, and so on, the court and the prosecutor will ordinarily agree to introduce only a sample and photographs of the total quantity, or the bulky exhibits are introduced and received in evidence, and pictures are made by the Sheriff's Department photographer. On the record the attorneys will agree that all but a small sample will be withdrawn and the photographs substituted.

Keeping Track of the Exhibits. Every reporter must check carefully at every recess and adjournment to ensure that he or she has every exhibit entrusted to him or her. Never let any exhibits lie around where they may be appropriated by anyone or inadvertently destroyed. Be sure (do not guess or assume) that an identified exhibit has actually been received in evidence by the Court. Usually the last thing the official does at a trial is check over the exhibits with the worksheet to separate those offered and received from all the rest because only those exhibits offered and received in evidence are allowed to go to the jury. If, by mistake, other exhibits go to the juryroom, this could result in a mistrial.

It is good practice, before the parties rest their cases, to go over with the judge the exhibits which are and are not in evidence, as there may be exhibits upon which ruling was reserved.

These items may be ruled on at that time. Also, the attorneys will probably come up to you just before resting and ask you if all their exhibits have been offered and received into evidence. A quick glance at your worksheet will indicate the status of each exhibit.

Some judges always send exhibits directly to the jury; others wait until they specifically request all exhibits or just part of them.

In some jurisdictions the reporter charged with responsibility for exhibits is required to store small valuables in safety deposit boxes at a bank. These are rented by the county for the court from the judge's budget. Normally, a vault is provided at the courthouse for these articles.

When weapons or narcotics are received in evidence, keep a record on a file card to save much time later when these are collected to be destroyed or auctioned off.

Check carefully how long you must retain exhibits and what the procedure is for disposing of them if their care and custody is delegated to you.

Exhibits on Appeal. Of course, exhibits go along with the other records to the appeals court. Large, bulky exhibits pose a problem when sent with the appeal transcript, so most appeal courts now permit the appellant to photograph the item and substitute a photograph for the original item.

In one of my Minnesota cases, plaintiff's counsel had a life-sized blowup of a picture of a tractor-trailer wedged into the trunk of plaintiff's car before the jury throughout the trial. It was so large a boxcar had to transport it to the Supreme Court. In most states the clerk of court arranges for transportation of the exhibits to the appeals court, thank goodness!

Returning Exhibits to Attorneys. It may be your duty to see that exhibits are returned to the lawyers who presented them in evidence, although usually the clerk of court attends to this. If this is part of your job, be sure to secure a receipt for each and every one of the exhibits at such time as the attorneys take possession of them.

Exhibits in Trial Transcripts

In the body of the trial transcript, insert the appropriate parenthetical statements concerning exhibits:

> (Said documents were marked for identification
> as State's Exhibits Nos. 5 through 15.)
> (A pistol was marked for identification as
> State's Exhibit No. 1.)
> (State's Exhibit No. 1 was received in evidence
> by the Court but is not included herein because
> it is physical evidence.)
> (State's Exhibits Nos. 5 through 10 were received
> in evidence by the Court, and copies thereof are
> attached hereto.)
> (Said photograph was marked for identification as
> State's Exhibit No. 13, was received in evidence by
> the Court, and a copy thereof is attached hereto.)
> (Defendant's Exhibit No. 56 was marked for
> identification and received into evidence and is
> attached hereto.)

Insertion of Exhibits in Record

Copies of exhibits should be inserted at the end of the transcript of the hearing or trial before the court reporter's certificate unless the statute directs otherwise. If you have several short hearings in one cover, place exhibits at the end of the hearing where the exhibits were introduced and before the next preface sheet.

In rare cases with many exhibits, make a separate volume of just the indexed exhibits.

Exhibit Index

Every trial transcript should have a separate index of exhibits, which should show: whose exhibit (for the plaintiff, for the State, for the defendant); exhibit number; description; page identified; page received; and page bound in.

The reporter must fill out the worksheet fully on all exhibits so the preparer of the index need only fill in the numbers of pages. If the transcript is prepared by a notereader or transcriber, he or she should prepare a rough penciled index as transcription is accomplished, and this will make final preparation of the index easy at the end of the job. If the transcript is done by computer, key in items for the index, and at the end of the transcript, print it out.

Copies of Exhibits

If you are required to make copies of exhibits, it is customary to charge the regular page rate for each page. However, if you are authorized to do this work on courthouse equipment at no cost to you, no charge should be made.

Securing Exhibit Information

When you take a new job, you will not always have someone to ask for answers to all the little questions that arise. Go to depositions and trial transcripts in the files and spend time studying how other reporters handled similar records. The files of district clerks, court of civil appeals clerk, and the others are all public records, and most clerks will cooperate willingly in showing you these.

The court, or the judge, is the authority for the official court reporter. If you have an important question as to how to handle something, be sure to check with the judge, who has the final responsibility.

Responsibility for Exhibits during Recess

In federal courts and many other courts, the clerk of courts is charged with marking and maintaining the exhibits. However, if it is your responsibility to retain the exhibits, never leave for recess or at adjournment and permit any exhibits or notes to remain on your table or elsewhere in the courtroom.

One day in our court, the clerk of courts in a case left the exhibits on a table in the courtroom while he got a cup of coffee. The judge came in and saw one of the attorneys destroying the photographs the other side had introduced as evidence in the case. Had the judge not caught counsel, the clerk of courts charged with responsibility for care, custody, and control of the exhibits would have been accused of losing the exhibits. Use care, and protect yourself at all times.

On your worksheet put a brief description of the exhibit by the number when it is identified. Then, check the number when it is received. As the trial progresses, it is good to write in "no" when the court does not allow the exhibit in evidence or "not offered" when the attorney has it marked and never offers the exhibit in evidence.

At noon, and at the close of the day, return exhibits that have been marked for identification but have not been received in evidence to the attorneys offering them. This lets them know what your understanding is as to whether the exhibit has been received in evidence or not. If you are in error, you will discover it then. If the attorneys cannot agree, check your notes.

At the end of the day, always take the time to get all the exhibits in numerical order and check carefully to make sure you have them all. Sometimes the judge will ask the attorneys to wait for this to be done. Retrieve any missing exhibits from the attorneys' files. If you are charged with care and custody of the exhibits, have the bailiff take narcotics, guns, money, and so on, to the sheriff's vault at night, but be sure to get a receipt from the bailiff. Keep two forms of receipts for exhibits at your desk in the courtroom, releases for officers or others and releases for the court reporter. Figures 57 and 58 show suggested forms of receipts.

Substitute Reporter's Duty Regarding Exhibits. If you substitute in a court for part of a trial, when you wind up the day's work be sure to leave a copy or a list of all exhibits showing which have been received in evidence. Leave the exhibits in numerical order if possible.

Storage and Disposition of Exhibits

If it is your responsibility to store exhibits, be sure that safety of all objects is ensured. Keep offense reports with your machine shorthand notes on guilty pleas. Keep your regular file cabinets holding exhibits locked. File the file folders of exhibits numerically by cause number. Keep an extra lock and bar on cabinets containing weapons and small amounts of narcotics.

FIGURE 57
Form of Receipt for Exhibits

```
                          NO. _____

THE STATE OF TEXAS,                    IN THE 158TH DISTRICT COURT

          Plaintiff,                   OF HARRIS COUNTY, T E X A S

     -vs-                              _____ TERM, A.D. 19__


     Received of:







  the above items introduced into evidence and kept in possession of

  the court reporter.


  Date: _____
                              _____
                              WRITING PRETELY
                              Official Court Reporter
                              158th District Court
```

FIGURE 58
Form of Receipt for Exhibits

```
                          NO. _____


THE STATE OF TEXAS,                    IN THE 158TH DISTRICT COURT

          Plaintiff,                   OF HARRIS COUNTY, T E X A S

       -vs-                            _____ TERM, A.D. 19__


       The evidence in the above entitled and numbered cause being:




was released to me this date by the Court Reporter of the 158th

District Court of Harris County, Texas.


Date:   _____
                                 _____
                                 Name


                                 _____
                                 Title


                                 _____
                                 Address
```

Chapter 26   *Reporting Objections*

Fear of Handling Objections

To the beginning court reporter, objections of counsel and the ensuing arguments and rulings present a frightening challenge. Even though the neophyte has had much exposure to them in four-voice classes as a student and a substantial internship period with practicing reporters, the burden of producing the record is totally upon the individual at that point.

On depositions the experience can be difficult at first when one counsel insists on trying to get material in and opposing counsel is just as determined to keep it out. After a day of this, reporters feel that their minds are Ping-Pong balls that have been bounced one too many times.

An example of what may happen is this: A graduate who was hired by one attorney was told by the other not to write certain testimony. When the hiring lawyer insisted that he wanted that part of the testimony on the record, she began to write. Opposing counsel then clutched her hands firmly and forbade her to write. When I asked her how she handled the situation, she said, "Oh, I memorized it. As soon as the attorney let go of my hands, I wrote what the other attorney had wanted. The attorney who objected thought I was just writing the next question. Now, I know why you told us we had to write fast."

Usually, on depositions, since the reporter is the one in control of the proceedings, if he or she does not keep order and do what is necessary to get a good record, it is the reporter's fault. You cannot be too timid and be a fine reporter. You simply must let the attorneys know you cannot take constant overlapping, but do it with tact and courtesy.

Reporting in the courtroom presents more of a challenge than deposition reporting because objections and arguments come up often and are ruled upon by a fourth person, the judge.

The examining attorney tries rapidly to sneak his or her unacceptable or at least potentially doubtful question in; opposing counsel cuts in with an objection at the speed of light. The witness tries to serve his or her own ends by getting a self-serving answer in even faster, and the judge breaks in to rule—all at the same time, it often seems.

The key words here are: Stay calm. Never panic.

A Personal Experience

I had been a judge's official only a short time when one day, right at the end of a question, the witness answered as opposing counsel objected frantically, all at the same time. The other attorney began to argue, and I never did get the answer. But I did get all the objections and ensuing colloquy, and even got the judge's ruling sustaining the objection.

Then, the objecting attorney said, "Your Honor, I move to strike the witness's answer from the record." The judge said calmly, "Mrs. Reporter, what was the answer counsel moved to strike?" All I could say was, "I was just going to ask the witness to repeat it myself. I couldn't hear it because of counsel's objection."

Everybody laughed, and the witness quickly made some reply—probably not the previous answer, as people seldom give an answer the same way twice—and the judge ruled it stricken from the record.

Shortly, the judge looked over at me and said, "See me in my chambers at recess." Right then I knew I'd done something wrong. In chambers, he started off diplomatically by saying, "I admired the way you handled that readback because I guess you retrieved the situation about as well as anyone could have, but let's talk about it a little bit." He went on, "In the future, in periods of stress, always get the question and answer because they are essential. If you can, mark them somehow because they may be asked for later on. Then, get the fact that there was an objection and as much of the grounds for the objection as you can. Then you have preserved the record in case the matter is appealed.

"The next important thing is my ruling, so be sure to get that. You can tell what the ruling was. If no answer has been given, and I sustain the objection, there will not be an answer. If an answer has been given, and I sustain the objection, the objecting lawyer will move to strike it if he or she is smart, and I will allow it to go out. If I overrule the objection, there will be an answer following my ruling. If the question has already been answered prior to the objection, the answer will remain in the record and nothing more will be said concerning the answer."

As the judge and I drove home together that day, he went into a number of grounds for objections, and within a few weeks I found it was so easy that I wondered why it had seemed to hard at first.

One thing that helped was that I could now anticipate what was going to be objectionable. At such times I would keep right up with the speaker, focusing my attention on what was being said. I managed to push myself beyond my regular speed because just when I thought I could not keep up any longer, the speakers would pause, and I would have time to catch up even though they were going fast, overlapping, and talking at the same time.

That judge also gave me more good advice that day. He explained that although he was in charge of the whole proceedings in court, it was my job to work with him as a team to make the record. He told me to interrupt only when absolutely necessary—never during opening and closing statements or jury charge—but to get his attention whenever I felt anything important might be slipping away. He urged me to bring my problems to him and agreed to give me any support and good advice he felt any occasion merited. In days to come that judge taught me more than any school could. That is the kind of rapport you must have to work satisfactorily as a judge's official reporter.

Marking Objections

You will get so you can sense that objections are about to occur by the line of questioning and the tenor of the testimony. Stenograph Corp., 1500 Bishop Court, Mount Pleasant, IL, has perfected a most helpful device called the "Steno-Mark," which places a spot of red ink on the edge of machine shorthand paper, where it is readily seen. It is placed at the top of the plate on the shorthand machine, and can be used not only for marking trouble spots at objections, but also to identify direct and cross-examination beginnings and names and words that must be verified as the case goes along.

My method was to keep on the table in front of me a number of brightly colored manila cards about 1½″ by 3″ in size. The second an attorney objected, I would throw one of these in my tray. At the end of objections, colloquy, and ruling, the question and/or question and answer could be found immediately. This also worked very well for me. However, we owe a debt of deep gratitude to Stenograph for the "Steno-Mark," which seems to serve so well for these several functions.

Rules of Evidence

It will aid you greatly in producing your records if you understand a little about the Rules of Evidence. The Rules of Evidence fill many books and state what is allowed and what is not allowed in presentation of a case so as to keep within the issues of the case and limit testimony to direct facts seen or heard by the witnesses. These Rules of Evidence have been developed over many years to determine what testimony will best help the Court and jury decide the issues in lawsuits. Evidence includes all the means by which any alleged matter of fact, the truth of which is submitted to investigation, is established or disproved. Evidence includes both oral testimony and the physical objects introduced in a case such as exhibits.

Attorneys are expected to protect their record by making timely use of objections and motions to strike during any deposition or hearing. These objections are essential to preserve the rights of the litigants. When one party attempts to offer evidence which is not admissible under the Rules of Evidence, the other party must object, giving a precise reason, if he or she wishes to keep such evidence out of the case.

Objections should be made to questions immediately before an answer is made, for once testimony is heard by the jury, they cannot lightly dismiss it from their minds even though the judge should rule that they must.

A lawyer who fails to object to evidence ordinarily waives claim as to its inadmissibility. The judge will rule on all objections, sustaining proper ones and overruling bad ones. Sometimes objections are stated as motions, in which case the judge will grant or deny the motion stated.

In some states, opposing counsel is considered to have an automatic exception to court rulings adverse to his or her side of the case. In other states, he or she must say, "I respectfully except to the Court's ruling," or, "Exception," or, "I take an exception," or something similar to preserve his or her record. This procedure is referred to by the Court and counsel as "protecting the record."

The purpose of taking an exception is to put the trial judge on notice that an attorney does not agree with the Court's ruling and will use that as a point should he or she appeal the case.

Motion to Strike

The Court may grant a motion to strike out evidence:

1. When the evidence was apparently proper when received but later shown to be objectionable.
2. When evidence is admitted subject to the understanding that it will be ruled on later in the trial.
3. When a witness makes a voluntary statement or testifies when there is no question pending.
4. When an answer is not responsive to a question.

When an attorney promises to connect objectionable matter up later, the Court may permit a question and answer subject to later connection.

As far as the court reporter is concerned, he or she writes all testimony included and all discussion concerning striking matter from the record and the Court's ruling and includes all this information in the transcript. The Court's ruling that matter is stricken or may go out merely means that the jury is to disregard it.

The only things the court reporter omits from the record are off-the-record discussions and matter expunged from the record. For example, one day in the midst of a case, the judge realized that the individuals had the matter hopelessly turned around and the record would be undecipherable by an appeals court. It was before the Court only, so the judge, with consent of counsel, asked to have the proceedings thus far ignored. I threw out my notes in full view of everyone, and we started again and secured a clear record of the matter.

Sometimes it may seem that lawyers overlook possible objections, for there is a potential objection to almost every question that could be asked. Usually counsel purposely overlook many objections because they weigh the effect the evidence is having on the jury and consider the damage that might be done by interjecting an objection at the time. Jurors often feel that the frequently objecting lawyer is trying to keep something from them, so that attorney has to weigh this consequence. At other times it will seem to you that some attorneys, particularly new ones, object to everything in an anxious overeagerness to protect their record.

Grounds for Objections

Attorneys voice both general and specific objections. An attorney who simply says, "Objection" or, "We object" or states that he or she objects to the form of the question without defining specifically what in the form is objectionable is making a general objection.

An attorney who points out in detail the grounds or reasons why an objection should be sustained is making a specific objection.

In the following paragraphs examples will follow each item of objection.

Blanket Objection

The most commonly used general objection remarks that the proposed evidence is incompetent, irrelevant, and immaterial. This statement is what is called a "blanket objection," and the courts prefer a more specific reason why counsel deems the proposed evidence improper, so further objections are usually tacked onto this one.

The words of this objection are similar in meaning, but not identical. The word "incompetent" means not proper to be received, "irrelevant" means not relating to or applicable to the matter at issue, and "immaterial" means not important or pertinent.

Q: To your knowledge, is Eileen Gray a prostitute?

> MR. DISSENT: I object to that as incompetent, irrelevant, and immaterial. How could it matter in a robbery case what her profession is, Your Honor?

or

Q: In your work with polygraphs, have you ever determined results that have led to dismissal of charges against any defendant?

> MR. DEMONSTRATING: I object to that as incompetent, irrelevant, and immaterial. It has no relevance to the case at hand anyway.

All evidence must be relevant and germane to the issues of the case at hand, so objection is frequently made solely on the grounds of relevancy.

Q: Was the apprehension of Dale Morgan in Wyoming reported in the newspapers, to your knowledge?

> MR. JUMPUPP: I object. That is not relevant in this hearing.

or

Q: You have given us a lot of your professional qualifications and experience, Doctor. Did you mention your great experience in testifying in trials?

> MR. BOLDGUY: I don't think that is relevant, Your Honor; and I object to the implication contained therein.

Objections to Leading and Suggestive Questions

Another very common objection is: "I object to the question as leading and suggestive." This statement is often prefaced by the words, "I object to the form of the question."

Questions are leading when they clearly indicate to the witness the answer desired by counsel. For instance, a lawyer should not say, "You knew your wife was going to meet this man at 8:00 o'clock the night of March 23, 19—, at Carmelita's Corners, didn't you?" The question should be phrased: "To your knowledge, what was your wife going to do on the night of March 23, 19—?"

Q: Your doctor told you that you were to do no heavy lifting when you saw him on December 22, 19—, didn't he?

> MR. SNARLING: I object to the question as leading and suggestive.

Leading questions are allowed when the witness is old and infirm, a young child, a very illiterate person, or one suffering from a language barrier (as in the case of a foreign merchant seaman or a migrant worker involved in litigation in this country). Leading questions are also proper on cross-examination, and the Court may ask leading questions of a witness in order to bring out the truth in a case. The Court will also allow leading questions to be asked by counsel on direct examination when a witness becomes hostile or appears evasive.

Objections to Nonresponsive Answers

When a witness does not clearly respond to the question asked, counsel may object to the answer as not responsive and ask the Court to strike the nonresponsive matter.

Q: What is your name?

A: Well, I was standing right there by the stove in the kitchen when all of a sudden I heard this loud "Boom," and I just went out right away; and my daughter was laying there in the yard, and I could see she had been shot—

> MR. STOPPEM: Your Honor, I object to the answer as unresponsive and move to have it stricken.
> THE COURT: Sustained, and it may go out.
> Mrs. Smith we will let you tell your story, but listen to what this attorney asks in his questions, and just answer them one at a time. Don't volunteer anything until it is asked for.

Objections Due to Lack of Proper Foundation

Sometimes attorneys will object to questions because no proper foundation has been laid for them. Evidence should proceed logically, and a foundation must be laid step by step.

Ordinarily, witnesses are asked their names, addresses, businesses, and qualifications, if experts. Then their connection with the matter at hand is established before they tell what they have seen or heard regarding the matter. An attorney cannot elicit that a man saw another murdered until he or she establishes that the man was at the spot where the incident took place.

Often counsel will frame questions while rattling papers vigorously as they try to enter in evidence photographs, documents, X-rays, and other exhibits before they have been identified and prior to any foundation having been laid to make them material to the case at hand.

Q: Do I understand, then, that the only way you advertise is by brochures sent to customers?

> MR. STRIKEITT: I object. No foundation has been laid to show the company has any brochures or has ever sent any to prospective customers.

Objections to Facts not in Evidence

A closely allied objection to the one regarding improper evidence is made to assuming facts not in evidence. A hypothetical question which does not parallel the case at hand will be objected to as assuming facts not in evidence.

Q: Did you see Mr. Johnson in the same car that you saw the stolen lawnmower in?

> MR. IRONSIDES: Your Honor, I object. He has not testified that he ever saw either him or the lawnmower in any car, so that is assuming a fact not yet in evidence.

Objections to Repetitious Questioning

Repetitious questioning is objectionable because it takes up the valuable time of the Court, the litigants, and their witnesses.

Q: Do you know why it was determined that the back flow preventer should not be put on this system?

> MR. ENNUI: I object to this as repetition. That is the third time that question has been asked and answered in some form or other.

Objection to Hearsay Evidence

Hearsay evidence is frequently objected to by counsel. Hearsay is a term given to testimony offered by witnesses who testify not to what they know personally, but to what others have told them or what they have heard said by others. It is secondhand evidence.

Exceptions to the hearsay rule are dying declarations, confessions, admissions, statements against interest, res gestae, business entries, public records, former testimony, reputation, and statements about physical condition or mental state.

Witnesses often given hearsay answers in response to good questions because they do not know what is admissible and what is not. Hearsay answers lead to motions to strike the answer and a ruling of "sustained."

Q: When was the first time you saw Mr. Johnson that day?

A: Someone called from room 39 and reported he was in there.

> MR. GUTSY: Excuse me. I object to what was reported as hearsay, and the answer is also unresponsive.
> THE COURT: I will sustain it.

or

Q: Do you know what was the spark for this fire?

> MR. SUNDANCE: Objection. The witness was not present when the fire was ignited;

and it would be strictly hearsay and the rendering of an opinion on his part, which he is not qualified to give in his answer.

or

Q: Did the girl say anything at that point?

A: Well, she said someone told her John broke the glass to get in.

    MR. BLISTER: I will object to the answer as hearsay and move it be stricken from the record.

Hearsay statements include those saying "I understand," "I understood," "It is my understanding," "I was informed," "I was notified," "It was reported to me," "I have heard," and "I was told." Witnesses may ordinarily testify only to what they have knowledge of through their own senses and not as to what others have told them.

Objections to Self-Serving Answers

Self-serving statements and self-serving documents are objectionable as they serve no purpose other than to bolster the person's case who offers them. Often during the trial of a case, the plaintiff or the defendant will try to show that at some time prior to the present testimony he or she told the same story as is being told now. This type of maneuver is self-serving and an improper offer of proof.

Q: When you came to the hospital, you told them that Mr. Hittem ran you down, didn't you?

A: Yes, I certainly did. He did it on purpose.

    MR. WRAPPEMGOOD: I object to the question and answer as self-serving.

or

Q: Did you notice that there was considerable business activity in my client's store at the time you were there?

    MR. ALERT: I object on the ground that the amount of business can't be shown by this witness, and it is self-serving.

Compound and Complex Questions

Compound and complex questions may call for involved compound and complex answers, which become so confusing that much questioning is required to straighten them out. Counsel often become so engrossed in trying to elicit all the facts that they tack several questions together, thereby making the resulting answers unintelligible. Usually, upon objection to such questions, the judge will simply say, "Sustained. Counsel, rephrase the question."

When you are asked to read back such questions, they will frequently be unclear; and the attorney will say "I will restate the question."

Q: Did you stop the car at that time to have more kisses or to do what any man under those circumstances would do?

    MR. LA POINTE: I am going to object to that as calling for two answers in the same question. It is a plural question.

or

Q: Do you know when they were tested, and do you know why they were picked up to be tested?

      MR. SKAIREM: I object to that as a double question.

Ambiguity Leads to Objections

Vague, uncertain, and ambiguous questions are also objected to because an indefinite, uncertain question cannot elicit an intelligible answer. Ordinarily, the Court will request that such questions be rephrased.

Q: Would you say that there is a great likelihood of assuming small particles of sand or other debris get in the system, that there would be fairly good possibility of the valves wedging closed? Would you say this is a very, very, very remote possibility?

      MR. TRYING: I object to the form of the question. It is broad, vague, and indefinite. The witness would have to know the location of the material, the exact size of the material, and under what conditions the valve was operating at the time.

or

Q: Did you talk to Mr. Anderson about this matter?

      MR. SHUSHUPP: I object to this as too vague. There are three Mr. Andersons in this case: John, John, Jr., and Bill. Which one are you referring to?

Objections to Other than the Best Evidence

Sometimes attorneys will present carbon copies of letters or instruments or photocopies of checks and documents as exhibits when the originals could be made available. Also, counsel will sometimes bring in a secondary witness to testify to a matter which could be better answered by another. Opposing counsel will object to such presentations as not the best evidence.

Q: I am going to show you what has been marked as "Defendant's Exhibit No. 1 for identification, a rental schedule of the building in question, and ask you to tell us what Mr. Jay's rent was during January, 19—.

      MR. SMART: We object to it as not the best evidence. His lease would be the best evidence.

or

Q: I show you a photocopy of the ledger sheet of Readers' Book Company regarding Willie Paymee as of October 26, 19—

      MR. SNIDELY: To which I object as not the best evidence.

Objections to Conclusions and Opinions

Objections are commonly made to questions calling for conclusions, opinions, or speculations on the part of a lay (not expert) witness. Opinions are inferences or conclusions drawn by a witness from facts. Ordinarily, witnesses may give only facts, not opinions or their conclusions drawn from them.

When a witness states, "I think he went in the back door because I saw it was open," or, "I wasn't there, but he must have been running across the street at the time," he or she is stating a conclusion, which is not permissible.

Q: What does this photograph show?

A: It shows evidence of blood on the front seat on the passenger side.

> MR. UTELLEM: I object to that as a conclusion of the witness. That spot could be anything, and from that picture, he cannot possibly tell whether it was blood or not.

or

Q: What was his conviction for on June 19, 19—?

A: I believe Escape in the Second Degree.

> MR. PICKEE: I object to it unless the witness can be more precise. That is merely his opinion, and the answer, "I believe," is insufficient.

or

Q: All you're saying is that there's a possibility that the gas could have been in that lower bottle and that this gas could possibly have escaped through the top?

> MR. BRIGHT: I object to this line of questioning as being highly speculative.

Objections to Illegally Obtained Evidence

A valid objection is often made with regard to evidence which is illegally obtained and, therefore, not admissible. This objection is frequently made against inclusion in evidence of confessions obtained under circumstances where there is doubt as to whether the accused was properly advised of his or her rights.

Q: I show you now your statement which has been marked as State's Exhibit No. 1 and ask you if you can identify it.

> MR. BARBELL: Your Honor, I object to the introduction of this exhibit because it was illegally secured. My client was not properly advised of his Constitutional rights prior to this interrogation, and he gave that statement not knowing that he was entitled to the services of an attorney before he said anything and that an attorney would be provided for him if he could not afford to procure one from his own funds.

Objections to Self-Incriminating Testimony

A person does not have to give incriminating testimony against himself or herself and can claim privilege against self-incrimination (take the Fifth Amendment). Any client's attorney will quickly object to any question calling for the individual to testify against his or her self-interest.

Q: Did you enter a motel with Sally Forthe in the city of Winthrop, Louisiana, at 9:30 P.M. on the evening of July 20 of this year?

> MR KRAFTY: My client refuses to answer that on the grounds that it might tend to incriminate him since he is currently under indictment on a charge of adultery.

Objections to Cross-Examination Beyond Scope of Direct Examination

A frequently used objection on cross-examination is that the testimony goes beyond or outside the scope of the direct examination, or that the question is improper cross-examination. An attorney may cover only the subject matter already covered on direct examination in his or her cross-examination. New subject matter may not be developed on cross-examination except in the case of an adverse witness.

Q: Are you able, Doctor, to form an opinion of your own, based upon the reports of the latest laboratory examinations, as to the need for more tests?

    MR. SNAPPER: I object to this as going beyond the scope of direct examination.

Objections to Expert without Qualifications

Questions may be asked of a lay witness which call for more than a factual answer, and these will be objected to by counsel as calling for expert testimony. If the witness on the stand can be qualified as an expert, an answer will be allowed. Otherwise, the objection will be sustained. The following question asked of a lay witness would be clearly objectionable:

Q: What is the value of this property next to your home?

    MR. LASHINGOUT: I am going to object because the witness has not been qualified as an expert in the matter of appraisals.

Objections to "Fishing Expeditions"

On depositions and in court cases, attorneys will object to questions not germane to the issues as "fishing expeditions," and use such terms as "rewarding the lazy and punishing the diligent," and "usurpation of the work product of opposing counsel." Questions objected to for this reason are asked by attorneys who hope that the answers will turn up some information by chance which might be helpful to their cases.

Objections to Badgering the Witness

Attorneys are not allowed to argue with the witnesses because this tends to produce inferences, not facts. Neither are lawyers allowed to badger the witness or demean any person who is testifying in any way. Counsel are quick to object to such treatment of witnesses by an opposing attorney.

Q: Your answer is you think so? Is that all you can say? You think so. Come on, now. You know that to be a fact, don't you?

    MR. MERUIT. Your Honor, I object to counsel's arguing with the witness and badgering him in this manner. The witness has answered the question.

Objections on the Grounds that the Evidence Speaks for Itself

A common objection is that the evidence speaks for itself when counsel tries to adduce lengthy explanations concerning material which is readily discernable from documents, photographs, and such items.

Q: What does the scene depict other than the roadway?

    MR. JUMPUPP: I will object to that, if the Court please. The picture speaks for itself.

or

Q: I am going to show you the contract in question and ask you whether contained therein is a provision for locking block valves in this installation.

MR.OBJECTOR: I object to the question because the document speaks for itself and is the best evidence of what it contains.

Objections to Privileged Information

Information is privileged between husband and wife, attorney and client, clergy and parishioner, and physician and patient. The objection regarding privileged information may be invoked only by the person making the confidential communication by his or her lawyer on the individual's behalf.

Q: Have you discussed with your attorney whether either one of these tests was made in this case?

> MR. NETTLES: I object. You are asking him for privileged matter in an attorney-client relationship. Don't answer that question.

or

Q: What did your husband tell you as to his plans to commit this bank robbery?

> MR. FURY: I object. That question is asking for privileged matter between husband and wife.

Objection to Narrative Form of Testimony

An attorney may object to rambling, narrative-type testimony, which many times will get into inadmissible matter or add to the expense of trial because of excessive verbiage. Counsel are instructed by the court to ask specific questions and get concise answers that do not unduly prolong trial of a case.

Objections to Expert Witness

Should an expert witness not be qualified by questioning which elicits his or her training and experience sufficient to satisfy opposing counsel or the Court, an objection may be made by opposing counsel. When a particularly outstanding expert in any field is placed on the witness stand, counsel usually stipulate as to the qualifications of the witness, agreeing that he or she need not list training, experience, and accomplishments.

Objections to Mention of Insurance

Should the word "insurance" be mentioned during a trial, defense counsel will immediately rise and make vigorous objection, which will result in the judge's removing one juror from the jury box and declaring a mistrial. The reason for this is that if a jury knows a big insurance company may be paying the award, they may decide to give an excessive amount to the plaintiff as compared to the figure they would decide upon it it were to be assessed against an individual.

Objections as a Result of Surprise

An interesting objection is the claim of surprise on the part of attorneys. This claim means that one of their own witnesses has changed his or her story or introduced material not previously known to their attorneys, contrary to what the attorneys were led to believe the testimony would be. When the attorneys are surprised, they are forced to plan a whole new line of strategy and attack, necessitating continuance of the lawsuit to allow preparation time.

Objections to Exhibits

Attorneys may object to exhibits such as photographs and photocopies on grounds of clarity or that they are not an accurate representation of the thing purported to be reproduced.

Objections to an Attempt to Impeach a Witness

Should an attorney try to impeach a witness he or she has called to testify for his or her side of the case, opposing counsel will object to this tactic, since attorneys are supposed to bring in witnesses favorable to their own sides to strengthen their cases. They are expected to be familiar with the testimony the witnesses will give.

The previous objections are by no means the only objections you will hear. There are a myriad of others, but you will hear these common ones very often, so familiarize yourself with them and be prepared.

Chapter 27 *Jury Charge and Directed Verdicts*

Jury Charge

Following the closing arguments the judge delivers his or her charge to the jury. The jury charge, also called jury instructions, sets forth the principles of law governing the lawsuit in progress for the jury's application in their deliberations toward reaching a verdict in the case.

The judge ordinarily prepares his or her charge, and the lawyers provide the Court with instructions they would like to have charged. The Court then meets with the attorneys in chambers before presenting the charge to discuss those proposed by each side.

Occasionally an attorney will rush in to the court reporter with a request that the official type some suggested charges or changed wording, for which service the attorney will usually offer a nice gratuity. Being capable of doing such spur-of-the moment work engenders good public relations and endears the reporter to counsel.

The jury charge must be reported verbatim by the reporter, plus any exceptions of counsel to any part made at the end of the charge and any further requests of the attorneys for further specific items, together with the Court's rulings on these items. All exceptions taken to the jury instructions are a vital part of the transcript, and the proper parenthetical expressions must appear in the record showing where the jury is at all times. The discussions regarding exceptions to the charge out of the presence of the jury may take place in chambers, although the judge will often send the jury out and call the official to the sidebar or bench to report the exceptions and rulings.

Whether or not attorneys place an order for transcript of the jury charge in a case, the official almost universally is requested to transcribe a copy of it for the judge's files unless he or she has done so prior to its reading to the jury by the Court.

A nice service to provide a judge is to type up boilerplate (standard charges used over and over) in personal injury, criminal, and civil cases on 4″ x 6″ cards, assigning a number to each. Then, in uncomplicated cases, it is a simple matter of pulling cards the judge designates to prepare charges quickly.

Sometimes the reporter is as familiar as the judge with the jury charge by the time it is delivered in court, as in complicated cases it may be drafted and redrafted several times to secure the exact wording His or Her Honor wants.

More appeals are taken from jury charges than any other part of trials, which makes the wording very important. This is why the official reporter must record the charge in shorthand exactly as read, since an error or an omitted or added word may reverse a case in the appeals court.

If the judge has a secretary, the reporter may hear the charge for the first time when it is read in court; but in many places the official is the judge's secretary.

If the jury charge is prepared before the appeal transcript is transcribed in a case, it should be numbered at the top in the margin on the left-hand side so the proper numbers may be inserted on the right-hand side or center as the completed transcript is prepared to fit in with the correct numbering sequence.

A cover or blue legal back is not placed on the jury charge when it is prepared for the judge because most judges prefer to file these charges in notebooks for future reference.

Allen Charge and Admonishments

Occasionally it may be necessary for the judge to give a supplementary charge because the jury may have sent in a note requesting further clarification, or they may indicate that they are deadlocked. If the jury cannot agree, and so inform the Court, the judge may give what is known as an "Allen Charge," or "Dynamite Charge," which will ask that the jurors continue deliberations and try to reach a verdict if they can conscientiously do so.

Special charges are given at noon and evening recesses also, admoninshing jurors not to discuss the case among themselves or with others, and not to read newspapers or listen to the radio or watch T.V. newscasts regarding the case under consideration.

Parantheticals for Jury Charges

The reporter must note carefully the time the jury begins its deliberations. Also, each time the jury reenters the courtroom and leaves it again, the time should be carefully recorded as well.

A proper parenthetical expression must be inserted in the record concerning these comings and goings, such as:

> (At 3:30 P.M., the jury retired to
> deliberate upon a verdict.)

or

> (At 2:00 P.M., the jury retired to
> commence deliberations)

Procedures Regarding the Jury

Each note sent in by the jury is marked as an exhibit, and proper parenthetical expressions must be included in the transcript regarding such markings. Of course, the court reporter must be readily available during jury deliberations to read requested material and to report additional instructions and, ultimately, the verdict. If the official is asked to read to the jury one or several days' testimony of a witness or witnesses, the jury will be brought back into the courtroom. The testimony is read back, but objections, rulings, and material objected to are omitted in reading at this time.

The rules previously given as to reading back are particularly applicable at such times. The reporter should read at such a speed as allows constant looking ahead, scanning material to come in order to decipher poor outlines or unusual words without pausing.

Hung Jury

The jury may find for the defendant (not guilty in a criminal case; no cause of action in a civil trial) or find for the plaintiff. Or, it may be unable to reach a verdict, in which case the court will declare a mistrial. Should this happen, the case must be tried again before a new jury. A jury which cannot reach a verdict is referred to as a "hung jury."

Publication of the Verdict

When the jury has reached a verdict, it is returned to the courtroom to have the verdict published (announced). The jury may announce the verdict through its foreman, or the clerk of court may read the written and signed verdict of the jury. Sometimes the verdict is sealed and opened at a later session of court in the presence of the parties, counsel, the jurors, the judge, and the reporter, particularly when it is reached very late at night.

The reporter must record the verdict and the polling of the jury if this is requested. Polling of the jury simply means that each juror is asked whether he or she individually agrees that this is his or her verdict. In some places a civil trial verdict may be reached by a majority or designated number, such as ten of the twelve jurors.

Transcribing Jury Charge in Advance of Trial

The official reporter must be most meticulous in transcribing or typing the judge's jury charge in advance if this is one of his or her duties, not only to ensure correct wording, but to insure perfect agreement of verbs, antecedents, and correct punctuation. In case of an appeal the RE-PORTER series may perpetuate any flaws forever, and the judge will not appreciate your making him or her appear less than expert in usage of English.

While on the topic of editing, you will never make an enemy of counsel either if you edit to the extent that they appear literate, as long as you change nothing material. However, witnesses are not ordinarily edited except in the occasional case of an expert witness. Editing is a matter most agencies prefer to guide their newcomers in very carefully. Remember, though, no one should make Mortimer Snerd sound like H. L. Mencken. Editing requires a lot of common sense.

Figure 59A through C on pages 244 through 246 shows a brief, typical jury charge transcript. The samples in Figure 60 on page 247 represent the verdict forms sent out with the jury to be returned into court, signed by the foreman. Some judges will have all the possible verdicts typed on one sheet of paper, while others prefer to have each form of verdict on a separate sheet of paper.

Directed Verdict

After plaintiff has rested, and again after both sides have rested, either party to a lawsuit may move for a directed verdict because it feels the case is so one-sided that the judge should make the decision instead of the jury, or that only questions of law remain, and the judge should decide them.

It sometimes becomes apparent that a case will be decided upon special issues, and that there will be a directed (or instructed) verdict in the lawsuit based upon these issues. In this event the jury is given a series of questions to answer, and there can be but one decision in the matter as a result of these answers. Counsel may bring in prepared special issue questions, but the judge may call the reporter in and dictate the special issues to be resolved by the jury, or he or she may have jotted them down in handwriting for you. There are commercial forms available also in which only issue number and question need be inserted.

Typing the Special Issues

To prepare a set of special issues, cut half sheets of 8½″ x 11″ plain white typing paper, making at least an original and as many carbons as there are attorneys, plus one for the judge and one for yourself. The originals go to the jury room with the jury.

FIGURE 59-A
Jury Charge

1   NO. 356,938

2   THE STETE OF TEXAS   )   IN THE 180TH DISTRICT COURT
)

3   Plaintiff,)   OF TRAVIS COUNTY, T E X A S
)

4   -vs-   )   NOVEMBER TERM, A.D. 1982
)

5   ROBERT EARL BRENTWOOD,)
)

6   Defendant.)

7

8   CHARGE OF THE COURT

9 Members of the jury:

10   The defendant, Robert Earl Brentwood, stands charged

11 by indictment with the offense of theft, a felony, alleged

12 to have been committed in the County of Travis and State of

13 Texas on or about the 8th day of July, A.D. 19__.

14   To this charge, the defendant has pleaded "not

15 guilty."

16   Theft is the fraudulent taking of corporeal personal

17 property belonging to another from his possession or from

18 the possession of some person holding the same for him without

19 his consent with the intent to deprive the owner of the

20 value of the same and to appropriate it to the use and

21 benefit of the person taking.

22   By "fraudulent taking," as used in this charge, is

23 meant, first, that the person taking knew at the time of the

24 taking that the property was not his own; second, that the

25 property was taken without the consent of the owner; and,

FIGURE 59-B

1 third, that the property was taken with the intent to

2 deprive the owner of the value of the same and to ap-

3 propriate it to the use and benefit of the person taking.

4   Now, if you believe from the evidence beyond a reason-

5 able doubt that the property mentioned in the Indictment

6 belonged to Edward Hardesty, Jr., and was of the value of

7 $50 or over and was in his possession and that on or about

8 the time and at the place stated in the Indictment the

9 defendant did fraudulently take said property from the

10 possession of said Edward Hardesty, Jr., without his consent

11 and with the intent to deprive him of said property and

12 its value and to appropriate the same to the defendant's

13 use and benefit, then you will find the defendant guilty

14 as charged in the Indictment and so say by your verdict.

15   If you do not so believe, or if you have a reasonable

16 doubt thereof, you will find the defendant not guilty and so

17 say by your verdict.

18   The Indictment in this case is no evidence of the

19 defendant's guilt, and you will not consider the Indictment

20 nor the fact that the defendant has been indicted as any

21 evidence in this case; but you will wholly disregard the

22 same and pass upon the guilt or innocence of the defendant

23 wholly and solely from the evidence given before you in the

24 trial of this case and the law as given in the Court's

25 charge.

FIGURE 59-C

1   In all criminal cases, the burden of proof is on the

2   State. The defendant is presumed to be innocent until his

3   guilt is established by legal evidence beyond a reasonable

4   doubt; and in case you have a reasonable doubt as to the

5   defendant's guilt, you will acquit him and say by your

6   verdict "not guilty."

7   You are the exclusive judges of the facts proved,

8   of the credibility of the witnesses, and of the weight to

9   be given to the testimony; but you are bound to receive

10 the law from the Court, which is herein given you, and be

11 governed thereby.

12

13

14
                              _____
15   JURIS PRUDENCE, JUDGE
                              180th District Court
16   Travis County, Texas

17

18

19

20

21

22

23

24

25

FIGURE 60
Verdict of the Jury (Guilty)

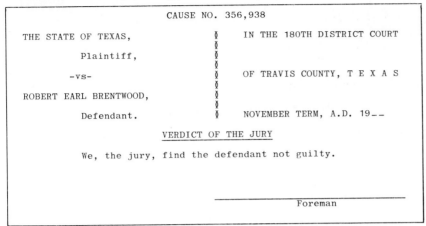

Verdict of the Jury (Not Guilty)

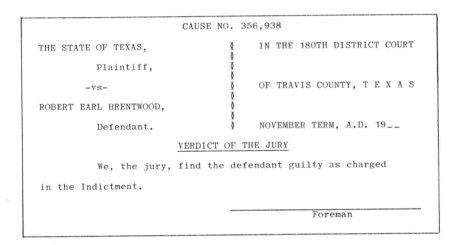

Center the title "SPECIAL ISSUE NO. 1" at the top of the first half page. Drop down a double space, indent, and type the first special issue, single- or double spacing the issue depending upon its length.

Your first one will look like the example in Figure 61. Proceed with other required issues using successive numbers.

FIGURE 61-A
Special Issues

SPECIAL ISSUE NO. 1

Do you find from a preponderance of the evidence that, at the time and on the occasion in question, Gertrude Holmes failed to leave and abandon her stalled automobile?
Answer "We do" or "We do not."
We, the jury, answer, _____ .

Usually each question proceeds from the prior one and is contingent upon how the last query was answered. Your second special issue will look like this:

FIGURE 61-B
Special Issues

If you have answered Special Issue No. 1 "We do," and only in that event, then answer:

SPECIAL ISSUE NO. 2

Do you find from a preponderance of the evidence that the failure of Gertrude Holmes, at the time and on the occasion in question, to leave and abandon her stalled automobile, if you have so found, was negligence?
Answer "We do" or "We do not."
We, the jury, answer: _____.

The last special issue in this case would appear like the following:

FIGURE 61-C

If you have answered Special Issue No. 2 "We do," and only in that event, then answer:

SPECIAL ISSUE NO. 3

Do you find from a preponderance of the evidence that such negligence, if any, was a proximate cause of the injuries, if any, sustained by Gertrude Holmes?
Answer "We do" or "We do not."
We, the jury, answer:_____

Chapter 28

Legal Citations

Attorneys who enter citations into records are sometimes inclined to read the material rapidly. Reporters who get the citation reference in their notes can look up the citation, check the accuracy of their notes, or fill in any parts they might have missed. Reporters, therefore, need to understand the meaning of the codes used in citations.

Federal Codes

The Constitution and every law that the Congress of the United States passes are published in a set of books called the United States Code. The laws are systematically arranged under subject headings, called "titles," and then into sections and subsections. The titles are arranged alphabetically and given a number. No matter how many separate statutes are placed under one title and how many books those statutes may fill, the title number remains the same. United States Code Annotated contains, in addition to the text of the statutes, references to decisions rendered on particular states.

The United States Code and United States Code Annotated are cited as follows:

> 28 U.S.C. 2254   or
> 28 U.S.C.A. 2254

The 28 is the title number and is always placed first; 2254 is the section number. If there is a subsection number in the citation, it would be added as follows:

> 28 U.S.C.A. 2254b

The United States Constitution and its amendments are cited as follows:

> U.S. Const. art. I, sec. 9. (If your typewriter has a section sign, use the sign in place of "sec.")
> U.S. Const. amend. XIV.

State Codes

Each state has its own method for compiling and codifying its laws. The following is a list of the accepted methods of citing them:

State	Title	How Cited
Ala.	Code of Alabama, 1940	Code of Alabama, Title 10, Sec. 101
Ariz.	Arizona Revised Statutes Annotated	RSA Sec. 10-101
Ark.	Arkansas Statutes Annotated (1947)	Ark. Stats. (1947) Sec. 10-101
Calif.	Deering's California Codes (Code of Civil Procedure)	CCP Sec. 101
Colo.	Colorado Revised Statutes, 1953	101-10-1, C.R.S. '53
Conn.	General Statutes of Connecticut Revision of 1949	Conn.G.S. 1949 Sec. 101
	1949 Supplement to the General Statutes	C.S. Supp. 1949 Sec. 101(a)
Del.	Delaware Code Annotated (1953)	10 Del. C. Sec. 110
Fla.	Florida Statutes Annotated	F.S.A. Sec. 101
	Florida Statutes, 1953	Florida Statutes, 1951, Sec. 101
Ga.	Georgia Code Annotated	Ga. Code Ann. Sec. 10-1010
Idaho	Idaho Code	Idaho Code, Sec. 101
Ill.	Illinois Revised Statutes 1951 Ill.	Rev. Stat. 1951 Ch. 10, Sec. 101
	Smith-Hurd Illinois Annotated Statutes	Smith-Hurd Anno. St. Ch. 10, Sec. 101
	Jones Illinois Statutes Annotated	Jones Ill. Stat. Anno., Ch. 10, Sec. 101
Ind.	Burns Indiana Statutes, Annotated, 1933	Sec. 10-1011 Burns Ind. Stat. Ann. 1933
Iowa	Code of Iowa	Code of Iowa, 1954, Sec. 110.10
Kan.	General Statutes of Kansas, 1949	G.S. 1949, Sec. 101
	1951 Supplement to General Statutes 1949	G.C. 1951 Supp., Sec. 101
Ken.	Kentucky Revised Statutes	KRS 101.010(1)
	Kentucky Civil Code	Civil Code, Sec. 101
La.	Louisiana Revised Statutes of 1950	R.S. 10:101
Maine	Revised Statutes of Maine, 1954	R.S. of Maine 1954, C. 10, Sec. 11
Md.	Flack's Annotated Code of Maryland, 1951	Md. Code (1951), Art. 10, Sec. 101
Mass.	Massachusetts General Law	G.L. (Ter. Ed.) c. 10 Sec. 101
Mich.	Michigan Statutes Annotated	Stat Ann Sec. 10.101
	1948 Compiled Laws of Michigan	C L 1948, Sec. 10.101
Minn.	Minnesota Statutes 1953	Minn. Stat. 1953, Sec. 101.10
	Minnesota Statutes Annotated	M.S.A., Sec. 101.10
Miss.	Mississippi Code, 1942, Annotated	Miss. Code, 1942, Ann., Sec. 101
Mo.	Missouri Revised Statutes 1949	R.S. Mo. Sec. 101
Mont.	Revised Code of Montana of 1947	RCM 1947, Sec. 10-101
Nebr.	Revised Statutes of Nebraska, 1943	Sec. 101, R.S. Nebr., 1943
	Reissue Revised Statutes of Nebraska, 1943	Sec. 101, R.R.S. Nebr., 1943
Nev.	Nevada Compiled Laws, 1929	NCL 1929, Sec. 1010
	Nevada Compiled Laws, Supplement 1953	NCL Supp. 1953, Sec. 1010.10
N.H.	1955 New Hampshire Revised Statutes Ann.	RSA 101.1
N.J.	Revised Statutes of New Jersey	N.J.R.S. 10:101-10
N.M.	New Mexico Statutes Annotated	1953 Comp., 1-1-10
N.Y.	McKinney's Consolidated Laws of New York	(Corporation) Law, Sec. 101
N.C.	General Statutes of North Carolina	G.S. 10-101
N.D.	North Dakota Revised Code of 1943	Sec. 10-1010 of NDRC 1943

Ohio	Ohio Revised Code, 1953	O.R.C. Sec. 1110.10
Okla.	Oklahoma Statutes Annotated	10 O.S. 1951 Sec. 101
Ore.	Oregon Revised Statutes, 1953	ORS 11:010
Penn.	Purden's Pennsylvania Statutes	10 P.S. Sec. 101
R.I.	General Laws of Rhode Island of 1938	Gen. Laws 1938, c. 1, art 10 Sec. 101
S.C.	Code of Laws of S.C. 1952	1952 Code, Sec. 10-101
	1952 Code Supplement	1952 Code Supp. Sec. 101
S.D.	South Dakota Code of 1939	SDC 10.1010(10)
Tenn.	Tennessee Code Annotated	Code, Sec. 10-101
Tex.	Vernon's Texas Statutes, Annotated	Vernon's Ann. Civ. St., art. 1010
Utah	Utah Code Annotated, 1953	UCA 1953, 10-10-1
Vt.	Vermont Statutes, Revision of 1947	V.S. 47, Sec. 1010
Va.	Code of Virginia, 1950	Code, Sec. 10-101
Wash.	Revised Code of Washington	RCW 10.11.101
W. Va.	West Virginia Code of 1955	Code Sec. 1010(1)
Wis.	Statutes of Wisconsin	Section 101.10(1) Stats. of Wis.
Wyo.	Wyoming Compiled Statutes, 1945	WCS 1945, Sec. 10-1010

Citing Foreign States

Sometimes the laws of a foreign state are cited. If the name of the state does not appear in the citation, it should be added. For example, if the document is to be filed in Texas and a Louisiana statute is cited, it should be "La. R.S. 9:103." However, if the document were filed in Louisiana, the citation would be "R.S.9:103."

Vernon's Texas Statutes, Annotated, are arranged similarly to U.S.C.A. The civil statutes have titles, chapters, articles, and sections, but in citing them, it is necessary to give only the article and section number. For example: Vernon's Ann.Civ.St., art. 1223, Sec.2. The Texas Legislature is in the process of codifying the statutes, and at present there are twelve codes which are to be cited as follows:

Tex.Bus. & Comm. Code Ann. Sec.16.16(a)(1)(A)(i) (1968).
Tex.Bus.Corp. Act. Ann. art. 206A(2) (1956).
Tex.Code Crim. Proc. Ann. art.3607 (1965).
Tex.Educ. Code Ann. Sec.33.09 (1972).
Tex.Election Code Ann. art. 3.55 (1962).
Tex.Family Code Ann. Sec.22.42 (1974).
Tex.Ins. Code Ann. art. 3.55 (1963).
Tex.Penal Code Ann. Sec.2.18 (1974).
Tex.Penal Code Aux. Laws art. 11, Sec.3 (1973).
Tex.Prob. Code Ann. Sec.27 (1956).
Tex.Tax.Gen.Ann. art. 3.01 (1960).
Tex.Water Code Ann. Sec.17.52 (1972).

Vernon's Texas Statutes has been nicknamed the "black statutes" because the binding on the books is black.

Statute books are kept up to date by means of supplements which are printed annually and inserted into special pockets in the binding of the back cover of the books. They are called "pocket parts."

Whenever a judge sits in a judicial proceeding and renders a decision, that decision is recorded for guidance of the courts in deciding future cases. Each appellate court has a reporter who is responsible for seeing that the decisions are published at regular intervals. These publications are called the official reports and the following is a list of those reports:

CITATIONS FOR OFFICIAL REPORTS

Title	*Citation*
Alabama Reports	Ala.
Alabama Appellate Reports	Ala. App.
Arizona Reports	Ariz.
Arkansas Reports	Ark.
California Appellate Reports	Cal. App.
California Appellate Reports, Second Series	Cal. App. 2d
California Reports	Cal.
California Reports, Second Series	Cal. 2d
Colorado Reports	Colo.
Connecticut	Conn.
Delaware Reports	Cited by name of reporter
Delaware Chancery Reports	Del. Ch.
Florida Reports	Fla.
Idaho Reports	Idaho
Illinois Reports	Ill.
Illinois Appellate Court Reports	Ill. App.
Indiana Reports	Ind.
Indiana Appellate Reports	Ind. App.
Iowa Reports	Iowa
Kansas Reports	Kan.
Kentucky Reports	Ky.
Louisiana Reports	La.
Maine Reports	Me.
Maryland Reports	Md.
Massachusetts Reports	Mass.
Michigan Reports	Mich.
Minnesota Reports	Minn.
Mississippi Reports	Miss.
Missouri Appellate Reports	Mo. App.
Montana Reports	Mont.
Nebraska Reports	Neb.
Nevada Reports	Nev.
New Hampshire Reports	N.H.
New Jersey Equity Reports	N.J.Eq.
New Jersey Reports	N.J.
New Jersey Superior Court Reports	N.J. Super.
New Mexico Reports	N.M.
New York Appellate Division Reports	N.Y. App. Div.
New York Miscellaneous Reports	N.Y. Misc.
New York Reports	N.Y.
North Carolina Reports	N.C.
North Dakota Reports	N.D.
Ohio Appellate Reports	Ohio App.
Ohio State Reports	Ohio St.
Oklahoma Reports	Okl.
Oklahoma Criminal Reports	Okl. Cr.

Oregon Reports	Ore.
Pennsylvania Reports	Pa.
Pennsylvania Superior Court Reports	Pa. Sup.
Rhode Island Reports	R.I.
South Carolina Reports	S.C.
South Dakota Reports	S.D.
Tennessee Reports	Tenn.
Tennessee Appeals Reports	Tenn. App.
United States Reports	U.S.
United States Court of Appeals, District of Columbia	U.S.App.D.C.
Utah Reports	Utah
Vermont Reports	Vt.
Virginia Reports	Va.
Washington Reports	Wash.
Washington Reports, Second Series	Wash.2d
West Virginia Reports	W. Va.
Wisconsin Reports	Wis.
Wyoming Reports	Wyo.

Not all states have an official reporter, but rely instead upon publishing companies to print them. Texas discontinued its official reports in 1963.

Decisions Published By Publishing Company

West Publishing Company publishes the decisions of all of the federal and state courts by means of a system called the NATIONAL REPORTER SYSTEM. A list of the separate sets of reporters, the courts they cover, and the abbreviations used in citing them are as follows:

CITATIONS FOR NATIONAL REPORTER SYSTEM

Title	Courts Covered	Citation
Supreme Court Reporter	United States Supreme Court	S.Ct
Federal Reporter	United States Circuit Courts of Appeals U.S. District Courts	Fed.
Federal Reporter, Second Series	U.S. Courts of Appeals U.S. Court of Customs and Patent Appeals	F.2d
Federal Supplement	U.S. District Courts U.S. Court of Claims	F. Supp.
Atlantic Reporter	Connecticut	Atl.
Atlantic Reporter, Second Series	Delaware Maine Maryland New Hampshire New Jersey Pennsylvania Rhode Island Vermont	A.2d
New York Supplement	N.Y. Court of Appeals	N.Y. Supp.
New York Supplement, Second Series	Appellate Division of the Supreme Court Miscellaneous Courts	N.Y.S.2d

Northeastern Reporter	Illinois Indiana	N.E.

Northeastern
    Reporter, Second
    Series
	New York
	Massachusetts
	Ohio
		N.E.2d

Northwestern Reporter	Iowa Michigan	N.W.

Northwestern
    Reporter, Second
    Series
	Minnesota
	Nebraska
	North Dakota
	South Dakota
	Wisconsin
		N.W.2d

Pacific Reporter	Arizona	Pac. California
Pacific Reporter, Second Series	Colorado Idaho Kansas Montana Nevada New Mexico Oklahoma Oregon Utah Washington Wyoming	P.2d
Southeastern Reporter	Georgia North Carolina	S.E.

Southeastern
    Reporter, Second
    Series
	South Carolina
	Virginia
	West Virginia
		S.E.2d

Southern Reporter	Alabama Florida	So.
Southern Reporter, Second Series	Louisiana Mississippi	So.2d
Southwestern Reporter	Arkansas Kentucky	S.W.

Southwestern
    Reporter, Second
    Series
	Missouri
	Tennessee
	Texas
		S.W.2d

Some of the REPORTERS are designated "Second Series." The designation is for numbering purposes and indicates that the numbers of the volumes have started over with number one. Care should be taken that the "2d" is added when so dictated—32 Fed. and 32 F.2d are two separate books.

Each week West publishes the decisions in paperbacks called advance sheets. These advance sheets are mailed to the lawyers subscribing to the service. When enough decisions have accumulated to fill a bound volume, they are published and mailed to the subscriber. The page numbers of the advance sheets correspond with the page numbers of the permanent volumes.

Cases in REPORTERS are cited as follows:

Black v. White, 124 S.W.2d 357 (Tex.Ct.App. 1967)

Black v. White is the style of the case; 124 is the volume number; S.W.2d is the abbreviation for SOUTHWESTERN REPORTER, Second Series; the material in the parenthesis signifies that the Texas Court of Appeals rendered the decision in 1967. It is necessary to indicate the court rendering the decision only if the citation itself does not indicate it. For example, it would not be necessary to add "S.Ct." in parenthesis because the citation 52 S.Ct.321 indicates it is a Supreme Court case.

Sometimes notes are added indicating the history of the case. The following are some of the frequently used abbreviations:

aff'd	affirmed
aff'g	affirming
app.	appeal
cert.	certiorari
cor.	correct
den.	denied
juris.	jurisdiction
n.r.e.	not reversible
prob.	probable
rev'd	reversed
rev'g	reversing
w.o.j.	want of jurisdiction
w.o.m.	want of merit

If more than one citation is given, they are separated by semicolons.

The U.S. REPORTS prior to Volume 91 carried the name of the REPORTER in the citation, and they should be cited that way. The following are the names of the old REPORTERS, the corresponding U.S. REPORTS volume numbers, and the way they should be cited:

CITATIONS FOR UNITED STATES REPORTS

Volume	No. Volumes	Reporter	Citation
1 U.S. to 4 U.S.	4	Dallas	1 Dal. 10
5 U.S. to 13 U.S.	9	Cranch	1 Cranch 10
14 U.S. to 25 U.S.	12	Wheaton	1 Wheat. 10
26 U.S. to 41 U.S.	16	Peters	1 Pet. 10
42 U.S. to 65 U.S.	24	Howard	1 How. 10
66 U.S. to 67 U.S.	2	Black	1 Black 10
68 U.S. to 90 U.S.	23	Wallace	1 Wall. 10

Some law book companies publish only selected cases. Two examples of these reporters and the way they are cited are as follows:

American Law Review: *Black v. White*, 1967 A.L.R. 123 (U.S.Ct.App.)
Law Reports Annotated: *Black v. White*, 1967 L.R.A. 123 (U.S.Ct.App.)

Indices

Another type of books which lawyers use in preparing their cases are legal indices. CORPUS JURIS SECUNDUM and AMERICAN JURISPRUDENCE are legal encyclopedias which are arranged alphabetically by subject matter and have an index, just as do regular encyclopedias. They are cited as follows:

12 Am.Jur. *Contracts* Sec. 74 (1938)
88 C.J.S. *Trial* Sec. 192 (1955)

A set of books which is also invaluable to the lawyer is SHEPARD'S CITATIONS. It is a list of cases with cross references to other decisions on the same subject matter, plus notes as to the final outcome of the case. Lawyers call the use of these books "shepardizing a case," and they are referring to the necessity of checking SHEPARD'S to make sure a decision has not been reversed by a higher court before they use it in their argument.

Chapter 29

Testifying on Past Proceedings

Many judges do no allow their official reporters to take outside work because it may involve something which will come up in court later on. A problem exists when a reporter must be a witness and report the record at the same time. Judges may also feel that reporters who do outside work may be less dedicated to their courtroom reporting.

In many places, however, the official reporter must do the freelance reporting of interrogatories, statements, and depositions, since there is no other reporter readily available. These matters must be arranged around the court schedule in such areas.

Procedures for Testifying

I shall never forget the first time I was called to testify on my notes. The attorney who had hired me to report some statements six months or so before telephoned and asked me to bring my notes concerning the matter to court the next day to testify regarding them.

Up until then I had no idea that I could be asked to testify. Needless to say, that night I compared everything on the typed transcript with my shorthand notes and memorized them.

The next day I was seated in a front row of the courtroom right on time, nervous, but ready. We had hardly finished the preliminaries when opposing counsel, for whom I reported a few times a month, looked my way and said, "I see Mary is here, and I assume she is here to testify regarding something she reported in this matter. We will certainly stipulate, if that is the case, that she took the notes accurately and they were transcribed correctly." So, I spent that half day shopping and received in the mail a nice appearance fee from the counsel who had called me.

I was called a few other times to testify on my notes during my reporting career, but it never seemed scary again.

It is quite common for reporters to be called to prove their work. Attorneys request reporters to testify in order to impeach witnesses, to resolve contradictory facts, to inquire as to circumstances surrounding the taking of the matter (mental or physical capacity of the witness as it appeared to the reporter), or even to try to prove incompetency on the part of a court reporter who does not have a good reputation for accuracy. A graduate from an approved school, who has taken exams, such as the CSR, CP, and CM if possible and who maintains a high standard in all work has the greatest credibility.

The following paragraphs describe some procedures to follow when testifying on your notes.

Reporting and Testifying

Should you ever be the official who is called to testify regarding your notes taken during some assignment, you can report and testify at the same time. As the attorney asks you a question, write his or her question. Then, write your answer and read what you have written from the tape. This method will assure you that your testimony is recorded in a verbatim manner and that questions are not asked you before you have completed writing your answers in the record.

Take Your Notes Along and Go Early

If you are called to testify regarding a matter you have reported, take your original shorthand notes to court with you. Arrive early as counsel requesting your presence may want to go over spots in questions with you in advance to save time.

You should never get into the habit of writing insertions and/or changes in your notes, as the opposing attorney may notice these changes and suggest that you have filled in something or that you make mistakes in writing shorthand. Some attorneys, who see marked-up notes, may even ask for portions from other parts of the proceedings to be read, hoping to confuse the reporter or to spot errors in the typed transcript they are holding. However, the opposing counsel who is alert will object to this maneuver as immaterial. The judge will usually sustain this objection.

Show That You Are a Professional

Answer all questions forthrightly and courteously. Stay calm, and do not become flustered. Read in a loud, clear voice in even tones at a moderate rate of speed if requested to read. Look far enough ahead to avoid embarrassing pauses.

Should attorneys become rude or seem to deprecate your ability, do not retaliate. They are only harming their own cases, and the judge will not let them badger you very much. Take this part of your duty seriously. Do not act belligerently or take questions lightly, as then either attorneys or the judge might take exception to your behavior. You might be discredited before the jury.

Always be a professional.

Dress Carefully for Testifying

Your appearance will be very important on such an occasion. Your best understated businesslike attire which blends in well with the formal atmosphere of the court is in order here. Remember, it is always easier to believe in someone who looks and acts like an expert.

Preliminary Questioning of the Reporter

Should a lawyer demand that you be tested with your machine and that you write a test to prove your competence before the Court and jury, the judge and the attorney for the other side will not permit it. You must stand on your rights and refuse to be tested because you can readily see all the ramifications of submitting to such an ordeal.

After you are placed under oath, you will be asked to state your name, address, and business or profession. Next, you will be questioned about your education, qualifications, and experience. Be totally honest, but not so modest that you do not prove you are capable of doing your job and doing it well. Tell about the rigorous training you had in school, the testing you have undergone, the awards, if any, the experience you have had — in other words, sell yourself and your ability right there.

You may be asked if you or your transcribers or scopists ever make any mistakes. Assure them that you proofread all work carefully to be sure no material errors exist on delivered transcript. Tell the questioner frankly "Occasionally I hit a wrong key, but from context I can always determine what the stroke should be."

Were Any Errors You Made Ever Brought to Your Attention? If you are ever asked if any errors have been brought to your attention, be careful. Maybe none have ever been pointed out to you. Then, your answer is, "No." Be careful, though, because counsel may point to some inconsequential error in the very transcript he or she is holding, and you will be discredited. If you are reporting day in and day out, even the best reporter may mishear something or let some other insignificant error slip by. If an attorney asks that question, he or she may have knowledge of some error you have made, so a good answer is: "No material error has ever been brought to my attention."

Do Witnesses Ever Talk So Fast that You Cannot Keep Up? This question is very common. Your answer should be: "I stop the witness when that occurs and have the testimony repeated. However, I have enough reserve speed due to my training that this almost never happens."

What Do You Do When Three or Four People Speak at Once? The answer to this question is: "I ask them to speak one at a time, and I have them repeat anything I could not hear because of the overlapping. Since I write well over 225 words per minute, this speed allows me to get most overlapping without interrupting."

How Much Experience Have You Had as a Reporter? If you have had a great deal of experience, the answer to this question will be easy. If you have not had a great deal of experience, stress your fine training and the fact that you have reported many mock trials and have had a lengthy period of internship with practicing reporters while you were in training. Stress the demanding testing program you have had to go through to secure your CSR or your NSRA Certificate or Certificate of Merit.

This is also the place to bring out any college, business school, or other training you have had and the continuing education work done through NSRA, state and local reporting organizations. Do not be meek and modest here, but let everyone present know that it takes a lot to be a professional court reporter.

Did You Report Anything about the Case Being Tried? After your qualifications as a reporter have been established, you will be asked if you were the court reporter in the matter concerning which you were called to testify. Dates, places of taking the notes, names or persons present at the time of taking, and other such details will be determined.

Testifying on Your Notes

Your notes will usually be marked for identification as an exhibit at this point, after which you will be asked to identify them as your shorthand notes pertinent to the case under consideration. You will be questioned as to whether you truly and accurately took the testimony. You may be asked if you recall all the questions asked by counsel and all the answers of the witnesses. Of course, your answer must be "No." Then, usually you will be asked to turn to the relevant portions of your notes and answer questions as to whether or not the witness was sworn and how he or she testified. You may be asked to read from your notes in some instances at this point.

Questioning Concerning Transcript

The attorney may now ask you if you prepared a transcript of your own notes or had another person under your direction do so and when this was done. The transcript will normally be marked for identification as an exhibit at this point.

You will be asked if the transcript you have identified as your work is a true and correct transcription of your original notes and, specifically, the particular portion in question. There may be quite some questioning regarding your method of producing the transcript and qualifications of the typist, scopist, proofreader, or other person working on the transcript.

You will then be asked if the witness testified certain things in response to certain questions.

Is the Transcript the Best Evidence? An objection may be made by some attorneys that the transcript is not the best evidence, but that the testimony should be elicited from the original shorthand notes. However, the Court has ruled in *People v. Colon*, 119 NYS. 2d 503, that a court reporter may use a transcript instead of his or her notes.

Always go in prepared with your notes, for the attorney asking you to appear may feel that your reading from your notes is much more effective than your being questioned concerning the typed transcripts.

General Guidelines

Always be totally honest in all your answers. If there is anything that you do not remember, say so. If you don't, it may boomerang when other witnesses testify differently. Testify directly and confidently.

Keep in mind always that judges, attorneys, juries, and the general public want to believe that you, as a court reporter, do a fine job day after day. You must do your part to help them believe in you by being a good witness when called upon to testify.

Treat testifying on your notes as a routine part of your job. You read back every day, and testifying on your notes is really no different except that your notes are usually much older.

Remember, people in court often try to change their stories to help their own causes. Lying often comes easily to such individuals. Your testimony will help bring out the truth. If you have completed your education in a good school and worked diligently, you have nothing to fear when you get called upon to testify regarding your records.

You may be a student today, but think how you would handle this situation before you are placed on the stand. Know yourself so that you can state your qualifications and abilities clearly; then, know that your records are impeccable and unimpeachable, and you will never go wrong. INSTEAD, YOU WILL GO FAR!

Chapter 30   *Indexing the Transcript*

An essential part of the reporter's transcript of any proceeding before the court except the most simple case consisting of only one witness and no exhibits or unusual happenings is a complete, properly typed index which shows fully what took place at the hearing.

Contents of a Good Index

A proper index will list the page at which each item is found. Items in the index will include the following:

(1) Docket call.

(2) Jury selection (voir dire) if transcribed or the fact that the jury was impaneled and sworn if it is not transcribed.

(3) Invocation of the Rule.

(4) Motions in limine and other motions occurring throughout the hearing and rulings thereon.

(5) Opening statements by counsel representing plaintiff(s) and defendant(s).

(6) Plaintiff's and defendant's witnesses for both sides, listing direct, cross, redirect, recross, rebuttal, and surrebuttal examinations.

(7) Points at which plaintiff and defendant rest.

(8) Summations of counsel for plaintiff(s) and defendant(s).

(9) Charge to the jury.

(10) Exceptions to the court's charge.

(11) Verdict.

(12) Polling the jury.

(13) Adjournment.

(14) Reporter's certificate.

(15) Agreement of counsel and court on the Order for Settled Record, where applicable.

Other pertinent items, such as reading into the record of depositions, interrogatories, and the like, are also properly included in the index.

Indexes may be very simple or very lengthy depending upon the type of case, number of witnesses, and physical exhibits produced. As the transcript is prepared, a rough index should be made up. Then, at the end of the transcript, it is a simple matter to print and paginate an attractive summary of events.

The statutes or manuals of many states prescribe the form of index shown in Figure 62. It is neat and complete, but not easily read when repeated redirect and recross-examinations take place. You will notice the witness's sections are single spaced to get the entire index on one page.

Always prepare an attractively arranged index page or pages. The index is one of the first items that the judge and counsel see, and it is frequently referred to.

Numbering of Index

The index is numbered with lower case Roman numerals since it is prepared last and comes at the beginning of the transcript. In billing, the number of index pages is added to the total of other transcript pages to be charged to the client.

FIGURE 62
Index

	Direct	Cross	Redirect	Recross
I N D E X				
Jury impaneled and sworn	3			
Plaintiff's opening	5			
Defendant's opening	16			
Plaintiff's witnesses				
Tunis Willingham	24	36	40,48	46,50
Iva Hadditt	56	60	72	81
Ura Coldnotes	85	88	91	93
Plaintiff rests	96			
Motion and ruling	96			
Defendant's witnesses				
Eukelia Kubes	97	103	109	137
Also A. Square	195	199	207	222
Ima Deere	245	298		
(Deposition)				
Defendant rests	335			
Plaintiff's rebuttal witness				
Harry Lee	335	367		
Defendant's surrebuttal witness				
Summitt Upp	367	378		
Motion and ruling	387			
Plaintiff's summation	388			
Defendant's summation	401			
Charge to the jury	459			
Verdict and motions	491			
Adjournment	494			

Indexes in Cases Requiring Several Volumes

In large cases, transcript is often bound in a number of volumes. This is particularly true in the U.S. District Courts (federal courts) where highly technical cases may involve weeks and months of trial.

A master index of transcript of trial and exhibits covering the entire trial must be included within the cover of Volume I of the proceedings, and an index must be included within each volume of the transcript of trial outlining all proceedings and exhibits covered in that specific volume.

Attractive Index for Federal Court Case

Figure 63A through C shows a proper summary index in a United States District Court case. Notice that no reference is made to the court reporter's certificate at the end because this item is on the front page of a Federal case transcript. This particular form of index is easy to read and appealing to the eye.

FIGURE 63-A
Index

```
 1                        I N D E X

 2                                                       Page

 3   Motions Disposed of:
         Motion for Bill of Particulars Declared
 4           Satisfied  . . . . . . . . . . . . . . . .     3
         Motion to Produce Exculpatory and Mitigating
 5           Evidence Declared Satisfied  . . . . . . .     3
         Motion for Separate Hearing to Determine
 6           Existence of Conspiracy for Invocation
             of Rule 801(d)(2)(e) . . . . . . . . . . .     3
 7       Court's Decision ot Carry Motion with Case  . . .  9

 8   Opening Statement by Mr. De Luna on Bahalf of
             the Government  . . . . . . . . . . . . . .   14
 9
     Opening Statement by Mr. Rodriguez on Behalf of
10           the Defendant . . . . . . . . . . . . . . .   20

11   Rule Invoked . . . . . . . . . . . . . . . . . . .    23

12   GOVERNMENT'S WITNESSES:

13       Lex Henderson
             Direct Examination by Mr. De Luna  . . . . .  24
14           Cross-Examination by Mr. Rodriguez . . . . .  50
             Redirect Examination by Mr. De Luna  . . . .  65
15           Recross-Examination by Mr. Rodriguez . . . .  70
             Redirect Examination (Cont'd.) by
16               Mr. De Luna . . . . . . . . . . . . . .   72

17       Allen Tittle
             Direct Examination by Mr. De Luna  . . . . .  73
18           Cross-Examination by Mr. Rodriguez . . . . .  78

19       Michael Harper
             Direct Examination by Mr. De Luna  . . . . .  80
20           Cross-Examination by Mr. Rodriguez . . . . .  83

21       Eugene Dan Habib
             Direct Examination by Mr. De Luna  . . . . .  87
22           Cross-Examination by Mr. Rodriguez . . . . .  94
             Redirect Examination by Mr. De Luna  . . . .  96
23
         James V. Glazener
24           Direct Examination by Mr. De Luna  . . . . .  97

25
```

FIGURE 63-B

FIGURE 63-C

```
 1                    I N D E X (Cont'd.)

 2                                                              Page

 3    Requested Instructions . . . . . . . . . . . . . . . .     231

 4    Closing Argument on Behalf of the Government
             by Mr. De Luna . . . . . . . . . . . . . . . .      237
 5
      Closing Argument on Behalf of the Defendant
 6           by Mr. Marsh . . . . . . . . . . . . . . . . .      254

 7    Closing Argument on Behalf of the Defendant
             by Mr. Rodriguez . . . . . . . . . . . . . . .      265
 8
      Closing Argument on Behalf of the Government
 9           by Mr. De Luna . . . . . . . . . . . . . . . .      274

10    Charge of the Court  . . . . . . . . . . . . . . . .       283

11    Exception to Charge of the Court . . . . . . . . . .       306

12    Dismissal of Alternate Juror by the Court  . . . . . .     307

13    Verdict of Jury  . . . . . . . . . . . . . . . . . .       309

14    Jury Polled  . . . . . . . . . . . . . . . . . . . .       310

15    Jury Excused . . . . . . . . . . . . . . . . . . . .       312

16    Bond Set for Defendant by the Court  . . . . . . . .       316

17    Sentencing . . . . . . . . . . . . . . . . . . . . .       321

18    ADJOURNMENT  . . . . . . . . . . . . . . . . . . . .       322

19

20

21

22

23

24

25
```

Index for State District Court Case

Figure 64A through C on pages 266 through 268 is a neat, explicit, complete index for a State District Court case. This style index is favored by many court reporters, as it shows at a glance who is examining each witness at all times, and it presents a superior appearance. It may take longer to prepare such an index, but the result is certainly worth the effort involved.

Methods of Indexing Vary Widely

You will find methods of indexing vary greatly from place to place. Follow the system employed wherever you work as dictated by the judge or your firm.

The Los Angeles County reporters' manuals detail their system precisely, and if you intend to work in California, get these books and study them well.

Figure 65A through F on pages 269 through 271 shows pages 123–128 of the Los Angeles Reporter's Criminal Manual, which exhibits its style of transcript index. The index is very complete. It seems complicated and difficult to understand without some study, but it demonstrates the system used. You will notice that this form provides an original of the Master Index to be inserted in the original copy of Volume I and a carbon or photocopy of the Master Index to be inserted

FIGURE 64-A
Index

1 I N D E X

2 CAPTION   Page
                                                                       1

3   PLAINTIFF'S EVIDENCE

4 WITNESSES:

5   FLORENCE ROSS

6   Direct Examination by Mr. Kidd   2
         Cross-Examination by Mr. Maroney   16
7   Redirect Examination by Mr. Kidd   27
         Recross-Examination by Mr. Maroney   28
8   Redirect Examination by Mr. Kidd   29

9   LOUELLA LATTISON

10   Direct Examination by Mr. Kidd   29
         Cross-Examination by Mr. Maroney   43
11   Redirect Examination by Mr. Kidd   54
         Recross-Examination by Mr. Maroney   59

12   JOHN W. CAIN

13   Direct Examination by Mr. Kidd   61
14   Cross-Examination by Mr. Maroney   76
         Redirect Examination by Mr. Kidd   89
15   Recross-Examination by Mr. Maroney   91
         Redirect Examination by Mr. Kidd   94

16   JOSEPHINE SMITH

17   Direct Examination by Mr. Kidd   94
18   Cross-Examination by Mr. Maroney   102
         Redirect Examination by Mr. Kidd   106

19   JULIUS SHUTZE (by written interrogatory)

20   Offered by Mr. Kidd   107

21   JAMES G. HAMER

22   Direct Examination by Mr. Kidd   111
23   Cross-Examination by Mr. Maroney   122
         Redirect Examination by Mr. Kidd   132
24   Recross-Examination by Mr. Maroney   141
         Redirect Examination by Mr. Kidd   142
25   Recross-Examination by Mr. Maroney   143

FIGURE 64-B

FIGURE 64-C

1
2
3
4
5
6
7
8
9
10
11
12
13
14
15
16
17
18
19
20
21
22
23
24
25

FIGURE 65-B
(California)

INDEX - (CONT'D.)

MASTER INDEX

CHRONOLOGICAL (Cont'd.)

3 WEDNESDAY, JUNE 15, 19__ P.M.
   (Volume 2, page 421)
4 MOTION UNDER 1118.1 PENAL CODE
5 THURSDAY, JUNE 16, 19__ A.M.
   (Volume 3, page 430)
6 OPENING STATEMENT (Defense) (If included)
7 DEFENSE:

DEFT'S(S') WITNESSES	DIRECT	CROSS	REDIRECT	RECROSS	VOIR DIRE	VOLUME
8						
9 JAMES, Carl	452	470 478	483	494	476(S)	3

10 (Etc.)

12 FRIDAY, JURY 27, 19__ A.M.
   (Volume 9, page 2101)
   MOTION FOR NEW TRIAL
13 PROBATION AND SENTENCE HEARING
14 (Volume 9, 2158)

ALPHABETICAL WITNESS INDEX

PEOPLE'S WITNESSES	DIRECT	CROSS	REDIRECT	RECROSS	VOIR DIRE	VOLUME
17 ANDREW, Melvin	314	323	340 353	351	351(S)	2
19 JONES, John (1538.5)	85	89	93	95		1
(trial)	245 249	255	258	260	247(S)	1
20 (Examination by the court at page 263)						
21 LYON, Ida M.	353	370	393	399		

22 DEFENDANT'S(S') WITNESSES

	DIRECT	CROSS	REDIRECT	RECROSS	VOIR DIRE	VOLUME
23 JAMES, Carl	452	470 478	483	494	476(S)	3

25 (Etc.)

26 REBUTTAL WITNESSES
27 (If pertinent)
28 (Set up SURREBUTTAL WITNESSES in same manner if pertinent)

FIGURE 65-A
Master Index (California)

INDEX - (ONE ORIGINAL MASTER INDEX INSERTED IN ORIGINAL COPY OF
VOLUME 1; XEROX OR CARBON COPY OF MASTER INDEX INSERTED
IN EACH REMAINING VOLUME OF APPEAL TRANSCRIPT.)

MASTER INDEX

CHRONOLOGICAL

3 FRIDAY, JUNE 10, 19__ P.M.
4 (Volume 1, page 1, Dept. 120, Judge Smith)
   MOTION UNDER 995 PENAL CODE
5 MONDAY, JUNE 13, 19__ A.M.
6 (Volume 1, page 85, Dept. 120, Judge Smith)
   MOTION UNDER 1538.5 PENAL CODE:

PEOPLE'S WITNESSES	DIRECT	CROSS	REDIRECT	RECROSS	VOLUME
8					
9 JONES, John	85	89	93	95	1

10 ARGUMENT (a538.5)
   (Volume 1, page 96)
11 TUESDAY, JUNE 14, 19__ A.M.
12 (Volume 1, page 122, Dept. 125, Judge Keene)
13 TRIAL:
14 JURY VOIR DIRE
   (Volume 1, page 122)
15 OPENING STATEMENT (People's only)
16 (Volume 1, page 234)
17 TUESDAY, JUNE 14, 19__ P.M.
   (Volume 1, page 245)
18 PEOPLE'S CASE IN CHIEF:

PEOPLE'S WITNESSES	DIRECT	CROSS	REDIRECT	RECROSS	VOIR DIRE	VOLUME
20 JONES, John	245 249	255	258	260	247(S)	1
21 (Examination by the court at page 263)						

22 WEDNESDAY, JUNE 15, 19 A.M.
   (Volume 2, page 294)

	DIRECT	CROSS	REDIRECT	RECROSS	VOIR DIRE	VOLUME
24 ANDREW, Melvin	314	323	340 353	351	351(S)	2
25 LYON, Ida M.	352	370	393	399		2

26 PEOPLE REST
   (Volume 2, page 420)

FIGURE 65-C
(California)

INDEX - REPORTER'S APPEAL TRANSCRIPT (CONT'D.)

MASTER INDEX

EXHIBITS

PEOPLE'S EXHIBITS	FOR IDENTIFICATION Vol.	Pg.	IN EVIDENCE Vol.	Pg.	WITHDRAWN OR REJECTED Vol.	Pg.
1 - Magnifying glasses	2	286	2	291		
2 - Child's coat	2	286	2	291		
3 - Key	2	286			2	320
4 - Map/City of L.A.	2	295	2	298		

DEFENDANT'S(S') EXHIBITS						
A - Photograph of kitchen	3	513	3	513		
(Etc.)						

FIGURE 65-D
(California)

INDEX - (SEPARATE INDEX FOR EACH VOLUME IN TRANSCRIPTS WITH 1,000 PAGES OR LESS)

INDEX FOR VOLUME 1   Pages 1 to 220

DAY	DATE		PAGE
Wednesday	June 28, 19--	A.M.	1
		P.M.	9
Thursday	June 29, 19--	A.M.	44
		P.M.	51
Friday	June 30, 19--	A.M.	54
Monday	July 10, 19--	A.M.	55
		P.M.	74
Tuesday	July 11, 19--	A.M.	134

MOTION UNDER 995 PENAL CODE (Dept. 123, Judge Ritzi)	1
MOTION UNDER 1538.5 PENAL CODE (Dept. 123, Judge Ritzi)	9
Argument	32
OPENING STATEMENT (People's)(Dept. 134, Judge Brandler)	45

CHRONOLOGICAL INDEX

PEOPLE'S WITNESSES	DIRECT	CROSS	REDIRECT	RECROSS	VOIR DIRE
SNYDER, Joseph N. (1538.5)	12	24	29		
GREENFIELD, Harry	74	77	83	84	
HARRISON, Julie	84 / 88	89	98	120	86(M)

ALPHABETICAL INDEX

	DIRECT	CROSS	REDIRECT	RECROSS	VOIR DIRE
GREENFIELD, Harry	74	77	83	84	
HARRISON, Julie	84 / 88	89	98	120	86(M)
SNYDER, Joseph N. (1538.5)	12	24	29		

PEOPLE'S EXHIBITS	FOR IDENTIFICATION	IN EVIDENCE	WITHDRAWN OR REJECTED
1 - Police report	201	202	

FIGURE 65-F
(California)

INDEX – (FOR SEPARATE INDEX USE; TOTAL LIST OF EXHIBITS TO BE INCLUDED IN VOLUME 1 ONLY.)

EXHIBIT INDEX

	FOR IDENTIFICATION		IN EVIDENCE		WITHDRAWN OR REJECTED	
PEOPLE'S EXHIBITS	Vol.	Pg.	Vol.	Pg.	Vol.	Pg.
1 – Police report	1	201			1	201
2 – Xerox copy of confession	2	374			2	374
3 – Records from Dept. of Motor Vehicles	2	489	2	489		
(Etc.)						
DEFENDANT'S(S') EXHIBITS						
A – Records of Vale High School	3	789	3	860		
(Etc.)						

FIGURE 65-E
(California)

INDEX – (FOR SEPARATE INDEX USE – CONT'D.)

INDEX FOR VOLUME 2   Pages 221 to 499, incl.

DAY	DATE		PAGE
Wednesday	June 12, 19--	(A.M.)	221
		(P.M.)	297
Thursday	June 13, 19--	(A.M.)	362
		(P.M.)	433

CHRONOLOGICAL INDEX

PEOPLE'S WITNESSES	DIRECT	CROSS	REDIRECT	RECROSS	VOIE DIRE
HARRISON, Julie (Resumed)				221 237	232(M)
GREENFIELD, Harry (Recalled)	243	245	250	268	
THOMPSON, George N.	305		362 447		385(M)

ALPHABETICAL INDEX

PEOPLE'S WITNESSES	DIRECT	CROSS	REDIRECT	RECROSS	VOIE DIRE
GREENFIELD, Harry (Recalled)	243	245	250	268	
HARRISON, Julie				221 237	232(M)
THOMPSON, George N.	305		362 447		385(M)

PEOPLE'S EXHIBITS	FOR IDENTIFICATION	IN EVIDENCE	WITHDRAWN OR REJECTED
1 – Xerox copy of confession	374		374
2 – Records from Dept. of Motor Vehicles	489	489	

in each remaining volume of appeal transcript. This index is set up in the statutory form used in many states. In California, if transcript indexes are not set up according to their procedures, the transcript will be turned back to the reporter for inclusion of a proper index.

The rules of some other states are equally as rigid, but it is impossible here to include every rule concerning each one. My personal experience has been that attorneys seem to like and prefer the types of indexes presented here as Figures 64A–C because of their legibility, but it must be emphasized that you must conform to the rules, customs, and wishes existing where you are employed.

Index of Exhibits

All exhibits introduced during proceedings are indexed. Should the index of witnesses and proceedings be very short, the exhibit index may be placed on the same page as the witness listing. However, be sure your exhibit index also looks neat and easy to read.

Included in the exhibit index should be identification of the party presenting the exhibit, number and description of the physical evidence represented, the page at which the exhibit is identified, the page at which the exhibit is received in evidence, (if it is), and possibly the page at which the exhibit is bound into the record.

Many exhibits are identified which are never received into evidence. This makes it incumbent upon the reporter to keep a very accurate record of the status of the exhibits and to index the exhibits accurately. Be sure the index of exhibits clearly shows the correct listing as to each one.

Figure 66 shows a sample form of index for a trial transcript set of exhibits.

FIGURE 66
Index of Exhibits

1

2   INDEX OF EXHIBITS

3

4   PLAINTIFF'S EXHIBITS

5

Exhibit Number	Description	Page Ident.	Page Rec'd.
P-1 - P-6	Photographs of Finishing Room at Marvco Film Company	8	9
P-7	Invoice for Medical Expenses of Sarah Long	15	15
P-8 - P-9	Work Records of Sarah Long	109	122
P-10	Autopsy Report of Sarah Long	146	147

* * * * *
* * *
*

             DEFENDANT'S EXHIBITS

Exhibit Number	Description	Page Ident.	Page Rec'd.
D-1 - D-2	Adding Machine Tapes Run in Computing Sarah Long's Time and Wages	272	274
D-3	Death Certificate of Sarah Long	282	
D-4 - D-6	Photographs of Interior of Finishing Room of Marvco Film Company	326	326

* * * * *
* * *
*

Chapter 31

Court Transcripts

Orders for Transcripts

As a trial progresses, attorneys for either side may request excerpted testimony, motions, etc., to be prepared by the official reporter to assist them in further preparation of the case. Sometimes this work is done over noon recess, sometimes overnight.

However, the real test of the reporter's transcription abilities comes when long records must be prepared. In case of a mistrial, lawyers may order transcript of the proceedings in order to better retry the case the next time around. Sometimes a case is dismissed without prejudice, and transcript is ordered so when the case is scheduled again, the trial may well be successful for the plaintiff. Attorneys may also have transcripts prepared in a case because there are companion cases yet to come, and a study of the completed case record will assist in representing other clients.

The record is most often ordered from an official reporter because an appeal is to be taken because of some exception defense counsel takes to something which occurred during the proceedings or some outcropping misconduct, or the plaintiff may feel the verdict was excessive or contrary to justice. In some states an appeal is mandatory in criminal felony cases.

Get Orders for Transcript in Writing!

As you leave the courtroom after a vigorously debated civil case, an attorney may say to you in a moment of anger "I am going to make an appeal. Get me out a transcript right away." Always tell such attorneys to have their secretaries write you a letter on their office stationery ordering the transcript because they may later decide the case was not quite such a good appeal prospect as they had thought at first. When you deliver the transcript, they could say, "I was only joking. I didn't order that transcript, and I won't pay for it." Then, you may have to pay your scopist or transcriber and bear the cost of supplies to produce a worthless transcript.

Deposit May Be Secured before Transcript is Produced. In most jurisdictions the reporter has the right to ask for a deposit of the estimated cost of a transcript before commencing transcription of the case. In some other places the money for the estimated cost of transcript may be required to be placed on deposit with the clerk of court before the reporter begins transcription of the case.

Confirm Orders for Court Trial Transcript by Letter. When the official court reporter receives a letter ordering transcript, he or she should write a letter on his or her letterhead to counsel confirming the order and stating that upon receipt of the estimated sum, transcription of the case will begin and that delivery date may be anticipated by a stated date. Of course, the definite stated date must come within the cut-off date for the appeal.

Keep Deposits in a Trust Account. When the court reporter receives a transcript deposit, it must not be placed in the reporter's personal account, but it must be maintained in a trust account. This money may be used to purchase supplies, to pay transcribers or scopists, and for any other purpose related to producing the transcript; it cannot be used for a new car, a mink coat, or whatever until the record has been accepted by the court and the attorneys as correct.

Payment for Records of Indigents

Most states allow for payment of the court reporter for preparation of a record in the case of an indigent under the Pauper's Oath. In such cases, the reporter is paid at the statute rate by the County. Figure 67 shows a typical Order issued by the court to allow payment for such a transcript.

In other states these transcripts are produced by the official as pro bono work.

Estimating Transcript Costs

Early in your career you should learn to estimate how many pages of transcript your notes will produce.

When you have prepared several sizeable transcripts, locate page 100 on one that is of moderately dense material. Take a ruler and measure on the notes for that transcript where page 100 ends, and in this way you can determine that 100 pages is equal to a certain number of inches of tape (or inches plus a fraction thereof). Again, using the same transcript and the same notes, measure the notes to one inch; and at one inch of notes, see where that is in your transcript. In that way you can tell how many pages of transcript you get to an inch.

This ruler method is fine for the ordinary case, but you must keep in mind the fact that technical cases, medical Q and A, or solid matter will result in greater number of pages, and this type of material will yield fewer pages to the inch. Conversely, it will take a greater amount of stenotype notes per 100 pages for dense material. Matrimonial cases and negligence lawsuits will normally yield more pages to the inch of notes than technical and medical material.

Really short cases will require you to use a manual method of estimating transcript pages from your stenotype notes. Grasp the bottom fold of your notes and open them so the bottom fold is the top fold. Count it as one. Grasp the next bottom fold and move it to the top, counting that as two. When you finish counting the folds, divide the total by two. This is your approximate number of pages, allowing again for the type of case and considering your system of shorthand—do you use lots of phrasing or do you write everything out, and how close a spacing do you have your machine set for?

You should also occasionally measure entire pads of notes and compare them to the amount of transcript produced by an entire pad. If you do this with a number of pads and transcripts, you will get a pretty good average.

Many times counsel will inquire as to the cost of a record, talk it over with the client, and decide not to appeal a shaky case.

In giving an estimate of the cost of a transcript to an attorney, always make the estimate liberal because you will refund any money over what the actual transcript costs, but you may never collect the balance if you underestimate. Somehow, it makes everyone feel good to get some money back, even if it is only a few dollars.

Preparing Transcripts

You will normally prepare all transcripts in order of sequence in which they come up in court, perhaps doing pleas, sentences, and minor transcripts as they come along. You must keep

FIGURE 67
Order Issued to Allow Payment of Pauper's Record

```
 1   THE STATE OF MINNESOTA,X   IN THE 95TH DISTRICT COURT
                           X
 2                Plaintiff,X   OF BLUE EARTH COUNTY, MINNESOTA
                           X
 3          -vs-           X   APRIL TERM, A.D. 19--
                           X
 4   JOHN R. SHAW,         X   No. 125,656
                           X
 5                Defendant.X

 6

 7

 8                    O R D E R

 9

10       On the 10th day of April, A.D. 19--, came on to be

11   heard evidence concerning the defendant's motion that he

12   be declared a pauper and an indigent, as provided by

13   the Code of Criminal Procedure of the State of Minnesota;

14   and the Court on that date found the defendant,

15   JOHN R. SHAW, to be a pauper and an indigent and hereby

16   orders the court reporter to prepare a transcript of the

17   trial in the above cause as provided by law for presentation

18   and filing before the Court of Criminal Appeals in St. Paul,

19   Minnesota.

20   DATED:  April 10, 19--

21

22                         _____
                           RIGHTEOUS N. PROPER, JUDGE
23                         95th District Court
                           Blue Earth County, Minnesota
24

25
```

track of when appeal dates run and turn out transcripts in a timely manner, as the case will be thrown out at the higher level due to your negligence if you do not follow the statute very carefully as to delivery. Then, you may be the object of a malpractice suit.

You can write perfect notes, turn out perfect transcripts, but that is no guarantee that some disgruntled losing litigant will not hire an attorney to sue you for some alleged mistake in a record. Regardless of how good you are, you absolutely must avail yourself of malpractice insurance available through the National Shorthand Reporters Association.

Securing Transcript Time Extensions

During a busy term of court, you may be in court day after day and still get orders for thousands of pages of transcript to complete within statute time. Therefore, you may have to ask for an extension of time to complete some of them. With the advent of Computer-Aided-Tran-scription, this is not so likely to happen, but Figure 68 shows an affidavit such as might be prepared in this situation, and Figure 69 shows the judge's order approving the extension.

Transcript Requirements

NSRA has set down the proper format for transcripts. The NSRA guidelines for transcripts were listed in the chapters on depositions, and you should follow these wherever possible. Typed copy appears on only one side of the paper and is always double spaced. Trial transcripts should be labeled on the cover as Volume I, and so on. Stamp ORIGINAL on the first copy cover with a large rubber stamp, and place the word COPY on the cover of all other copies. Some reporters have the word COPY imprinted on sheets used for copies.

FIGURE 68
Affidavit Prepared for Extension Request

```
1   IN DISTRICT COURT                 COUNTY OF BURKE

2   NINTH JUDICIAL DISTRICT           STATE OF UTAH

3

4   Dearborn Chemical Company,    *
                                  *
5              Plaintiff,         *
                                  *
6        -vs-                     *     C.A. No. 14,875
                                  *
7   John P. Pearsoll, d/b/a       *
    Employers Insurance Company,  *
8                                 *
               Defendant.         *
9

10              A F F I D A V I T

11      Before me, a Notary Public in and for said County and
    State, on this day appeared Mr. Hand E. Writer, known to
12  me to be the person whose name is subscribed herein, and
    after being by me duly sworn on his oath stated as follows:
13

14      I am the official court reporter charged with the
    responsibility of preparing the trial transcript in the
    above-captioned and numbered case for filing in the Court
15  of Civil Appeals.  Because of the press of official
    business, it will be impossible for me to prepare and file
16  such trial transcript within the original sixty (60) days
    allotted by the Rules, and it is my best estimate at
17  this time that I will need until approximately November 1,
    19--, to prepare and file the same.
18

19

20                      _____
                        HAND E. WRITER
                        Official Court Reporter
21                      Ninth Judicial District

22  SWORN TO and subscribed before me this 1st day of September,
    19--.
23

24                      _____
                        SIGNED N. SEALED, Notary Public
25                      Burke County, State of Utah
                        My Commission Expires May 1, 19--
```

FIGURE 69
Judge's Order Approving Extension

```
1   IN DISTRICT COURT                 COUNTY OF BURKE

2   NINTH JUDICIAL DISTRICT           STATE OF UTAH

3

4   Dearborn Chemical Company,    *
                                  *
5               Plaintiff,        *
                                  *
6        -vs-                     *     C.A. No. 14,875
                                  *
7   Jason P. Pearsoll, d/b/a      *
    Employers Insurance Company,  *
8               Defendant.        *

9

10

11                  O R D E R

12

13     BE IT REMEMBERED, on this, the 1st day of September,

14  19--, for good cause shown, the time for filing of the

15  trial transcript in the above-entitled and numbered

16  cause is extended for a period from this, the 1st day

17  of September, A.D. 19--, to the 1st day of November,

18  A.D. 19--.

19

20

21                       _____
                         FINDING RIGHTLY, JUDGE
22                       Ninth Judicial District

23

24

25
```

It is often not physically possible or practicable to assemble a record on appeal under one cover because of the bulk of the record. Therefore, when the record will be in excess of 2½" thick, the volumes are designated as "Volume I of IV Volumes," and so on. Each page of the transcript must be properly numbered chronologically, and an index must be included of all proceedings and exhibits.

In most states detailed instructions exist regarding preparation of trial transcript, and the proper formats are detailed in manuals. For instance, the Los Angeles Superior Court Reporters have compiled three separate manuals, CIVIL-CRIMINAL, and TRANSCRIPT FORMAT AND DAILY COPY PROCEDURES, which cover every format and index to be used there. Wherever such manuals are available, they should be studied carefully by the new official reporter.

The reporter's certificate will appear at the end of the testimony (except in Federal Court). Figure 70 gives an example of a trial record certificate.

FIGURE 70
Reporter's Certificate at End of Testimony

```
 1

 2

 3    THE STATE OF TEXAS)
                       )
 4    COUNTY OF HARRIS  )

 5

 6        I, Verbatim S. Possible, official court reporter

 7    in and for the 183rd District Court of Harris County,

 8    State of Texas, do hereby certify that the above and

 9    foregoing _____ pages contain a true and correct

10    transcription of all the proceedings (Or all proceedings

11    directed by counsel to be included in the statement of

12    facts, as the case may be), in the above-styled and

13    numbered cause, all of which occurred in open court

14    or in chambers and were reported by me.

15        I further certify that this transcription of the

16    record of the proceedings truly and correctly reflects

17    the exhibits, if any, offered by the respective parties.

18        WITNESS my hand this the _____ day of _____, 19--.

19

20

21                            VERBATIM S. POSSIBLE
                              Official Court Reporter
22

23

24

25
```

In some states an Order for Settled Record is required, in which the attorneys and the Court certify their approval of the transcript. More and more states are ceasing to require this form as provision exists for objection to the record to be made, making this procedure unnecessary. Figure 71 shows a typical Order for Settled Record.

Formal notice must be prepared and filed for each completed transcript on appeal in some jurisdictions. Figure 72 on page 282 shows an example of the notice that must be filed for records on appeal.

Appearance of Transcripts. Before you deliver any transcript, pause for a moment and think that some 50 years from today someone may look at one of your records and judge you by it, so it behooves you to make an excellent transcript at all times.

A truly fine, conscientious reporter may be sleeping soundly in bed and, all of a sudden, he or she will sit upright, wide awake, and start stewing about something in a transcript that just for

FIGURE 71
Order for Settled Record

```
 1  STATE OF WISCONSIN !
                        !
 2  COUNTY OF MANITOWOC!

 3     We, the undersigned attorneys of record in the above-

 4  entitled and numbered cause, do hereby agree that the

 5  foregoing 619 typewritten pages constitute a full, true,

 6  and correct transcript in question and answer form of all

 7  proceedings had and all documentary evidence introduced

 8  during the trial of said cause, if any, and all objections

 9  to the admission or exclusion of evidence, rulings of the

10  Court thereon, and bills of exception taken thereto, and

11  evidence in connection therewith, if any, and hereby agree

12  that the same may be filed as such among the papers in

13  this case.

14

15                          _____
                            CHARGE M. PLENTEE
16                          Counsel for Plaintiff

17

18                          _____
                            LEIF A. LOOPHOLE
19                          Counsel for Defendant

20     The above and foregoing 619 pages, having been

21  examined by the Court, are found to be true and correct

22  and are hereby ordered filed as the transcript of the

23  Court Reporter's notes in this cause on this the 16th

24  day of November, A.D. 19--.

25                          _____
                            A. BENCH SNOOZER
                            Presiding Judge
```

some unknown reason does not make sense and will start thinking about how to solve the dilemma. I often transcribed for my husband, and he would wake me in the middle of the night to remind me "Say, I just remembered: Where I dictated 'Edmonton,' it should be 'Edmundsen.' I checked it with him at recess, and I just didn't get a chance to write it down," or some similar bit of information.

The time to worry about a transcript is before you deliver it, not after. When you deliver it, say to yourself "I am proud of this job. It is absolutely the best I can do."

In the rush of taking shorthand and getting out transcript (and getting the money) some reporters are too prone to take shortcuts with the final product, the transcript. It may be that your notereader, transcriber, or computer operator is so good you can read 200 pages and find only one or two errors. As a result, you come to the conclusion you can save a lot of time by not even reading transcript before delivering it. Keep in mind that those "one or two errors" could

FIGURE 72
Notice Filed for Records on Appeal

```
 1            IN THE CIRCUIT COURT OF THE STATE OF OREGON

 2                      FOR DOUGLAS COUNTY

 3   THE STATE OF OREGON, X
                          X
 4           Plaintiff, X            No. 487346
                          X
 5           -vs-         X         NOTICE OF FILING and
                          X
 6   JANICE KAYE OBREGON, X         PROOF OF SERVICE
                          X
 7           Defendant. X

 8       I certify that the original transcript on appeal in the
     above-captioned case was filed in the Circuit Court Clerk's
 9   office on March 22, 19--.

10       I further certify that I served a true copy of the said
     transcript on appeal on Squarely Litigating, District
11   Sttorney for Douglas County, attorney for Plaintiff-
     Respondent, and Carrie DeBurden, Public Defender, attorney
12   for Defendant-Appellant, on March 22, 19--.

13       I further certify that, in compliance with O.R.S.
     19.078(1), I have this date served a copy of this
14   certificate on Squarely Litigating, District Attorney,
     attorney for Plaintiff-Respondent, in the Courthouse in
15   Wilton, Oregon, and on Carrie DeBurden, Public Defender,
     attorney for Defendant-Appellant, at 110 Labor and
16   Industries Building, Salem, Oregon, by personal delivery
     to Squarely Litigating and upon Carrie DeBurden by United
17   States mail deposited at the United States Post Office
     in Wilton, Oregon, with the proper amount of postage
18   attached.

19   Dated this 22nd day of March, 19--.

20

21                          _____
                            PRECISE N. ACCURATE
22                          Official Court Reporter

23

24

25
```

also be monumental errors which you will have to live with the rest of your career. No matter how accurate you and the others who work with you may be, mistakes can and do happen, but careful proofreading will minimize them. The transcript that goes out has your name on the certificate, and you are the one responsible if there is a complaint.

I cannot reiterate too often how important the appearance of the reporter's transcript is. The appearance of pages has suffered from use of continuous computer paper quality, but reporters must use ribbons and printers that produce sharp, clear copies. No overprints should exist, and errors must be corrected on the computer, not with Liquid Paper or correction tape.

Computer and other transcript papers are now delivered with holes punched in the left-hand side. Some reporters use very heavy binders with a light-weight subcover underneath to keep the first few sheets of the transcript from creasing. Filler strips, cut the same length as the transcript paper, punched like the paper, about three-fourths of an inch wide, inserted every 25 to 40 pages will help make the volume lie flat.

Many reporters use transparent plastic front covers because they make typed covers unnecessary since the title pages show through, but these covers become brittle and break easily. Others use medium-weight covers with the reporter's or firm's name, address, and telephone number printed thereon and have the scopist or other worker prepare the cover information.

Velo-Bind provides a punching machine which places evenly placed holes along the left side of a transcript and seals plastic prongs in these holes. Volumes bound this way look very professional, but, like all plastic materials, these plastic strips eventually break with hard use.

Attorneys become irate when pages in volumes they are reading from come loose, so do find a good-looking, permanent means of binding your transcripts. My husband and I had a local printer bind all copies of larger transcripts, which may have taken away a bit from the fees received, but counsel always remarked on the beautiful appearance of the work.

Never allow staples, fasteners, or brads to protrude from the back of transcripts to scratch desks or the hands of the people handling the transcripts. Acco fasteners work well when used with a cover which keeps them inside. Star fasteners, two-piece screws, and even shoestrings are used for various types of transcripts. Just be sure your binding is neat and permanent.

Two-inch Mystic Tape is used by many reporters to seal the back of transcripts. This tape is self-sealing, and when cut to the length of the volume, it can be applied easily. Before applying it, simply place a dot evenly at top and bottom of the volume with a pencil and press evenly to smoothly seal the tape.

A machine manufactured by Standard Duplicating Machines Corp., 10 Connector Road, Andover, MA 01810, called the Bind-Fast II, has many advantages:

1. It is easy to operate.
2. There are no holes to punch as it seals the transcript in book form by use of hot plastic adhesive.
3. There are no metal fasteners to scratch desks and cut fingers.
4. Transcripts so bound cannot be easily taken apart or rebound, which prevents attorneys from copying transcripts and thus cheating the reporter out of fees.
5. The binding is durable and attractive.
6. The Bind-Fast II consists of machinery that does not break down.

Securing Transcript when a Reporter Leaves. If an official court reporter moves for any reason, his or her notes remain filed at the last duty station. A proper forwarding address should always be provided the judge in the former location so notes may be transmitted for transcription to the reporter who originally took the matter. These transcripts should be done promptly and with as great care as those from the place where the reporter is presently employed.

In the past some former officials have refused to or neglected to do such transcripts, and the former judge has ordered them to jail with their notes, a typewriter, carbon, and transcript paper until the required transcript is completed. The publicity surrounding these rare cases is very harmful to the profession, and such situations should be avoided.

If the former reporter cannot be located, great effort is made to discover a person who can transcribe the matter. With Computer-Aided-Transcription and the current uniformity of notes, this should not be the problem it was at one time. There is no excuse for anything but excellent notes in these days of CAT, so to be on the safe side, never let your notes deteriorate.

Chapter 32 ## Reporting Interpreted Proceedings

If participants in any proceeding do not speak English, they have an absolute right to a translation of the trial. In some jurisdictions the absence of an interpreter at trial or during any other critical stage of the proceedings has been held to be a denial of due process even though no objection was made at the time.

Qualifying the Interpreter

Attorneys may hold voir dire, testing the qualifications of the court-provided interpreter or an interpreter produced by opposing counsel, delving into whether or not the interpreter is related to the attorneys or parties or a friend of any of the participants in the matter, how he or she is being paid (by the hour or by a contingent fee), how familiar he or she is with the case, and so on. If any interest or bias on the part of the interpreter can be elicited, he or she may be disqualified.

Interpreting Procedure

When examining the witness, counsel normally use direct questions as though the interpreter were not present.

The interpreter is supposed to give the answers in the first person, although sometimes uninformed ones will answer "He says he was not present," at which point counsel or the judge may request that the interpreter answer in the translated direct words of the witness.

Most attorneys are very careful to avoid attacking or building up the interpreter when a jury is present because they might harm their case.

Oath Used for Interpreters

If an interpreter should be needed during a grand jury case, the oath administered by the judge, the foreman, or the prosecutor (depending upon the jurisdiction) is as follows:

Example

I do solemnly swear (or affirm) that I will interpret truly, faithfully, and fully all the matters and things which may be stated to the witness, _____, and all the matters and things which may be stated by the witness, _____, in response thereto; and that I will not disclose any testimony or the name of any witness before this grand jury except when testifying in court, so help me God. (If the interpreter is affirming, the "so help me God" is omitted.)

In a court case, the interpreter is usually sworn by the clerk of court, but may be sworn by the judge. When an interpreter is requested during a deposition, the court reporter swears the interpreter as follows:

Example Do you solemnly swear that you will well and truly translate from English to Spanish (German, sign language, Russian, Greek, etc.) and from Spanish (German, sign language, Russian, Greek, etc.) into English in the cause now pending before the court, so help you God?

The same rules as to affirmation apply here also.

Parenthetical Inserted in Record

A proper parenthetical remark must be placed in each record by the court reporter similar to the following:

> (Rosario Juan Benevides was sworn by the clerk of court to interpret Spanish into English and English into Spanish.)

Witness Resworn if Sworn in English

If the witness was previously sworn in English due to the fact that counsel or the Court were not aware of the need for an interpreter, the witness should be resworn by the clerk of court through the interpreter in the usual manner, and the court reporter must reflect this happening in the record.

Placement of Interpreter

The interpreter ordinarily sits beside the witness if the testimony is lengthy. If the required examination is to be short, the interpreter stands beside the witness, between the witness and the jury.

Correcting the Interpreter

It is generally held that if the court reporter knows material is not being translated correctly by an interpreter, the reporter is to do nothing about it, as to do otherwise violates the reporter's required impartiality.

However, some very fine reporters feel that the reporter's duty, as an officer of the Court, is to inform the Court (out of anyone's hearing) of this fact and let the matter be handled by the Court from that point.

Of course, if counsel both speak the foreign language or each side has its own interpreter, this matter will be disposed of very rapidly.

Presence of Two Interpreters

There may be many objections to translations of the official interpreter when there are two interpreters present. Then, the court reporter will be asked by the Court to read the question of counsel and the interpreter's English answer. The Court will ask the interpreter if that is the proper answer as given by the witness, sometimes admonishing the interpreter to be more exact in translation. This material must be taken down by the reporter and placed in the printed record.

When two sworn interpreters are used, all conversation in English between the interpreters that is loud enough for the jury to hear must be in the record for consideration by the appellate court. Likewise, should an interpreter add his or her own explanations of a witness's answer (which should not be done), this matter should be taken down by the reporter and placed in the record in toto (in its entirety). The reporter must take down the exact statements of an interpreter and may not convert any of the material to the first person.

Sometimes a witness testifying through an interpreter will answer some questions in English. In the record, this may be indicated by use of an asterisk before the answer sign and a footnote "Answer by the witness in English," or after the answer sign the typed parenthetical "(In English)."

If part of the translation is given by the interpreter and the rest is in English by the witness, the parenthetical (In English) should precede the portion of the witness's remarks given in English, as shown below:

Example

JOSE DE DIOS GARCIA,

having been first duly sworn by the clerk of court through the interpreter to tell the truth, the whole truth, and nothing but the truth, was examined and testified upon his oath as follows:

DIRECT EXAMINATION

BY MR. LEADING:

Q: What is your name?

A: Jose de Dios Garcia.

Q: Where do you live?

A: I live at 1616 Briarglen, Tucson, Arizona.

Q: How long have you lived there?

A: (In English.) Seven years.

Q: Please speak through the interpreter.

A: I would have to ask my wife. She would know that. About seven years.
   (In English.) No. Six years.

Q: Before the accident happened that we are here about today, did you ever see the car that collided with your vehicle?

A: (In English.) I saw the car.
   (By the interpreter.) It was going very fast.

How and Why Interpreters Are Found

In some cases, opposing counsel is taken by surprise by the appearance of a foreign-speaking witness. Counsel will then ask for a short recess in order to secure his or her own interpreter, perhaps requesting the services of the consulate, a university, a school of foreign languages, or a professional person who speaks the language. In some places, counsel may be able to find such a suitable person among court employees.

If an interpreter speaks broken English, as many of them do, the court reporter must make sure that he or she understands all utterances of the interpreter just as he or she would with any other witness.

Interpreters may be required to translate not only for evidence of those speaking an alien tongue, but also for persons physically unable to use words and persons unable, through diffidence or illness, to speak loudly enough to be heard distinctly.

Chapter 33

Daily Copy Reporting

With the advent of CAT, many reporters are handling daily copy all alone with the aid of a scopist (sometimes called a text processor). However, many times the necessary equipment is not at hand and teams of court reporters who employ transcribers turn out daily copy efficiently, with three reporters being the optimum, but a team of two being quite adequate for the task.

Some reporters never secure daily copy assignment. Some others, although very experienced, do not wish to take part in a proceeding where daily or immediate copy might be requested because it is stressful work. Many avoid these situations because they lack experience and confidence.

In this book, I will go into daily copy using transcribers because for some time to come reporters will be forced to use this system due to unavailability of equipment. However, with lowered prices, more CAT daily copy will become the rule.

How Daily Copy Is Secured

A law firm will contact the reporting firm it customarily uses and request daily copy services, or sometimes a reporter taking depositions or an official reporting a court case of some magnitude will be requested to provide daily copy.

Sometimes the reporter suggests that he or she can furnish daily copy, and the attorneys immediately take up the offer.

Be sure to establish a definite understanding in advance as to how much your charges will be for furnishing it. Also, be very sure to get a commitment from the person hiring you as to exactly when payment will be forthcoming.

Personnel Required

Two reporters and two or three typists are the norm for dictated daily copy transcript.

Be sure the reporter you choose to work with is someone you work well with. Select your typists carefully, remembering you need people who can produce quality work rapidly and can withstand the pressure of deadlines. The transcribers are a vital part of any daily copy operation.

Some reporters handle daily copy alone by using two notereaders who alternate in entering the hearing room and tearing off notes to transcribe at convenient spots. Most people are not so lucky as to have notereaders, however.

A useful member of the daily copy team may be a "go-fer," called a "roust" by one Texas firm, I suppose as a derivative of "roustabout." Often students do this work for experience, but all teams do not have go-fers available, and the burden for all big and little chores then falls upon their shoulders. The types of activities these people do varies. If the typists do not prepare the stacks, the go-fer may make up the typing paper and carbon sets used, staggering them so there is a continuous supply of stacks with the right number of carbon copies. Other reporters use continuous paper purchased with the correct number of copies as a part of the pack.

The typists blind number all pages in the left top margins after the first take as, for instance 5-M-10-L might mean "Take 5, Mildred (the reporter), page 10, Linda (the typist)"; but in the final transcript numbering, the page may be 85. The go-fer may be the person selected to type proper page numbers in the proper place, remove carbons, and sort the pages (face down so the reporters can turn them right-side-up for easy proofreading). If errors are found, the go-fer may be the one to pull all sheets with that page number and return them to the typist for corrections (even sometimes helping to make corrections).

The go-fer may also go among reporters and typists to pick up dictated tapes, return blank ones, and pass along information about court recesses and start-up times of other reporters. He or she may also photocopy exhibits, go out for food, or supply cups of coffee and Cokes to the workers.

Preparation for Daily Copy Reporting

To ensure a well-run daily copy, a certain amount of advance preparation is required. Before the starting date, the reporters should:

1. Get together a glossary of names and terms if possible and study them, alphabetize them, and type them double-spaced to leave room for additions. Copies should be run for each reporter and typist who will be working on the case, plus a few spares. At the end of each day, these information sheets should be retyped with additions to speed the typists' work.

2. Work out a system to be used when relieving other reporters, such as a tap on the shoulder or a nod of the head.

3. Decide in advance what formats are to be used for setting up witnesses, exhibits, off-the-record discussions, margins, and so on, and supply each typist with a sample.

4. Check all shorthand machines including the essential spare one and typewriters and dictating machines that will be used in advance of the starting date. Things like extension cords should be secured in advance.

5. Label the dictating tapes in order of takes.

6. Gather lists of attorney's names and addresses and get an understanding as to just when and where complete transcripts are to be delivered.

7. Have enough stacks made up so the typists can start immediately when the first reporter returns from the hearing room and so there will never be any waiting during the whole procedure.

8. Before the session commences, turn typewriters and dictating machines on and have the belts on the machines threaded and numbered so time will not be wasted doing these things.

9. When everyone arrives, make a seating chart. Most daily copy cases involve a number of attorneys, so be sure every reporter has a copy of the chart.

Daily-Copy Procedures

A decision must be made in advance as to who will record the first take. The "first-take" reporter will then do all the odd-numbered takes, and the "second-take" reporter will do all even-numbered takes. Take No. 1 should be no longer than five minutes so the typists may begin work as rapidly as possible.

Usually the "second-take" reporter sits in during the first take to make sure of the starting time. At a prearranged signal, he or she will begin to take in shorthand, and the "first-take" reporter will return to the office to dictate the notes taken during the first five minutes. In taking over from another reporter, reporters try not to break in the middle of a question or an answer sequence because if readbacks are requested, it could be very embarrassing. If, however, an answer goes on for pages and pages, and reporters must break in the middle, the transcript indicates "A (Continuing)" to keep a clear record.

Since reporters relieve one another at intervals, a number of partial pages result where these breaks are made. Reporters keep track of the number of lines on these partial pages, and they are computed out to full pages. The reporters and typists are then paid on the basis of these computed full-page figures. At such times as a take ends in the middle of a page or a few lines from the top, the typist types "(Continued on next page)" so the attorneys and the judge will not think anything is missing from the transcript. Some reporters have typists type "(Continued with no omission)" to be sure no misunderstanding results.

The first reporter, upon returning to the hearing room, will now write for about ten minutes, after which the second reporter will come in and take over. These short periods are necessary at first in order that typists will be constantly working.

The takes will stretch out from this point on to 15 to 20 minutes, becoming somewhat longer during the course of the session because of the time it takes to get back to the office, dictate, and return to the hearing room.

Lunchtime is usually a very busy period on a daily copy, as it provides a chance for reporters and typists to catch up in order to start off even at the afternoon session.

Transcribing the Copy

On the first take, if there are two typists waiting, the "first-take" reporter should split his or her take and dictate half on each of two tapes so each typist can get started working as soon as possible. This practice helps to ensure that each typist will get about the same number of pages.

The first typist will number the transcript pages in the proper place on the page. The second typist will blind his or her pages, placing number and identifications on the left-hand side where they will be hidden when the transcript is collated and bound.

Carbons are left in until numbering is done by the typist or go-fer. If typists do their own final numbering, they put the last number of their pages on the list so the other one can merely consult the list at such time as they are in a position to number their pages.

Dictating Daily Copy. The following timesavers will help produce daily copy more efficiently.

1. Reporter 1 should announce clearly "Transcriber, I am dictating Take 1, Belt 1," at the same time numbering the reel of tape "1-1." ("Belt" is used as opposed to "Tape" to avoid conflict with "Take.")

2. Reporters should have a notepad handy to write out spellings for typists. The same number should be put on each sheet as on the belt so typists can readily match the belt and the spelling sheet. The typists should be instructed to add these spellings to the master long sheet.

3. Unusual terminology may be spelled out on the dictated belt, but it should always also be placed on the pad because it is faster and safer. Once it is written down, the terminology need not be repeated for the typists. They are able to refer to the pads when necessary.

4. Reporter 2 should start out by alerting the typist that he or she is dictating Take 2, Belt 1, at the same time marking the reel of tape 2-1.

5. It is extremely important that reporters do not dictate beyond the five-minute mark on any belts so both typists can keep working.

6. Reporters, immediately upon dictating a take, return to the courtroom to relieve the duty reporter.

7. Before returning to the hearing room, each reporter should put a properly numbered belt on the dictating machine so when he or she returns to dictate, this chore will have been accomplished.

8. Reporters should keep their voices modulated because both reporters are dictating at the same time. In addition, over the course of a long trial the reporter's voice will give out. Furthermore, one can dictate faster and more distinctly in a modulated voice.

9. Reporters should punctuate as much as possible while actually recording the shorthand. This practice will facilitate dictation. This remark is primarily directed to unusual punctuation, such as dashes, a question mark following an answer, a semicolon, or a colon. All usual punctuation should be inserted in all reporting as a matter of course.

10. Reporters should tear off notes and prepare paper in the tray before leaving the machine in the hearing room so upon returning, they will be ready to go.

11. An extra pad should be in the hearing room at the reporter's desk or table so that helpful information can be written down to alert a colleague when he or she returns to the courtroom. For instance, Reporter No. 1 may have departed while Attorney A was questioning the witness on direct and return to find Attorney B questioning the witness. If Attorney B has the witness merely on voir dire, Reporter No. 2 should write this information on the pad so that when Attorney A resumes, Reporter No. 1 will not set such questioning up as redirect.

12. Reporters cannot be timid in asking politely and diplomatically for spellings, copies of exhibits read from in length, copies of citations, and copies of depositions read into evidence or indictments.

13. Reporters should dictate very distinctly in order to avoid having typists wasting time puzzling over indistinct portions of any belts.

14. All reporters should establish a good rapport with counsel because a relaxed mood will make everything go better. Then, when reporters want to secure information, such as spellings, counsel will gladly supply it.

Typists' Time Savers

1. Typists should report half an hour early or more to check on setups and equipment.

2. Typists should tape information given them before the start of the daily to the wall in front of them or keep it readily available for ready reference. This information includes style of the case, venue, appearances, and any unusual words, names, or phrases known then.

3. One typist should type a style page, indicating Volume No., commencing Page No., blank for ending Page No., and date. This procedure should be followed each morning and each afternoon.

4. Each typist should type the "take" and "belt" number worked on and identification letters at the extreme left-hand top margin of the page. The blind numbers should follow.

5. If the typists are doing all page numbering, as soon as Typist No. 1 completes Take 1 (or any other take, for that matter) he or she should give Typist No. 2 a page number.

It is also imperative that the typists communicate with one another, especially regarding numbering if that is their responsibility alone. They must also share information such as names; words; what attorney is examining the witness as to direct, cross, redirect, or recross-examination;

and marking and admitting of exhibits. This information will also be needed for indexing purposes. In other words, typists must cooperate in making entries on the Daily Copy Log and in anything that will make the entire operation run more smoothly.

Typists Must Keep Records. Typists are expected to keep a record of exhibits, witnesses, and other matters to be indexed so an index can be made easily at the end of the session or day. They also must keep a record of the takes they have done with corresponding page numbers in order that they may bill the reporters correctly. This also helps keep the transcript straight for collating.

All Typists Must Be Kept Busy. The reporters' dictation takes should be kept short to ensure that typists are kept working at all times. The typists do not work for just one reporter because they would then be idle a certain amount of time.

The reporters should try to see that all typists get about the same number of pages to type. If they do not, and if it is a long daily, animosity may develop that will impede the orderly, congenial handling of the whole assignment.

Figures 73 and 74 illustrate forms which might be kept to handle daily copy efficiently.

FIGURE 73

```
┌─────────────────────────────────────────────────────────────────────┐
│                         DAILY COPY LOG                                │
│   VENUE OF CASE:                     DATE:        TIME:               │
│                          Day Totals: Reporters: ____ ____ pages       │
│                                                 ____ ____ pages       │
│   TITLE OF CASE:                                                      │
│                                      Typists:   ____ ____ pages       │
│                                                 ____ ____ pages       │
│   ─────────────────────────────────────────────────────────────────  │
│   Take    Reporter's  Typist's    Pages   Pages   Witnesses, Direct, Cross,  │
│   No.      Initials   Initials                     Motions,  Voir Dire, etc.  │
│   ═════════════════════════════════════════════════════════════════  │
│   1. _____   │
│   2. _____   │
│   3. _____   │
│   4. _____   │
│   5. _____   │
│   6. _____   │
│   7. _____   │
│   8. _____   │
│   9. _____   │
│  10. _____   │
│  11. _____   │
│  12. _____   │
│  13. _____   │
│  14. _____   │
│  15. _____   │
│  16. _____   │
│  17. _____   │
│  18. _____   │
│  19. _____   │
│  20. _____   │
│                                                                       │
└─────────────────────────────────────────────────────────────────────┘
```

FIGURE 74

```
                    DAILY COPY LOG
                       Page 2


                        EXHIBITS

    PLAINTIFF'S                           DEFENDANT'S

  Id.       Rec'd.                       Id.       Rec'd.

   1          1                           1          1
   2          2                           2          2
   3          3                           3          3
   4          4                           4          4
   5          5                           5          5
   6          6                           6          6
   7          7                           7          7
   8          8                           8          8
   9          9                           9          9
  10         10                          10         10
  11         11                          11         11
  12         12                          12         12
  13         13                          13         13
  14         14                          14         14
  15         15                          15         15
  16         16                          16         16
  17         17                          17         17
  18         18                          18         18
  19         19                          19         19
  20         20                          20         20
  21         21                          21         21
  22         22                          22         22
  23         23                          23         23
  24         24                          24         24
  25         25                          25         25

  Line to be drawn through number as exhibit occurs.

  NOTES:
```

Daily Copy Supplies Checklist

For Reporter:	Stenograph and tripod
	Stenopads
	Extra ribbon
	Marking pen
Dictating Supplies:	Dictating machines
	Dictating tapes or cassettes
	Extension cords
For Typist:	Typewriters (if not brought by typists)
	Typewriter pads
	Typewriter tables and chair
	Transcribing machines
	Earphones
	Foot pedals
	Typewriter ribbons
	Dictionary
	Towelettes

Transcribing Supplies:	Masters
	Backing sheets
	Razor blades
	Spirit master hand cleaner
	Transcript paper
	Carbon or carbon sets
	Erasers and shields
	Medical, unabridged, and technical dictionaries
Duplicating Supplies	Xerox machine with or without collator
	Duplicating paper
Miscellaneous:	Covers and backs
	Brass fasteners or Acco fasteners
	Brass washers
	Hammer
	Scissors
	Scotch transparent tape
	Stapler and staples
	Paper clips
	Rubber bands
	Name stamp
	Stamp pad
	Legal-size scratch pads
	Collator
	Envelopes for transcripts
	Labels
	Rags
	Alcohol
	Pencils and pens
	Marking pens
	Box of tissues
	Multiple outlet plug
	Business cards
	Petty cash
	Billheads

Money Can Be Saved by Photocopying

Photocopy requires typing of originals only. Typist production is increased 15 to 20 percent in this way if the typists are paid by the hour. This method assures a uniform appearance of all copies and eliminates cost of carbon paper. Photocopy paper is also less expensive than regular transcript paper.

Daily Copy on the Computer

CAT is very beneficial to the official reporter when producing daily copy transcripts. Once a reporter has achieved a good quality translation, transcript can be produced much more quickly on the computer than by any other method. Several options are available as to production depending on the delivery time requirements, the skill of the reporter, the equipment available, and the number of hours the reporter desires to work.

It is possible, though not always advisable, for a reporter to produce a day's proceedings alone. The length of the hearing or testimony and the requested delivery time should govern what help is needed. One experienced text processor and one experienced reporter should not have difficulty producing an average day's testimony within a couple of hours after the proceedings recess.

The key is to get the data to the text processor to begin translating and working on as early in the day as possible and utilize all recesses for production of the transcript.

Two reporters and one text processor can easily handle a day's proceedings, especially if the reporters are able to help with part of the editing functions. Having two scopes available during daily copy is extremely beneficial.

Two reporters with two text processors who each have a scope should be able to produce a daily copy transcript very easily without working into the evening. This is an ideal setup for long days or immediate delivery of the transcript. If the reporters' "takes" are broken into 30-minute segments, the morning session should easily be completed before the afternoon proceedings begin and another delivery made shortly after the afternoon recess is taken.

Daily copy on systems with only one scope requires careful management and an awareness of Murphy's Law. The other reporters using the system must be aware that a daily is going on and try to schedule their work around that.

During extended dailies, it may be necessary to allow the other reporters an hour in the morning and one in the afternoon to produce some of their work during daylight hours. This is a time when a late-night text processor is desirable and sometimes a necessity.

Daily Copy Procedure for Pool System Utilized by the Court Reporters' Division, Superior Court of the District of Columbia

Example   When word is received that a specific case is going daily copy, the supervisor in charge of scheduling reporters ascertains from the judge, government and defense counsel exactly which portions are requested on a daily basis, duration of the case, as well as hours court will be in session, number of copies of transcript needed and any other pertinent information. He then selects his reporter team (usually 4) from among the qualified and available reporters. The reporter who has been assigned to that court for that particular month is always the "lead" reporter and works with the supervisor in making certain that transcript payment is guaranteed in advance by obtaining orders signed by the appropriate approving officials, and also sees that witness lists, copies of indictments or other information valuable to reporters is secured.

On the first day, the lead reporter reports the first take and begins keeping a witness sheet in the courtroom. On this he shows the status of the trial such as which witness is on the stand, the examining attorney, and so forth, thereby giving ready reference to reporters who follow him. He remains in the courtroom until he has taken as much as he can transcribe by 9 A.M. the following morning. This runs from 40 to 80 pages, depending upon the reporter's individual skills and his transcript backlog, as he may receive other daily copy requests for cases he reported earlier and he is expected to produce them also. When he reaches his maximum, he signals the courtroom clerk, who calls the supervisor. The next reporter on the list is told to report to the courtroom, and the procedure is repeated for the remainder of the day. When each reporter comes from the courtroom, he sees the supervisor, who notes on a daily copy record sheet the time the reporter was in the courtroom. The supervisor also records the number of pages the reporter estimates he took, and based upon that estimate, assigns page numbers (such as 1–60 for the first reporter, 61–106 for the second reporter, etc.). If the reporter has under-estimated his pages, he adjusts the pagination, for instance making the last page 55–60. If he overestimates, he adds letters to his last number: 60A, 60B, 60C, etc.

If court continues longer than expected, the first reporter is reassigned, although this is infrequent. Reporters on standby for daily copy are assigned to other courts for short matters such as sentencings, status calls, etc., as are those who have had their takes for the day.

All reporters on the team hand their completed transcripts to the first reporter, who early the next morning prepares a table of contents, assembles the transcripts and gives the original to the supervisor. The copies are handed to the reporter who will report the first take that day, and he carries them to the courtroom, along with a receipt for counsel to sign so no payment problems develop later on. This signed receipt is returned to the supervisor.

On the second and subsequent days, the supervisor rotates reporters' take positions, that is, the reporter who was first the previous day moves the last, while the reporter who was second goes into the courtroom first. Thus, no one reporter has the first (or last) take every day. Also, the supervisor makes a new daily copy record sheet and completes the first day's sheet by counting the actual pages prepared by each reporter and placing the sheet in a file. At the end of the case, these sheets are handed to clerical personnel who utilize the information for billing purposes. The sheets then go into our permanent files, along with transcript receipts and any other documents. If the case goes on appeal, the original transcripts are transmitted to the Court of Appeals.

Prepared by:
Mrs. Louise A. Koniarski, Deputy Director
Court Reporter Division
District of Columbia Courts
613 G Street, Northwest
Washington, D.C., 20001

A Reporter's Comparison of the Operation of a Pool System Vìs-a-vís One-to-One System

Pool System	One-to-One System
Supervised atmosphere	Unsupervised atmosphere
Regular working hours	Irregular working hours
Shared workload	One-person workload
Relief from extended in-court duties when backlog dictates	No relief reporter when backlog too large to complete on timely basis
Daily copy in limited quantities rather than bulk	Reporter responsible for all daily copy transcripts
Reporter relieved from in-court duty, at expense of the Court, when reporter is on sick or emergency leave	Must furnish substitute reporter if ill, or emergency arises, often at own expense
Friendly exchange of courtroom duty for evening hours or Saturday-Sunday-Holiday sessions, on a voluntary basis	Reporter is required to attend court until adjournment regardless of personal commitments
Vacation time flexible	Vacation time must coincide with judge's plans
Not subject to whims of individual judge if you are employed by the system	Always at beck and call of judge
Supervisor can intercede in case of dispute with the judge, such as a request for a change in transcript outside the Rule of the Court	Possibility of dispute with judge, resulting in dismissal

A Reporter's Comparison of the Operation of a Pool System
Vis-a-vís One-to-One System (cont'd)

Pool System	*One-to-One System*
Transcript production geared for maximum efficiency wherein supervisor is responsible for the mechanics of delivery, enabling reporter to spend less time with administrative duties	Reporter is required to prepare and file necessary paper work regarding everyday administrative duties, including deadlines and extension in the Appellate Court
No secretarial work	Secretarial work likely even though judge has a secretary
Personal social relationship with judge not likely	No opportunity to develop close personal relationship with judge and staff
Reporter may volunteer for added courtroom duty or different case-type reporting	Reporter has no control over hours in court and type of cases to be reported

Another method of balancing the workload is to organize the reporters into a pool and have the administrator or managing reporter assign reporters to courtrooms based on their backlog. A reporter with a substantial backlog would be assigned to a court unlikely to produce transcript or might be able to be relieved of reporting duties (if a judge is on vacation or a court is not sitting) and thereby work on the backlog. By the same token, a reporter with no backlog can be assigned to a heavy transcript court.

Pooling, however, is not a panacea. If the main purpose for pooling is to assure an even distribution of transcript resulting from time spent in court, the administrator must first consider whether some reporters are, in fact, overburdened with in-court time.

Another reason for pooling is to enable reporters to get transcripts finished on time. However, if all reporters in the court are habitually late in filing transcripts, the problem may be insufficient staffing, and pooling alone will have little positive effect. Similarly, if only some of the reporters are consistently late in transcript production, the administrator must consider whether it is due to overwork or poor work habits, requiring a different solution.

Pooling does require more administrative time, whether it be the time of the court administrator or a separate managing reporter. Record keeping, assignments, and monitoring of in-court time and pending transcripts must be done consistently and accurately for pooling to be successful. Pooling also requires changes on the part of the reporters. Rather than adjusting to the work habits of one judge, they must be prepared to work for a number of judges. Pooling may have distinct advantages for a court, provided it is implemented to solve the problems it is designed to address.

Effective use of reporting services may not be under the complete control of the administrator. Often the administrator may not have the authority to make changes in the existing system. However, if transcript delay is a problem and reporting services are not being efficiently used, the administrator has an obligation to the judicial system to attempt to make the changes necessary to use the available resources more effectively.

Chapter 34

The Use of Videotaping

Videotape Technology

Videotape is an audio-visual medium by which a machine electronically records and stores a picture with sound on a magnetic tape. Videotape is not like film in that it involves electronic rearrangement of particles on magnetic tape, which makes developing unnecessary.

Videotaping may be done in color or in black and white. Most videotape machines record sound only on one track (monaural). The tapes used for videotaping normally last one hour, although half-hour tapes are available.

Fear of Being Replaced by Videotape

Many reporters have, from time to time, feared that videotaping would sound the knell of doom for their profession. However, in all jurisdictions where videotaping has been tried without a transcribed record by a reporter, the result has been unsatisfactory. As an adjunct to the transcribed record, videotapes can be most useful, and many reporters offer videotaping services either in their offices or at the client's location. This has become a very profitable business for many individuals and firms.

It is doubtful that a beginning court reporter will be called upon to report simultaneously with videotape for a time after leaving school, but every student and reporter should have familiarity with this process.

Why a Reporter Should Be Present

There are many excellent reasons it is important to have a court reporter present making a shorthand record at the same time a videotape is being made, among them, the following:

1. Electronic malfunction may occur, or a poor quality videotape may result from using an inadequate operator.
2. The typewritten transcript enables the Court to rule on potentially objectionable testimony without having to view the entire videotape.
3. Costs are saved when the technician has a typewritten transcript for editing purposes.
4. Typing a transcript from a videotape alone is a very difficult, slow, laborious task.

5. It is difficult to locate portions of videotaped testimony or colloquy in a hurry.

6. If a judge wants to review testimony, there may not be an operator available or equipment there to view the videotape.

7. Extraneous noises, such as the rustling of papers or moving of chairs may block out the sound on a videotape, but the reporter would ask the witness to repeat an answer otherwise lost to the record.

Applications of Videotape

Innovative reporters and members of the bar have found a number of uses for the comparatively new videotape technology, and others are sure to follow. Some applications currently in vogue are:

1. Expert witnesses may have their depositions taken prior to trial. Having videotaped testimony results in cost saving and time convenience.

2. Doctors' depositions are taken for the previous reason, and presentations of x-rays and slides can be shown more effectively through videotapes than by ordinary courtroom presentations.

3. Demonstrative evidence can be presented showing laboratory experiments that would be impossible to perform in the courtroom.

4. Segments of a trial have been prerecorded and played to a jury in proper sequence in short trials, although the results have been generally poor in the few instances where this has been tried.

5. Demonstrations of evidence showing handicaps of injured people in daily situations are shown effectively to juries.

6. Individuals are having videotapes made as they read aloud and sign a "living will" to ensure that their wills will survive any attacks.

7. Freelance court reporting firms use videotapes to teach new employees how they want transcripts prepared and to demonstrate office procedures.

8. Confessions are videotaped by police departments.

9. Court reporting schools use videotapes as instructional tools.

Securing the Use of Videotape Equipment

There are several methods of securing the use of videotape equipment:

1. Purchase.

2. Lease.

3. Rental.

4. Subcontracting.

The volume of a reporter's business will determine whether outright purchase of equipment is practical. Some firms buy such equipment under a lease-purchase agreement. If the volume does not materialize by the end of the lease period, the equipment goes back to the leasing agent.

Rental is the cheapest method, but the equipment may not be available at the proper time, or it may be of inferior condition and reliability.

When videotape work is subcontracted, the reporter contracts with a professional cameraman or a firm specializing in video services to do the videotaping while the reporter takes the proceeding in shorthand.

The technologies are advancing so rapidly it is difficult to project what equipment will be foremost in years to come. Reporters can only keep current by reading the *National Shorthand Reporter* (*NSR*), attending seminars, and keeping in touch with reporters who furnish such services regularly.

Producing Videotape

Both competent reporters and trained video-production personnel are required to produce a good videotaped deposition. NSRA holds excellent seminars on videotaping in selected cities of the United States throughout each year and at the NSRA Convention annually. They also have a fine CLVS testing program. Every reporter should avail himself or herself of such updated training.

An excellent article by H. Allen Benowitz in the *NSR* described and diagrammed his videotape deposition studio, which is 23 feet long by about 15 feet wide. Behind the witness's location there is an "exhibit wall" with burlap over drywall to accommodate tacks for charts. Above this wall is an electronic movie screen for movie or slide demonstrations that can be lowered by pressing a button. It also serves for contrast if the witness appears in a plaid sports coat or wants to use skeletal models, which do not usually show up well.

There is also an easel with pointer and an X-ray shadowbox available to the witness. The background of the video room should be a solid color in order to maximize contrast and minimize brightness or glare, such as a light blue or light green drape behind that end of the conference table.

Two-Camera System Is Recommended

Some reporters use a single-camera system to videotape, but a two-camera setup is preferable because it enables the cameraperson to set one camera forward for a closeup of the witness and the other at a wide angle to present a view of all participants.

At the time of objections, a flick of the input selection switch on the recorder from closeup position to wide angle results in immediate pre-focused view of the deposition scene with all participants in view for the colloquy exchange. When colloquy ends, at the first question, the input selection switch on the recorder is again moved to the original position for closeup of the witness.

Suggestions for Securing Satisfactory Videotapes

Cooperation among the attorneys and the reporter is essential to have a good videotaped proceeding. The following suggestions have been made by experts to help provide a near perfect service:

1. All speakers must speak loudly enough to be heard, and they must avoid overlapping by giving the previous speaker an opportunity to complete his or her statement.

2. The witness should occasionally glance at the camera in order to relate to the jury who will view the deposition.

3. The attorneys should sit close to the witness for maximum effectiveness. The camera is set for closeups of the witness a great deal; but in colloquy, the camera will go to long range and all parties will appear on the screen. In exchanges between the witness and the questioner, the camera will be at medium range, showing both on the screen.

4. Counsel should be advised to speak assertively and to enunciate clearly because the jury will lose interest in material that is not easily understood.

5. Attorneys should ask short, direct questions that require short, precise answers.

6. Material should be organized in advance and lawyers should avoid looking through files and reports or having witnesses read long passages. The camera will pick up the crown of a witness's head when he or she looks down, and the audio from a lavalier microphone on the lapel exaggerates the rustling of pages.

7. If viewboxes are used, or other such equipment, these items should be close to the participants.

8. Written documents shown on camera should be displayed so they can be easily seen and read on playback.

9. On pauses in excess of 60 seconds, filming should be halted:

   a. When the court reporter is directed to mark exhibits,

   b. During off-the-record discussions,

   c. When searching through documents and records.

Forms and Stipulations Used in Videotaping

The following forms and stipulations in Figures 75–80 on pages 302 through 308 will prove of value in videotaping situations.

FIGURE 75
Sample Form for Videotape Technician

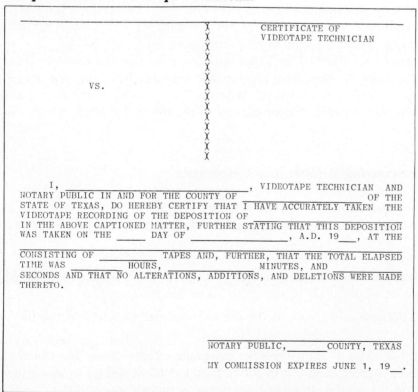

```
_____     X     CERTIFICATE OF
                                  X     VIDEOTAPE TECHNICIAN
                                  X
                                  X
                                  X
                                  X
                                  X
              VS.                 X
                                  X
                                  X
                                  X
                                  X
                                  X
                                  X

     I, _____, VIDEOTAPE TECHNICIAN  AND
NOTARY PUBLIC IN AND FOR THE COUNTY OF _____  OF THE
STATE OF TEXAS, DO HEREBY CERTIFY THAT I HAVE ACCURATELY TAKEN   THE
VIDEOTAPE RECORDING OF THE DEPOSITION OF _____
IN THE ABOVE CAPTIONED MATTER, FURTHER STATING THAT THIS DEPOSITION
WAS TAKEN ON THE _____ DAY OF _____, A.D. 19___, AT THE
_____
CONSISTING OF _____ TAPES AND, FURTHER, THAT THE TOTAL ELAPSED
TIME WAS _____ HOURS, _____ MINUTES, AND _____
SECONDS AND THAT NO ALTERATIONS, ADDITIONS, AND DELETIONS WERE MADE
THERETO.




              _____
              NOTARY PUBLIC,_____COUNTY, TEXAS

              MY COMMISSION EXPIRES JUNE 1, 19___.
```

FIGURE 76-A
Sample Stipulation for Videotape Technician

(TITLE OF COURT AND CAUSE)

It is stipulated by and between the undersigned as follows:

1. That the deposition of _____, a witness produced by the _____, be taken at _____ o'clock __.m. on _____, the _____ day of _____, 19___, at the office of _____ at _____.

2. That the deposition of said witness be taken in the usual manner, under Rule 30, Federal Rules of Civil Procedure (Section 2019(c) California Code of Civil Procedure), before _____, a qualified deposition reporter, and that the proceedings, including the swearing of the witness, be videotaped for use at the trial in lieu of reading the transcript of the witness' testimony.

3. The deposition reporter will take the stenographic record and will hire, control, and be responsible for providing an experienced camera operator for making the videotape.

4. The videotape shall be timed by a timedate generator that shall show continuously each hour, minute, and second of each tape.

5. The camera operator shall take an oath to record all proceedings accurately and completely, and certify as to the correctness and completeness of the videotape.

6. At the beginning of the deposition, the parties and counsel shall be shown in the visual portion of the deposition.

7. During the deposition the witness shall be recorded in as near to courtroom atmosphere and standards as possible. There will not be any procedures to give undue emphasis to any portion of the testimony. The camera shall focus as much as possible on the witness and the lawyer asking the questions. If it is not possible to do both, then the camera will focus on the witness.

FIGURE 76-B

8.   Each attorney and the witness shall be provided with an individual microphone.

9.   The person operating the video camera shall give a two-minute warning before the end of each tape.

10.   It shall not be necessary for the witness to view and/or approve the videotape.

11.   At least one original videotape record must be made and shall remain in the custody of the deposition reporter until trial or until the Court has ruled on any objections and an edited copy of the original has been prepared for presentation to the jury, whichever shall sooner occur, at which time the original and the edited copy, if any, shall be filed with the Clerk of the Court and kept in a place suitable for preservation of magnetic tape.

12.   Any party may purchase a duplicate original or edited tape from the reporter, at any time.

13.   The deposition reporter shall be responsible for providing equipment and facilities to edit the tape and to play back and show the videotaped deposition.

14.   Objections shall be ruled on in camera prior to showing the videotaped deposition to the jury. Any editing of the tape that becomes necessary as a result of the trial Court's rulings shall be done immediately after the in-camera hearing and prior to the presentation of the videotape deposition to the jury. Editing costs may be assessed against any party participating in the deposition as shall be determined by the Court.

15.   For showing of the videotape deposition to the jury, the deposition reporter shall furnish a television screen at least 19 inches corner to corner, with a suitable stand.

FIGURE 76-C

16. If the jury requests that any portion of the videotape deposition be read back, the court reporter shall read back from the stenographic record or from the edited transcript, as the Court shall direct.

17. Except as provided in Paragraph 14, only the stenographic record of the deposition shall be taxed as costs.

18. After time for appeal has expired, appeal has been concluded or settlement effected, the videotape shall, on request of _____ , be delivered to him or, if no request is made in 60 days after such final determination of the case, then to the deposition reporter.

DATED this _____ day of _____ , 19___ .

_____

_____

FIGURE 77
Title Page of Videotaped Deposition

```
 1                          NO. 67-33572-75

 2   JOHN A. WALKER              )(      IN THE DISTRICT COURT OF
                                 )(
 3        VS.                    )(      TARRANT COUNTY, TEXAS
                                 )(
 4   INSURANCE COMPANY           )(      67TH JUDICIAL DISTRICT
     OF NORTH AMERICA            )(

 5

 6

 7

 8

 9

10

11

12        DEPOSITION OF WILLIAM ROGER BERNELL, M.D.

13                   TAKEN FOR PLAINTIFF

14                        VIDEOTAPED

15

16

17

18

19

20

21   REPORTER:  GLORIA CARLIN, RPR, CP, CM

22   VIDEOTAPE TECHNICIAN:  DOUGLAS MORRIS, RPR

23   DATE:   FEBRUARY 18, 19__.

24

25
```

FIGURE 78

NO. 67-33572-75

JOHN A. WALKER	X	IN THE DISTRICT COURT OF
	X	
VS.	X	TARRANT COUNTY, TEXAS
	X	
INSURANCE COMPANY	X	67TH JUDICIAL DISTRICT
OF NORTH AMERICA	X	

- - -

ANSWERS AND DEPOSITION OF WILLIAM ROGER BERNELL, M.D.,

a witness produced on behalf of the Plaintiff, taken by

shorthand and videotape in the above styled and numbered cause

on the 18th day of February, A.D. 19_ _, commencing at 2:00 P.M.,

before Gloria Carlin, a Notary Public in and for Tarrant County,

Texas, at the office of Dr. William Roger Bernell, M.D.,

located at 622 S. Henderson, in the City of Fort Worth,

County of Tarrant, State of Texas, in accordance with the

agreement hereinafter set forth and the accompanying Notice

hereto attached.

- - -

APPEARANCES:

    For the Plaintiff:

        DUSHMAN, GREENSPAN & FRIEDMAN,
        By: Lowell E. Dushman, Esq.,
        920 Commerce Building
        Fort Worth, Texas 76102.

    For the Defendant:

        STREET, SWIFT, BROCKERMEYER, BELL & WARD,
        By: Richard E. Ward, Esq.,
        515 Fort Worth Club Building,
        Fort Worth, Texas 76102.

FIGURE 79
Opening Statement Form

(Prior to opening the record, the video technician will give general instructions to all parties and the court reporter will secure the agreement the deposition is being taken under. After receiving the signal from the video technician to begin, the court reporter will read the following opening statement. Be sure to speak slowly and distinctly and with plenty of volume.)

AT THIS TIME THE DEPOSITION OF _____, A WITNESS

PRODUCED BY THE _____, IS BEING TAKEN IN CAUSE NO._____

STYLED _____ VS. _____

COMMENCING AT _____ O'CLOCK (A.M.) (P.M.) ON (DAY) _____,

THE _____ DAY OF _____, 19___, AT THE OFFICE OF

_____, LOCATED AT _____, IN

THE CITY OF _____, COUNTY OF _____, STATE OF

TEXAS.

THE COURT REPORTER TAKING THIS DEPOSITION IS _____

AND THE VIDEO TECHNICIAN OPERATING THE CAMERA IS _____.

WILL COUNSEL PLEASE STATE THEIR APPEARANCES FOR THE RECORD?

(After this statement is read, appearances are given. After this, the witness is sworn and the deposition begins.)

FIGURE 80
Additional Procedures

You will have to signal the attorneys that there are two minutes left on the videotape, when signaled by video technician, so they can finish their line of questioning before changing tape.

Any time there is a record of off-the-record discussion, be sure and give time on camera when you go off and when you start back. When the tape is changed and we go back on the recrd, give time and tape number.

EXAMPLES:

WE ARE GOING OFF THE RECORD AT (10:45) _____.

WE ARE BACK ON THE RECORD AT (10:52) _____.

WE ARE GOING OFF THE RECORD TO CHANGE TAPE AT _____.

WE ARE BACK ON THE RECORD AT _____ AND THIS IS TAPE NUMBER TWO OF THE DEPOSITION OF _____.

Chapter 35

Dictating for a Transcriber

Court reporters have been dictating into machines and having transcribers type from their dictation for many years. Although notereaders are used by some reporters and most reporters are on a CAT system of one type or another, the dictation method will be used by lesser-volume reporters for some time to come. Its advantages are economy, comparative ease of training the operator, and satisfactory work product turned out within reasonable time incorporating the brain power of another intelligent, thinking person.

Every reporter should be able to dictate well for a transcriber because notereaders may come and go and computers have "down time." The dictation method provides a suitable alternative system and can save many positions from going to electrical recording where, in the mind of the reporter, volume does not merit purchasing a CAT or word processing system.

Preparation for Dictation

The reporter should set aside sufficient work space where it is quiet for dictation work to allow efficient layout of materials and equipment required for the job. He or she should have a special desk or table for dictating only so time is not wasted searching for an extension cord, finding an outlet, setting up a lamp, unpacking the machine, finding Stenorette tapes, going elsewhere for notes, and so on.

Proper lighting and a comfortable chair are musts. Reference materials and a telephone to be used for business purposes only should be close at hand.

It helps to keep a pitcher of room temperature water handy as the throat becomes dry, and hoarseness may result during long stretches of dictation; or the reporter should break occasionally to drink some hot tea or coffee. Iced drinks are not advised because they tend to constrict the throat muscles. Hot liquids, on the other hand, relax the throat muscles and allow the reporter to continue dictating much longer.

Some reporters prefer to dictate standing up part of the time because they feel alternating sitting and standing prevents a groggy feeling after some time has elapsed.

Select a Good Dictating Machine

There are a number of transcription units on the market, but the Dejur-Grundig Stenorette has long been the machine of choice of most reporters. This machine requires a special tape. The unit consists of a basic machine, microphone, earphones, and foot pedals, all of high quality.

Analyzing Your Dictation Techniques

In order to dictate well, you must start with accurate well-written notes. You should practice so that you can translate your notes fluently. Before you dictate for a typist, dictate a full 30-minute tape from your notes into the dictating machine you intend to use. Run your 30-minute, dictated tape back and listen carefully to your voice and consider whether you would want to type from your dictation hour after hour. Better yet, type the whole tape from your own dictation and note your flaws.

1. Is your delivery monotonous? Use inflection, emphasizing words by saying them at a little higher pitch and employing pauses. Do not overemphasize.

2. Do you keep the volume constant? A voice that is too loud is harsh and irritating, while a voice that is too low makes understanding difficult. If a transcriber cannot hear and understand a word or phrase, the tape must be played over and over, which wastes time. Transcribers are paid by the page, and they resent wasted moments.

3. Is the pitch of your voice high and shrill? Try to speak in a normal, modulated conversational tone.

4. Do you slur word endings, such as plurals, past tenses, and words ending in "-ing" and say "thuh" instead of "thee" for "the"? Do you dictate "haive" for "have" to avoid any possible conflict with "has" or "had" and the article "a" as a long "a"?

5. Can you distinguish between all the like-sounding words such as "an" and "and" and "in"? How about "if" and "it"?

6. Do you dictate so rapidly that words are garbled, or do you dictate so slowly that the typist is forced to wait constantly for the material?

7. When you stop to verify a word, make a notation on your information sheet, or look ahead to help you translate a faulty outline, do you let the machine run, causing the typist to waste time?

8. Do you drop your voice at the ends of sentences? Trailing off makes dictated matter unintelligible.

9. Do you dictate all the required punctuation and clarify homonyms?

10. Do you maintain your dictating machines and tapes in good order so legible dictation results?

11. Do you spell out unnecessary words? An experienced transcriber should be able to distinguish from context such words as there/their.

12. Do you always remember to say "Question" or "Answer"? Likewise, do you forget to erase errors because you are dictating too fast?

13. Did you hold the microphone too close to your mouth causing the words to slur and echo?

Practice Pronunciation

Some principles of correct pronunciation follow:

1. Increase your working vocabulary by reading and study.

2. Vary your speech rate and avoid sameness of tone in delivery.

3. Open your mouth when you talk, and relax your jaws. Speak from the diaphragm, not from the throat.

4. Use tongue and lips to make speech sounds.

5. Do not slur sounds.

6. Pronounce every syllable in every word.

7. Pronounce all final consonants and endings.

8. Avoid careless, lazy speech.

9. Pause between sentences. A pause affords emphasis and opportunity for you to relax.

Working With a Transcriber

Before you hire a new transcriber, prepare a test so you can be sure he or she can handle the job. This will assure that you will not waste valuable time trying to train a person incapable of handling the job.

Testing

Devise a comprehensive spelling test, and do not consider an individual who does not pass that examination with a score of 90 or better. Give a typing test and make sure the applicant can type at least 60 words per minute with no more than five errors for five minutes; the higher the speed, the better.

Next, let the person under consideration copy a couple of form pages, such as a title page and a page setting up a witness and containing colloquy. After that, let the applicant type a couple of half hour selections from a dictating machine and then compare the typed product with the original transcript from which they were taken. The test will tell you whether the person has the ability to follow directions.

Finally, there is one other factor to consider. It is very important that you consider whether the person's personality harmonizes with yours, as the two of you will work closely as a team.

Establishing Procedures for Your Transcriber

Start your beginning transcriber off on smaller depositions or pleas and sentences and gradually increase the volume of work if you can possibly do so. Explain to your operator that you will supply all punctuation, spellings of uncommon words and proper names, and that he or she is never to deviate from your instructions in this regard.

Give your ground rules at the start. Be sure your typist understands how carefully all carbon copies must be corrected and the importance of perfect, well set up originals. Have an understanding with your typist that if work must be retyped, if it is because of a transcription error, you will pay for one page only. If it is due to the reporter's fault, the operator will be paid for two pages if required to redo any such page.

Payment of the Transcriber

Typists are usually paid by the page, but now and then the transcriber is paid an hourly rate, particularly if other duties are performed in the office. When the transcriber delivers transcript, payment should be made at that time because the reporter receives much more for those pages than the typist. Reporters have always maintained a good record for paying their typists immediately, so do keep it that way.

The reporter is responsible for furnishing paper, carbons, Stenorette tapes, covers, and notesheets. If the typing is done in the reporter's office, the reporter may or may not furnish the typewriter or word processor and Stenorette the typist uses, depending upon their agreement. Home typists ordinarily furnish their own Stenorette playback unit and typewriter. The required typewriter today will be an IBM 10-pitch Pica type machine or a conforming word processor. In some states a "cheater ratchet" is installed to space the material to fit on a 25-line double-spaced sheet of ruled, numbered paper.

Form Book

You should have a reporting form book prepared in advance for the use of your operator and any fellow reporters who may later join you. This book should include pages showing margins and tab stops for each type of work you do, indicating that the first tab stop is used for indentation of Q and A, and where further tab stops are for colloquy and parenthetical remarks of the reporter. These sheets should be in loose-leaf form so the typist can place them in the typewriter to insure uniformity of all work.

Your form book should include pages showing setups for the opening session of the day, opening session for afternoon of continued case, further session setups for cases lasting several days, caption pages of various types, certificates for sworn and unsworn statements, depositions, court cases, and so on. Sample indices of proceedings and exhibits will be invaluable time savers. Typical appearance pages and cover formats and examples of how recesses, exhibits, colloquy, examination headings for witnesses, and other general information forms will save your answering many questions and prevent transcription errors. After your typist becomes knowledgeable, you will simply say "Type the Certificate of Non-Attendance just like the one on pages 75 and 76 of your form book using this information sheet for titles, venue, times, and dates."

Information Sheet

Always provide a properly filled out information sheet for every assignment you give your typist with all the items previously mentioned on it. The operator should not have to spend valuable time wondering, searching, or worse still redoing pages because of your neglect.

Always number the words on your word list, which should always be typed, not handwritten. If you spell words on your tape, also place them on the information sheet.

Mark on the information sheet the number of copies you need as well as dictating it on the first tape. Include on the dogsheet an estimate as to the number of pages the transcript should run so your transcriber can make up the correct number of stacks at the beginning and allocate time according to work load.

If your index pages follow the title page, indicate how many pages to leave for the index. A rule of thumb is 10 exhibit descriptions usually fit on one page, depending on the length of the description of each exhibit.

Advantages of Having Only Original Typed

To reduce transcription time, most reporters now have only the original of transcripts typed, and they use photocopy and collators to run copies, sort, and prepare transcripts for binding, all automatically. This saves correction time, and there is no need to make up stacks. The pages are sorted automatically, and copiers produce a "printed" look transcript. After the equipment is paid for, copies can be produced at a cheaper rate than when prepared by a transcriber, and automation speeds up the whole process and does it more efficiently.

Achieving Required Transcript Appearance

The appearance and readability of a transcript are affected greatly by a number of small things. Instruct your transcriber to erase neatly, leaving no "crumbs" or smudges or visible erasures. Instruct him or her also that correction paper or fluid cannot be used and that strikeovers are not allowed. Inserting typewritten words between lines may not be done except in very rare cases on daily copy.

Insist that your operator keep the type clean and that he or she changes the typewriter or word processor ribbon when it gets light, even in the middle of the transcript.

Teach your typist to type the number in the same place on each page and that the paper must be fed into the typewriter straight. Be sure whoever binds up completed transcript tamps the pages so a tight, orderly volume results.

Tell your transcriber all material must be typed in final form the first time, as it is costly and time-consuming to do anything over. Instruct him or her to leave a space for a word or group of words that cannot be distinguished and mark the place in the margin with a paper clip, if possible, typing the number of the tape far out in the left margin. Then, this part of the tape can be checked and the proper wording inserted when proofreading is done. The typist should be reminded that if proofreading is done while the page is still in the machine, time will not be wasted reinserting and realigning the paper.

Addressing the Transcriber

Reporters are somewhat divided as to whether the term "Operator" or the word "Transcriber" should be used before giving instructions to the typist to get his or her attention. The advantage of using the word "Transcriber" is that in patent and industrial cases where the word "Operator" is used frequently when referring to the operation of some machine, the use of this term when addressing the typist may cause confusion.

Identification of Tapes. At the beginning of the first dictation tape in a matter, say, "Transcriber (or Operator), this is Tape No. 1 of the deposition of Samuel Johnson in the case of Johnson versus Smith. Make an original and three copies. Do the title page as indicated and then insert the usual stipulations."

Of course, you have typed the caption on your information sheet and given the typist the form for the usual stipulations. If usual stipulations do not apply, dictate the stipulations that should be inserted. At the end of this tape, let your typist know by saying, "Transcriber, that is the end of tape 1, continued on tape 2, Thank you."

At the beginning of the next tape, state, "Transcriber, this is Tape No. 2 in the deposition of Samuel Johnson. Transcriber, repeating: Answer I was not at home when he called on Sunday. Transcriber, continuing: Question Had you left because you were afraid he would come around?" and so on.

At the end of each succeeding tape, close in the same way, and begin new tapes being careful to keep the numbers in succession. Finish the last tape in the matter by saying, "Transcriber, this is the end of the job and the end of this tape. Thank you." Be careful not to tape over any finished tapes, and be sure to wind tapes back for your typist when dictation ends midway into the reel.

Setting Up a Witness. Instruct the typist thoroughly as to setups, but at first give full description in your dictation as to just how headings, and so on, should be done. For instance, in setting up a witness, dictate as follows: "Transcriber, set up the witness. Solid caps and center Joseph E as in Edward period Jones comma margin called as a witness in his own behalf comma having first been duly sworn by the clerk of court comma testified e-d on his oath as follows colon."

Later, you may not have to tell your typist to write the witness's name in solid caps and to center it, but it will always be your responsibility to give your transcriber all spellings of the names, whose witness is taking the stand, and who swore the witness.

Spellings and Initials. Witnesses spell their names very rapidly. After all, they have been doing it all their lives. If you get the name phonetically but miss the spelling, you may be combing through telephone books and directories uselessly at midnight, for even the best reporter now and then does not have time to mark the notes. Get the spelling because the spelling of the name is sufficient.

Dictate words you spell out using hyphens between each letter, prefacing with "Transcriber" at first. When dictating initials or spelling out words, designate by associative names or words because many letters sound alike. It saves typists' time if these words are also placed on the information sheet.

The following are standard alphabetic identifications:

A as in Alice	B as in boy
C as in Carl	D as in David
E as in Edward	F as in Francis
G as in George	H as in Henry
I as in Irene	J as in John
K as in Kenneth	L as in Louis
M as in Mary	N as in Nevada
O as in Oscar	P as in Patrick
Q as in Quincy	R as in Robert
S as in Sam	T as in Thomas
U as in umbrella	V as in victory
W as in William	X as in X-ray
Y as in yellow	Z as in zebra

Be alert to the fact that the letters "b," "v," "d," and "c" are often hard to distinguish on the dictated tape.

Soundalikes should be spelled out for the typist. Dictate one letter at a time the following words: two, too, to; their, there; four, for, fore; red, read; ink, inc.; weigh, way; whole, hole; oh; few; site, cite, and sight. If you do this, the typist will not start out and have several incorrect letters typed before he or she realizes what the correct word is.

Bear in mind also the following conflicts: many and any, seven and several, a and eight, day and date, some and one, and conceive and concede. Distinguish between "extensive" and "expensive" by saying: "Transcriber, extensive, t as in Thomas" or "Transcriber, expensive, p as in Patrick." Never hesitate to spell any word that you think the typist might have difficulty in understanding.

Capitalization. Dictate all capitalizations except the very obvious: city names, state names, months, days of the week, colleges, and prominent names. Keep capitalization consistent and minimal. Follow the *Government Printing Office Style Manual.*

In a doctor's testimony, dictate the abbreviation Dr. before his name, but when the doctor is addressed as: "You are aware comma Transcriber initial cap Doctor spelled out comma that this test should have been run comma are you not?" Dictate initial cap or lower case at the beginning of a quote or after a colon as you decide it should be. The typist should not be expected to make such decisions.

Past Tenses. Indicate past tenses by saying: "work-ed," "park-ed," and in some instances where there might still be difficulty understanding, say: "walked Transcriber e-d" or simply "walked e-d."

Plurals. Dictate all plurals. Pronounce the word "plural" very clearly and not too rapidly because it is difficult for the typist to understand if you slur the pronunciation.

Contractions and Apostrophes. Say "I didn't Transcriber n apostrophe t." Do the same for wouldn't, shouldn't, can't, won't, etc. Accentuate the "ent" sound at the end to alert the typist. Dictate all apostrophes as: "That's Transcriber t apostrophe s right," for "That's right." For possessives say: "girls apostrophe s," for "girl's," and "girls s apostrophe" for "girls'." Dictate "ten days s apostrophe time" for "ten days' time." Say: "It's transcriber initial caps i-t apostrophe s a rush job."

Dashes. If you want your transcriber to type a dash, don't say "dash." Instead, dictate "dashes." This makes for greater clarity, as the typed dash consists of two hyphens. Some reporters have a space precede and follow the dash although properly this is incorrect. However, follow the wishes of your employer in this regard.

Parenthesis. In dictating parentheticals, say "paren," which is shorter; and keep parentheticals short. When parentheses are used with chapter designations or in sentences, state whether it is an opening or closing parenthesis.

Certified Questions. When lawyers have certified a question during a deposition, dictate "Transcriber, type a 'C' before the 'Q' for 'Question' because this question is certified, and do not forget to note it on the index." If you have more than one certified question, dictate "Transcriber, type 'CQ1' for the first certified question", and then "Transcriber, type 'CQ2' for this certified question," and so on numerically until all are dictated.

The index should have these questions listed by number as well as page. Be sure to maintain a copy of these questions for your use in preparing the excerpted certification of questions.

Figures. You can dictate time figures in one of three ways:

1. Transcriber, time figures, four o'clock.

2. Transcriber, one colon three zero.

3. Transcriber, five o'clock.

Any one of these three ways is easily comprehended by the typist. Tell your typist whether you want time figures typed in figures with a colon between hours and minutes or in words.

In dictating money figures, for $475.96, say, "Transcriber, dollar mark four seven five point nine six; repeating four hundred seventy-five dollars ninety-six cents."

For round figures, you may say, "Transcriber, fifty dollars; repeating dollar sign five zero." The problem is that the typist may type the 50 before he or she hears the dollars and will have to erase to insert the dollar sign. Be very careful about fifty and fifteen and sixty and sixteen; likewise forty and fourteen. Always say "zero" rather than "oh."

Labeling of Media

Always number your tape boxes or dictated cassettes carefully and fasten them inside the information sheet with elastic bands so they cannot get separated.

Always be certain your transcribers return all transcribed Stenorette tapes or cassettes with each transcript. Note on the last tape in an assignment by a penciled arrow where the dictation ends to help your transcriber allot his or her time. Watch that you do not record over a tape you have just finished.

General Guidelines

You must dictate "Question" for every question and "Answer" for every answer. Do not leave it up to the transcriber ever to figure this out. The typist was not there, and serious error could occur in the record if an improper designation were made.

In dictating ending punctuation, it is not necessary to dictate "Interrog" at the end of a question or "Period" at the end of an answer. However, when the question becomes a statement, the "Period" must be dictated; and when the answer becomes a question, it is necessary to dictate "Interrog." Wherever a period or an interrog occurs within a question or answer, it must be dictated without fail.

Tell your typist you will not dictate a comma between "Yes, sir," "No, sir," "Yes, ma'am," and "No, ma'am," but that it should always be inserted. Give him or her the spelling of "ma'am" and "you-all."

In dictating colloquy, always indicate solid caps, the person's name, and then say, "Colon," as: "Transcriber, solid caps, Mr. Anthony, colon."

Dictate a term properly once, type it on the instruction sheet, and expect the operator to type it properly thereafter, as: "Transcriber, single caps Concrete Workers' Union."

A pause between common expressions written as two words helps ensure correct transcript, as "All (pause) right." However, in instances where there may be doubt as to whether expressions are one word or two, it is the reporter's responsibility to dictate the proper form: payoff, pay off; liftoff; recheck; and so on.

When you have quotations, say "open quotes" and "close quotes." For quotations within a quotation, dictate: "Transcriber, open single quote" and "Transcriber, close single quote."

Most transcribers would rather have more short tapes than a few long ones, as they experience a feeling of satisfaction each time they complete a unit.

Communicate Frequently with Your Transcriber

Always tell your typist to let you know if there are any ways you can make the job easier or if he or she cannot understand your dictation.

If your transcriber does a particularly good job for you, be sure to say some words of praise. Better yet, give a small gift or a bonus for super speedy rush work or exceptional performance. Let a good typist know that you really appreciate the great work.

As your rates increase, remember costs go up for your transcriber also, and consider giving a raise. You can help your typist make more money by dictating carefully, so check to see if he or she is having problems every once in awhile.

Communication does not mean hanging over the transcriber on rush jobs and grabbing every page to proofread and interrupting the typist every few minutes with directions and corrections. Communication means establishing the kind of rapport where you can talk to each other about your common problems and solve them as a team with good feeling between you.

Be Businesslike in Handling Corrections

Explain at the beginning that you will place transcript to be corrected in an out box which should be checked and handled each day. Do not ask the typist to make changes in single pages as you proofread except on the most urgent transcript, as much time will be wasted by constant interruptions. Check to be sure all copies are corrected.

Proofread Carefully

Again, the reporter is responsible for any errors that may go out on the final transcript, so you must proofread carefully. You may read 500 pages and find only one or two errors; those errors could be crucial, so never neglect this phase of your work. Proofreading transcripts and making corrections is time-consuming, but it must be a part of every court reporter's routine.

The rate of proofreading varies quite a bit, depending on the density of the material and its technical nature. About the top limit for careful proofreading is 150 pages per hour, and to achieve anything like this average, it must be done without interruptions. The ideal time for proofreading is at night or on weekends. Reading notes for a whole day's sessions at one time is best as a continuity exists. The same is true of proofreading.

The reporter should watch for page misnumberings, repeated words or lines from one line or page to the next, misspelled words, and typographical errors. Proofreading may also show that a fold of tape was missed, a word or phrase was misread, a word or phrase was misheard during the taking, or the reporter was on automatic pilot during a long dictation session. Figures, directions, dates, proper names, addresses, and anything that does not seem to fit into context should be doublechecked while proofreading.

Advice to Reporters Who Dictate

Avoid unnecessary remarks to your typist. When my husband would be traveling in his district, he would often dictate transcript to while away lonely hours in hotel and motel rooms at night. While I would answer office phones for him and the Judge, I would noteread or type from his dictation. On many occasions he would often make little side remarks of a very personal nature to me, which I would omit from the transcripts.

One day I was typing along on some colloquy, and I found myself typing into the record, "What do you think of the way this dodo is trying this case, Kid?" I tore the sheets of paper from the typewriter in a state of shock, thinking what would have happened if that had gone out. We laughed about it, but he was more careful about remarks in the dictation after that.

Write it down, even if it is in the middle of the night. As another personal reminiscence, every once in a while my husband would jab me in the ribs in the middle of the night and say, "Say, I just remembered where I wrote 'carburetor' in my notes this afternoon, it was 'carborundum,' and I never did write it down or change it," or some such remark. I always kept a pad and pencil on the dresser, and I would get up, turn on the light, and groggily jot down the message to put with the notes for transcription in the morning.

No matter when something like that occurs to you—and it will—write it down and place it with the notes where it belongs right away. You will certainly be glad you did later.

When you hit a snag, don't panic. Sometimes if you have difficulty reading an outline as you dictate, it can be located in various forms or other material concerning the case. First, try it for context. Then, look back of it and ahead to see if it recurs written in a more correct form or decipherable from context elsewhere. Consult your dictionary or other reference books and go to words that mean approximately the same if you have a general idea of the significance of the expression. Consult your thesaurus.

If all these fail, get up and leave the material while you walk around the block, get a cup of coffee, and sit back down. Often, it will pop out of the notes at you.

As a last resort, substitute a word known to have the proper meaning.

No, that's not right! There is a last, last resort. Sometimes you will come across a few strokes of pure gibberish that you cannot possibly make anything of no matter what you do. If you cannot possibly decipher it and it is not material to the transcript, leave it out. Someone will notice if they are not translated into sense, but if they seem unimportant, you may be better off omitting them.

Wouldn't You Rather Be a CAT Reporter?

When you consider all of the above, the advantages of being a CAT reporter should be most evident. You can see how much drudgery the computer has cut out of producing the record. Make yours your friend.

Chapter 36 *Writing for a Notereader*

Advantages of Using a Notereader

Some reporters prefer to use notereaders for production of transcript, particularly where their volume of transcript is not heavy, for the following reasons:

1. The writing, dictating, proofreading cycle is cut to writing, notechecking, and proofreading.
2. More free time is available for the official and freelance reporter.
3. It means earning more money for the freelance reporter.
4. The reporter's backlog is reduced.
5. The notereader is a thinking person who can use initiative and prevent errors from slipping through.
6. Daily copy can be turned out with less effort than by the dictation method.
7. The notereader makes a better page rate than a transcriber from a dictating machine and is, therefore, more likely to stay with the job.
8. Reading notes is faster than transcribing from dictation which results in increased production for both reporter and notereader.

Requirements for Noteread Reporters

Writing for notereaders is not quite as easy as it may seem. The notereader was not present at the taking of the material, so certain things are necessary in the interest of producing an accurate record:

1. The reporter must read the notes and edit them carefully.
2. The use of long vowels is mandatory.
3. Clean notes are a must.
4. Conflicts should be avoided (were/with; and it/the).
5. Outlines should be consistent. If the reporter changes an abbreviation or phrase, the notereader should be informed orally and on the information sheet.

6. The reporter should strike the speaker's name, city, and state abbreviations twice.

7. A flagged alphabet must be used. When an acronym is pronounceable, it may be written by sound; otherwise it is written with flagged letters, using either the period or the asterisk.

8. All parenthetical remarks should be placed in the notes for marking and receiving exhibits, off-the-record discussions, in camera sessions, and so on.

9. After colloquy in Q and A, the reporter should identify the questioner again when returning to Q and A.

10. The reporter must prepare a complete and detailed typewritten information sheet using upper and lower case. If a word is to be capitalized, it must not be written with a lower case letter on the dopesheet (and vice versa). All pertinent data must be provided by the reporter. The reporter should always type the caption and appearances for the notereader, showing the outline the reporter used for each lawyer (written next to the lawyer's name), and a word list with correct spellings of all proper names and uncommon words that occur in the body of the proceeding.

11. The line spacing of the reporter's shorthand machine should be wide enough for easy reading, and the keys should be clean, as reading inkspots is time consuming. The shorthand machine should also be well inked.

12. All unusual briefs should be listed with their translation on the information sheet. The more standard the reporter's system, the quicker the transcription can be completed.

13. The reporter should edit the notes carefully before turning them over to the notereader to cross out false starts, put in necessary punctuation, and add parentheticals that may have been omitted during taking the matter in shorthand.

14. Trouble spots in the notes should be flagged so the reporter and notereader can resolve any difficulties to avoid wasting time having pages retyped.

Should the notereader have difficulty reading outlines or understanding the format or have other problems, he or she should be instructed by the reporter to put paper clips on those spots on the notes, write the transcript page number down, and clip the transcript page where it will not leave a mark when bound. Then, the notereader should leave a blank and continue typing the transcript.

When the reporter proofreads, he or she can easily check the clips first and note the necessary corrections. This procedure is especially important when the notereader first starts working, but the notereader must be admonished never to type anything that seems like gibberish without verifying the translation with the reporter.

Finding Notereaders

Notereaders are often students who have been excellent in English but have been forced to drop out of school for financial reasons or personal problems. Reporters sometimes find note-readers by contacting court reporting schools, advertising in NSRA Employment Referral Service Bulletins, or advertising in the newspaper.

Some schools that teach court reporters offer training in notereading.

The person being interviewed for training as a notereader should have a vocabulary of no less than 50,000 words and should have a college degree or work experience of an equivalent nature. Sometimes people who have dropped out of court reporting schools are not good note-readers because the reason they quit training was their lack of English skills and other necessary background. People who have worked as proofreaders and can type accurately and rapidly or liberal arts college graduates who majored in English are excellent prospects.

No reporter should hire a person to noteread without administering typing, spelling, and English tests. Valuable time can be wasted in trying to train the wrong individual to do this important work.

Some Reporters Train Their Own Notereaders

It is a good idea to have the intended notereader work through the theory books the reporter used in school, not for speed, but to learn the briefs, phrases, and general system the notereader will use.

At present a notereading book which may be secured to help with the training of notereaders is *Notereading—From Student to Professional* by Helen Riedel, P.O. Box 335, Lebanon, OH, 45036. An investment of time must be made to train a good notereader, but there are benefits to be derived when the reporter and a competent notereader work together.

Chapter 37 *Computers and Reporting*

Computers have significantly affected all aspects of a reporter's work. Computers are used for the following:

1. Organizing and running an office or agency—Office/Agency Management Systems;
2. Transcribing transcripts—Word Processing Systems or Computer-Aided Transcription Systems (CAT);
3. Capturing a speaker's words on a computer screen in various settings—Computer-Aided Transcription Systems with Real-Time Capabilities;
4. Providing attorneys with electronic transcripts for searching and locating key issues—Litigation Support Systems;
5. Providing courtrooms with real-time capabilities plus instant litigation support for judges and attorneys—Computer Integrated Courtroom Systems (CICS).

All computers are really computer systems that consist of physical equipment (hardware), programs that make them run (operating system software or operating systems), and programs that perform various tasks (application software). The following sections describe the various types of hardware and software that reporters must be aware of today.

The Computer System

The computer equipment that a reporter uses is similar and, in many cases, the same as computers used both in other professions and in the home. It consists of a screen, the computer itself, a keyboard, a printer, and perhaps a modem. A modem is a device used if the reporter has someone else working on his or her transcript at another location. It allows the reporter to send the transcript from one computer to another electronically.

The screen may be any one of four different types of screens (also known as display monitors): monochrome, CGA, EGA, and VGA. *Monochrome monitors* are generally a one color combination such as black and green or black and orange. *The Color Graphics Adapter* (CGA) is an early color screen that was not very readable for text purposes. It was replaced by the *Enhanced Graphics Adapter* (EGA), and then by the *Video Graphics Adapter* (VGA). By far the best monitor is the VGA. Unfortunately, it is also the most expensive.

The computer itself is really the processor unit that consists of a boxlike structure that usually has one or two disk drives into which floppy disks of either 3.5″ or 5.25″ disks are inserted. (See Figure 81.) The disks are used to store transcripts after they have been worked on inside the memory of the computer. The *memory* is the temporary storage area used where all application programs are stored while in use and where all work that is being done is held temporarily.

Memory should not be confused with hard disk storage. *Hard disk storage* is permanent storage that resides within a computer. You may also store application programs that you use frequently and transcripts that you wish to store permanently on a hard disk. The difference between items stored in memory or those items on a hard disk is that if the computer is turned off while work resides in memory, the work will be lost. If it resides on a hard disk, it will not be lost. Some newer CAT systems, however, invalidate this statement. They automatically save work that is being done in the event that there is a loss of power or that someone accidently unplugs your computer while you are working.

FIGURE 81
Transcripts are stored on either 3.5″ or 5.25″ disks (Courtesy of Johnson Court Reporting.)

Keyboards can be standard computer keyboards similar to a typewriter keyboard but with a set of function keys (keys labeled F1 through F10 or F12 and a keypad) keys that have a dual function to type numbers and to move the cursor. These keyboards usually have specially marked keys that have such labels as ALT, CTRL, Caps Lock, Enter, Ins, and Del. Such keys are used to make the operation of application software easier. In addition to this type of keyboard are various other keyboards that are modified for special purposes. For example, some may have a programmable touch keypad for moving the cursor or for performing commands easier or some other variation.

Printers are used to produce the paper copy of the transcript. The two types of printers that are generally used for this purpose are impact printers and laser printers. *Impact printers* print a character at a time by hitting the paper through an inked ribbon. *Laser printers* use a photocopy process and print a page at a time. Laser printers are faster but more expensive than impact printers.

More and more reporters are using modems to send transcripts from one location to another. Some reporting agencies provide people to finalize the transcript of the reporter. This person may work out of his or her home or at the agency. A modem on the computer lets the reporter receive the transcript from any location.

In addition to equipment, reporters need to have the programs that make their computers run and to perform the tasks which they need completed. With computers that are IBM or IBM compatible, one computer may be sufficient to perform all the different types of tasks described in the following sections. In addition to separate programs for the tasks that will be described, a reporter needs to have an operating system such as *DOS* (Disk Operating System) that is used to start the computer, manage the operation of the parts of the computer, and perform house-keeping tasks on the disks. The following sections deal with the types of tasks that a reporter can do using this basic type of equipment, an operating system, and a program designed for the intended task.

Office/Agency Management Systems

If you decide to handle your own clients, you will need some type of application program that will help you schedule your depositions, track your jobs, and bill your clients. If you work alone, this type of program will help you get organized. If you decide to open an agency and have others working for you, this type of software is essential.

Office/Agency Management Software generally consists of at least the following modules:

1. A calendaring module to allow you to set court or deposition appearances.
2. A tracking module to allow you to track who is transcribing or scoping your transcript and what stage it is in. Is it being proofread or has it already been sent?
3. A billing module to allow you to bill your clients automatically and figure out what is owed to your employees.
4. An accounts receivable and aging module to let you know who still owes you money.

Office/Agency Management Systems are designed to give you management reports and to let you know who are your best customers and best employees.

Transcribing Transcripts

Reporters today use either *word processing* or *Computer-Aided Transcription* (CAT) systems to transcribe their notes. Word processing can be done on a special type of computer known as a *dedicated word processor* or on a computer that uses a word processing package such as

WordPerfect, Word Star, Microsoft Word, and so on. The advantage of using one of these packages over a dedicated word processor is that your computer can then also be used to do the other tasks that are described in this chapter.

The disadvantage of using a word processor or word processing package that does not have CAT capabilities is that someone still has to read or listen to the reporter's notes and transcribe the notes. The majority of this nation's court reporters are on some type of *Computer-Aided Transcription System* (CAT). A CAT system is a system designed to take the outlines captured by a reporter on magnetic media such as a tape or disk and translate them into their English equivalents. In other words, it is a system that eliminates (1) the need for the reporter to dictate notes into a dictation machine, and (2) the need to have someone transcribe them.

A CAT system is really a word processor that also possesses the ability to translate the reporter's notes automatically. The word processing portion of the CAT system is known as the *editor*. Therefore, the features of a word processor or word processing package will be described in the following chapter where the editor of such CAT systems is described.

Computer-Aided Transcription With Real-Time Capabilities

Reporters now find themselves with opportunities to use their skill in capturing a speaker's words as they are spoken. Reporters use *computer-aided transcription systems* with *real-time capabilities* for courtroom or deposition testimony. Only reporters who have excellent skills can write real-time, as accuracy is essential. You do not have time to read and decipher *untranslates* (words not in your dictionary) or resolve *conflicts* (homonyms that you write alike or other outlines that you may write the same).

Real-time writing is also used with Captioning Systems by real-time writers who do captioning for the hearing-impaired in classroom (see Figure 82), other live situations, or closed captioning— captioning on videotape for television purposes.

Another use of real-time is for *rapid text entry systems*. These are systems that allow word processing editing commands to be issued from the steno machine keyboard rather than from the computer keyboard. The use for rapid text entry is to enter text rapidly into a word processing environment (such as WordPerfect) faster and easier than from the computer keyboard. Rapid text entry is now being used for medical transcriptions and in other places where fast text entry is desired. (See Figure 83.)

The basic differences between a CAT system that has real-time capabilities and a rapid text entry system is that a CAT system produces a note file and a rapid text entry system does not. It translates the notes immediately and displays them on the screen of a popular word processing program. The reporter using the CAT system with real-time capabilities can refer to the note file at a later time. On CAT systems with real-time capabilities, generally the reporter is able to back up and erase a stroke or two but is not able to perform the extensive editing such as blocking and moving a paragraph, erasing a block of text, or inserting into the middle of a paragraph. These commands can be accomplished on a rapid text entry system.

Litigation Support Systems

Attorneys want what reporters have, namely, transcripts stored electronically. Attorneys are willing to pay, and in some cases, quite generously for such transcripts. Agencies have come to think of themselves not as transcription services but as attorney support service centers with litigation support being one of the services provided. On a lesser scale, the individual reporter can also provide this service by having a CAT system that can convert the electronic disk to an ASCII (American Standard Code for Information Interchange) format. An ASCII format is simply a disk containing the transcript without the special formatting codes placed in the transcript by the word processor or editor that is used. In this format, the attorney can then use whatever litigation support system that is available in order to perform a search on the transcript for issues or other items desired. Litigation support systems enable the attorney to locate and to summarize information without having to read tediously through the entire document looking for important items.

Computer-Integrated Courtroom Systems

The application of the latest technology in combining real-time writing, litigation support for attorneys and judges in the form of computer-assisted research, the ability to search the testimony in progress, and other related technologies new to the courtroom is known as *Computer-Integrated Courtroom Systems* (CICS) or, sometimes, simply called *Computer-Integrated Court-*

FIGURE 82
Real-time is used for captioning for the hearing-impaired
(Courtesy of Jerome Woods.)

room (CIC). The CIC courtroom is not a new concept. A number of these courtrooms exist throughout the country and others will emerge as the need dictates. In Chapter 39, you will learn more about CIC courtrooms.

FIGURE 83
RapidText TM is used for medical transcription (Courtesy of Stenotes, Inc.)

Chapter 38

Computer-Aided Transcription

The most important tool for the reporter is the reporter's steno writer. (See Figure 84 on page 330.) Next to this tool is the reporter's CAT system. Although many reporters wish to spend their time recording transcripts rather than transcribing them, someone needs to perform this activity. The fastest way to get the final transcript produced is by using a CAT system. Often a reporter works in conjunction with a *scopist* (a person trained to proofread and edit the transcript while it is on the computer screen). The scopist looks for *untranslates* (words that may have not translated either because they were misstroked or because no matching entry exists for them in the reporter's dictionary), such as [SKWOEPBZ], or *unresolved conflicts* (words that may be written the same in the reporter's dictionary), such as [pass|past].

CAT systems have the ability to allow the reporter to do the following:

1. Build a dictionary that consists of the outlines written the way the reporter writes them.

2. Read in steno notes taken from electronic writers.

3. Translate the steno notes into English.

4. Edit the document.

5. Update the reporter's dictionary.

6. Print the document.

Build a Dictionary

All CAT systems allow you to build a dictionary that consists of the outlines written in the way that a reporter writes them. The CAT system company provides a dictionary build program that consists of an English word list and reporters stroke in their equivalent outlines. Usually the way it works is that the dictionary building program is started, an English word appears on the screen, the reporter strokes the English word, then strokes a separator stroke, and a new English word appears. Sometimes it is possible to misstroke a word. With some programs, if you discover that you have misstroked the word before the separator stroke is entered, you can stroke an asterisk or some other designated stroke to remove the misstroke. On most programs, once the separator stroke has been entered, you need to continue entering your dictionary equivalents until you are finished building the entire dictionary. Then you can obtain a printout of the dictionary and edit the dictionary using a special dictionary edit module in the CAT system. If you should overlook or not edit the dictionary and a word does not translate properly in the editor, you can

FIGURE 84
The most important tool for the reporter is the reporter's steno writer (Courtesy of Jerome Woods.)

always fix it in the editor. Note that once the dictionary is built, it is then used in the translation process. Sometimes vendors provide specialized dictionaries which can be built in the same way for medical or technical purposes.

Read Steno Notes

The reporter normally captures notes electronically on a disk located inside an electronic steno writer. The notes are generally taken during a court session or deposition and not translated until later. When the reporter is ready to translate the notes, the notes are read into the computer in one of two ways:

1. Some CAT systems read notes using a cable linked from the electronic steno writer to the computer. First a disk is placed inside an electronic writer. The reporter then takes notes. The same disk that is used to capture the outline is kept inside the computer while a cable is linked from the electronic writer to the computer. Normally, you are able to select an option on a menu which says: Read Steno Notes or something similar and begin the read-in process.

2. Some CAT systems read notes directly from a disk. First a disk is placed inside an electronic writer. The reporter then takes notes. The same disk that is used to capture the outlines is then transferred to the disk drive inside the computer and the notes are read in. As in the previous item, normally you are able to then select an option on a menu that says: Read Steno Notes or something similar and begin the read-in process.

Translate the Steno Notes into English

During the translation process, the steno outlines are matched to the outlines in the reporter's dictionary. If a match is found, translation occurs. If a match is not found, an untranslate appears on the screen. If several outlines are used to represent the same word, a conflict appears. The translation process can usually be selected from a menu that contains a *Translate the Document* option. When this option is selected, the transcript can be translated against one or several dictionaries. The CAT system user usually selects the name of the dictionaries that will be used in the translation process at this time.

Edit the Document

The editor of a CAT system is really a word processing program specifically designed to handle specific problems peculiar to reporting such as untranslates and conflicts, in addition to the more common word processing capabilities that all word processing programs have. In addition, the editor enables you to see line numbers, a feature that most word processors do not have. (See Figure 85 on page 332.)

An editor has features that are similar to a word processor in that it allows you to do the following:

1. Move through the transcript a character, a word, or a line at a time.
2. Move to the top or bottom of the page or document.
3. Insert and delete characters, words, phrases, or whole paragraphs.
4. Center text automatically.
5. Perform block copy, move, and delete copy and move or delete a block of text.
6. Spell check a word or a block of text while you are editing.
7. Copy text to/from another file.
8. Double-space text on the screen for ease of reading.
9. Change margins and tabs.
10. Find a particular word or phrase.
11. Search for a word or phrase and replace it with another (called *global search and replace*).
12. Capitalize or decapitalize a character, a word, or a line.

In addition, the editor has special global features which only a CAT system would need. These global features include the ability to do the following:

FIGURE 85

Notice the line numbers at the left side of the screen. The reporter is also able to pull down the steno notes in the editor or to remove the steno notes from the screen (Courtesy of Jerome Woods.)

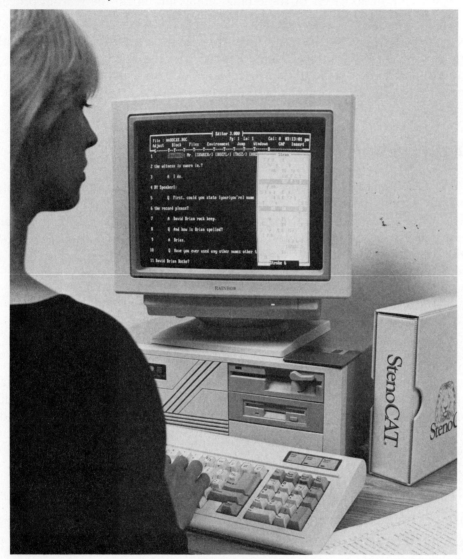

1. Find untranslates and allow you to supply English equivalents, add the entries to your dictionary, and allow you to make the change throughout the rest of the transcript.

2. Correct mixed English and steno outlines that may appear on the screen, add the correct entry to your dictionary, and allow you to make the change throughout the rest of the transcript.

3. Resolve untranslates by selecting the word that makes sense in context.

4. Perform automatic punctuation changes by enabling you to locate a word and change the punctuation next to it to the punctuation of your choice. It can automatically adjust the spacing and capitalization or decapitalization that the next word needs.

5. Format colloquy automatically by placing the proper indentations in the text.

6. Update the reporter's dictionary with all the job, case, or master dictionary entries that you make as you edit the document.

Other CAT Features

In addition to the specifically CAT functions that can be performed in the editor, most CAT systems allow the reporter to perform other functions related to reporting. On the menu of CAT system, you can usually find choices that will allow you to do the following:

1. Automatic batch spell checking and proofing.
2. Index creation and keyword indexing.
3. ASCII disk creation for litigation support.
4. Telecommunications.
5. Artificial Intelligence Conflict Resolution (AICR).
6. Real-time capabilities.
7. Print feature.

Automatic Batch Spell Checking and Proofing

The *automatic batch spell checking feature* on a CAT system generally is more than a spell checker. It also enables the reporter to do some functions that are designed specifically for reporting such as locate the presence of two words that are written together such as "the the." This feature is invaluable because reporters often mistakenly stroke the same outline twice. The proofing feature allows you to not only identify the location of the words but decide whether you wish to keep the two together. Sometimes words such as "that that" legitimately belong together. This feature also often finds repetitive occurrences of a Q or an A and lets you change the incorrect one.

Index Creation and Keyword Indexing

Since transcripts begin with a page or two which resemble a table of contents but are called an index, most CAT systems have an *automatic index creation feature*. This feature allows you to search for speakers, exhibits, and so on and automatically print out a list of pages on which the items can be found. Sophisticated index creation features also allow you to add a heading above certain areas.

Keyword indexing is a similar feature that may be combined with the index creation feature or presented as a separate feature. Attorneys who do not have litigation support software may request that reporters give them a printout of the location of certain key words that they request.

ASCII Disk Creation

An attorney who requests an electronic transcript often is given an ASCII disk that is generated from an option on a menu within the CAT system. Although some CAT systems have this capability, attorneys or reporters may also have specific litigation support software that will make conversions of their CAT system disks to ASCII disks for litigation support purposes.

Telecommunications

Since modems are generally not easy to connect or to make operate easily, a telecommunications connection through a CAT system is desirable if you are going to be sending transcripts over phone lines. Most CAT systems have telecommunications features that can easily be accessed through a menu option.

Artificial Intelligence Conflict Resolution (AICR)

In addition to being able to choose the conflict resolution that fits best in the context of a transcript manually, reporters who have CAT systems with an *Artificial Intelligence Conflict Resolution* (AICR) feature are also able to resolve conflicts by choosing a menu option that will resolve conflicts with a high degree of accuracy and highlight questionable ones for you to check. For reporters who did not learn a conflict-free theory and who resist going onto computers because they write with too many conflicts, this feature is invaluable.

Real-time Capabilities

A *real-time capability* is generally an optional feature that can be added when you purchase a CAT system. It usually can be accessed by connecting your steno writer and selecting an option from a menu within the CAT system. As soon as you enter the editor, you can begin to write and your notes are translated on the screen. On some systems, you can translate an untranslate while writing and enter it and the English equivalent into your dictionary. On some systems, you can even resolve conflicts manually. On still others, you can switch on the AICR and have your conflicts be resolved automatically. A new device has also been added to work with CAT systems that have real-time capabilities. The feature is called an *impact device*. The impact device consists of a tiny box that contains a keypad. It is connected to the CAT system. The purpose of the device is to allow attorneys to insert codes in the transcript to make it easier for them to locate items that they wish to note. (See Figure 86 on page 335.)

Print Feature

Although the *print feature* is a standard feature on all word processing programs, the print feature on a CAT system is usually more sophisticated than on some word processors. It enables you to set up and save a variety of formats and choose the format that you desire. You can also merge documents together while printing, insert index pages and other documents that may have to be included, such as sworn statements, and perform the normal print functions such as:

1. Place a header at the top of the document—a standard portion of text usually the name of the agency or something else that you wish repeated at the top of each page.
2. Place a footer at the bottom of the document—a standard description that you wish to appear at the bottom of each page.
3. Print a single page or the entire transcript.
4. Print multiple copies of the same document.
5. Print while working on another document (background printing).

Networking Capabilities

Since many agencies use CAT systems, it is helpful if several computers can be linked together to share the program, transcript files, and printers. Not all CAT systems work when linked together

FIGURE 86
The attorney holds the impact device and inserts codes in the transcript. When the transcript is produced, he can search for the items he marked in the transcript (Courtesy of Jerome Woods.)

through a network. Therefore, if you intend to use a CAT system in this type of work arrangement, be sure to see that it does have *networking capabilities*.

Roles of Reporter and Scopist

Although a reporter may choose to take notes and produce the final transcript, many reporters find it more economical and more revenue producing to hire a scopist. The reporter then takes notes. The reporter then either translates the notes or gives a copy of the disk to the scopist to translate and edit. Many reporters translate the notes because the systems that scopists use are partial systems often called *edit systems*. Scopists are allowed to edit a transcript that has been translated, but they cannot translate on their own edit systems.

The scopist generally makes the editing changes to the document but does not place the new dictionary entries into the reporter's dictionary. The reporter usually wishes to make these decisions. Therefore, most CAT systems have a feature that saves the dictionary updates in a temporary list that can be reviewed by the reporter and then omitted. Since reporters also must certify their transcripts, many of them wish to proofread the final transcript.

Role of Scopist

The *scopist* is the person who cleans up the reporter's notes and finalizes the transcript. The scopist translates untranslates and resolves conflicts and, therefore, must know the theory that the reporter writes. Other than these activities, the scopist's job is similar to that of a word processing operator. The extent to which the reporter relies on the scopist depends upon the trust that the scopist instills.

Procedures for Using CAT

When CAT systems are used, certain procedures need to be established. If you work with a scopist, your procedures have to be more defined because another person is involved. Some of the items that you need to consider are the following:

1. Writing for CAT.
2. Establishing procedures for building a dictionary.
3. Establishing procedures for handling disks.
4. Labeling and storing disks for your electronic steno writer and your computer.
5. Establishing procedures for coordinating your work with that of a scopist and establishing a set of proofreading marks.
6. Using work logs.

Writing for CAT

The National Court Reporters Association, formerly the National Shorthand Reporters Association, recently established that in order for schools to be approved by their association, they must use a theory that is relatively conflict-free. (See Figure 87 on page 337.) Such a theory should do the following:

1. Use both long and short vowels. Words such as pal and pale would not be written the same and distinguished in context.
2. Distinguish between high-frequency conflicts such as:

it/the	oh/on/owe
had/did	his/is/as
a/an/and	of/have/very
be/been	am/him/many
were/with	two/to/too

FIGURE 87
Students can learn to write conflict-free theories using computer tutorials *(Courtesy of Jerome Woods.)*

3. Differentiate words such as the following:

inform/information   communicate/communication
your/you are   per/perfect
sub/subject   well/we will
our/hour   co-/could/company

4. Distinguish the article *A* from *A* in a word such as:

a lone/alone
a dress/address
a way/away

5. Distinguish endings such as:

-T/-TH   -S/-Z
-ES/-S   -S/-ST

-T/-TY
-L/LY

-F/-V
-SHAL/-SHUS/-SHUN

6. Distinguish long *E* and *EA* conflicts:

hear/here
week/weak
steel/steal

sea/see
sealing/ceiling
break/brake

7. Distinguish alphabetical letters.

Distinguishing Long and Short Vowels

All newer theories use both long and short vowels. If you write a theory that does not distinguish between long and short vowels, you need to start differentiating between the vowels. It is critical, when writing for CAT at this time, that long and short vowels be written differently.

Avoiding High-Frequency Conflicts

High-frequency conflicts may arise from either homonyms or sound alike words such as hear and here or from phrasing two words and creating a conflict such as "to the" and "tot." See Figure 88 for a list of homonyms and some proposed solutions.

FIGURE 88
Ways to resolve some homonyms

English	Outline	English	Outline
beach	BAEFP	beech	BAOEFP
beat	BAET	beet	BAOET
breach	BRAEFP	breech	BRAOEFP
creak	KRAEK	creek	KRAOEK
dear	DAER	deer	DAOER
feat	FAET	feet	FAOET
flea	FLAE	flee	FLAOE
grease	GRAES	Greece	GRAOES
heal	HAEL	heel	HAOEL
knead	NAED	need	NAOED
leach	LAEFP	leech	LAOEFP
peal	PAEL	peel	PAOEL
read	RAED	reed	RAOED
real	RAEL	reel	RAOEL
sea	SAE	see	SAOE
seam	SAEM	seem	SAOEM
sear	SAER	seer	SAOER
shear	SHAER	sheer	SHAOER
steal	STAEL	steel	STAOEL
tea	TAE	tee	TAOE
team	TAEM	teem	TAOEM
weak	WAEK	week	WAOEK
weal	WAEL	we'll	WAOEL
lean	LAEN	lien	LAOEN
mean	MAEN	mien	MAOEN
peace	PAES	piece	PAOES
tear	TAER	tier	TAOER
hear	HAER	here	HAOER
cede	SAED	seed	SAOED
scene	SAEN	seen	SAOEN

Writing the Article A

Various methods are used to distinguish the article *A* from the syllable *A* that begins a word. The most common methods are either that *A* is written *A EU* when written by itself and *A* when it appears in a word or the reverse; *A* is written *A* by itself and is written *A EU* when it appears as the first letter of a word.

Adding Missing Endings

Many older shorthand theories did not supply endings for *TH*, thus words such as *PAT* and *PATH* were written identically. Newer theories either use the * to distinguish the two words or use an alternative ending such as *-PBLG*.

Other words that fall into this category are words ending in *ST*. In some theories, words such as *PASS* and *PAST* are written the same. Newer theories either use the * or *-FT* for the *ST* ending. Sometimes conflicts may be created when the *-FT* ending is used, but when this happens the conflicts are so few that they can easily be resolved.

The following are examples of conflict resolution using the *.

English	Outline	English	Outline
fate	FAIT	FAITH	FA*IT
debt	DET or DEBT	death	D*ET
boot	BAOT	booth	BAO*T

Differentiating Endings

Many earlier theories did not distinguish between other endings such as *-S* and *-Z*; *-L* and *-LY*; *-T* and *-TY*; *-ES* and *-S*; and *-SHAL/-SHUS/-SHUN*. Many problems occur when these endings are not differentiated.

Using the Reversal Principle AE

The *AE* reversal can be used both to resolve conflicts in homonyms in which at least one of the words contain *AE* and in which the long *E* sound is heard, such as: hear and here. It can also be used to resolve a conflict when words are merely spelled with an *AE*, but in which the long *E* sound does not appear such as: bred and bread and herd and heard.

Distinguishing Alphabetical Symbols

Upper case letters and upper case letters followed by periods are distinguished in different ways depending upon the theory used. In one method, the asterisk is used to indicate the period and space used. The asterisk is handy because it can easily be stroked with any single letter on the alphabet to clearly distinguish the letter. For example, *Mr. P. O. Lee* can be written *MR/P*/O*/LAOE*.

The asterisk is also used in abbreviations:

English	Outline	English	Outline
United States	*US	U. S.	U*/S*
Multiple sclerosis	M*S	tuberculosis	T*B
electrocardiogram	E/K*G	EKG	E*/K*/G*

Other Ways of Resolving Conflicts

Sometimes conflicts occur when words have a double consonant such as *allot* and *a lot* or *affix* and *a fix*. To resolve conflicts of this type, simply double the consonant and write *AL/LOT* and *A/LOT*.

Conflicts may also arise if you write your contractions and phrases the same such as: *I had* and *I'd*. Contractions should always be written differently.

Proper names and common names can easily be distinguished, if there is a problem, by simply using the asterisk as in writing bill *(PWEUL)* and *(PW*EUL)*. Another method is to write a stroke that stands for an uppercase letter before stroking the word that is to be capitalized.

Building a Dictionary

Building a dictionary can be quite tedious. Therefore, it is important that you take it seriously. Remember that whatever you enter as an outline for an English word will be there until you change it. Since it is a time-consuming activity, prepare yourself for how you are going to approach it.

1. Set aside enough time so that you are not hurried.
2. Bring a notepad and supplies with you to the computer.
3. Write each outline carefully.
4. If you make an incorrect entry, and it is too late to catch it, write down the word so you can locate it easier later.
5. Bring a dictionary and look up any words that you do not know.

Handling and Storing Disks

If you use disks, you need to take some precautions to follow when using them and to set up a procedure for labeling and storing them.

Some items to note when using disks:

1. Use a felt-tip pen when labeling disks.
2. Avoid the use of any type of fastener on a disk.
3. Keep your disks out of sunlight or excessive heat.
4. Keep your disks away from magnetic surfaces.
5. Avoid touching the exposed part of the disk.
6. Never smoke, eat, or drink when handling disks.

Working With a Scopist

Before giving your work to a scopist, it is important that you develop procedures for how your work is to be handled, what is to be done by the scopist, and what control you feel you must exercise. The use of consistent proofreader marks helps you to coordinate with the scopist. (See Figure 89 on page 341.) Written procedures are best so that both people are doing what is expected.

Establishing Work Flow

If you do not already have an Office/Agency Management System, you will need to work on designing and developing forms that will help your work flow, track your scopist's work, and ensure that your job is getting done on time. In addition, if you are to be successful on your own, you must learn how to bill and collect the money owed to you. Some forms that may be helpful in giving you ideas for developing your own are shown in Figures 90 and 91 on page 342.

FIGURE 89
Common Proofreader Marks.

```
                    PROOFREADER'S MARKS

1.   ⌐       Move to the right.    10.  ⌀      Take out character,
     ⌐       Move to the left.                 word, or line

2.   ⌐⌐      Center                11.  /      Put in lower case

3.   ◯       Spell out             12.  #      Insert a space

4.   ∼       Transpose either one  13.  ⌒      Close up; print as
             letter or whole words                one word

5.   ≡       Put in upper case     14.  STET   Do not make correc-
                                                  tions
6.   ⌿       Paragraph             15.  CT     Change type style
7.   ∧       Insert here
                                   16.  ∧∧∧∧   Insert punctuation
8.   DS      Double Space                         as noted

9.   SS      Single space          17.  ⌐⌐     Close up paragraph
```

⌐Proofreading Corrections Symbols⌐   Center; close up
         (Explanation)   CT   Change type face

⌿Using proofreading symbols will   Paragraph

  make the job of editing   Close up; print as
                                            one word
  and the tasks of revising   Transpose

  easier. an originator doesn't   Put in upper case
            ≡
  have to spend time writing out

  longhand corrections; and   Delete

  ✗ typist can quickly   Put in lower case

  scan a typewritten copy and
  make corrections where the DS   Double space

  symbols occur instead of   Insert punctuation
               ∧
  reading a whole explanation
  reading a whole explanation   Take out line

  of what to do.⌐   No paragraph
  ⌐Using proofreading

  correction#symbols presents   Space
  tremendous
  a savings for the   Insert word
   ∧
                          STET   No correction
  originator and the transcriptionist.⌀

  Michael Cunningham   Single space
                       SS
  Word Processing Supervisor CT ⌐   Move to the right

  ⟨Jan.⟩ 10, 19 ___   ⌐   Spell out

The Future of CAT

Today the burden is still on the reporter to produce clean, shadow-free notes, resolve conflicts while writing, and add untranslates to the dictionary when they occur. Some vendors have already begun to utilize artificial intelligence to some extent in resolving conflicts both in editing in CAT and in real-time writing. As the technology becomes more sophisticated, the application of artificial intelligence will go beyond conflict resolution to the translation of untranslates automatically. Artificial intelligence programs will be able to decipher a word in context and apply it directly to the reporter's dictionary in both editing in CAT and in real-time writing modes. In addition, many new peripheral programs will be developed to assist reporters such as pop-up windows that will

FIGURE 90
Scopist Time Sheet

Oper. ID	Time In	Time Out	No. of hrs.	Reporter's Name	Number of Pages

FIGURE 91
Work Flow Record

DATE	REPORTER	FILE NAME	LIST	CS	FINAL	ROUGH	PROOFER	PAGES	REPRINT

allow you to organize your notes and other peripheral programs. In addition, it is likely that the real-time reporter will be captioning onto videotape and the attorney will be using litigation support systems that search video instead of electronic transcripts. The reporter's job will continue to become more challenging and exciting.

Keeping Up With Reporter Technology

The best way to keep up with reporter technology is to belong to reporter associations, attend seminars, visit vendor booths, and read about the technology. The National Court Reporter, formerly the National Shorthand Reporter, is a good source for state-of-the-art information on technology. The annual *July Technology* issues are specifically devoted to the latest developments in computers, litigation support, and other technology. Your local court reporting associations also hold seminars and conventions, produce newsletters, and often even publish periodicals. If you wish to be the best—you will need to keep up with the advances in reporting.

Chapter 39

The Computer-Integrated Courtroom

The computer-integrated courtroom (CIC) makes available the wonders of computer technology to the judge and the trial lawyer in both the courtroom and the judge's chambers, and these are being implemented in new courts with increasing frequency. In addition to working with computer systems, support for these projects has come from Mead Data Central, West Publishing Company, and the American Bar Association as they have sponsored the addition of LEXIS, WESTLAW, and ABA/Net to the systems.

Applications of this technology include: realtime translation, courtroom litigation support, pacer, computer-assisted legal research, U.S. Sentencing Commission's ASSYST program, ABA/Net, word processing, desktop utilities, judicial applications, and confidential uses.

Components of the Computer-Integrated Courtroom

A computer-integrated courtroom is a combination of hardware and software designed to accomplish specific tasks in the courthouse setting. Limitless variations can and no doubt will be created and placed into operation in courtrooms and courthouses in a wide variety of jurisdictions throughout this country.

The advanced system used in the Phoenix computer-integrated courtroom (CIC) uses a Novell local area network (LAN) linking ten DOS 286 work stations. These are located on the judge's bench, at each counsel's table, at the courtroom deputy clerk's station, the court reporter's position, the secretary's desk, and at each law clerk's desk. In addition the judge has a work station in chambers, and the court reporter, as local area network manager, has a work station in the reporter's office, along with a 70 megabyte DOS 386 Fileserver. This local area network permits sharing of the database by all users, thereby greatly enhancing the efficiency of the court in the disposition of business.

Realtime Translation

Realtime translation is the ability of the court reporter to use a computer-assisted stenograph machine and have the testimony of a witness appear on the computer monitor in plain English text within a matter of seconds from the time the words were spoken. This "computer magic" is accomplished by the matching of the reporter's stenographic keystrokes with the same stroking already stored in the reporter's computer dictionary and associated with a specific English word. If a "match" occurs, the English word appears on the monitor. If a match does not occur, an "untranslate" appears on the screen in the form of the stenographic keystrokes which, of course, are unreadable to the untrained eye, but which can later be corrected by the court reporter or a "scopist." Ordinarily, untranslates will occur when new words are presented to the court reporter which are not already in his or her computer dictionary.

Court reporters who write "realtime" are highly skilled members of their profession in that they are required to differentiate or discriminate between all homonyms such as to, two, too, and 2, so that these will translate in appropriate form. Reporters lessen the occurrence of "untranslates" by requesting attorneys to give them in advance a list of names of witnesses, geographic locations, or new technical terms which are expected to be used in the testimony so these new words can be placed in the reporter's computer dictionary.

Realtime translation has a number of significant benefits for the judge, the lawyers, the litigants, the jury, and others in the courtroom setting.

No More Readbacks. Realtime eliminates the need for readbacks by the court reporter. If the judge or an attorney misses or doesn't hear any portion of the proceedings because of crosstalk or a muffled statement, they need only refer to the monitor to be fully apprised of the content of the statement.

Objections. In considering an objection, the Court has the benefit of referring to the precise formulation of the question or statement before making a ruling; and while this may not be of great significance in each instance, it is of enormous benefit when the content of a lengthy question or statement is at issue. In the long run, it is clear that this use of realtime will enhance the quality of judicial rulings.

Bench Conferences. Realtime permits second-chair lawyers, paralegals, and the parties in civil and criminal cases to "be present" at bench conferences by remaining at counsel's tables and reading the content of the sidebar conference on the monitor. This can be of particular benefit in a criminal case where a defendant has a constitutional right to be present at all critical stages of his trial.

Hearing-Impaired Litigants and Jurors. Realtime translation permits hearing-impaired litigants and jurors to take part in trials in a new and more meaningful way than was heretofore possible. By providing the hearing-impaired individual with a computer monitor, the realtime presentation permits full participation in all aspects of the trial proceedings.

Court Interpreters. In many trials simultaneous translation is required in order to permit non-English speaking parties to understand all that is taking place during the court proceedings. While certified court interpreters must and do rely upon what is said by the witness as the source of their translation, they nonetheless find it helpful to be able to refer to the realtime monitor in order to confirm what they have heard from the witness stand and to enhance their recall, particularly when dealing with testimony that involves a great deal of numbers.

Courtroom Litigation Support

Computers, together with realtime translation and appropriate additional software, have transformed the courtroom into a new venue for "litigation support" and have given the term an entirely new meaning. In the past litigation support has generally been understood to include the ways in which computers permit court reporters and lawyers to create, edit, store, and retrieve voluminous discovery materials in preparation for litigation. The process was largely confined to the offices of the court reporters and the attorneys.

The CIC permits the lawyers to bring the full text of their depositions, discovery summaries, legal memoranda, and other trial materials to the courtroom on diskettes and to "load" these materials onto the hard disk or memory system of the computer that has been assigned to their side of the case. The computers used by the parties and the Court are separate, each having its own database and security code in order to ensure that proper handling is accorded to these confidential and privileged litigation materials.

The trial begins, and at the close of each day a complete record of the proceedings is loaded onto the database of each computer, so that as the trial expands from days to weeks or perhaps even months, the trial participants have not only their own trial materials but a complete record of the trial itself on the hard disk of the computer.

Software has been developed which permits the Court and counsel to review independently the database on their computer, thus enabling the participants to study and compare the material while the trial is in progress and while the realtime is being displayed on an alternate selection on their monitors. The litigation support software also permits the parties to search the database using Boolean logic in a manner that is somewhat similar to the process used in conducting searches on the computer-assisted legal research databases. This review and search capacity gives the trial lawyers and the judge a remarkable new ability to deal with the facts of an extended or complex case with a speed and accuracy that was heretofore unattainable.

This litigation support system virtually eliminates the need for the judge to take trial notes since he or she has available not only a complete record of the proceedings but, in addition, the ability to search it with infinite precision. The software also permits the judge and counsel to insert notes of their own in the testimony as it unfolds and to program the computer to highlight any keywords which they expected to occur during the trial.

The realtime portion of this litigation support system permits creation of a simultaneously printed copy of the proceedings which can be made available to the lawyers immediately after the close of the court session so that it could be used, for example, to prepare for cross-examination of a witness, to prepare a written order form the Court's orally announced decision, or for any other purpose that court transcripts are traditionally used. The record prepared in this fashion is referred to as "dirty copy," since it has not been edited to eliminate the "untranslates." Notwithstanding these imperfections, the dirty copy can effectively be used by anyone who was present at the trial since they would have heard the "untranslates" during the presentation of the case.

The review and search capabilities of this system are of great benefit in preparing for and presenting motions and are invaluable to appellate counsel in preparing briefs on appeal. This new system of litigation support transforms the court reporter into what we might call a data management specialist, who, for the first time, can now capture, store, issue code, search, cross-reference, compare, annotate, sort, edit, file, retrieve, print, fax, and/or telecommunicate trial proceedings with heretofore unattainable speed and accuracy.

Pacer

Pacer is a program that permits users at each work station to access the Court's computerized civil docketing system by modem and to view and/or copy the docket entries for any case. In the near future, this capability will be available to lawyers anywhere via modem.

Computer-Assisted Legal Research

A major aspect of the computer-integrated courtroom is the availability of computer-assisted legal research for the judge and for the attorneys in the courtroom. Two systems are available: LEXIS and WESTLAW, and both are excellent. These services provide the user with a remarkably complete "computer library," which is immediately available in the courtroom and in chambers. These services provide full text of all reported state and federal cases, electronic citations to unreported cases, rules of Civil and Criminal Procedure, ALR annotations, selected law reviews, and specialty materials on a wide variety of subjects. In addition to these traditional legal research materials LEXIS and WESTLAW and associated gateway services provide the opportunity to search or view in full text an enormous number of magazine articles and newsletters. Additional materials include biographical profiles, an index to legal publications, as well as a whole series of files on medical and pharmaceutical subjects. An extensive list of expert witnesses is also available on many specialized subjects.

For lawyers who want an insight on the judge who will be presiding over their case, the Federal Judicial Almanac can be searched. For judges who want to know the track record of the lawyer who is going to appear before them, a segment search of all state or federal cases can be made to examine the type and depth of litigation experience they have had.

Computer-assisted legal research is a magnificent technology and a great benefit to the justice system.

United States Sentencing Commission's ASSYST Program

The U.S. Sentencing Commission has developed PC software for computing sentences under the new sentencing guidelines that went into effect in November 1987 and which were held to be constitutionally valid by the U.S. Supreme Court in January 1989. The ASSYST program permits the judge to enter and thereafter vary any of the nearly infinite factors that go into the computation of sentences under the newly mandated guideline system. The program will permit the judge to keep a record of all the sentences he or she has imposed for purposes of review and comparison.

ABA/Net

The computer-integrated courtroom has on its terminals the American Bar Association's ABA/Net. Many services are provided including electronic mail, PC to FAX transmission, computerized legal research on an as-needed basis, electronic conferencing, a wide variety of specialty services including a schedule of information on American Bar Association meetings and programs, a complete presentation of airline schedules and more than a thousand different public and private databases.

The electronic mail capability of ABA/Net not only permits lawyers and judges to have virtually instantaneous communications, but, in addition, this service provides a vehicle for experimenting with new rules and procedures that would permit electronic filing of pleadings and other documents from the lawyer's office to the courthouse.

Word Processing

At each work station in the computer-integrated courtroom, word processing software provides the user with the opportunity to create correspondence, pleadings, or other documents with the style, speed, and accuracy that in the past was only available from a highly skilled executive legal secretary.

Desktop Utilities

The term "desktop utilities" includes a large number of software programs that are available to assist the Court and its staff in the discharge of routine office tasks. The Court's calendar, for example, can be entered on the computer and, if networked, all members of the staff from all work stations have the ability to check the Court's schedule and to make timely and appropriate additions or alterations thereto.

Each day a current copy of the schedule can be printed and distributed as needed. A computer-generated Rolodex with names, addresses, and telephone numbers can also be made available on all CIC terminals. With a modem and a telephone handset available at the terminal, calls can be automatically placed by the computer.

Other features of a desktop utility software traditionally include a sophisticated calculator and the ability to generate and transmit notes and to "post" them in a timely manner on the addressee's computer screen.

Judicial Applications

A computer-integrated courtroom enables a judge to accomplish many of his or her responsibilities at new levels of speed and efficiency. For example, requesting the submission of proposed jury instructions on a diskette as well as in hard copy permits the Court to consider submitted instructions "on line" and to make appropriate modifications in chambers with the lawyers present and to then send the material directly to the printer. Further, stock jury instructions can be placed in the database of the computer, thus greatly facilitating the review and selection of appropriate pattern instructions. These practices can be of great benefit to the Court during the process of settling jury instructions.

Following bench trials the Court can require submission of proposed Findings of Fact and Conclusions of Law in computer format, thereby enabling the judge to incorporate such portions of the document as may be appropriate in the materials created by the Court on its word processor.

Additional uses might include the use of computer-generated minute orders by the courtroom deputy clerk, development of a control or monitoring system for keeping track of matters under submission, the entry of frequently referred to rules of evidence, rules of procedure, and local rules of practice on subdirectories of a word processor.

The foregoing are just a few examples of the vast number of ways the computer can help judges discharge their judicial responsibilities.

Confidential Uses

From time to time all judges have occasion to deal with confidential or sensitive information which, if presented in computer format, should be placed in a discrete and secure portion of the Court's computer database. Examples of this kind of information might include presentence reports containing unduly sensitive material, applications for wiretaps, commercial trade secrets, and other information of a sensitive nature that may have been submitted for in-camera inspection. We are all aware of cases that are national in scope and that require very secure handling of material involving issues of national defense or other classified subjects.

What Lies Ahead?

The future is bright for the computer-integrated courtroom. Networks, PC to FAX, and other forms of telecommunication will allow us to transmit and share information with unprecedented speed and accuracy.

Optical scanning technologies will allow direct input of documentary exhibits to the trial database. Monitors for the jury and other trial participants will permit simultaneous viewing of documentary exhibits, videos, and other computer-generated graphics. Pleadings will be "filed" electronically, and court calendars will be set without conflicts and viewed by counsel from the comfort of their offices.

The Justice System will, indeed, benefit as new computer technologies are introduced—it's just a matter of time and money.

The computer-integrated courtroom is a reality in an increasing number of locations throughout the nation. The computer has changed, in a very real way, the manner in which we can discharge our responsibilities to those we serve. There is a great deal of underutilized computer equipment in the courthouses of this country, and it is suggested that computer-integrated courtrooms are potentially available in a great number of these locations and need only the focus and direction of an interested judge to make them a reality.

Tribute for the Above Information

I am deeply appreciative of the sharing of the above information concerning computer-integrated courtrooms by The Honorable Roger G. Strand, United States District Judge, Phoenix, Arizona.

Certainly, as more and more courtrooms become computer integrated, the true worth of the court reporter will become evident not only to the participants in trials but to the general public as well.

Essentials for CAT Success in the Courts

Critical elements in the success of a CAT system are proper management and education. Reporters must be properly educated so as not to become disillusioned, because some have become discouraged with CAT by expecting either too much from the equipment or themselves. Both hardware and personnel have limitations.

Judges, attorneys, and court administrators also must be educated as to how the equipment works and what it entails to produce a transcript. They often are of the opinion the reporter simply feeds his notes into a computer, and the printer spits out the transcript.

Judges and court administrators must know there is a learning phase where production is slowed. CAT is not an instant answer to backlogs in the courts. They must become aware of the assistance they can provide the reporter through properly controlled proceedings which will enable the reporter to write clean notes and foresee conflicts.

With proper management, the right equipment, and a positive attitude by all involved, CAT will ultimately make a great contribution to the efficiency of the modern court system as nothing else can, and it will greatly enhance the professional reporters' production capabilities.

Chapter 40 *Realtime Writing*

Within the near future, it is anticipated that most freelance reporters and many of our courts of any size will go to realtime writing with no more than a five-second lag time between the spoken word and its appearance on a screen properly translated for all participants to see. The reason for the necessity of this is evident: Only in this way can reporters prove that with CAT (Computer-Aided Transcription) can they provide a cheaper, more accurate, quicker transcript than can be had by any other method. It is their hope of survival!

Today, many reporters are using scopists and proofreaders to assist in turning out the heavy workload which has resulted from attorneys' ability to receive prompt, usable transcripts. This, in turn, has led to more reporting work being done. Scopists trained in all phases of computer translation have become invaluable because of their keyboarding, proofreading, and other skills, which take away much of the drudgery of turning out transcripts.

However, realtime writing is becoming more prevalent. Reporters are now showing by their ability to write for instant translation that one person can accurately write material for viewing at the time it is written, provide key word searches, and save time, since few readbacks are required with the material readily visible on each monitor screen. Soon after a realtime job is written, the printed copy can be made available promptly.

Prior to taking realtime matter, pertinent data, such as the petition, the response, interrogatories, names, curricula vitae of witnesses, and so on, should be furnished the reporter for inputting into his or her dictionary (which should contain well over 50,000 entries before a person even considers doing realtime). Also provided should be unusual technical and medical and drug terms.

Of course, of paramount importance is ensuring that all necessary gear, including backups of everything, be brought to the site of taking.

As the material begins, the words appear on the TV screen monitors for everyone to see, and every 25 lines, the laser printer will turn out a page. With realtime writing, a laser printer is a must because of its silent action. The system can automatically print at the bottom of every page printed in realtime "Rough Draft."

When repeats of questions or answers are required, the attorneys simply take the necessary page (or pages) out of the printer and hand it to the witness so that the witness can read the exact material.

During a noon hour, preparation of the final transcript of the morning's proceedings can be made. At the end of the day, within a short time, daily copy transcript can be provided.

Of course, where hearing-impaired parties are concerned, they can take an active part in the trial of the case, whereas previously they had no means of knowing what was going on in a lawsuit.

Unfortunately, cost will be a factor in incorporating realtime in courtrooms because government is slow to appropriate money for computer systems or to move rapidly in incorporating new methods. Surely, however, any student of court reporting must be aware today that realtime writing is the wave of the future!

Instant Transcripts From An Attorney's Viewpoint

by Jerry Kelley, CSR

Q: What is instant transcript?

A: Instant transcript is when, during deposition or trial, the court reporter writes on his shorthand machine what is being spoken and his personal computer instantly translates it into English and beams it into a small TV screen located in front of the attorney and/or judge, then prints it on a silent laser printer which can be located at counsel table.

Q: Why should I order instant transcripts?

A: For several reasons:

1. The cost involved for instant or daily trial transcript more than pays for itself in the event we have to appeal, because instead of having to wait for the transcript to be prepared, with post-judgment and/or prejudgment interest running, we already have the transcript. Example: $1 million @ 10% = $100,000.

2. During depos or trials, transcripts are ready immediately to share with my client, house counsel, legal assistants, experts, litigation support systems, co-counsel who must cover for me tomorrow, and so on.

3. I can simultaneously get a computer diskette for my use, which sometimes can be much more valuable than the paper transcript.

4. The computerized transcript can be phoned electronically or faxed to the client, general counsel, legal assistant, or experts anywhere in the country each evening or twice daily for review and recommendations on strategy.

5. There's no need to ask the reporter for a search and readback of the question when the witness wants a long, but perfect, question repeated or says "That's not what I said."

6. If the jury wants something read back, the judge can look at the actual written transcript and decide what, if anything, to read to them in response to their request rather than having the court reporter search for it and read from his notes.

7. Rather than asking the court reporter to mark something special for me in his shorthand notes, perhaps divulging my strategy to my opponent, I can mark it myself on my paper copy of the English printout.

8. If I'm asking questions, my second-chair associate or legal assistant can ensure I don't miss something on paper that perhaps was glazed over by gestures, innuendo, the bravado of counsel-opposite or otherwise.

9. If someone else asks questions first, I have an instant transcript to use for cross-examination, follow-up or impeachment; and as really great questions come to me, I can make notes on the instant transcript of what I want to ask later without simultaneously losing what the witness is saying.

10. I don't take off down so many rabbit trails, because many times otherwise disputed points become insignificant when seen in the transcript.

11. If it becomes necessary to argue a motion before the court during deposition or trial, we have in our hand the same transcript the trial court or court of appeals will have rather than the court and counsel having to rely on the respective advocates' memories.

12. I can see what the record looks like as it is made.

13. In a matter where a deaf or hearing-impaired witness, attorney, or party is involved, they can see the exact words being used rather than relying on someone writing notes or the paraphrasing of sign-language interpreters.

Litigation Support

Q: Why should I use litigation support?

A: Ordering my transcripts delivered on computer diskette as well as on paper allows me:

1. In searching through several weeks or months of deposition or trial transcripts, to plug in key words or phrases and immediately open up on the one spot or all the spots in the transcript I need rather than making a time-consuming manual search and risk missing something. Also, this can be printed out in index form, giving me the page and line number of any testimony or exhibit I wish to find instantly.

2. I can get up to 30,000 pages, including exhibits that have been scanned into the computer, on a laptop computer for doing word- or phrase-searching, chronological searches, alphabetizing, digesting, summarizing, etc.

3. I can do issue coding. For example, what did a specific witness or every witness say about X date or X amount of money or X person or X anything?

4. During my questioning, I can use key words or phrases I have decided on *beforehand* (Example: "Very well, sir") to assist me in finding what I need *after* the testimony. I then use computer indexing to have the computer print out the page and line number of my key words or phrases, which is also where I needed to mark something for my attention later.

5. While taking testimony, when counsel-opposite or I fail to use the same name each time, defaulting to pronouns such as "he, his, him," I can instruct the computer to change those pronouns temporarily to "Mr. X" for the purposes of my search and other computer capabilities.

6. My associates or assistants and I can make "blind" notes in "windows" on the computer for our benefit only.

Chapter 41   *Closed Captioning*

One of the greatest services performed by a reporter today is that of the closed caption television writer, since television is the paramount mass communications medium, and hearing impairment is the nation's most prevalent disability. Closed captioning makes television information, news, and entertainment available to ten million deaf Americans.

This new profession for reporters began in 1970, when the Caption Center started captioning Julia Child's *The French Chef*. Today, a number of captioning agencies provide television closed captioning of presidential addresses, newscasts, Wall Street Week, the Oprah Show, 60 Minutes, Charles Kuralt, Science Journal, awards programs, game shows, sports events, Miss America Pageant—in all more than 175 hours every week with over 97 percent of network prime time programs captioned. In addition, thousands of commercials and home videocassettes are captioned.

Captions display television's auditory information in visual form. Similar to subtitles, captions translate spoken dialogue into printed words on a screen. They also identify speakers and indicate additional information, including sound effects and mood music. Captions can be synchronized with speech patterns and changes in camera angles to convey a sense of rhythm and pace.

Closed captions are seen only on television sets equipped with special decoders. Captions appear as white letters against a black background. These one-half-inch high letters are usually displayed at the bottom of the screen, although they are sometimes placed in other positions to identify speakers or to avoid interference with graphics or text. Musical notes accompany song lyrics.

Captions are timed to match audio and lip movements, then carefully placed to indicate the speaker. Reviewers proof the completed show at least twice before final approval. Finally, encoding can take up to 30 hours for a one-hour program to make the data ready for broadcast or duplication.

Approximately 250,000 decoders are used by an audience of over 800,000 hearing-impaired viewers in our country. The TeleCaption adapter (decoder) is purchased through AT&T's Special Needs Center, Sears, hearing-aid distributors, organizations serving deaf consumers, and consumer electronics stores.

Realtime captioning is done for news, sports, and other live programs, whereby reporters take words as they are spoken, producing captions that appear with live programming.

The cost to caption a one-hour program is approximately $2,500, and it costs about $235 to caption a 30-second commercial.

The Caption Center has made available the job qualifications for real-time Stenocaptioners as follows:

Speed of 225 WPM on two-voice Q&A, 180 on literary.

Accurate, consistent writing with minimal shadows and conflicts.

Excellent command of spelling, grammar, and punctuation.

Experience on a Computer-Aided Translation (CAT) system.

Willingness to refine theory and eliminate conflicts.

Strong transcription skills.

RPR or CSR certification preferred.

A person who plans to become a closed caption writer should also have a wide knowledge of current events, an extraordinary vocabulary, and familiarity with names of personages in the news, company titles, and the classics.

The Caption Center lists its salary range for full-time Stenocaptioners as $35,291-$45,041, and undoubtedly other firms would offer similar salary incentives. The training period is paid, and two annual step increases are provided per year. All equipment, software, updates, and maintenance are provided by them, together with other benefits.

For the highly knowledgeable reporter with excellent skills, closed captioning for television offers an interesting alternative to other forms of reporting.

Chapter 42 *Voice Recognition Technology*

Many experiments are being carried on today in the field of voice recognition to develop computers capable of understanding the natural English language.

Such a system would possess an unlimited vocabulary and would understand and separate English spoken by people of varying accents and speaking patterns. It would be able to translate this oral information into transcribed output at triple the rate of the fastest keyboardist.

Experimental voice-activated systems have been tried for at least the last ten years in several locations. The user's voice is electronically photographed, and the computer associates the dictated sounds with a set of keystrokes. The system compares the user's voice to electronic graphs stored in the system and keys the corresponding words.

Insurance adjusters already use a voice-activated hand-held device to input data relating to car damages using a set of codes for specific car parts, adding data of estimated labor rates and repair costs, and the computer prints a repair estimate.

Voice-activated systems understand spoken words by comparing patterns of sound with speech patterns stored in memory. Experts are still working for a significant breakthrough that will enable all types of machines to obey a user's every spoken word.

A great problem is the ability of the voice recognition system to string sounds together to make words. Another problem is the enormous vocabulary required in the system. So far, the systems developed are limited to about a 15,000-word vocabulary.

Currently, users of voice recognition systems must use excellent diction and pause between command words to avoid slurring, which results in incorrect translation. Also, systems must yet be developed to understand speech patterns of more than one user. Until voice-activation systems can understand concurrent dictation from multiple users, the systems will be of little use in court reporting situations.

The costs of implementing voice-activated systems may prohibit their use for sometime in the future, but as the technology becomes more refined and more companies enter production, costs should decline. However, so many problems exist in securing a system that will differentiate between voices and apply formats required in court reporting, that many years of refinement will be required to make voice activation a viable instrument for reporting work. Not long ago, researchers predicted the paperless offices of the 1980's, which did not develop. It may be that the same fate will overtake voice-activated systems for the entire future.

Chapter 43 **Convention Reporting**

Some reporters, after doing a certain amount of general reporting, develop a clientele sufficient to devote themselves to a certain field of work which particularly appeals to them, such as medical reporting, workmen's compensation hearings, maritime work, or government contract hearings.

One type of specialized reporting preferred by many reporters who have a broader than average background and a desire to travel about the country or abroad is convention reporting. Some firms are widely known for expertise in this field, but there is always the chance that every reporter may be called upon to report a convention at some time.

It may be hard to a beginner to turn down any work that is offered, but when it comes to taking aerospace conventions and conferences, highly technical medical conventions, and meetings of high technology groups, a beginner should probably work with an experienced reporter unless the individual possesses extraordinary background and initiative.

Securing Convention Work

Organizations that have their proceedings reported usually hire the same firm or reporter year after year. Reporters may be requested to report the proceedings of a convention by a client, friend, another firm, or by a group meeting in a certain city that is seeking to have a record of the proceedings made.

As in all other types of reporting, personality plays a large part in securing convention business and in retaining the business in the future, but convention reporting is a real test of true ability.

Normally, the person in charge of securing the reporter for a convention will telephone or write the reporter requesting coverage of the meetings. The reporter should get the proper name of the organization and the name and spelling of the person's name who is calling and determine whether that individual is to be the contact person. He or she should also get the dates and location of the convention, time of the first session, the approximate number of reporting hours, and date and ending time of the last meeting.

Immediate inquiries should be made with airlines to take advantage of lowest available fares, and early reservations should be booked GLA—guaranteed late arrival—on the day preceding the convention opening. If reporting is to be on a daily basis, reservations should be made for rooms for other reporters, if any, notereaders, or typists at the same time.

At booking time the convention reporter must inquire regarding delivery time (normally 14 days). Quotations should take into account whether the convention will be technical, how long it will be, how many copies will be required, and what delivery date is expected. Extra copies can be decided later, but there should be an understanding at the outset that at least an original and one copy will be the base.

The reporter should secure the name of the head of the hotel's audiovisual department, including his or her phone number or extension, as reporters invariably use headset earphones to ensure clear voice reproduction undisturbed by the distances over which voices may travel. Convention centers and auditoriums may accommodate as many as 5,000 delegates. Microphones, placed at strategic locations, provide all delegates access to the proceedings. The headsets are connected to the communication system so the reporter can hear each speaker clearly without the extraneous noises of the convention.

If the convention is to be a daily copy affair, the reporter should be sure his or her hotel room is not adjacent to that of the typists so he and they will not disturb each other. However, the typists should have adjacent rooms with doors between to expedite collating, indexing, and so on. Their rooms should be provided with secretarial chairs and typing tables.

The reporter should ask the person arranging the convention reporting to mail, as soon as it is printed, at least two copies of the printed program, indicating sessions to be covered or a rough draft when available. One should be left with the typists and the other taken with the reporter so all can be familiar with the program and names.

Traveling and Hotel Preparation

A smart reporter will pack light, easy-care clothing in a readily distinguishable suitcase for quick check-in and check-out at the airport. Of course, the shorthand machine will accompany the reporter at all times.

At the hotel, prior arrangement for VIP check-in will prevent waiting in line and allow the reporter to ask the assistant manager for just the key and no bellboy, facilitating getting settled in the hotel room.

Clothes should be hung up, personal items put away, and the hotel room rearranged by the reporter for work right away. A table must be setup to use for checking and mailing notes and, perhaps, dictating. Housekeeping should be notified if light bulbs are not working and if there are not enough clothes hangers, towels, and washcloths.

The reporter should now check where the icemaker is on the floor and get some ice and go to a nearby shop and get juices and other beverages for refreshment in order to save time later.

Check In and Register for the Convention

The reporter can ascertain from the call board or the hotel operator where the registration desk for the meetings is located. The personnel at the registration desk will give the reporter a badge which will admit him or her to all functions and exhibits. A visit to the exhibits will provide reference material to assist in preparing a good record. The badge will also help the reporter get into hotel executive offices to make copies of reports and prepared addresses. These costs can be charged to the master account of the association.

The registration desk should also provide the reporter with a packet given to members, extra programs for typists and other reporters, a membership directory, and a pre-registration list. Copies of these should go to the typists in the first mailing, along with the first notes or dictation. The reporter should also secure names of people who may ask questions or carry on discussions after the speakers have completed their addresses.

Arrange to Meet Audiovisual Personnel

Upon arrival at the convention hotel, the reporter should arrange for a meeting with the hotel's audiovisual person in the meeting room. This meeting may be pre-arranged by telephone.

Some reporters take their own stereo earphones and mixer (custom-made for use with any system in the world) and ask the audiovisual person to connect them directly to the public address system for the following day, giving that individual the starting time. Then, the sound system is checked out for each microphone at the table or on the floor. There should be individual volume controls on the earphones and also on the mixer. This unit should have three different-sized plug-in receptacles to fit any system. For security reasons, the equipment should be taken by the reporter to his or her room at day's end, advising the sound person what time sessions will begin the next day.

Usually earphones are not used in reporting a board or committee meeting because microphones are not usually used during these sessions. A U- or V-shaped table arrangement allows the reporter to be placed in the center, directly facing the nameplates in front of the persons to be identified. There will normally be much back-and-forth conversation and many interruptions during this type of reporting.

Get to Know the Convention Staff

If reporters identify themselves to the association staff members and get on a first-name basis with them, these people may be available to help copy or to assist with other chores during proceedings.

The reporter should meet with the person who originally arranged for the convention, reporting in person to exchange room numbers as soon as possible. Information for that person can be left, telling him or her that the reporter has arrived. The room number can also be left in the person's mailbox if he or she is in a pre-convention meeting.

Arrangements should be made at the pressroom to have a file made in the reporter's name and a copy of everything that passes through the pressroom placed in it, to assist in transcription.

Check Out the Convention Meeting Room

The reporter should check the convention room in advance to note the size of the room and where the podium will be. A small cloth-covered card-table sized table should be requested to be placed in a spot in front of and adjacent to the head table, about 4 to 6 feet to the right of the lectern, and on the main floor. A comfortable chair should be at the table site.

If panel discussions are on the program, the reporter should arrive early and arrange seating at a table to the right of the panel, partly facing the panel and partly facing the audience from the side for easy viewing of panel members and speakers from the audience. The reporter must never sit directly between the panel and the audience.

The panel members should be requested by the reporter to sit in the order listed on the program for identification as 1, 2, 3, and so on. However, if they do no sit in that order, a mark on the program should be made indicating who sat in each seat or a diagram should be drawn so the typist can make proper identifications.

Be Early for Each Session

The reporter should appear for the first day's session at least an hour early to check everything and to meet the president or chairperson and others at the head table. A fresh pad of shorthand paper should be in the machine for every session and another open and ready to use on the table.

Get All Names Right

The reporter must obtain the correct name spelling for any speaker. Normally, the chairperson or another assigned person will be seated beside the reporter to help in this regard.

The reporter should check with the chairperson before the session begins as to whether speakers from the floor should be identified by name. If so, the chairperson should ask them to give their names and companies or cities clearly. If speakers are not identified, the reporter must call out clearly and courteously "Name, please," in the interest of having a good record.

Practice for Invocations

The reporter will take in shorthand invocations which are normally quite lengthy at the beginning of a convention. Practice for invocations by securing some Congressional Records and writing daily invocations given in the House and Senate.

Secure Items that Must Be Included

During business sessions of a convention, reports are read, and it is customary for copies of these to be furnished to the reporter. People giving reports often read rapidly, sometimes mumbling and speaking indistinctly. If a speaker is reluctant to give the reporter an only copy of a report, the speaker should be assured it will be returned at the first break or lunch hour. The name and room number of the speaker should be marked on the report. Then, at the first break, a copy should be made (perhaps by the executive office personnel) and charged to the association's account. Finally, the report should be returned as promised.

If arrangements have been made to return reports at the time transcript is prepared, the person's business card should be attached with notation that the report is to be returned immediately by the typist as soon as she is finished with it.

Each speaker should be asked by the reporter if he or she has a prepared text to give the reporter a copy of. Those to be returned should be placed in the speaker's hotel mailbox or mailed the next day to the address supplied.

Sometimes speakers will instruct the reporter to place in the record the prepared text provided rather than what was said at the podium. Should such a request be made, the reporter should show only what the paper states.

Keep a Strict Record of the Time

The reporter should place an accurate wristwatch or travel alarm clock on the table and record the exact minute the meeting begins and when it adjourns. Starting and ending times for lunches and other recesses should also be carefully noted.

Verify Important Information

Any time a name, place, or word comes up that the reporter is unfamiliar with or feels he or she could not find the spelling of, the place should be marked with a "Stenomark." At the first break, all such spots should be checked and verified with the speaker or someone who knows the answers.

If a speaker is to leave instantly after speaking, any verifications should be made at the very first break. If handed any materials to copy information from, have it done right on the spot and return the document immediately.

Get the Transcript Started Right Away

At the end of any session or dictation session, the reporter should have checked the location of the nearest post office. The notes for a notereader or dictation belts and information materials should be placed in a pre-addressed padded envelope and mailed back to the office from the post office. This material should never be mailed from the hotel.

Edit Convention Records Carefully

Delete false starts and clean up bad grammar, unless it is used to make a joke. Speakers should be made to sound intelligent.

Arrange for a Speedy Check-Out from the Hotel

The reporter should take advantage of VIP check-outs, which allow the person merely to drop the key off. Usually the charge will be on the association's account; if not, the bill will arrive in a few days charged on the reporter's credit card.

Selling Copies of the Record

The reporter must check with the convention administration to find out whether it is permissible to sell copies of speeches or the entire record. If it is, a round-figure cost is given, estimating approximately 55–60 pages per hour. The information as to the parts desired and names and addresses are taken, together with the money, and the typist is instructed to type and mail out the ordered portions or whole record.

Associations always pay, so there are normally no unpaid bills.

Package Deals May Be Made

In some instances the reporter is requested to provide copies of the proceeding for all members of the group. To make a package deal with a client, the number of reporting hours is translated into number of pages. The type of transcript reproduction is settled with the client, and the transcript is typed so as to be adaptable to a printer's camera-ready method. The price per page, based on the number of pages and number of books to be run is obtained, and a package price is given.

Transcripts should be mailed first class, special delivery, and billing should be made after the client has received the transcript and says he or she is happy with it.

Don't fail to consider the glamorous field of convention reporting!

Chapter 44

Legislative Reporting

One of the more interesting specialties of court reporting is performed by reporters in the United States Senate and House of Representatives.

Thanks to my good friend, Grant Perry, a retired Senate Reporter, I am able to acquaint my readers with this fascinating and glamorous work. His description of the development and present-day reporting of the CONGRESSIONAL RECORD FOLLOWS:

Establishment of the Congressional Record

Once upon a time many verbatim or near-verbatim reporters worked for newspapers, and in those days one could expect "the news" to be an account of what had actually happened, rather than a version slanted to conform to the perspective of a particular newsperson or publication.

It was through the efforts of such reporters that the Lincoln-Douglas debates, the sermons of Phillips Brooks, and many of the great speeches which have become part of our literary heritage were disseminated and preserved for posterity.

For many years, too, the debates in Congress were reported in private-enterprise newspapers—successively the *National Intelligencer* and the *Congressional Globe*—until the establishment of the *Congressional Record*, printed and published by the Government Printing Office (GPO), in 1873.

Though the publishing arrangements differed, the same reporters, at that time, continued to do substantially the same job under public instead of private auspices; and the *Congressional Record* still retains traces of its newspaper past.

So, it is not surprising that there, more than anywhere else, the functions of newspaper reporter and verbatim reporter, as we usually understand the term nowadays, converge. And thus, it should not be surprising that legislative reporting, as performed in the U.S. Senate and the House of Representatives, differs from ordinary court and convention reporting in a number of ways.

Since I was a Senate Reporter, I shall refer hereafter to the Senate and Senators, though much or most of what is stated will be equally applicable to the House.

Function of the Senate Reporters

The Senate reporter is not, quite frankly, an impartial guardian of the public's interest, as is the court reporter. People's lives, liberties, and fortunes do not depend upon the accuracy of his transcript. He or she is first, last, and always an employee of the Senate, and his or her primary function is to reflect credit upon that institution and its Members.

This type of work often involves more time spent in research and editing than in actual reporting and dictating. Many people, both in and out of the government, carefully study the *Congressional Record* and depend on it for information and guidance in their fields of employment or interest. It is often relied on by the executive departments and agencies of the government, as well as the courts, in trying to determine, through study of the legislative history, what Congress really intended when it passed some piece of legislation.

Therefore, the *Record* must be accurate in all its facts, figures, and quotations; and if a Senator misspeaks or uses words which, in cold print, will not convey accurately, precisely, and according to the rules what he and his staff of experts intended that he say, it is the duty of the floor reporters, the chief reporter, the parliamentarian, the legislative assistants, the Senator himself, and on occasion even the GPO to see that the *Record* is kept straight and that it is in conformity with the *Journal*, which has always been the official formal record of the proceedings. (The *Journal* is a summary of proceedings something like a secretary's minutes. At the beginning of every legislative day, the reading of the *Journal* for the previous day is routinely dispensed with by unanimous consent—except during filibusters, when, if one Senator objects, the transaction of other business must wait while the whole thing is read. Fortunately that rule does not apply to the *Congressional Record*.)

The Senate reporters have a very good reference library immediately available in their office—including three unabridged dictionaries, five versions of the Bible, and numerous books of quotations—as well as the facilities of the Senate library in the Capitol and the Library of Congress across the street.

It is usually possible to check the source and text of any quotation heard in the Chamber, though in a few cases the reporters have found it worthwhile to develop a file of a particular Senator's favorite quotations and stories. For example, Senator Robert C. Byrd, the Senate Democratic leader, can quote poetry—and sometimes quite obscure poetry—by the page, and his file often comes in handy.

Adherence to Parliamentary Procedure

In the *Congressional Record*, many parliamentary niceties and distinctions must be maintained by the reporters whether observed in practice or not.

Every bill and joint resolution must be shown, at the appropriate places, as having been read three times; though if this were to happen in actual practice, nothing else would ever be accomplished. Nowadays every piece of legislation and most amendments are printed and are readily available to every Senator to read for himself; but the old rule prevails as far as the *Record* and the *Journal* are concerned. The only reading heard in the Chamber, except when the bill or other matter is taken up, when it is identified by title, is a perfunctory and abbreviated reading of the title—called the "third reading"—at the time the matter is voted on.

The reporter must remember that amendments, simple resolutions, and concurrent resolutions are agreed to and bills and joint resolutions are passed, regardless of what the Presiding Officer may say happened; that resolutions and their preambles are agreed to separately and in that order; and countless other particulars.

A uniform form book compiled by the chief reporter has been helpful in recent years; formerly every reporter made up his own.

The rules require that Senators, in debate as well as otherwise, address their remarks to the chair (which, of course, means that they refer to one another only in the third person); and whether they do so or not in practice (actually, they usually do), it is expected that the *Record* will show that they did.

While the House of Representatives appears to be more flexible in this respect, Senate reporters are taught that the word "you" should legitimately appear only in such expressions as "pay-as-you-go," though lately an occasional impersonal "if you please" has been permitted to appear in the *Record*.

Any Senator wishing to interrupt or comment upon the remarks of another rises (the rules require that they always rise and speak from their own seats), and, addressing the Chair, inquires, "Mr. President, will the Senator yield?" The Senator who has the floor may yield or not, as he chooses, and he may yield on condition that he not lose his right to the floor (since no Senator is permitted to speak more than twice on the same measure on the same day).

All of this, of course, makes the *Record* seem stilted, old-fashioned, quaint, courtly, and more in keeping with the bowing and scraping and the powdered wigs of 200 years ago than the fast-paced rush of today.

After a time, the reporter learns to be grateful for these decorum-preserving formalities, as he comes to realize that, granted the impatience and the cavalier attitude of many Senators, the alternative would often be parliamentary chaos.

Preservation of Tradition

Despite the nonchalance of some of its Members, the Senate as a body attempts, at all levels, to preserve decorum and tradition. Each Senator's desk in the Chamber is equipped with an inkwell and a shaker of blotting sand—though the march of progress somewhere along the line did lead to the abandonment of the goose quill for the wooden penholder.

Next to each of the entrance doors to the Chamber may be found a lacquered snuffbox, and until recent years those boxes were kept filled with snuff.

The original ivory gavel, though now shattered and unusable, is nevertheless preserved in a glass case and is always present on the Presiding Officer's desk when the Senate is in session, and the Senate is called to order with a substitute.

Reporting Difficulties

Every politician loves to talk, and were it not for the rule that remarks must be addressed to the Chair, several debates could be going on at once in different portions of the Chamber. (I have seen this happen.)

What does the reporter do in such a case? Report the debate being engaged in by the Senator last recognized by the Chair and such portion of the "other" debate as you are able; and, in the case of unreportable pandemonium, insert the sentence "Several Senators addressed the Chair."

The reporter will shortly be rescued by one of the Senators inquiring "Mr. President, who has the floor?" The Chair will respond, and all will be well.

Some Senators are able to think clearly and express themselves precisely even in the heat of debate, and naturally they become the reporters' favorites.

Some, on the other hand, seem to delight in trying to confuse the reporter with regional dialect, individualized rhetoric, and obscure colloquialisms. Others are sometimes confused.

In such cases, staff people, including the reporters, all strive to keep the Senators on the right track and to straighten out the *Record* if they wander too far.

The hapless reporter, too, has his guardian angels. Senators who read their speeches ordinarily given them to the reporters when they have finished, and some thoughtfully have a copy prepared beforehand.

Aides, who often are permitted to sit beside their Senators while they speak, are helpful in obtaining needed papers or information, and a clerk from the reporters' office is available when needed.

The floor reporter's transcript is prepared on legal-sized paper, quadruple-spaced, by typists working as a pool. (If the recent order standardizing the size of government stationery applies to the reporters and the GPO, I have not heard about it.)

Some of the reporters dictate everything, some are noteread part of the time, and some have their notes read all the time. Most of the typists are competent notereaders.

This is no job for reporters who cherish their transcripts. Considerable editing and interlineation occurs before the transcript goes to the GPO for printing—sometimes to the point that it is a marvel how the printers can read it.

Editing is done with a pencil, first by the floor reporter, then by the chief reporter, then by members of the Senator's staffs or the Senators themselves, who use a conference table in the reporters' office for that purpose (which sometimes becomes crowded toward the end of a busy day).

Sometimes an entire speech will be withdrawn and a prepared copy substituted. Sometimes, by unanimous consent, speeches and statements of Senators are placed in the *Record* without having occurred on the floor.

All of this is a part of the Members' effort to polish their "image," and I suspect it is sometimes overdone. The practice is more frequent by some Senators than by others, and those who feel most secure seem to do the least in the way of editing or supplementing the *Record*. One of the principal functions of the *Congressional Record* is to impress the voters.

The *Record,* published under Congressional control by the Government Printing Office, was established originally because Congress was dissatisfied with the arrangement of having commercial newspapers publish its proceedings.

Positive and Negative Aspects

As a job, Senate reporting has positive and negative aspects. The pay is good; and, like any straight salary, it is dependable. There is a good deal of time off, but when it occurs is not subject to the reporter's control.

The official hour for beginning the day's proceedings is noon, but by unanimous consent, Senators may change it, day by day, to some more convenient hour—such as 7:30 a.m.

The reporter never knows, when he goes to work in the morning, when that day's proceedings will be finished. Proceedings on the Senate floor on a given day may consist of a series of droning speeches, or a reporter may enter the Chamber for his "turn" on the floor in the midst of what, except for the knowledge he acquires of the rules and procedures would be a totally incomprehensible parliamentary tangle.

Sometimes the only person in the Chamber who seems to know what is going on is the parliamentarial—a trained professional who is thoroughly familiar with the rules and precedents of the Senate; and at such times he may be seen whispering frantically to the Presiding Officer, who himself·is often bewildered.

For the reporters, other than perhaps occasionally the chief reporter, there is no necessity, as with many of the Capitol Hill jobs, to play politics or pull strings. A convenient parking place is provided; but as for prestige, it probably exists only in the eyes of other reporters.

Nor surprisingly, perhaps, not every reporter feels comfortable in this environment. Some Merit writers have spent a week or more trying out for prospective vacancies and then rejected employment. Others seem to find the job beyond their comprehension.

Freelance reporters who have done Congressional committee reporting seem to have a better "feel" of what the job requires, and they now constitute the principal source for recruitment of new floor reporters.

The House has historically had official committee reporters, while for the Senate that work is done by freelance firms.

Computer-Aided Transcription is now used, in part, in reporting and printing the proceedings of the House committees, and there is probably no reason why it could not be used for the floor proceedings, thus eliminating the reporters' office typing pool, except that so many persons are involved in the editing process that CAT probably could not, without radically altering long-established procedures and inhibiting some Senators' free-wheeling styles, be used to set the type or prepare the offset masters for the printing of the *Congressional Record*.

Anyone interested in further information on this subject might enjoy reading an address by Gregor Macpherson, then Chief U.S. Senate Reporter of Debates, at the Denver convention of the NSRA on August 3, 1960, published in the proceedings of that convention at pages 52 to 67.

Figure 92 presents some practical pointers on parliamentary procedure, since knowledge of this is so vital to the legislative reporter.

FIGURE 92
PRACTICAL POINTERS ON PARLIAMENTARY PROCEDURE

From: Walter Rochow, CSR
Court Reporter
Superior Court
New Haven, Conn. 06510

The motions or points listed below, 1 through 9, are in order of precedence.
In other words:
ONE
A. When anyone of them is pending, you cannot introduce one that is listed BELOW it.
B. You can introduce one that is listed above it.

YOU WANT TO:	YOU SAY:	May You Interrupt Speaker To Make This Motion?	Is A Second Necessary?	Is The Motion Debatable?	Can This Motion Be Amended?	Is Vote Required? What Percent Required?
1. Adjourn	I move we adjourn	No interruption permitted	A second is necessary	Not debatable	Not amendable	Majority vote required
2. Recess	I move we recess until . . .	No interruption permitted	A second is necessary	Not debatable	Amendable	Majority vote required
3. Register a complaint	Point of privilege, Mr. Chairman . .	Yes, you may interrupt	No second needed	Not debatable (any Resulting motion is debatable)	Not amendable	No vote required (chair decides)
4. Suspend further consideration of a matter (to Table)	I move we table this matter	No interruption permitted	A second is necessary	Not debatable	Not amendable	Majority vote required
5. End discussion or further debating of a matter	I move the previous question	No interruption permitted	A second is necessary	Not debatable	Not amendable	Two-thirds vote required
6. Postpone consideration of a matter	I move we postpone this matter until . . .	No interruption permitted	A second is necessary	Debatable	Amendable	Majority required
7. Have further study on a matter	I move we refer this matter to a committee	No interruption permitted	A second is necessary	Debatable	Amendable	Majority vote required
8. Amend a motion	I move this motion be amended to read . . .	No interruption of speaker permitted	A second is necessary	Debatable	Amendable	Majority vote required
9. Introduce a matter or business (A primary motion)	I move that	Cannot interrupt speaker	A second is necessary	Debatable	Amendable	Majority vote required

(Continued)

FIGURE 92 *(Continued)*

PRACTICAL POINTERS ON PARLIAMENTARY PROCEDURE

THESE ARE GENERAL POINTS, PROPOSALS AND MOTIONS AND HAVE NO ORDER OF PROCEDURE OVER ONE ANOTHER, YOU MAY INTRODUCE ANY ONE OF THEM AT ANY TIME, EXCEPT:

TWO

A. When Motion To Adjourn is Pending
B. When Motion To Recess is Pending
C. Point Of Privilege is Pending

YOU WANT TO:	YOU SAY:	May You Interrupt Speaker To Make This Motion?	Is A Second Required?	Is The Motion Debatable?	Can This Motion Be Amended	Is Vote Required? What Percent Required?
1. Object to error in procedure or to a personal affront	Point of order	May interrupt speaker	No second	Not debatable	Not amendable	No vote required, Chair decides
2. Request for information	Point of information	If urgent and to the point	No second	Not debatable	Not amendable	No vote required
3. Verify voice vote by taking actual count	I call for a division of the house	No interruption permitted BUT division must be called by Chairman before new motion can be made	No second	Not debatable	Not amendable	No vote required UNLESS someone objects THEN majority required
4. Object to consideration of a matter you consider improper or undiplomatic	I object to consideration of this question	May interrupt speaker	No second required	Not debatable	Not amendable	Two-thirds vote required against consideration
5. Take up a matter which has been previously tabled	I move we take from the table	May not interrupt the speaker	Must be seconded	Not debatable	Not amendable	Majority required
6. Reconsider something already disposed of	I move we reconsider our action relative to . . .	May interrupt the speaker for record only. (Business at hand takes precedence)	Must be seconded	Debatable IF original motion was debatable	Not amendable	Majority required
7. Consider something out of its scheduled order	I move we suspend the rules and consider . . .	May not interrupt the speaker	Must be seconded	Not debatable	Not amendable	Two-thirds vote required
8. Vote on a ruling of the chair	I appeal the chair's decision	May interrupt speaker	Must be seconded	Debatable IF original motion was debatable	Not amendable	Majority vote required

Published by the Secretary General, Junior Chamber International
Box 1250, Miami Beach, Florida, U.S.A.

Chapter 45 *Testing*

At some point in every student or reporter's life, the fact must be faced that a test of some sort looms ahead: For a reporter, it may be the CSR of the state he or she plans to report in, if such a test exists or is instituted. Next, there should certainly be the NSRA Certificates of Proficiency and Merit, and who knows? Why not the NSRA Championship test?

Since this book is aimed primarily at students, let's talk about how to prepare for school tests first.

Academic Subject Tests are Most Important

Every student feels that if he or she could just get the required speed on the shorthand machine, he or she would be the greatest reporter in the world and get in the big money.

Judges and the better firms, however, are looking beyond mere machine shorthand speed in selecting a court reporter these days, so let's talk about how you are to study to get the most out of your academic and machine classes.

You may ask why this chapter was not at the front of this book. Well, when you get to the higher speeds, you must be the one to decide if you are going to put forth the effort it takes to do this job and do it well. If you really want to make it, here are a few tips you can follow:

1. Put forth your utmost every minute in every class, whether it is English, medical or legal terminology, machine shorthand, or any other subject. At the end of every hard take in machine shorthand, you should have put so much effort in striving to get it that you feel absolutely drained. Less is not enough!

2. Attend every class every day. One of the first things potential employers ask in most cases is "How was this person's attendance?" The next is "What about punctuality."

3. Set a place at home or in a local library and always study there. This place should have a desk or table, a chair with good support, excellent lighting, and should also be where no distractions, such as telephone, callers, radio, or television can intrude.

4. Take a long look at your day and plan your study schedule, considering what your assignments are and the length of time each will require. Study hard for about an hour and then rest for ten minutes or so before studying again so your mind will remain fresh.

5. Do the work you find most interesting first to attain a positive feeling of accomplishment. Next, do your hardest subject to get it over. Finish with work that requires less concentration.

6. Do not waste a lot of time planning what to study. Start studying!

7. Get everything done before you start to study that might take your mind from your work. Drink the Coke; go to the bathroom; make that telephone call. But when you start to study, let nothing interfere.

8. Keep a notebook for each course. Maintain all your notes regarding that subject in that one neatly arranged notebook.

9. Review your class notes and textbook daily. Figure out what you may not have understood. Don't tell yourself you'll learn things before the test. That is too late!

10. Concentrate totally during your study time. Write down questions, spellings, and outlines. Repeat important rules out loud and test yourself.

Written Knowledge Tests

State and NSRA tests include a written knowledge examination, and rightly so! Reporting is technical and complex today, and employers are not interested in hiring half-trained reporters with high machine shorthand speed but lacking the common sense to know what they do not know. Included on the WKT's are questions regarding English grammar, punctuation, spelling, and vocabulary; reporting procedures; medical and legal terminologies; and government and current events.

Insofar as possible, secure copies of old CSR and RPR written knowledge tests from NSRA, state associations, and the *NSR* and state publications, and your instructors and reporter friends.

When you appear to take a Written Knowledge Test, observe the following suggestions for a successful examination:

1. First, write your assigned number or name, as required, on your Scantron card, answer sheet, or test papers.

2. Read the directions to each part carefully before answering any questions. Be sure to answer in the way specified. Occasionally, individuals fail tests because they do the reverse of what is asked of them on a large section of a test. FOLLOW DIRECTIONS!

3. Glance through the questions on the test to get an overview. You will see what to expect and where the hard parts are.

4. Answer the easy questions first.

5. Any time you are not certain of an answer, place a check mark beside the question. After you have answered all the easy questions, come back to these. Otherwise, if you spend too much time puzzling over a few difficult questions, you may run out of time and fail even though you knew enough answers to have a comfortable passing margin.

6. Allocate your time. If you have an hour to do 100 questions, you must do almost two questions a minute.

7. If there is no penalty for guessing, answer every single question, or you are bound to lose points by leaving some questions unanswered.

8. After the examination is over, study to find the answers to any questions you were not sure of.

Prepare for the Test Well in Advance

Most days in the court reporting field are, in effect, machine test days, but somehow they don't seem formidable to most people. However, when someone mentions that one word TEST! everyone panics. Then, the ones who are well prepared settle down and get the take.

I will say one thing, and that is: If a person is overtrained, tests will not hold the same terrors as they do for a person with the bare minimum speed to get through them. Even if your school does not require stricter test performance than will be required on CSR and NSRA tests, demand it of yourself. It is better to spend a few more months in school to acquire the requisite speed and accuracy. It will eliminate the possibility of having to struggle every day of your life on rapid medical or technical cases.

Get Your Machine Ready for the Big Day

If you feel your shorthand machine may need any mechanical repairs or adjustments, have them done at least a month before the test, not a week prior to the test. You should have used it enough to be familiar with the touch and to be sure that it is going to function properly during the dictated test.

If you must furnish your own typewriter or computer for the test, the same applies to that.

Psych Yourself Up in Advance!

Be sure you have enough reserve speed, and then start about a month before simulating actual tests from beginning to end to put yourself in the right frame of mind for the test. Transcribe your mock tests within the time limits of the actual test, and check your papers carefully to be sure spellings and typing errors will not be your downfall.

Review legal and medical terms, spelling, punctuation, and grammar also.

Relax the Day Before the Test

Do not arrive for any test in a state of exhaustion. Relax the day before the test, knowing you have prepared fully in advance.

Check your machine(s). Take a pack of paper and tear off an amount more than you think will be sufficient for the test. Label that pack "Test." Label the balance "Practice." Carefully go through the "Test" pack to be sure there are no folds stuck together or cut.

Bring both the "Test" and "Practice" packs to the test. Use the "Practice" pack for warm-up dictation and the "Test" tape for the actual test.

Don't Overink Your Machine for the Test

Overinked letters and numbers may come out as unreadable blobs and smears, so do not overink your shorthand machine in anticipation of the examination. Should overinking cause numbers to run together, a little blip mark appears above the correct number, but tests are no place to waste time deciphering such things.

Test Day

Get to the testing room early, and get a good seat as close to the speakers as possible. Do enough preliminary writing to get the rhythm of the speeds established in your mind, but not so much practicing that you are exhausted mentally or physically before the test begins. How much this will be for you is pretty much an individual matter. Take your cassette recorder and tapes with you if you want some warmup and are not sure any is being provided at the test site.

Say to yourself "I know I am ready because I have done this over and over again. I am as ready as anyone could ever be." Keep away from all the nervous, unsure, pessimistic doomsayers who will undoubtedly be there, for they always abound at any test to act as "downers." Keep your positive mental attitude high.

Now, write a good test. Keep your mind firmly on the dictation so nothing those around you can do will disconcert you. If you should drop or misstroke, get right back in the writing of the test as soon as you can, and you will come through with flying colors.

Transcribing Suggestions

1. Should you come to an illegible outline or trouble spot, leave a blank space on your typing paper and place a paper clip at the margin beside it. Don't spend a lot of time on it. Just keep going, or you may run out of time with just a fold or so to transcribe.

2. After transcribing, go back to spots with paper clips and try to fill in the spaces. Do not edit or add words. Assume the words before and after the outline are correct. See if the expression came up before, or occurs again, or if context can give you a clue. Don't puzzle too long on it, but go on to other sections.

3. After you have finished all three (or whatever) sections of the test, read each transcript for typographical errors and spelling errors or run-on sentences, since gross punctuation errors count off. Check for proper ending punctuation at all points.

4. Do not stop at the end of any one section and try to look up word after word as you go along. You will run out of time.

5. Compare your notes to your transcript. You may notice words you have omitted or other corrections to be made. You should have drawn a line through the notes as you typed. Make a careful check of these to be sure you have not omitted any folds.

Testing May Vary from State to State

Most CSR state tests and the NSRA Certificate of Proficiency dictated examinations require five-minute takes of 225 WPM on testimony, 200 WPM on jury charge, and 180 WPM on solid literary material with at least 95 percent accuracy. The NSRA Certificate of Merit requires five-minute takes at 260 WPM on testimony, 240 WPM on jury charge or legal opinion, and 200 WPM on literary matter with the same standard. Some states require four-voice testing, medical dictated material to be transcribed, oral readbacks on jury charge or other matter, and have grades of tests for advancement in the system.

Find out about these requirements long before you plan to take the required tests to avoid testing without adequate preparation.

Start Practicing for Your Next Test!

When you have sailed through that first test, it will be time to start practicing for the next step up!

Epilogue

As I reluctantly close this first revision of THE COMPLETE REPORTER'S HANDBOOK, I again agree with my good friend Dick Mowers, who was originally of such help to me in producing the first edition of this book. He then wrote me that writing a book about court reporting must be like a perpetual Christmas, as each topic might open up a whole new package of goodies.

He was right, and I leave this project again feeling that there is much more to be added. Court reporting technology has moved light years ahead since the first edition came forth, and new wonders are surely ahead in the days to come. Reporters are going to have to be willing to change and enlarge their capacities to keep up with technology and save our profession, but they have proved themselves to be equal to every task in the past, and I have wonderful faith in them in the future.

Perhaps I have succeeded in whetting the appetite of students, and perhaps some reporters, to the point where they will aim to be great reporters and they will go forth better prepared because of this production. If so, this book will have accomplished its purpose!

Index

De bene esse depositions, 65
Decisions published by publishing company,
  citations for, 253
Default judgment, 133
Defendant, presence of, 201
Delivery of depositions, 123–28
Deportment, 3–7
Deposition
  appearance page, 93
  certification of signing witness, 108
  collection procedures, 103
  colloquy, 98
  corrections to, 109–14
  filing, 126–28
  final preparation of, 115–21
  handling the reading and signing, 108
  indexing, 115
  information sources, 103
  multiple attorneys and, charts as visual
    aids, 82
  one step at a time, 93
  other guidelines, 98–101
  preparation of printed forms, 120
  preparing your first, 93–103
  procedure for reading and signing, 105–08
  proofreading, 101
  reading, signing, and making
    corrections, 105–14
  refusal of witness signature, 108
  setting up a witness, 97
  stipulation page, 96–98
  taking the, 81–91
  testimony by, 196
  title page, 93
  transcribing legal papers, 120
  transcription advice to students, 118
  transcription pointers, 117
  witness changes, 108
  written notice of, sample, 67
Deposition exhibits, 115–17, 217
Depositions
  billing of, 123–28
  certifying and filing, 32
  company transcribed, 102
  concluding, 89
  delivery of, 123–28
  examinations before trial, 65–79
  multiple attorneys and, 82
  no shows, 88
  preparation for assignment, 68–69
  procedures used in taking, 66–67
  transcribing, 91
  types of, 65–67
Deposition worksheet
  contents of, 70
  preservation of, 71, 73
  sample, 74
Designation of counsel
  by numbers, 82
  first syllable, 81
  for deposition, 81
Desk dictionaries, 20
Desktop utilities, 346
Dictated stipulations, example of, 73
Dictating notes, 117
Dictating, for a transcriber, see "Transcriber,
  dictating for."
Dictionaries, 20–21
Dictionary, building a, 329, 340
Difficulties, reporting, in legislative
  reporting, 365
Diligence, as element of deportment, 6
Diplomacy, use of, 4
Directed verdicts, 241, 243–48
  typing special issues, 243
Directories, tabbing, 152
Discovery depositions, 66
Discrimination, absence of in profession, 9–10
Disks, handling and storing, 340
Dismiss complaint, motion to, 177
Dismiss for lack of prosecution, motion
  to, 176
Dismiss for want of jurisdiction, motion
  for, 176
Disposition of deposition exhibits, 217
Disposition of exhibits, 226
Documents, executing official, 31
Dog sheet, general, sample, 77

E

Editing, writing and, 84
Efficiency, as element of deportment, 6
Encyclopedias, 21
Endings, 339
Engineering, references on, 27

English skills, as element of reporting
  profession, 1
English sources, misc., 23
Entry cost, as incentive to enter reporting
  profession, 9
Estimate of transcript cost, 276
Etiquette, books about, 24
Evidence
  close of, motion to dismiss and, 196
  defendant's, 195
Evidence speaks for itself, ground for
  objection, 238
Ex parte hearings, 133
Examination, order of, 192
Execution of bond for notary publics, 31
Exhibit-related parentheticals, 209
Exhibits, 217–28
  checking, 220
  constitution of, 217
  copies of originals, 99
  copies of, 225
  courtroom, 217
  deposition, 115, 217
  ground for objection, 240
  in trial transcripts, 224
  index, 225
  information, 219
  insertion of in record, 224
  marking, 79, 221, 222
    at pretrial hearing, 22
    in advance of trial, 222
    types of, 219
  multipage, 219
  multiunit, 219
  premarking, 220
  procedures for marking, 222
  procedures to follow, 220
  re-marking at trial, 221
  responsibility for during recess, 225
  securing information, 225
  specific requests, 219
  stamps, 220
  storage and disposition of, 221, 226
  substitution of copies for original, 221
  supplies, 218
  writing about in the dark, 221
Expedited copy, charges for, 125
Expert without qualifications, ground for
  objection, 238
Expert witness, ground for objection, 239
Extension system phones, 149

F

Facts not in evidence, ground for
  objection, 234
Fascinating work, as incentive to enter
  reporting profession, 9
Federal codes, citations for, 249
Federal court notice, 50
Federal court procedures for
  interrogatories, 46–47
Federal courts, organization of, 130
Filing cabinets, 143
Filing depositions, 32
Financial texts, as reference material, 25
Findings of fact, 135
Fishing expedition, ground for objection, 238
Foreign languages, books about, 24
Foreign states, citations for, 251
Foundations, references on, 27
Freelance reporting, 11–13
  advantages of, 11–12
  disadvantages of, 12–13
  payment methods, 11
Freelance transcripts, binding, 98
Future considerations, 7

G

General local references, 21
Grand jurors, questions by, 156
Grand jury
  composition of, 155
  function of, 155
  justice reporters, 156
  procedure of, 155
  proceedings, 155–57
  transcripts of, 156
Grounds for objections, 232–40
  ambiguity, 236
  attempt to impeach witness, 240
  badgering the witness, 238
  blanket, 232
  compound and complex questions, 235
  conclusions, 236

cross-exam beyond scope of direct, 237
  evidence speaks for itself, 238
  exhibits, 240
  expert without qualifications, 238
  expert witness, 239
  facts not in evidence, 234
  "fishing expeditions," 238
  hearsay evidence, 234
  illegally obtained evidence, 237
  lack of foundation, 233
  leading and suggestive questions, 233
  mention of insurance, 239
  narrative form of testimony, 239
  nonresponsive answer, 233
  opinions, 236
  other than best evidence, 236
  privileged information, 239
  repetitious questioning, 234
  result of surprise, 239
  self-incriminating testimony, 237
  self-serving answers, 235
Guidelines, depositions, 98–101
Guides to proper English, 22–23

H

Habeas corpus, motion for writ of, 177
Handling objections, fear of, 229
Head shakes, problems with in
  depositions, 84
Hearings, in chambers, 207
Hearsay evidence, ground for objection, 234
High-frequency conflicts, 338
Hotels, books about, 25
Hung jury, 242

I

Illegally obtained evidence, ground for
  objection, 237
Impeaching the witness, ground for
  objection, 240
In chambers hearings, 207
Index creation, 333
Index, exhibit, 225
Indexing the transcript, 261–74
  attractive for federal court, 263
  contents, 261
  exhibits, 272
  methods vary, 265
  numbering, 262
  several volumes, 263
Index pages, numbering of deposition,
  100, 119
Indices, citations for, 255
Indictment, reading of the, 203
Indigents, record of, 276
Information securing exhibit, 225
Information sheet, sample, 78
Insurance, mention of, ground for
  objection, 239
Integrity, as element of deportment, 4
Interpreted proceedings
  parentheticals in, 212
  placement of interpreter, 286
  reporting, 285–88
    correcting interpreter, 286
    finding interpreters, 287
    guidelines, 288
    oath for interpreter, 285
    parentheticals, 286
    procedure, 285
    qualifying interpreter, 285
    reswearing witness, 286
  two interpreters, 286
Interpreter
  correcting, 286
  placement of, 286
  qualifying, 285
Interpreters
  finding, 287
  oath used for, 285
  presence of two, 286
Interrogatories, 43–57
  answers to, 44
  complications with, 44
  cost of, 44
  definition of, 43
  federal court procedures, 46
  in various-sized cities, 44
  points to observe, 47–49
  procedures to be followed regarding, 45
  purpose of, 45
  samples, 51–53, 55–57
  types of, 43
Interruptions, 83